THE MONS
MYTH

THE MONS MYTH

MYTH

A Reassessment of the Battle

TERENCE ZUBER

For the 9th (US) Infantry Regiment
Keep Up The Fire

First published 2010

The History Press
The Mill, Brimscombe Port
Stroud, Gloucestershire, GL5 2QG
www.thehistorypress.co.uk

British Library Cataloguing in Publication Data.
A catalogue record for this book is available from the British Library.

ISBN 978 0 7524 5247 0

Typesetting and origination by The History Press
Printed in Great Britain
Manufacturing managed by Jellyfish Print Solutions Ltd

Contents

Glossary

AK	*Armeekorps*	Army Corps
C, Cus	*Kürassier*	Cuirassier regiment
Drag	*Dragoner*	Dragoon Regiment
DOW		Died of Wounds
EM		Enlisted Men
FAR	*Feldartillerieregiment*	Field Artillery Regiment
FUSS	*Fussartillerie*	Heavy Artillery Regiment
H, Hus	*Husaren*	Hussar Regiment
ID	*Infanteriedivision*	Infantry Division
IR	*Infanterieregiment*	Infantry Regiment
	Jäger	Light Infantry battalion
	Jäger zu Pferde	Cavalry Regiment
KIA		Killed in Action
KTB	*Kriegstagebuch*	War Diary
L	*de Ligne*	Belgian Infantry Regiment
LH	*Leibgarde*	Lifeguard Hussars
MIA		Missing in Action
MG	*Maschinengewehr*	Machine Gun
OFF		Officers
RFAR	*Reservefeldartillerieregiment*	Reserve Field Artillery Regiment
RIR	*Reserveinfanterieregiment*	Reserve Infantry Regiment
sFH	*schwere Feldhaubitze*	15cm heavy howitzer
U, Ul	*Ulanen*	Uhlan Regiment
WIA		Wounded in Action

1

The British Description of Mons and Le Cateau

It was foreordained that British historians would enshrine Mons and Le Cateau in the storied succession of British victories in northern France and Belgium. During the rail deployment to northern France in August 1914 British officers were well aware that they had passed near Agincourt and Crécy, that on 20 August the 9th Brigade bivouacked on the Malplaquet battlefield and that Mons is just south of Waterloo. The battle of Le Cateau was fought on the 568th anniversary of Crécy.[1] These battles conjured up the names of the most famous of British commanders: Edward III, the Black Prince, Henry V, the Duke of Marlborough and the Duke of Wellington. Every British history of Mons and Le Cateau makes mention of these historic associations.

So it must follow that at Mons and Le Cateau another small professional British army, standing on the defensive and relying on training, discipline and firepower, delivered stinging defeats to a much larger continental enemy. As had the French at Agincourt, Crécy and Waterloo, so at Mons and Le Cateau the Germans attacked in solid blocks and were mown down in rows by precise British fire. This is what makes Mons and Le Cateau British victories, for even though the British were driven from their positions, the Germans suffered disproportionately heavier casualties.

One of the first histories of these battles was A. F. Becke's *The Royal Regiment of Artillery at Le Cateau*.[2] It was written during the war by a gunner officer and shows that the principal themes of the British description of these battles were established almost at once. The historical precedents for Mons are made explicit: early in the book there is a comparison of the British artillery at Le Cateau with that of Waterloo. Becke maintains that the British II Corps was outnumbered 2.5 to 1. Nevertheless, the decision of the II Corps commander, Sir Horrace Smith-

Dorrien, to fight at Le Cateau was the proper one; indeed, all of the British tactical decisions at Le Cateau were correct. The British gave the attacking Germans a fearful beating, so much so that II Corps was able to break contact and withdraw without any German pursuit, and the German army stayed a respectful distance away from the BEF until the British attacked at the Battle of the Marne.

The British official history was written under the guidance of Brigadier-General J. E. Edmonds in 1920–21.[3] He says little about British pre-war training or tactical doctrine, other than the fact that the British rifleman was trained to fire his weapon at a rate of fifteen rounds a minute or faster, and that this 'rapid rifle fire' was 'legendary and decisive'.[4] Edmonds says that the British riflemen were firing so quickly that 'The Germans imagined that they were everywhere opposed by machine guns only, not realising the intensity of British fire'.[5] The legend of 'rapid rifle fire' was also repeated by every subsequent Anglophone history of the battle.

The British official history says that German infantry tactics consisted initially of attacking *en masse* with the intention of simply overrunning the British position by weight of numbers. Only after the Germans felt the power of 'rapid rifle fire' did they sometimes disperse. Eventually, German numerical superiority would force the British to retreat, but the British would go in good order. The few British units that were destroyed died gallantly. Acts of British individual heroism feature significantly, especially that of winners of the Victoria Cross. There is no criticism of British tactics or leadership.

There were few German sources available in 1920–21. Walter Bloem, a novelist, playwright and reserve captain in the Grenadier Regiment Number 12 (2nd Brandenburg), published *Vormarsch* in Germany in 1916,[6] a lurid account of the 12th Grenadiers' action at Mons which suited Edmonds' purposes exactly. Bloem had published three fictional accounts of the Franco-Prussian War, and embellished his description of his regiment's battle at Mons to add more pathos and drama to what was otherwise a rather standard infantry firefight. According to Bloem, Mons was an epic battle, in which the 12th Grenadiers were nearly destroyed by British small-arms and machine-gun fire; the remnants of his regiment, to include the commanding officer and Bloem himself, were thoroughly demoralised. Edmonds liked Bloem so much that the book was translated into English by one of his former subordinates, G. C. Wynne, in 1930. Edmonds wrote the foreword.[7] The only other German sources that were used were carefully selected to confirm the official British account of these battles.

The British official history included a folder with thirty-four maps. The only conclusion one could draw from Map 11 is that at Le Cateau six German infantry divisions and three cavalry divisions had attacked the three divisions of the British II Corps. This map has been reproduced by every subsequent book on Le Cateau. It is completely wrong.

Edmonds' official history became the template for subsequent Anglophone histories of Mons and Le Cateau. All repeat that the 'the Germans thought British rapid rifle fire was machine-gun fire'. All quote Bloem. All contend that the Germans massively outnumbered the British, attacked in solid blocks and were mown down in rows.

Edmonds' description of Mons and Le Cateau has become 'common knowledge'. This seems to have discouraged further study of the battles. Modern accounts are short, populist and do not stray far from Edmonds' dogma. There has not been a new analysis of Mons and Le Cateau in the eighty-eight years since the British official history.

David Ascoli's *The Mons Star* does not footnote the sources, there is no bibliography and German sources are not used. The war to the Ypres Salient in November 1914 is covered in 244 pages. Ascoli's intent is to go one better than Edmonds. He is scathing concerning German generalship, as well as the generalship of the BEF commander, Sir John French. However, Smith-Dorrien, the commander of II Corps, is Ascoli's hero, a worthy successor to the British commanders who had been victorious on the north European plain. The formula 'British rapid rifle-fire = machine gun fire' is repeated. The Germans always outnumbered the British and their attacks were always conducted in massed formations, which eventually pushed the British back by sheer weight of numbers, but not until the Germans had taken awful casualties. 'The German answer [to firepower] was sheer weight of numbers. The infantrymen of the 3rd British Division at Nimy and Oburg were astonished to see the Germans advancing upon them in close columns.' He quotes one 'Pony' Moore of the 4/Middlesex: 'It was an unbelievable sight. You didn't need to aim. You just fired into the blue and they went down like flies, like a pheasant shoot without any beaters. After a bit they retired in disorder. In a way, it was sickening to see all those men lying there.'[8]

John Terraine's *Mons* was written with the express intent of highlighting 'great British battles' and gives admiring accounts of the deeds of individual British soldiers.[9] *Mons* covers the BEF from mobilisation to the Marne in 217 pages; the Battle of Mons takes eighteen pages, Le Cateau fourteen.

David Lomas's *Mons 1914: Britain's Tactical Triumph* is heavily illustrated, paying even more attention to British heroism and the deeds of the winners of the Victoria Cross. Lomas says that Mons was a British tactical triumph solely on the basis of body count: while the British lost precisely 1,642 men, Lomas says 'Most estimates agree that they [German casualties at Mons] were not less than 6,000 and could have been even as high as 10,000'.[10] His source for these estimates is not cited.

Mons by Jack Horsfall and Nigel Cave and *Le Cateau* by Cave and Jack Sheldon are part of the *Battleground Europe* series, intended primarily to serve as guides to tour the battlefields. Both focus on the actions of individuals and are also heavily illustrated.[11] The description of the battle in *Mons* is conventional. *Le Cateau* does not break the mould entirely, but does crack it. Jack Sheldon, who is a retired British colonel, was trained at the German General Staff Academy and was military attaché in Germany, and used individual accounts and maps from the German regimental histories. Sheldon's interest is, however, still on the individual, not tactical doctrine or the description of operations and combined-arms combat.[12]

Edmonds' picture of Mons and Le Cateau is pure patriotic myth. A professional military analysis, with impartial use of both German and British sources, comes to very different conclusions.

The Germans did not massively outnumber the British at either battle. In fact, at Mons the British and Germans were of roughly equal strength. The difference was that the Germans concentrated at the decisive point, while the British did not. At Le Cateau the British outnumbered the Germans.

The Germans never equated British 'rapid rifle fire' with machine-gun fire. British 'rapid rifle fire' was also not the wonder weapon that it has been made out to be. British artillery was rarely able to support the infantry, and 'rapid rifle fire' alone was usually incapable of stopping the German attacks.

Taken together, this means that the British did not inflict disproportionate casualties on the Germans. The casualties at Mons were roughly even; at Le Cateau British casualties were significantly higher than the Germans'.

Which leaves the question: How did the Germans push the British off their positions at Mons and Le Cateau? The answer is, that the Germans benefited from superior tactical doctrine and training. The Germans did not attack bolt upright in solid blocks, but by bounds in fire and movement. Moreover, the German infantry attacked as part of a combined-arms team, supported by artillery and machine-gun fire, which repeatedly allowed it to close with the British defenders.

Hidden under the Mons Myth, there is a great deal to be learned concerning German doctrine, tactics, training and performance on the battlefield.

German Sources

An accurate picture of Mons and Le Cateau can only be gained through the thorough use of German sources.

The war diaries and records for the German 1st Army units were destroyed in a British firebomb raid on the Reichsarchiv at Potsdam during the night of 14 April 1945. The only surviving German army primary documents are those at the archives of the individual German states at Stuttgart, Karlsruhe, Dresden and Munich, which contain a number of pre-war German tactical regulations, training regulations, range firing regulations and after-action reports from tactical exercises. Together they show in detail German doctrine and training at the company/battery, battalion and regimental levels.

Three books show what tactical doctrine was actually taught in the German army. On 29 May 1906 the Prussian War Ministry issued a new doctrinal manual for infantry tactics and training, the *Exerzier-Reglement für die Infanterie*.[13] This is our baseline document for studying German tactics and training. The *Leitfaden für den Unterricht in der Taktik auf den Königlichen Kriegsschulen* (Handbook for Tactics Instruction at Royal Military Schools)[14] was used to teach all-arms tactics to young officers. German officers who wished to be considered for acceptance in the Kriegsakademie, the General Staff College, were required to take a written examination in which they demonstrated their mastery of tactical doctrine. While there was no official text that they could use to prepare for this examination, Friedrich Immanuel's *Handbuch der Taktik*[15] was the most highly-regarded study guide. Lieutenant-Colonel Hein's *Kampfesformen und Kampfesweise der Infanterie* (Structure and Conduct of Infantry Combat), explained German infantry doctrine and training to the educated public.[16] Training was taken so seriously in the German army that many officers wrote books describing in detail effective training philosophies and methods. Our description of German training will also utilise these.

The German official histories are concerned with strategy and operations, and state expressly that they do not deal with events below corps level. They are therefore of little help in describing battles at the tactical level. The German official history also had an agenda: explaining why the German General Staff had lost the Battle of the Marne. The official history maintained that the younger Moltke had inherited the 'perfect plan', the Schlieffen Plan, but failed to understand the concept, which was to 'keep the right wing strong'. According to the official history, the only German generals who did understand the the Schlieffen Plan were the commander of the right wing 1st Army, Kluck, and his chief of staff, Kuhl. Therefore, Moltke, the OHL (Oberste Heeresleitung – the German headquarters) and the commander of the German 2nd Army are the fall guys and receive continual criticism, while Kluck and Kuhl are the German official history's heroes, who can do (almost) no wrong.

The German regimental histories published after the war give the best picture of tactical combat at Mons and Le Cateau. The quality of these histories is generally high: they were written by capable men who were simultaneously four-year combat veterans in wartime and professional men – lawyers, bureaucrats, university professors – in peacetime. Most of them also state the German casualties, which provide a corrective to the exaggerated casualty estimates of the British histories. The German description of their own tactics and the course of the battles from their perspective seldom corresponds to the British description. The Germans did not attack in solid masses, the British did not mow down rows of German troops. Instead, the German infantry attacked using fire and movement, and most of these attacks were provided with excellent support from machine-gun and artillery fire.

None of the German regimental histories mentions that the Germans thought the British had more than the usual number of machine guns, two per battalion. British rifle fire was judged to be very fast and accurate, but that is exactly what the Germans expected from an army of long-service professionals with experience in colonial warfare. In any case, the Germans were comparing British rifle fire to that of the Belgians and French, whom the Germans thought were miserable shots. The Germans were also quite proud of their own rifle marksmanship and fire discipline.

The 12th Grenadier regimental history was published in 1924. It gives a good description of the regiment's fight at Mons, including a map, and is an excellent corrective to Bloem's *Vormarsch.*[17] All the German histories asserted that Mons and Le Cateau were German victories. They observed, not unreasonably, that in both cases the British right flank had been completely driven in and that at the end of the day the Germans were masters of the battlefield.

Edmonds conducted a revision of the official history, which was printed in 1933, ostensibly to consider these new sources. This review had little or no effect on the 1921 text. Instead, he selected portions of those German histories, often quoted out of context, which would confirm the exceptional effectiveness of British rifle fire.

A serious study of Mons and Le Cateau, including a militarily and historically professional description and analysis of operations and tactics on both sides, is long overdue. It is the attention of this volume to correct this deficiency.

To accomplish this, it is first necessary to describe German offensive tactical doctrine and training. The conduct of the campaign will be described at the operational level, and the decision-making process and orders of both the German and British army and corps commanders will be critiqued. Most important, the British description of the battles of Mons and Le Cateau at the tactical level will be compared to the German accounts. This will produce a far more credible picture of both the campaign and the tactical conduct of these two important and instructive battles.

2

Tactics and Training

The German Army

After the First World War, German officers stated almost unanimously that the German army of 1914 was the best-trained and best-disciplined in the world, and that the peacetime tactical doctrine and training proved themselves unequivocally in combat, leading the German army to 'brilliant successes'.[1] Repeatedly, German soldiers of all grades said that their victorious engagements had been conducted 'just like in training'. Such opinions must be taken seriously, since they were made by some of the most combat-experienced soldiers in modern military history, who had the benefit of four years of high-intensity warfare to educate and refine their professional judgement.

The foundation for German success in combat in the First World War was laid in the forty-three years of doctrinal development and training prior to the battle. This chapter will concentrate on the final German tactical doctrine that was implemented in 1906 and used as the basis for subsequent training.

The German army was so serious about training that many German officers regarded combat as merely the final live-fire training test. The regimental historian of Hussar Regiment 12 wrote that combat was an opportunity for the regiment to 'show what it had learned and done in decades of hard peacetime work', an opinion also expressed by Otto von Moser, one of the most important German authors on tactics and training.[2]

The Art of War[3]

Combat was characterised by Clausewitz as the realm of friction and the clash of
two independent forces. The combat leader must comprehend what is happen-
ing on the battlefield in an environment where everything is uncertain and draw
conclusions based on limited information. War, in German doctrine, is an art;
decision-making and leadership in combat are creative acts.[4] War is not a science,
in which decisions can be made by following a set formula. Nor can a war be
fought, as some Western armies try to do, according to the principles of business
management.

After a long debate, the German Army rejected *Normaltaktik* – applying a
standard solution to tactical problems. Every German doctrinal manual emphasised that there was no *Schema*, no cookie-cutter solution to operational and
tactical problems. Each operational and tactical situation had to be evaluated on
its own merits. No two situations are alike. Doctrine, the study of military history,
and training exercises provide a framework for decision-making, but the soldier
uses his intellect and will to solve each tactical problem. Doctrine may emphasise
the offensive, but that does not mean that there is a knee-jerk requirement to
attack under all circumstances. A German combat leader therefore required clear
and sharp judgement and perception, but above all strength of character, determination, energy and equilibrium.

The Nature of Combat in 1914[5]

By 1914 firepower, in the form of magazine-fed small-calibre rifles, machine guns,
and quick-firing artillery pieces, dominated the battlefield. Whatever could be
seen could be hit. Smokeless powder made weapons-fire practically invisible and
counter-fire much more difficult.

Every army in Europe had drawn the consequences from the firepower-dom-
inated battlefield, both in defensive and offensive operations. They recognised
that it was necessary for all arms to use the terrain to provide protection against
observation and fire. Troops were dispersed in order to reduce casualties. Closed
formations could no longer be used if exposed in the open to effective enemy
fire. Units could be committed to combat only in broad lines, and had to be further broken down to the point that they could utilise the cover provided by the
terrain. In the defence, even thin lines could present significant resistance, especially if they were in tactically effective positions. The difference between armies
lay not in the recognition of the problem, but in the quality of the subsequent
training.

German doctrine emphasised that if the proper tactical precautions were not
observed, if units attempted to cross open ground under effective fire or failed to

adequately disperse, the result would be extraordinarily high casualties in a very short time. On the other hand, adequate use of terrain, proper tactical movement and dispersion would rob small-arms, machine-gun and artillery fire of much of their effectiveness; the casualties in Manchuria in 1904–5 were lower than those of the 1870–71 Franco-Prussian War.

Every army but the French adopted combat camouflage uniforms. The German army introduced the field grey combat uniform in 1907, after tactical tests had shown that it offered the best concealment, particularly against long-range or air reconnaissance when the troops were marching in column. The combination of camouflage uniforms, smokeless powder, dispersion and the use of the terrain meant that it had become extraordinarily difficult to discern the enemy's location, movement and strength. It was also difficult to tell if one's own fire was effective and if the enemy was taking casualties.

For these reasons, it was widely recognised that the battlefield had become 'empty'. Not only had the enemy become invisible, the only members of his own unit that the soldier could see were those in his immediate vicinity. Formal discipline became ineffective. The lethality of weapons fire eliminated the direct influence of the senior leaders over their men. The German army stressed that combat leadership would be provided by company-grade officers and NCOs. Everything depended on the qualities of the small-unit leader and the individual soldier. Training therefore had to emphasise and reinforce the soldier's ability to think and act – in particular, to fire and move – in small units or on his own initiative.[6]

The first principle of war for practically any army, at the strategic, operational and tactical level, is to have superior forces at the decisive place and time.[7] German doctrine highlighted that it was also important to conduct the main attack, if possible, against the flank and rear of the enemy. This, the *Handbook for Tactics Instruction* said, was 'the highest accomplishment in the art of war'. No other European army emphasised the flank attack and envelopment to the degree that the German army did. Units under effective fire could not manoeuvre against the enemy flank. Envelopments were generally only feasible if units not in contact marched against the enemy flank. For this reason the German army at the operational level marched on a very broad front, and at the tactical level deployed early from march column to combat formation.

In 1914, all European armies emphasised the offensive.[8] It was thought that the future war could be won quickly in big battles, but only by offensive action. The *Handbook* said that leaders and troops would never choose of their own free will to stand on the defensive. The attacker has the initiative; he can choose the time and place of the attack and mass his forces there, hopefully against weak points in the enemy defences. However, the attacker had to accept that he was going to take heavy casualties. Nevertheless, the will to win and ruthless determination would secure victory, which was all that counted. Initially the attacker might well suffer higher casualties than the defender, but once the defender was driven from his position his morale and cohesion would be degraded and he would be subjected to pursuit by fire. If the attacker continued the pursuit vigorously, the defender might be completely destroyed.

The German army, going back at least as far as Frederick the Great, had a bias in favour of offensive operations, and this bias was reflected in German training and doctrine before the First World War. The *Handbook* said that troops attack when they feel themselves to be superior to their enemy; the German army clearly thought that this feeling of superiority was most likely to arise not from superior numbers, though this was possible, but rather from high morale: from the soldiers' confidence in their leaders, their training, tactics and weapons. Attacking was more difficult than defending, but the act of going on the attack itself gave the troops a 'massive moral superiority'.

German doctrine acknowledged that modern firepower had reinforced the effectiveness of the defence. As the Boer War had demonstrated, even weak forces on thin, extended fronts could maintain themselves for a considerable time against a frontal attack by superior forces. But firepower could also assist the offensive. If the attacker used the terrain effectively, he could bring his firepower closer and closer to the enemy position. In particular, the attacker could concentrate his fire at a chosen place. If he could do so at vulnerable points, such as salients in the defensive position, or the flanks, then the firepower advantage would be on the side of the attacker. It might also be necessary to fix an enemy in place, that is, prevent him from moving his troops, usually to keep him from withdrawing or shifting forces. Fixing an enemy in place would be necessary in order to provide the time for an attack on his flank or rear to be effective. One could attempt to hold an enemy in place by conducting a feint attack, but as a rule the enemy would not be fooled for long and a serious attack would become necessary. In actual practice in August 1914 it was found that at all levels – strategic, operational and tactical – it was nearly impossible to keep an enemy in place. It was almost always possible to break contact and withdraw.

By adopting the defensive, the defender was acknowledging his inferiority. The defender could choose where he wanted to defend, and prepare his position and the battlefield in order to maximise the effectiveness of his fire, but having done so was forced to wait and react to the enemy's actions. The Russo-Japanese War proved, to the satisfaction of practically the entire European military community, that even if the defence were reinforced by modern trench works and machine guns the passive (Russian) defence failed and the (Japanese) offensive succeeded.

A successful defensive battle would only be decisive if it facilitated a counter-offensive. The idea that the defender can throw back the enemy attack, then go over to the offensive in turn (the elder Moltke's defensive-offensive concept) was appealing, but, as military history shows, was also unworkable. A better solution was to go on the defensive on one part of the front, perhaps on terrain not suitable for the offensive, where it was possible to employ fewer forces, which would allow stronger forces to take the offensive on another part of the front.

The Infantry Regiment[9]

The basic tactical unit was the infantry company. The wartime strength of a German infantry company was five officers (OFF) and 260 enlisted men (EM). The company commander was usually a captain who was responsible for individual, NCO, and squad and platoon training, particularly individual marksmanship and small-unit fire tactics. The company was broken down into a small company command group and three platoons of about 80 men (in practice, 64–72 men[10]), each platoon consisting of eight squads, each squad led by a sergeant or corporal.

Its non-commissioned officer corps was a particular strength of the German army. Each peacetime German infantry battalion had between 72 and 78 career NCOs, a war-strength battalion had 85 NCOs (including four medical NCOs). These were men who had re-enlisted expressly to become non-commissioned officers. They were carefully selected and provided with excellent training by the company commander and army schools. Training of the individual soldier was in their hands. The company first sergeant, the 'mother of the company', held his position for a considerable period and enjoyed immense prestige and responsibility.

The company also included the combat trains, which consisted of the ammunition wagon and the mobile field kitchen, and the field trains, which included a company supply wagon and a rations wagon.

The German infantry battalion consisted of four infantry companies and the battalion headquarters: 26 OFF and 1,054 EM. The battalion commander was usually a major, perhaps a lieutenant-colonel. He was assisted by the battalion adjutant, the most capable lieutenant in the battalion, who was the operations officer, and by a rations officer, in combat usually a reserve lieutenant, as well as a surgeon and a paymaster, who was also the NCO in charge of property. Each battalion had eight bicycle messengers, armed with carbines. The company trains were united under battalion control to form the battalion combat trains (four ammunition wagons, four mobile field kitchens, plus the battalion medical wagon) and the battalion field trains (battalion staff wagon, four company supply wagons, four rations wagons, one sundries – tobacco and similar personal use items – wagon, one battalion supply wagon), together with 19 vehicles, 38 horses and 47 men. On the march and in combat, while the battalion combat trains stayed close to the battalion, the field trains could be as far as a day's march behind.

The German infantry regiment was composed of three battalions and a machine gun company: 86 OFF, 3,304 EM, 72 vehicles and 233 horses. The regiment was the most important unit in the German army. The regimental commander was responsible for selecting and training the officer corps. The annual recruit, company and battalion inspections and range firing exercises took place in his presence and largely under his control. Unit pride was directed principally towards the regiment and its history. The regimental commander was a lieutenant-colonel or colonel. The regimental staff consisted of three lieutenants: the adjutant (operations officer), an assistant operations officer, and the leader of the field trains (which united all the battalion field trains) as well as the regimental surgeon. The regiment also had a large four-horse wagon with engineering tools: 1,200 small shovels, 275 large shovels, 288 pickaxes, 107 picks, 66 axes, 30 saws and 96 wire cutters. The regimental trains included 72 wagons, 165 EM and 210 horses. In theory the field trains would catch up with the regiment when it billeted or bivouacked, but that rarely happened in mobile operations.

German regiments generally had two designations, first their number within the German army, such as Infanterie-Regiment 154, and then their territorial name, in this case 4 Schlesisch (4th Silesian), or the name of the German state it belonged to, such as Infanterie-Regiment 100 (1. Sächsisches – 1st Saxon). The exceptions were the Prussian Guard and the Bavarian army, which were not numbered within the German army and used only their own designations. German regiments were also frequently given an additional name of famous generals or members of the high aristocracy. According to the history of the regiment, infantry units could also be called fusiliers or grenadiers. Hence the 6th Infantry Regiment was really Das Grenadier-Regiment Graf Kleist von Nollendorf (1. Westpreußisches) Nr. 6. In the full recognition that this is a cardinal sin against the traditions of the old Imperial German Army, for the sake of simplicity we will simply call this regiment IR 6.

Battalions were numbered with Roman numerals I, II, III, and referred to as I/IR 164 (1st Battalion, Infantry Regiment 164). Companies were numbered consecutively within the battalions: the 1st, 2nd, 3rd and 4th companies always belonged to the I Battalion; 5th, 6th, 7th and 8th II Battalion; 9th, 10th, 11th and 12th III battalion. 3rd Company, 1st Battalion, Infantry Regiment 164 was abbreviated 3/ I/ IR 164. The same system applied to cavalry, artillery and engineers.

An infantry brigade in the German army consisted of two infantry regiments and a small brigade staff, and was usually commanded by a brigadier general. An artillery section of three batteries was often attached to it for tactical control.

A German infantry division was a combined-arms force, consisting of two infantry brigades, an artillery brigade and a cavalry regiment; in total, twelve infantry battalions, three or four cavalry squadrons, twelve artillery batteries (seventy-two guns) and one or two engineer companies, plus service and support units. Most division commanders were former General Staff officers. The small divisional staff consisted of a General Staff major and the adjutant (personnel officer), surgeon, intendant, JAG and chaplain.

A German infantry corps consisted of two infantry divisions. An active corps included a heavy howitzer battalion and an aviation section: a reserve corps had neither. An active corps usually included 24 infantry battalions, 6 cavalry squadrons, 28 artillery batteries (144 field guns, 16 heavy howitzers), 3 engineer companies and an aviation section with 6 aircraft. The corps staff consisted of a chief of staff who was a General Staff colonel, and 4 sections: I, the General Staff proper, consisting of the Ia, a General Staff major responsible for tactics, and the Ib, a General Staff captain responsible for rations, billeting and intelligence; II (Adjutant); IIIa (Supply); IIIb (Surgeon).

German Marksmanship Training and Fire Tactics[11]

In his study of the effectiveness of German tactical training in 1914, Liebmann said that the German 1888 combat regulations had to be considered 'an extraordinary accomplishment'. It marked the decisive change from shock to fire tactics. It also put an end to parade-ground tactics (Revuetaktik) and canned tactical solutions (Normaltaktik). The new regulation fostered and required individual initiative and thought. The skirmisher line became standard in combat.[12]

The 1906 *Exerzier-Reglement für die Infanterie*[13] was the base doctrinal tactical document in the pre-war years: there was no combined-arms tactics manual. It is divided into three parts. The first part of the *Exerzier-Reglement* concerns individual and company training. Individual training includes the personal bearing and movements, as well as manual of arms and operating the rifle. Company training includes movement in closed order, in skirmisher line and fire commands. The second part of the *Exerzier-Reglement* covers combat doctrine at the company level. There is also a short third section covering parades and an annex for the drum and trumpet signals.

The first four paragraphs of the *Exerzier-Reglement* state the principles of infantry training and operations in the German army. The infantry was the principal arm on the battlefield, but fought as part of a combined-arms team. Infantrymen must be disciplined and determined, but 'in particular, combat requires leaders and soldiers who are trained to think and use their initiative'. Training must be thorough, but simple. Last, each leader must be granted the maximum amount of latitude to carry out his mission.

In mid-October of the year each German infantry company would receive about eighty recruits. Initially, they would be grouped together under a recruit training officer. The training day would start at 0530 when the troops were awakened by the NCO serving as the company CQ (Charge of Quarters). The troops would quickly wash, clean and put on their uniforms, make their beds (straw mattresses and wool blankets), clean their quarters and then go to the mess hall to get a breakfast of coffee and *komißbrot*, hearty dark bread. Bread is a staple of the German diet and the regimental historian of IR 156 said that the troops liked the *komißbrot*, and that, between the healthy rations and the *komißbrot*, the recruits thrived and put on weight, in spite of the heavy and continual physical labour. At 0700 they began recruit classroom training, focusing on the soldierly virtues: determination, courage in war, obedience to superiors, including the serious admonition that 'Duty was not an empty word'.

The discovery of smokeless powder in the mid-1880s allowed the development of small-caliber rifles which fired rounds with a muzzle velocity of over 600 metres/second, giving the round a much flatter trajectory and ranges over 2,000 metres. The first rifle to utilise this technology was the French Lebel 1886/93, an 8 mm bolt-action weapon which had an eight-round magazine in a tube below the barrel. The standard German rifle in 1914 was the Gewehr 98, which was issued first to the Chinese Expedition troops in 1900 and the regular army in 1901. It was a magazine-fed, bolt-action rifle, the five-round clip being inserted from above in front of the open bolt. This was a very successful weapon, and remained the standard German infantry rifle throughout both world wars.[14]

The recruit training emphasis was not on classroom work but on effective use of the rifle, and on learning how to use the terrain in combat conditions. After the recruit learned how to stand in formation (facing movements, manual of arms) and march, the recruit instruction quickly moved out of the barracks square and into the local training area and the surrounding countryside, which was especially useful for the men who were from the urban industrial areas.

The author of the IR 6 regimental history wrote:

> Commensurate with modern requirements, with the passing of time the training was increasingly conducted in the terrain; daily the recruit detachments could be seen in the very suitable terrain near [the barracks] ... running, bounding forward, crawling, aiming at targets and firing blank ammunition ... Training wasn't easy in our hard Posen winters, but given careful supervision by the medical personnel and the hearty meals our recruits, from the Lausitz and Silesia or from Rhineland-Westphalia, developed brilliantly. As soon as the first Christmas vacation every mother could see in this short time what a strapping fellow her son had become. For our splendid recruits from the coal fields the entire recruit period was easy; they were used to hard daily labour, but they benefited especially from lots of exercise in the fresh air.[15]

The soldier was taught to recognise what targets – human figures – looked like at distances of up to 2,000 metres and then to estimate the range to those targets. The soldier had to master range estimation if he was to be able to fire his weapon accurately. A rifle bullet travels in a parabola. In order to hit a target at an estimated range of 700 metres, the rifleman would set his sight at 700 metres (see Figure 1). This sight setting would cause him to raise the barrel, ensuring that if the weapon were fired accurately the bullet's parabola would pass through the target at that range. He would also adjust the sight picture so that the sight was

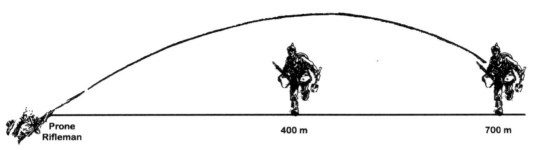

Fig. 1: Trajectory of a rifle bullet at 700 metres range. The parabolic arc taken by the bullet causes it to pass over a target at 400 metres away.

oriented on the middle of the target. However, if the sight was set at 700 metres and the target was 400 metres away, the bullet would pass over its head. If he had estimated the range to be 400 metres when it was 700, the bullet would hit the ground well in front of the target.

In three months the recruit period was ended with the Recruit Inspection (*Rekrutenbesichtigung*) which was held by the regimental commander himself in the terrain, usually the garrison's local training area. Frequently companies would be inspected by more senior officers: the regimental historian of IR 156 told of *Rekrutenbesichtigungen* held by the corps commander. This had to be an advantage for all concerned; the senior officers came into immediate contact with the troops and vice versa, in spite of the stress such an event put on the company commander's nerves. Chosen individuals (in some regiments every recruit) were tested on their conduct as a rifleman. The recruit had to show that he could move forward, low-crawling if necessary, and assume a firing position while using the terrain for cover and concealment; that he could identify targets that appeared unexpectedly, estimate the range, set his sights, accurately aim his rifle, and squeeze off his shot; that he could bound forward as part of a squad conducting fire and movement; and that he could give an accurate tactical report.

After recruit training was concluded the company would train as a unit. At 0600 the company would fall in under the first sergeant for morning formation. When the company commander approached, mounted on his horse, the first sergeant commanded 'Eyes Right!' The senior officer would report. The company commander would call out 'Good morning, Company!' and the troops would reply 'Good morning, Herr Hauptmann!' Then the company, musicians in the lead, would march through the streets to the local training area. Training in the LTA would last all morning. The company would march back to the barracks for lunch, which in Germany is always hot and the main meal of the day. It was a particular pleasure to march in behind the regimental band, which always drew the local girls' attention. The IR 24 historian noted that the troops wanted to put in a good appearance. Every shopkeeper and farmer had been a soldier and cast a critical eye at the troops as they passed by. Every girl was the daughter and sister of soldiers, could distinguish between the sharp soldier and the sloppy one and draw the necessary conclusions.[16]

Sometimes afternoon training included gymnastics using various pieces of equipment, or practice road marches. But once again, the most important training was rifle marksmanship. The rifleman was drilled endlessly on the technique of aiming and firing his weapon: sight picture, placement of the cheek on the butt stock (stock weld), breathing and trigger pull, reloading. Weapons were not locked in the arms room but kept in the hallway outside the squad bay: the soldiers even practised with their weapons during the evening. Individual dry-firing and live-fire was conducted at the garrison firing range. Each soldier was required to complete a prescribed firing table to at least minimum standards, and repeated it until he did so.[17]

IR 20 had an excellent local training area as well as access to large stretches of uncultivated heath. It used them to conduct field training in local security, winter exercises and bivouacs, night operations and combined-arms tactics with Cuirassier R 6 and FAR 74. The regiment was particularly proud of the local firing range, with shade trees and 'a friendly canteen'. The regiment took marksmanship very seriously, as the various shooting trophies in the barracks demonstrated.[18]

Although individual marksmanship was essential, the goal of German fire tactics was to direct the fire of the entire platoon against a specific enemy target. The platoon was the fire unit in German tactics and the platoon leader, through fire commands, designated the target and the range. The fire of eighty men would not fall at exactly the same range; some would go over and some fall short (see Figure 2). If the target were at 700 metres this dispersal would create a beaten zone, called a 'sheaf' (*Garbe*), from 640 metres range to 760 metres. The platoon would also spread its fire along the width of the target. The objective of German fire tactics was to place this beaten zone on the enemy unit. The impact of at least some of these rounds would throw up dirt, allowing the platoon leader to judge if his fire was landing properly and adjusting it if it was not. Squad leaders were trained to direct their squad's fire in the same manner. This system was especially important at medium range (800–1,200 metres): while individual aimed fire at medium range was difficult, the platoon's beaten zone could be effective.

The rate of fire had to be adjusted to meet the tactical situation. The firefight might well last for hours, so the rifleman could not be allowed to expend his basic load of ammunition in the first twenty minutes. The platoon leader would designate the rate of fire, but the rifleman was also trained to fire only when he thought he could get a hit, and on his own initiative to fire slowly or quickly as the tactical situation required. On the other hand, the troops were also taught

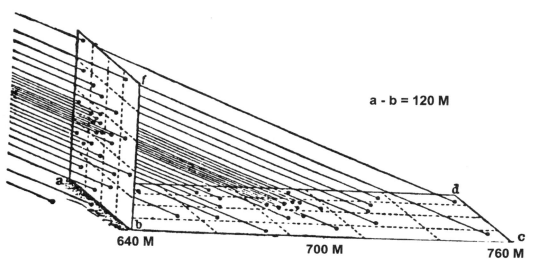

Fig. 2: Beaten zone at 700 metres. Dispersion of a platoon's fire: with point of aim at 700 metres, beaten zone extends from 640 to 760 metres.

that if the enemy was hard to see, fire could be directed at his suspected location (suppressive fire). The platoon leader had two range estimators, who acted as his assistants, watching the effectiveness of the platoon's fire, but also observing the company commander, neighbouring units and the enemy, in order to keep the platoon leader informed; their functions had to be practised. Platoon combat techniques were mastered as battle drills. Individual soldiers were taught to call out their observations and to pass orders down the firing line. As supports entered the firing line, nearby soldiers told them the target and range. Squad and platoon fire tactics were mastered as dry-fire training at home station and practised in live-fire exercises, which were conducted at the major training area.

Combat Gunnery[19]

With the introduction of the Model 1871 rifle, which was capable of accurate fire at ranges far exceeding those of the 1848 Dryse needle gun, the German army, with the Combat Gunnery School at Spandau in the forefront, became serious about combat marksmanship. The Spandau school developed squad, platoon and company graded range firing exercises which became mandatory in the entire army. In 1877 these were designated combat gunnery courses. Initially, they were held on temporary ranges established in manoeuvre rights areas (civilian land rented or sequestered for training). Beginning in the 1890s the establishment of the major training areas (MTA – dedicated manoeuvre areas usually about 8x8 kilometres in size) led to the creation of permanent ranges and an exponential increase in the effectiveness of gunnery training. The Spandau school also conducted demonstration all-arms live-fire exercises. All German company commanders attended one of the Gunnery Schools before assuming command, in a programme similar to the US Army's Master Gunner Course.

The German army taught that the ability of the individual rifleman to use his weapon, as well as the effectiveness of squad and platoon fire, was crucial to obtaining victory. To train and test this ability, the German army required that infantry, engineer and cavalry units fire annual combat gunnery qualification courses while at the MTA. The modern American army still uses a practically identical procedure. The regulations stressed that combat gunnery ranges were to be conducted in as realistic a manner as possible. The targets were not bulls-eye paper targets, but realistic tactical targets. They could be groups of man-sized silhouettes mounted on sleds pulled by long ropes that would move forward and backwards, and would also disappear and then appear for 10–15 seconds, as though the enemy were attacking by bounds. They could also be stationary head-and-shoulders or man-sized pop-up targets (introduced in 1898), which fell over when hit, and were set up depicting firing troops or troops in defensive positions. There were stationary targets that could be turned 90 degrees in order to appear and disappear, or set up in rows to depict advancing or withdrawing troops. Targets were also set up in mock villages. The targets were placed irregularly and in large quantity, up to three times as strong as the firing unit, in order to test the unit's fire control. Targets for squads and platoons were not usually at ranges greater than 1,200 metres. Since ammunition was in short supply, the troops would also conduct extensive dry-fire practices, or practices with blank ammunition, on these ranges.

The squad, platoon and company live-fires were conducted tactically. There were numerous realistic scenarios (attack, defence, etc: the regulation listed forty-three possible scenarios, and that was not exhaustive). The troops were given a situation and mission, the leader issued an order, deploying the troops in the defence or beginning a forward movement: in the latter case, the movement would commence some distance from the firing range. When the targets appeared the troops would assume a firing position, estimate range, pass orders (perhaps disturbed by drummers replicating combat noise) and open fire. Combat actions might include attaining fire superiority, advancing by bounds and control of fire. A leader could be 'killed' and his subordinate would have to assume control of the unit. The situation would dictate the rate of fire: slow fire (one and a half to three rounds per weapon per minute) against distant targets, in poor light and at targets that were difficult to see; high rate of fire (three to seven rounds per minute) against advancing infantry, artillery, machine guns, march columns, or to attain fire superiority and to cover troops making a bound; highest rate of fire (seven to twelve rounds) just before the assault, to defeat an enemy assault, or in sudden close-range contact. Units had to be able to conduct long periods of accurate rapid fire.

The umpire would tell the unit what effects the enemy fire was having on their own unit: none, a few casualties, or demoralising losses. The troops might have to dig in during a long firefight. Pursuit by fire was depicted in several of these scenarios. Experience showed that with 100 rifles firing at 100 head-and-shoulders targets set 1.6 metres apart at 1,000 metres range, twenty rounds per weapon (2,000 rounds overall) had to be fired to hit 25 per cent of the targets; 30 to 40 per cent of the targets hit denoted the attainment of fire superiority. The company would conduct two combat gunnery firings annually, once under battalion control and the second time as graded qualification firing during the regimental exercises. Live-fires always had the character of an inspection and all members of the unit were observed and rated. The evaluation was based first on whether the range estimation was correct and whether the unit's beaten zone was on target. The percentage of rounds that hit and the number of targets hit were both recorded: the overall evaluation, however, was dependent on the tactical conduct of the troops.

Many units conducted battalion and even regimental live-fire exercises. In 1887 the 1st Foot Guard Regiment held a battalion live-fire exercise against moving targets involving defence, attack and pursuit. In 1907 the Kaiser established a fund for this regiment to allow it to conduct an annual battalion-sized combat live-fire exercise, including 1,000 rounds per machine gun.

The German army was serious about marksmanship and fire tactics. Every soldier had a personal *Schiessbuch* (marksmanship book). The company's marksmanship results were kept in a company *Schiessbuch*. The best individual marksmen were awarded the *Schützenabzeichen*, a coloured cord attached to their epaulette on their Class A uniform. Officers annually qualified competitively with the rifle. Companies – and their commanders – were rated principally on the basis of their gunnery qualification results. The best company in every corps was awarded the prestigious *Kaiserpreis* (in Bavaria the *Königspreis*), which included a decoration for the company commander, a bust of the Kaiser for the officer's club and a cloth arm insignia for the members of the company.

Machine Guns[20]

Each active-army German regiment included a machine gun (MG) company with six weapons, three ammunition wagons, four OFF and ninety-three EM. The company also had a supply wagon, a pack wagon including engineer tools, and wagon for fodder, plus a mobile field kitchen. The guns were transported on wagons and dismounted to fire. The MG sections assigned to cavalry divisions could fire the weapons from gun carriages, like artillery.

The standard German machine gun in 1914 was the Maxim Maschinengewehr 08, which on its four-legged *Schlitten* (sled) mount, weighed 57 kg (126 lbs) and had a five-man crew.[21] The MG 08 was difficult to man-carry: two-man stretcher-carry was possible for short distances, but usually a four-man carry was used. In the four-man carry, each man would also carry a box of ammunition. The crew did not have to carry their packs, which were left on the MG vehicles. The gun commander, equipped with binoculars, directed the fire. The mount provided a very stable firing platform, allowing the gunner to precisely adjust fire using an elevation hand-wheel and making slight lateral adjustments by tapping the traversing handles. The ballistic characteristics of the MG round – muzzle velocity, trajectory and range – were basically identical to those of the rifle round. The gun was water-cooled, which provided a high rate of fire, but also required a supply of water. Steam rising from the gun could also give its position away. The German MG 08 fed ammunition from a 250-round belt.

European armies are often criticised for failing to recognise the destructive power of machine-gun fire. As a consequence, practically all historians maintain that the infantry attempted to attack machine guns in mass formations and were mown down in rows. In fact, German tactical doctrine fully recognised the power of machine guns. The *Exerzier-Reglement* was supplemented in 1909 to provide doctrine for the employment of machine guns: the German army therefore had more than three complete annual training cycles to practise with machine guns. The *Handbook* said that machine guns had attained an 'extraordinary importance'. They were capable of generating the greatest firepower in the smallest area and in the shortest possible time, quickly producing a decisive effect at the desired place. Immanuel said that 'the machine gun is the weapon of the future, of immense importance'.

The principal concern when MGs were introduced was the same as that after the fielding of rapid-firing rifles in 1848 and magazine-fed rifles in the 1880s – the troops would quickly shoot off all their ammunition. But aside from this restriction, the power of machine guns was clear. German infantry doctrine recognised that skirmishers advancing without cover in machine-gun fire would take heavy casualties at medium range. Given good observation, skirmishers lying prone could be engaged by MGs out to 1,000 metres range. An assault on machine guns would result in 'enormous casualties'. In an army whose tactics centred on directing rifle fire to the desired place and winning fire superiority, the ability to concentrate a high volume of MG fire (cyclic rate of 500 rounds per minute) in a small area was revolutionary. Six machine guns concentrating their fire on one target would 'produce a quick, decisive result'.

Machine guns would best be engaged with artillery or other machine guns. Since MGs could use cover effectively, they would present a difficult target, hard to find and just as hard to hit. Machine guns posed an even more difficult target for infantry fire, requiring a large number of rifles and high expenditure of ammuni-

Fig. 3: Machine-gun team advancing. In the background a second MG provides covering fire.

tion, whereas machine guns were able to inflict casualties on the infantry even at long range. Any infantry advance against machine guns required careful use of the terrain and unexpected, quick bounds forward, using the interruptions inherent in MG fire (changing of the ammunition belt and barrel). If movement by bounds were no longer possible, the skirmishers should low-crawl until they were within close range, at which point even a squad could take the gun under effective fire.

German infantry doctrine particularly emphasised that machine guns were just as useful in the attack, being able to suppress defensive fire and contribute significantly to winning fire superiority. Because of concern for ammunition resupply, doctrine called for MGs to be kept in reserve for use at the decisive place and time, and not be committed to long, drawn-out firefights. Unless MGs could find a good overwatching position, they were to be brought forward into the firing line. Although the water-cooled German MGs, their mounts and ammunition were heavy, doctrine required that the crews man-carry the guns forward by bounds to keep up with the attack. In the defence, MGs might be kept in reserve, but the emphasis of the regulation was to employ them from the outset in an overwatching position or on the front line: preparing fields of fire and digging the guns in was important. Choosing flanking positions that allowed fire across the defensive front was considered particularly effective.

An important advantage of the machine gun over rifle fire was that the impact of so many rounds in a restricted space made the fire usually easy to observe and adjust. MG fire could be moved quickly and accurately to the exact place that it was wanted, even at long ranges. The MG 08 was also not an infallible wonder weapon. The history of the 1st Foot Guard Regiment reported that it was too heavy to keep up with the advancing infantry, jammed frequently, and, in spite of the water cooling, required frequent barrel changes (every MG had six spare barrels!).[22]

For all of the machine gun's usefulness, only infantry could take and hold ground. An infantry regiment still consisted principally of infantrymen – 3,000 rifle-armed infantrymen as opposed to six machine guns. Machine guns were most proficient on exactly the kind of flat, open terrain that the infantry would try to avoid. In rolling terrain, in built-up areas or in woods, where infantry was most effective, the influence of machine guns would be much reduced.

The Infantryman's Combat Load[23]

The mobility of an army was based on the individual infantryman's ability to road-march as well as to move across country. The soldier's mobility depended on his physical fitness and the load he carried. Everything possible was done to lighten the German soldier's load, including constructing his canteen and canteen cup from aluminium. The German soldier's pack (in German infantryman's slang the 'Affe', the ape[24]) weighed 11 kg (about 24 lbs), in which he carried a change of underwear, a pair of lace-up boots, a field cap, two iron rations, a washing- clean- ing- and sewing-kit, tent pegs and rope and thirty rounds of ammunition. His coat, wrapped in his poncho, and his mess kit were attached on the outside. His weapon weighed 4 kg (9 lbs). On his combat harness he carried ninety rounds in ammo pouches, his bayonet, bread canister, canteen and entrenching tool. The spiked helmet, or *Pickelhaube*, was made of leather, not metal. The soldier also car- ried two combat wound dressings sewn into both front corners of his battle dress blouse. The total combat load, including clothing, was about 24–30 kg (53–66 lbs).[25] To make sure that he carried only that which was absolutely necessary, his combat load was minutely regulated by strict inspections.

In combat, unit commanders could direct that the soldier drop his pack. This would reduce his load by the most cumbersome one-third. The commanders thereby ran the risk that his soldiers would be separated from their packs for a longer period or lose them permanently, and with them the coats which kept the soldier warm, the ponchos which kept him dry and formed the bivouac tents, his iron rations and thirty rounds of ammunition. For those reasons, the German soldier almost always carried his pack into combat.

Before engaging in combat, the company ammunition cart would be unloaded and its contents distributed to the troops (about seventy rounds per man), who would carry the extra ammunition in bandoliers and stuff loose clips into pockets or bread canisters. Movement by bounds was therefore conducted by troops who were carrying sixty to seventy pounds of weapons, ammunition and equipment.

The Infantry Company on the Move [26]

The most common formations for cross-country movement were the squad column, the platoon column and the company column.[27] In the squad column, the squad moved in two ranks, the squad leader and four men in the first rank and four men in the second rank. In the platoon column, the platoon was formed in a line of squad columns. It therefore had two ranks and had a forty-man front. If the company were moving in platoon column, the platoons would move one behind the other. In the company column, the company moved with platoons abreast. The platoons were formed in squad column, one squad behind the other. Each platoon therefore had a five-man front. This formation was the easiest to use during an approach march. The company could also move on line. The platoons were then formed abreast, in two ranks. Finally the company could move in squad column, one squad behind the next. The road-marching column was a modified squad column, having a four-man front. As a practical matter, on trails in the woods tactical units could march in single file. There were no battalion or regimental movement formations: the battalions deployed individual companies, as the situation required.

These were movement, not combat formations. In enemy fire the only combat formation was the skirmisher line or swarm.

Our baseline for discussing German tactics will be the infantry company in the attack. The purpose of German offensive tactics was to place effective fire on the enemy in order to gain fire superiority, and then close with the enemy by means of fire and movement and destroy him in close combat. This litany can now be repeated by probably any infantry officer in the world.

The German army introduced the concept of fire superiority in the ground-breaking 1888 *Exerzier-Reglement*, and it remained the distinguishing characteristic and cornerstone of German tactics thereafter. Fire included machine-gun and artillery fire, but principally it meant rifle fire. Success would be dependent on the training, fire discipline and marksmanship of the individual rifleman. The final assault with the bayonet sealed the enemy's defeat.

Closed formations, such as march columns, were used for approach marches only and could not be employed under effective infantry fire. High and deep targets, such as standing or marching troops in closed formation, could be engaged successfully at long range, which was from 1,200 metres out to the maximum effective range of the weapon. At medium range (1,200 to 800 metres), such targets would be destroyed. Low, dense targets could also be engaged successfully at medium range.

When the company anticipated making contact it would deploy from company march column into platoon columns and then, if necessary, into squad columns. Smaller columns were easier to control and able to utilise the terrain and therefore allowed quick movement. Frequently, the company would deploy with two platoons in front and two platoons following about 300 metres behind in support (far enough not to be hit by the small-arms fire or artillery shrapnel fire directed at the lead elements), but any other formation that met the requirements imposed by the terrain and situation were permissible. The company would continue to close with the enemy while in platoon or squad column for as long as possible, until it received effective enemy fire. The company would then deploy into skirmishers.

The German army used only one infantry combat 'formation', and that was the skirmisher line or swarm. The 'normal' distance between skirmishers was two paces (1.6 metres, which sometimes grew to 2 metres), and was called a 'dense' skirmisher line, but this distance would be greater in more open terrain. One gunnery qualification problem called for a skirmisher line with four-pace (3.2 metre) intervals. Dense skirmish lines were easier to control and provided greater firepower, but were also better targets for defensive fire. Looser skirmisher swarms might theoretically suffer fewer casualties to enemy fire, but the looser they were the more difficult they became to control, while reducing the unit's firepower; too much dispersion compromised the unit's ability to accomplish its mission. It was also very difficult to significantly change the direction of advance of a skirmisher line, which is one reason why the approach march was continued in squad, platoon or company column for as long as possible.

Skirmisher lines moving in the open could be engaged at medium and even long ranges. It was important for skirmishers to move irregularly, by bounds, using all available cover and concealment.[28] The bounds would probably be by platoon, or by squad. If enemy fire was weak or inaccurate, the bounds could be as long as 80 metres: if it was strong and effective, much less. At the early stage, bounds might be made at a walk. Each platoon might also advance in several waves of skirmishers with 5- to 6-metre intervals between skirmishers. The company would advance as close to the enemy as possible and then take a position and return fire. A rule of thumb was that the range for opening fire should be 700 metres, but in terrain that offered good cover and concealment it might be closer, in open terrain further away. Behind the firing line the supports (successive waves of skirmishers from the same platoon) and reserve platoons would also advance by bounds, utilising all available cover and concealment. The reserve platoons could advance in skirmisher lines or as squad or platoon columns.

Effective use of terrain played an essential role in German offensive tactics. If possible, attacking units were to avoid open ground and use the terrain that provided the most cover and concealment. However, it was unlikely that the defender would be so accommodating; rather, he would strive to defend on open terrain that provided him with the best fields of fire. In this case, the attacker would advance in waves of loose, open skirmisher lines with expanded intervals between skirmishers. When the first skirmisher line had bounded forward to a position suitable for beginning the firefight, it would stop and take cover. It would not, however, immediately open fire. Rather, it would wait until the successive skirmisher lines had come forward to form the dense skirmisher line which alone could generate enough firepower to prosecute the firefight successfully.

The firefight was conducted at the platoon and squad levels.[29] The German infantry would be supported by artillery and machine-gun fire. The objective was to place effective fire on the enemy position, cause him casualties, but more important, make him take cover to avoid being hit and thereby spoil his ability to see his target and aim his weapon. When this occurred, the enemy fire would become weaker and less accurate: the enemy would fire too high. The Germans had gained fire superiority.

The German infantry – individuals, squads, even platoons – would seize this opportunity to bound forward as far as possible, covered by the fire of their comrades. They would then take up a firing position and resume fire. The rearward groups would bound level with or beyond the first group. This is called fire and movement. Determining whether your side had gained fire superiority would not be easy, and making the decision to bound forward would require courage. At medium and close range (less than 800 metres), the only manner in which long, dense, skirmisher lines could advance – and survive – was by fire and movement. Fire superiority might be lost: bounding forward reduced German fire and might give the enemy the respite he needed to allow him to expose himself to fire effectively, and it might be necessary to regain fire superiority. Key terrain would be seized that would give especially favourable points to provide fire support, and dug in to serve as offensive strongpoints.[30] As the tactics textbook, the *Handbook*, said: 'The modern infantry fight has the character of a long, hard struggle for fire superiority. The attacker's skirmisher line, carefully using the terrain and cover, can only advance slowly.'[31] Ammunition resupply would be difficult, if not impossible, and accurate fire and fire discipline were critical. There would be significant casualties; the strength of the firing line would be maintained by individuals, squads or even entire platoons moving forward from the supports or from the reserve platoons into the firing line. If the attack stalled, the German soldiers were taught to dig in with their entrenching tools and continue the fight in place. German doctrine was very cautious about individual units pushing forward ahead of their neighbours, for fear that this unit would be defeated in isolation. There was also a tendency at all levels to commit reserves in sectors where the attack had stalled or failed. The ideal was a uniform advance by all units.

Because formed bodies of troops could not survive in the face of modern fire, and all troops on the battlefield sought cover and concealment, the battlefield became 'empty'. Since the advent of smokeless power and the small-calibre rifle,

Fig. 4: The infantry is advancing in successive waves with large intervals between each wave. Supporting artillery fire is landing on the objective.

the firing enemy no longer gave off a cloud of white smoke, but was almost invisible. At the beginning of an engagement, it might not even be possible to tell where the enemy position was. The lethality of modern weapons made the transmission of orders from the rear to the firing line and reports from the firing line to the rear slow and difficult. The noise of weapons firing and artillery exploding was deafening. The company commander was the highest-ranking officer who was able to exercise real tactical control of his troops. Battalion and brigade commanders could commit troops to combat, but lost control of them once they were engaged. Combat leadership was actually the function of the platoon and squad leaders.

It is evident that if the unit was to succeed in these terrifying circumstances, the soldier had to be superbly trained and disciplined, and had to possess courage, high morale, determination, and individual initiative. All were needed if the soldier was to accurately aim, fire and reload his weapon, and then on command – or on his own initiative – jump up in enemy fire, run forward twenty metres (carrying pack, equipment, rifle and ammunition), then take up another firing position, fire, and then advance again. Drill occupies an essential role in making this possible.

Barracks-ground training – formal drill – was and is the foundation of military discipline. It involves standing and marching in formation, proper wear of the uniform and military courtesy, such as forms of address and saluting. Formal discipline was always important in the German army, but as of the 1888 *Exerzier-Reglement* less and less time was spent on formal drill in favour of combat training.

The German army used the term 'battle drill' (*Gefechtsdrill*) in its current sense – training and practising routine combat tasks until they become automatic.[32] Drill allowed the soldier to ignore the terrors of enemy fire, the isolation, the wounds and death of his comrades, sergeants and officers, the thirst, the heat, lack of sleep and fatigue, and carry out his combat tasks. He had been drilled to load, aim and fire his weapon accurately, shift and adjust his fire and clear stoppages in his weapon quickly. He had been drilled to bound forward skillfully. But drill and discipline alone are not adequate. Ultimately, the infantryman advanced because of personal motivation and morale. The best soldiers are, through drill, courage and dedication, able to apply their judgement and reason to master the tactical task at had, and to exercise their initiative. These men are the natural battlefield leaders.

Moreover – and this factor has been ignored by the critics of 'Prussian drill' – three quarters of the mobilised German army would consist of reservists, and in case of necessity even Landwehr troops would be committed to combat. These men had not had any military training in years, perhaps not in a decade or more. Yet their training had to have been so effective that they could quickly become soldiers again. German reservists proved decisively that they were able to do so. Only superb training – and drill – could have produced such reservists.

As the German firing line approached the enemy position the enemy would begin to crack, and individual enemy soldiers would be seen leaving their positions and heading for the rear. When the firing line had advanced close enough to the enemy position (in peacetime training, 100 metres), the final step was to take the enemy position by assault. The decision to conduct the assault could be taken by the leaders on the front line or by the battalion or (less likely) brigade commander to the rear. The leader deciding to assault would give the order to 'Fix bayonets!' which would be taken up by trumpeters and all leaders. At this time, all successive waves moved quickly forward, as did reserve platoons and companies. Riflemen, machine guns and artillery began rapid fire. The company or battalion commander would then give the command 'Charge!' (*Rasch Vorwärts!*). This signal was repeated by all drummers and buglers. The battalion standards were unfurled and the troops assaulted the enemy position shouting 'Hurra!'

When the enemy position had been taken, the troops advanced far enough to take a firing position and pursue the retreating enemy by fire. Since French doctrine emphasised the immediate counter-attack to retake a lost position, the assaulting unit would organise the conquered position for the defence. The actual pursuit would only begin after the unit had reconstituted itself, that is, brought the squads, platoons and companies back together, re-established the chain of command by replacing leaders that had been killed or wounded and resupplying ammunition.

This offensive combat drill has become the standard for all armies. This is the same combat drill – including the assault – that I was taught as a recruit in basic training in 1968, and that I used as an infantry platoon leader in 1973 and as a mechanised infantry company commander in 1980. Artillery was to do its best to suppress the enemy artillery, but its primary mission was to support the infantry by bombarding the enemy position. There was generally no 'artillery preparation' prior to the infantry attack. This was felt to be ineffective. The defender would hide or hunker down in his fighting position and the bombardment would waste ammunition and advertise the area of attack, while accomplishing nothing more than tearing up the shrubbery. Rather, the infantry advance would force the defenders to open fire, thus revealing their positions and establishing the targets for the artillery bombardment.

Victory would not come cheap and casualties, particularly in officers, would be heavy. The German army continually stressed that victory had to be obtained '*koste, was es wolle*' – cost what it may.

The friction involved in war itself and the power of modern weapons created an environment in which command and control in combat was difficult at best.[33] Especially within the zone of effective enemy infantry fire, and to some degree also of artillery fire, sending reports from the front to the rear and transmitting orders from rear to front was dangerous, time-consuming and very unreliable. Orders from superior commanders would be transmitted slowly and could easily be overtaken by events.

The German solution to this problem was *Auftragstaktik*, or mission-type orders. The commander not only gave his subordinates a mission but also explained his intent – his concept of the operation. At each level, subordinate leaders were given a mission, but the manner in which that mission was executed was left up to that leader, with the caveat that the leader was responsible for acting within the parametres of the intent of his commander. It was also possible that situations unforeseen by the superior commander would arise. The subordinate leader was then authorised to act on his own initiative and report to his superior as soon as possible.

The system of *Auftragstaktik* was emblematic of the German philosophy of leadership, training and war-fighting. To be effective, it required that leaders at all levels be thoroughly familiar with German tactical and operational doctrine. Producing the necessary level of tactical skills necessitated intensive tactical training, not just at schools but at the unit level. Commanders at all echelons had to be personally responsible for the tactical competency of their subordinates. Such a system gave wide scope in combat for company commanders, platoon leaders and NCOs, while requiring that regimental and battalion commanders pay close attention to their training.

Winter was used for the tactical training of NCOs and officers.[34] NCO training was principally a company matter, in which patrolling and tactical reporting played a large role. In the winter of their second year of duty, conscripts were given specialised training, such as first aid, use of field telephone and bicycle, or training to become an NCO candidate.

For the officers, in the winter, battalion and regimental commanders conducted tactical exercises without troops (TEWT) and assigned graded written tactical problems (*Winterarbeit*). In the 1880s war games (*Kriegsspiele*) became obligatory. The 1st Foot Guard Regiment held a war game almost every week, as well as a TEWT once a year.[35] The goal of these exercises was simple: training officers in the rapid analysis of the military situation and in writing short, clear, effective orders. This involved an analysis of the friendly and enemy situation, understanding the commander's concept of the operation and his specific orders to each unit, and analysing the terrain and weather and using the available time wisely. The factors the officer had to consider varied with each mission: defence, attack, movement to contact, etc. The officer had to arrive at his own decision and a concept of the operation for his unit and issue his order.

In the preceding century, no army mastered these troop-leading procedures as well as the German army. On the battlefield on 23 and 26 August 1914 the German tactical commanders concentrated superior force at the weakest part of the British position and crushed it.

Cavalry[36]

A cavalry squadron comprised six officers and 163 enlisted men. Every cavalryman was armed with a lance, which was considered the primary weapon, being thought particularly effective in mounted combat against enemy cavalry. He was also armed with a carbine, a shortened version of the standard infantry rifle.

German cavalry was divided into strategic cavalry (*Heereskavallerie*) organised into cavalry divisions, which comprised the greater part of the German cavalry, and divisional cavalry, which was organic to the infantry divisions.

Divisional cavalry consisted of one regiment with a command group (8 OFF, 30 EM) and three squadrons, about 26 OFF and 510 EM per infantry division, which conducted tactical reconnaissance, usually in conjunction with the division advance guard. Cavalry regiments assigned to reserve divisions were called half-regiments, but in fact had three squadrons. Divisional cavalry also provided messengers and carried orders. The cavalry regiment combat trains included two wagons with bridging material, a telegraph wagon, two packhorses with medical equipment and a cavalry medical wagon. The field trains included three wagons.

The strategic cavalry was organised in wartime into eleven cavalry divisions. A cavalry division had three brigades, each cavalry brigade being made up of two cavalry regiments, each regiment consisting of a command group and four squadrons: 36 OFF, 688 EM. For fire support the cavalry division had six machine guns and twelve 7.7 cm canon. For supply it included a cavalry truck column.

Compared to previous German cavalry formations, such as those used in the Franco-Prussian War, which were composed overwhelmingly of cavalry armed with sabres and lances, not rifles, and were therefore tied to the infantry corps for protection, the *Handbook* said that modern strategic cavalry had become an all-arms, flexible force, with greatly increased firepower and the capability for independent operations. In particular, each cavalry division included an organic machine gun company. The cavalry division possessed a significant communications capability, with a section of six horse-drawn wagons for equipment (telegraph, telephone, signal lamps and heliograph) and a communications equipment truck. Four passenger vehicles were available to carry messages. Wireless telegraphy equipment would also be assigned as needed. *Heereskavallerie* was further organised into four cavalry corps, each with two or three cavalry divisions, wireless telegraphy, a bridge train and engineers.

The *Handbook* stated that the horse defined the parameters of cavalry operations. The horse allowed cavalry to move quickly; the mass and the tendency of the herd to charge forward gave it force in close combat. On the other hand, horses were hard to control when under fire, especially from artillery, or when their rider was attempting to fire. Cavalry was expensive, and training the horse and rider required time. Cavalry operations were therefore characterised by speed of movement, and cavalry preferred to fight by attacking with the lance while mounted. Cavalry would, however, often be placed in the position where it needed to use its carbine on foot. Frequently, cavalry would use both mounted and dismounted combat in conjunction with each other. Cavalry was not suited to attrition battles. The *Handbook* did not mention an important drawback concerning cavalry's maintenance-intensive qualities. The horses had to be unsaddled, watered, fed, curry-combed and rested frequently if they were to remain healthy. This not only required time, but during this period the cavalry unit was immobile and practically defenceless. Standard operating procedures therefore usually prescribed that the cavalry withdraw behind the infantry to bivouac. This often involved exhausting and time-consuming marches each night and the next morning.

The usual description of German cavalry before the war emphasises Kaiser Wilhelm's penchant for conducting division- or corps-sized cavalry charges at the annual *Kaisermanöver*. From this, it is inferred that German cavalry trained principally for its supposed role as *Schlachtenkavallerie* – to attack infantry on the battlefield with mass cavalry charges. This is completely erroneous. All German doctrinal manuals agreed with the *Handbook for Tactics Instruction* which says that, 'The most important role for cavalry lies in reconnaissance'. At the beginning of the war, when the two armies were moving to contact against each other, the cavalry corps, usually moving in division columns, had the mission of gathering operational-level information concerning the movements of the enemy infantry corps.

The most effective means for cavalry to conduct reconnaissance was to first drive away the enemy cavalry. Cavalry combat would usually take the form of meeting engagements. German cavalry would attack enemy cavalry wherever they found it. The enemy could be fought either with the lance while mounted, or dismounted with the carbine, according to the situation. The carbine would principally be used not against enemy infantry but against enemy reconnaissance elements: mounted and dismounted cavalry, or light infantry and bicycle infantry.

Reconnaissance was conducted principally by patrols, usually of about twenty men led by an officer. If possible, cavalry patrols would attack enemy cavalry patrols. Of course, there was the caveat that such attacks could not compromise the reconnaissance mission, nor be tactically reckless, but the offensive tenor of the regulation was unmistakable. The officer patrols would be backed up by a reconnaissance squadron. Each reconnaissance squadron was responsible for a 15–20 kilometre sector. If the patrols ran into resistance which prevented them from carrying out their mission, the reconnaissance squadron's task was to clear away the enemy force, if necessary in dismounted combat. A reconnaissance squadron was to be able to advance 30–35 kilometres daily. It would pass the reports of the officer patrols to higher headquarters by means of field telephone, signal lamps or messenger. A specialty of the strategic cavalry was the long-range patrol to conduct operational reconnaissance or destroy sensitive targets deep in the enemy rear with explosives.

The *Heereskavallerie* was also to push back the enemy's advanced combined-arms units or bypass them and penetrate as far as his corps and divisional columns, and into his rear areas. As the two infantries closed in on each other, the cavalry corps lost their room to manoeuvre and were moved sideways to the army's flanks. From there, they would attempt to attack the enemy's flanks and rear, which was the best employment for cavalry in combat. There it was also well-positioned to begin the parallel pursuit of the defeated enemy. The most important combat role for the cavalry was in conducting the pursuit or covering the withdrawal.

When the opposing infantry corps closed on each other, the divisional cavalry's tactical reconnaissance role became vital. The cavalry patrols would be supported by the advance guard infantry. It was necessary to determine the enemy's strength and direction of march in order to decide where and when to deploy the corps and divisions. When contact was made, the divisional cavalry continued to conduct reconnaissance, now in the form of combat patrols, principally against the enemy flanks and rear. This might well require dismounted combat or even foot patrols. All cavalry also performed a counter-reconnaissance function, attacking enemy cavalry patrols to prevent the enemy from obtaining information concerning the locations and movements of the German infantry. The historian of the 20th Uhlan Regiment (27 ID, XIII Corps) says that the regiment's peacetime training in all sorts of patrolling and security missions (including cavalry night patrols) was outstanding, and that the regiment was liberally supplied with officer and NCO patrol leaders who wanted nothing better than to demonstrate their skills in combat.[37]

In German cavalry doctrine, therefore, mounted action would take place primarily against other cavalry, not infantry. Large-scale mounted attacks, said the *Handbook*, were a thing of the past, if only because it was no longer possible to find extensive stretches of open terrain to conduct them on. In the last century, buildings had sprung up everywhere, as had the barbed wire that was used to enclose livestock. Against cavalry masses, the infantry could use individual terrain features (such as small copses) as strongpoints. Immanuel said it was clear that attacks over open ground against combat-capable infantry 'could result in the complete destruction of the attacking cavalry'. Mounted attacks could still be conducted against targets of opportunity; in this case, a concealed approach and surprise were a precondition for success. Against infantry, machine guns and artillery the chances for the success of a mounted attack were greatest if the cavalry was able to attack a flank. Given the range and effectiveness of modern weapons, this would be difficult to achieve. It was still possible to charge weak infantry units; units whose morale had already been broken in combat or second-rate reserve and third-rate territorial units. If a charge had to be made frontally against infantry, very wide intervals had to be used at high speed (beginning gallop at a greater than usual distance) which 'provides a means to avoid casualties'. Infantry would usually be attacked in several waves, from two or more sides if possible. Against artillery, it was best to attack when the guns were limbering up, or unlimbering, or against the front of artillery which was a covered, defilade position. The *Kaisermanöver* cavalry charges were pure theatre, and the German army knew it.

For dismounted combat, a cavalry squadron with 160 men had two tactical options. Half the riders could dismount, forming two rifle platoons. Each remaining mounted man led one riderless horse, which allowed the horses to be moved at the trot or gallop. The horseholders would then move or remain out of the line of fire, probably at least 300 metres to the rear. This option optimised mobility (the ability to quickly bring the horses forward) at the expense of firepower. Or, three-quarters of the riders could dismount, forming four rifle platoons. The horseholders, again 300 metres or so to the rear, were then responsible for three horses in addition to their own, and they generally dismounted, too. The horses could then move only at a walk. This option optimised firepower at the expense of mobility. A cavalry division with six cavalry regiments of 700 men, 4,200 cavalrymen in total, could dismount 3,150 riflemen.

Dismounted cavalry used the same tactics as did the infantry, with the caveat that the cavalry did not have the depth or staying power that the infantry possessed, was unsuited to long drawn-out combat and was much more sensitive to casualties. Cavalry would most likely attack dismounted to remove obstacles to its reconnaissance or to seize key points, such as bridges or rail stations. The cavalry was to avoid frontal attacks and demonstrate with one element against the enemy front, while other elements used cavalry speed and mobility to manoeuvre and attack the enemy flanks and rear, before resuming mounted operations as quickly as possible. Cavalry would conduct a dismounted defence to delay the enemy, to hold key terrain or towns until the infantry could arrive, to block enemy reconnaissance forces, or to defend their bivouacs.

Whatever some cavalrymen might say concerning the possibility that cavalry still could successfully charge infantry, the infantry itself was unimpressed. The infantry was sure that it had no reason to fear cavalry, so long as it could use its weapons, even if the cavalry was much stronger in numbers. Weaker infantry could successfully conduct a firefight with dismounted cavalry; the horses presented a special weakness.[38]

Jäger Battalions

The German army formed separate light infantry (Jäger) battalions. These battalions consisted of a company equipped with bicycles, four light infantry companies and most important, a full machine gun company with six guns. They were about 1,500 men strong, although the bicycle company was often detached for reconnaissance duty.

In German, Jäger are hunters, and the German Jäger battalions specialised in marksmanship, individual initiative, patrolling and use of the terrain in very open-order formations. They considered themselves to be an elite unit, motivated by Jägergeist, the spirit of the hunter. The historian of Jäger-Bataillon 3 said: 'Outpost duty and patrols were great fun. Large numbers of Jäger would volunteer: those that were chosen were envied by the rest. Every day they would engage enemy cavalry patrols and security detachments, sometimes taking prisoners.'[39] This was an aggressive group of soldiers. They did not wear the Pickelhaube but a shako, and they had their own jargon: their rucksack was not the infantryman's Affe (ape) but the Dachs (badger). This mix of high morale, mobility, modern training and machine-gun firepower created very powerful units. Indeed, the Jäger battalions were the wave of the future.

Heereskavalleriekorps 2 (HKK 2, 2nd Cavalry Corps), which operated principally against the BEF, had five Jäger battalions attached. This provided HKK 2 with greatly increased firepower, 7,500 light infantrymen and the ability to take and hold ground. Operating in a semi-independent manner with the fast-moving cavalry suited the Jäger just fine: it was a *Jägerauftrag*, a light infantry mission.

It had originally been intended to provide *Kraftwagen Kollonen* (motorised transportation columns) to allow the Jäger to keep up with the cavalry. The Jäger histories show that only one of these ever materialised. Mention was made of one of the columns hauling ammunition for the heavy artillery at the bombardment of Liège and it is a safe bet that such ammunition supply missions became their permanent employment. The Jäger therefore had to keep up with the cavalry by foot-marching. They were aided by the fact that they could march independently, which was far easier and faster than infantry in a brigade or division column. Nevertheless, it is a tribute to the high quality of the training and morale of the Jägerbataillone that they were able to keep up with cavalry. When HKK 2 caught up with the British II Corps on 26 August, after three days of punishing forced marches, the Jäger were right there with the horsemen.

A distinctive characteristic of German tactics was the use of patrols at all tactical levels and by all arms.[40] Immanuel said that great care must be committed to training this difficult operation. At the army, corps and divisional levels, the principal mission of the cavalry was reconnaissance and counter-reconnaissance. Infantry regiments, battalions and companies made extensive use of tactical patrols both prior to making contact and during combat itself. Artillery batteries sent officer patrols far forward to acquire targets. Infantry patrols were seen as a method of discovering the location of enemy artillery so as to direct counter-battery fire. Engineer companies patrolled to prepare for their mobility/counter-mobility missions: in particular prior to river crossings, and clearing or constructing obstacles. Infantry, artillery and engineer company commanders were all mounted and routinely rode forward of their units in reconnaissance. If the enemy had constructed a prepared defence, all four arms patrolled extensively to determine as much as possible about the enemy position. Patrolling did not stop once contact was made: combat patrols were continually used to clarify both the enemy and friendly situation.

Artillery[41]

The mission of the field artillery was to support the infantry. The objective was also to bring a superior number of guns into action at the decisive place and time. In German doctrine the priority of fires was directed against the targets that were most dangerous to the infantry. At the beginning of an engagement, priority of fires was normally given to counter-battery fire, to cover the infantry approach march. The intent was to gain fire superiority over the enemy artillery. During the infantry firefight, priority of fires was generally given to fire on the enemy infantry, but counter-battery fire would continue to be conducted. Given the increased use of the terrain for cover and concealment by all arms, targets for the artillery would often be fleeting and there would not be enough time to eliminate the target entirely.

The French Model 97 75mm gun was the first to incorporate a recoil brake. Since the gun was now stable, the gun aimer and loader could remain seated on the gun, and an armoured shield be added to protect the crew. The new French gun could fire up to twenty rounds a minute, against eight or nine for the German Feldkanone 96, which had just been fielded. Given this increased firepower, the size of the battery could be reduced from six guns to four. The French also introduced the armoured caisson. The 75 caused a sensation and the French imagined it to be a war-winning weapon. French tactics prescribed that the 75 would provide the firepower necessary to support the infantry attack with rafales, intense bursts of fire, to shake the enemy infantry. This was area fire, which made up in volume what it lacked in accuracy.

German divisional field artillery consisted of two weapons: a 7.7 cm flat-trajectory gun (Feldkanone 96 n/A) and a 10.5 cm high-trajectory light howitzer (leichte Feldhaubitze 98/09). The maximum effective range of the 7.7 cm gun is a subject of some controversy. In fact, the theoretical maximum range was rarely relevant. In practice, the maximum effective range was variable, depending on the ability of the battery commander to acquire targets, see the fall of shot and adjust his shells onto the target. The author of the FAR 25 regimental history said that 4,400 metres was long range, and targets at 5,000 metres were out of range,[42] even though the maximum range of the shrapnel fuse for the 7.7 cm gun was 5,300 metres, and for the contact fuse 8,100 metres. The light howitzer was provided with a recoil brake and the tube could be elevated to a high angle, which allowed it to fire easily from covered positions. The parabolic arc taken by the shell made it very effective against targets behind cover and in field fortifications.

A wartime-strength German battery included 6 guns or howitzers, 5 OFF, 188 EM and 139 horses, the battery commander's observation wagon, two supply wagons, a ration wagon and a wagon for fodder. Each regiment had six batteries divided into two three-battery sections, which were commanded by majors. A field artillery regiment included 36 guns, 58 OFF, 1,334 EM and 1,304 horses, including 2 light ammunition columns, each with 24 caissons. There were 4 OFF, 188 EM and 196 horses to each ammunition column. Ammunition columns were formed only at wartime and for a few training exercises. The field artillery did not have mobile field kitchens, which was found to be a severe problem in mobile operations. In each active army corps there were three gun and one howitzer regiments; one division had two gun regiments, the second a gun and a howitzer regiment. Reserve divisions had only one gun regiment.[43]

A German field artillery piece was drawn by six horses and consisted of the gun, its limber and a six-man gun crew, and an ammunition caisson, with its own five-man crew. The gun and caisson were provided with armoured shields that protected the crews against small-arms fire and shrapnel. The gun could be operated even if 50 per cent of the crew were casualties. Artillery batteries could immediately replace losses in personnel and horses by drawing on the regimental ammunition columns, which took replacements from the divisional ammunition columns and so on. The gun commander rode on a horse, 'drivers' rode on the gun team horses, gunners rode on the limber or the gun itself. The German field artillery battery of six guns would generally deploy in firing position with twenty paces (about 13 metres) between guns. The caisson and two of the caisson crew would deploy to the right side of the gun. The gun and caisson limbers with the horses, 'drivers' and the two remaining caisson crew would pull back 300 metres to the rear so that they would not be engaged by counter-battery fire directed at the guns. In practice, this proved to be too close and the horses and limbers were often hit by fire aimed at the guns. When the battery needed to move, the horses and limbers would be brought forward. The light ammunition columns would deploy 600 metres behind the gun line and move forward based on flag signals. The horses were the vulnerable point in an artillery battery. The guns could not unlimber and go into position, or limber up to withdraw without significant horse casualties, if they were in infantry fire at medium range (800 to 1,200 metres). Subjected to close-range infantry fire (ranges less than 800 metres) the vulnerability of the horses immobilised the battery.

There were two types of battery position. In the open firing position the guns were not covered or concealed. The gunners could see to their front and directly aim the guns over open sights. The guns were also visible to the enemy. A battery could occupy an open position easily and could fire quickly and effectively, especially against moving targets. It could rely on the gun shields for protection against small-arms fire, but in an open position it was visible to enemy artillery and vulnerable to counter-battery fire. Open positions would be used in a mobile battle. In a covered (or defilade) firing position, the guns went into battery position behind cover or concealment (frequently on the reverse slope of a hill). The guns were aimed by the battery commander, who set up his command wagon in a position where he could observe the enemy; the guns were then laid in for direction from the battery command wagon using an aiming circle (similar to a theodolite), and firing commands (deflection and elevation, type and number of rounds, fuse setting) were usually transmitted by field telephone from command wagon to the guns. Covered battery positions were nearly invulnerable to counter-battery fire, unless the dust thrown up by the muzzle blast betrayed the gun's position. Frequently the enemy would be reduced to attempting to suppress guns in a covered position by using area fire based on a map reconnaissance of likely covered positions, a procedure that demanded large quantities of time and ammunition. The disadvantage of covered positions was that occupying them was time-consuming, because of the extensive reconnaissance needed to find a suitable position in the first place, followed by the time necessary to lay the battery using the aiming circle. Adjusting fire would take more time than in an open position. Covered positions would be used at the beginning of an engagement, in artillery duels, and against stationary targets and dug-in positions. There was also a half-covered position, in which the guns were defilade, but could be aimed by the gunners standing on the gun. Such positions were preferable to open positions while at the same time allowing a more rapid support of the infantry that completely covered positions. Guns could also occupy an overwatch position. The battery was then deployed in a covered position, laid on an azimuth in the general direction of the expected target. When the target was observed, the battery was man-handled into firing position.

If the time and suitable positions were available, the artillery would initially occupy covered positions, but in the course of the battle, the artillery would almost always be forced to displace and fire from half-covered or open battery positions. If necessary the artillery, like the infantry, was to advance by bounds. Some batteries might be moved forward to provide close-range direct-fire support. When the infantry began the assault, the artillery would fire on the enemy defensive position for as long as possible, until the danger of friendly fire became too great (usually at 300 metres) and then shift its fire to the rear of the enemy position. When the enemy withdrew, he would be pursued by fire, with the artillery moving forward at a gallop and on their own initiative, if necessary, to keep the enemy in range.

Prior to the introduction of long-range quick-firing artillery around the turn of the century it was common to employ artillery in long continuous lines. In order to use the terrain effectively and avoid counter-battery fire, artillery was now to be employed in groups. Enemy counter-battery fire was rarely able to destroy a gun or caisson; its usual effect was to suppress the guns by forcing the crews to take cover. For that reason, the crews were to dig revetments around the gun positions as soon as possible, even in the attack. If the guns came under effective fire, the artillery commanders had to decide, on the basis of the overall situation, whether the gunners could cease fire and take cover, which involved the crews' retreating several hundred metres, leaving the guns and caissons in place, or if the artillery had to continue to fire, even if it meant that the crews were destroyed or the guns were overrun. Under overwhelming fire the artillery commanders down to battery level were authorised to order the crews to take cover.

It was the responsibility of the artillery to maintain liaison with the infantry through the use of forward observers (FO). The FO would communicate with his battery through field telephones or signal flags. His most important mission was to keep the guns informed as to the relative locations of the friendly and enemy troops, so that as this distance was steadily reduced, the guns could place fire on the enemy for the longest possible time. The artillery also regularly sent forward officer patrols, frequently in conjunction with cavalry patrols, in order to develop targets for their batteries.

The standard shell for gun artillery was shrapnel with a time fuse. The shrapnel shell exploded above and in front of the target, covering the target area with metal balls. In practice, setting the time fuse was difficult and shrapnel often burst too high. There was also a high-explosive round with contact fuse, which was used by howitzers and also by guns.

Beginning in the 1890s the German artillery underwent a profound transformation.[44] In 1890 the cannons were not provided with recoil brakes and gunnery practice took place from open positions at ranges of less than 3,000 metres. Firing from covered positions was inaccurate and slow. Then the improvements came fast and furious. FAR 69 recorded receiving the light howitzer in 1899, with aiming circle and field telephones to facilitate firing from covered positions. In the spring of 1906 FAR 69 received the cannon with recoil mechanism and gun shield. In 1907 a new artillery regulation introduced a doctrine commensurate with the new equipment and made combat effectiveness the sole standard for training. Firing with time fuses became normal, the field guns received stereoscopic battery telescopes, field telephones (1908) and aiming circles, and armoured observation wagons. Reservists were recalled to active duty to receive training in the new equipment. The German field artillery in 1914 had good equipment and had plenty of time to train with it.

For over twenty years prior to the First World War, the German army worked to perfect its heavy artillery, which involved constructing a mobile 15 cm schwere Feldhaubitze 02 (sFH 02 – heavy field howitzer, 1902) for the corps artillery and a 21 cm mortar for the army-level artillery, and then creating the techniques and doctrine to use them.[45] Originally, the impulse for this development was the need to be able to quickly break the French fortress line, and in particular the Sperrforts located between the major French fortresses. This mission shifted to one which focused on destroying French field fortifications and finally to counter-battery fire. Particular emphasis was also laid on integrating the sFH into combined arms training, including live-fire exercises.[46] By the beginning of the war, the German heavy artillery was fully proficient in all three missions. No other country in Europe possessed such combat-effective heavy field artillery.

Every German active-army corps included a battalion of 4 batteries of schwere Feldhaubitze, each battery having 4 guns: 16 guns and 32 caissons in total. The battalion also had an organic light ammunition column. The reserve corps did not have this battalion, which significantly reduced its combat power.

The 15 cm gun was characterised by the destructiveness of its high-explosive shell (bursting radius 40 metres to the sides, 20 metres front and rear), combined with its long range (most effective range 5,500 metres, max effective range 7,450) and high rate of fire. It was particularly efficient against enemy artillery, which was otherwise protected by its gun shield, and against infantry in field fortifications (the shell came down nearly vertically and was capable of penetrating two metres of overhead cover) or in defilade behind masking terrain. It was less effective against moving targets than the field artillery. The heavy field howitzer was less mobile than the field gun, but nevertheless was able to move long distances at a trot. The sFH battalion normally fought as a unit, firing from covered positions.

The 7.7 cm gun fired a 6.85 kg (9.35 lb) shell at a rate of up to twenty a minute. The 10.5 cm howitzer fired a 15.8 kg (34.75 lb) shell at a rate of four per minute, and the heavy howitzer fired a 39.5 kg (87 lb) shell at a rate of three to six per minute.

By 1906, combined arms tactics meant infantry–artillery cooperation.[47] Infantry and artillery were to complement and support each other. Infantry protected the artillery; the principal mission of the artillery was to support the infantry. Artillery was to be deployed at least 600 metres behind the infantry so that the one arm would not suffer from fire directed at the other arm.

The writers of German doctrine did not fully recognise that in a mobile battle it was nearly impossible to maintain communications between attacking infantry and supporting artillery, which would become apparent only during the Battle of the Frontiers. This would lead to delays in the artillery supporting the infantry, as well as numerous incidents of friendly fire.

Infantry could minimise the effect of enemy artillery fire by careful use of the terrain, continual rapid movement, and dispersion. The history of *Infanterie-Regiment 127* said that this was commonly practised in peacetime.[48] In particular, platoons could be broken down into successive waves of open skirmisher lines with 300 metre intervals between lines to reduce vulnerability to artillery fire.

Nevertheless, the *Handbook* said that infantry could not advance in the face of strong, effective artillery fire. This presented a quandary. The preparatory bombardment by the friendly artillery had little chance of completely suppressing the enemy artillery, which was provided with armoured gun shields and deployed in covered positions. The infantry advance could not wait for the artillery to gain fire superiority, which might never occur. The infantry attack and the counter-battery battle would necessarily proceed in parallel to each other, and the infantry would almost surely have to advance under at least some enemy artillery fire.

Attack on a Deployed Enemy[49]

The infantry attack on a deployed enemy was the baseline tactic for all German attacks. The attack on a dug-in enemy followed the same principles, but was conducted even more slowly, with more preparation and heavier artillery support, and the infantry advance itself was probably conducted by night. A meeting engagement followed the same principles, but was conducted more quickly, with less reconnaissance and preparation time, and it was more likely to begin at short ranges, leading to a violent close-range firefight and quick assault.

The doctrine for an attack on a deployed enemy, as well as against a dug-in enemy, were directly derived from the older procedures for an attack on permanent fortifications, that is, from siege warfare, which shows that the German army recognised the strength of firepower and the protection afforded by field fortifications in the modern defensive.

In an attack on a deployed enemy, the attacker had the time to conduct careful reconnaissance with patrols led by infantry, cavalry, artillery and engineer officers, while the main body was still advancing. After adequate reconnaissance had been made, the first decision to be taken was whether the attack should proceed immediately, or if the approach march should be delayed to deploy under the cover of darkness. In either case, the first step was for the forward infantry elements to establish a protective screen behind which the artillery would deploy, usually about 3,000 to 4,000 metres from the enemy.

The artillery then would begin the preparation fire, primarily counter-battery fire, in an attempt to gain artillery fire superiority. However, it was unlikely that the enemy artillery could be suppressed. An hours-long preparatory bombardment by the artillery against the (suspected) enemy infantry positions before the infantry attacked was felt to be of little value. Only when the infantry attack began would the enemy occupy his defensive positions and open fire, thereby giving the friendly artillery targets to fire at. Initially, priority of artillery support would be given to counter-battery fire; as the enemy infantry began to fire, priority of artillery support would be shifted to the enemy infantry.

The infantry would then deploy, if possible on a covered and concealed position, protected as much as possible from enemy artillery by the terrain and friendly artillery fire. In open terrain this infantry line of departure could be as far as 3,000 to 5,000 metres from the enemy front line. The attack order specified each unit's mission and attack sector. The concept of an attack sector was an innovation of the 1906 Exerzier-Reglement. A war-strength company (250 men) would generally deploy on a 150-metre front, a battalion on a 300-metre front (with two companies forward) or 450-metre front (with three companies forward), and a brigade with six infantry battalions on a 1,500-metre front. The attack sectors were kept intentionally narrow to allow a deployment in depth, in order to have supports and reserves available to replace casualties on the firing line. In sectors where success could be expected, the forces were stronger, in sectors where success was unlikely, weaker. The infantry would advance systematically, from phase line to phase line designated on recognisable terrain features. Units would remain in march column for as long as possible, utilising the cover and concealment provided by the terrain, and preceded by a skirmisher screen and patrols. Units that could exploit favourable terrain were permitted to advance quickly, while those forced to use open terrain would advance more slowly.

When the infantry began to receive effective enemy infantry fire, the attack proper would begin with the deployment of the forward platoons into a skirmisher line, which would advance first by using the cover and concealment in the terrain, then by bounds. The objective was to advance until enemy fire became so strong that it would be necessary to occupy a firing position in order to suppress it. The manner in which the skirmishers were deployed and moved was dependent on the mission and situation. On terrain that provided cover and concealment, strong, dense skirmisher lines, moving forward in unison as far as possible, were employed. Open terrain called for an initial deployment that was weaker and further away from the enemy and the advance would be slower and more careful. In open terrain the platoon could deploy in waves of loose skirmisher lines. If a significant distance had to be crossed under effective enemy fire to reach the firing position, or if the situation was not clear or the engagement was to begin slowly,

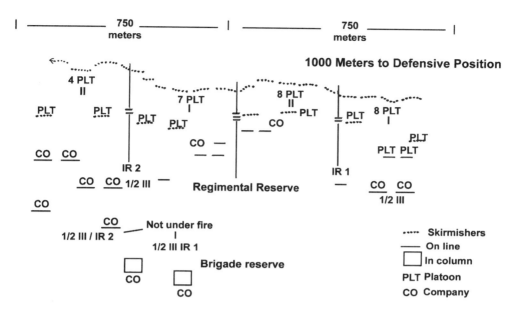

Fig. 5: Dispersion of infantry regiments in the attack. The attacker's front is 1,000 metres from the defensive position. The attack is making most progress on the left.

then the open skirmisher lines were to be committed carefully. However, the overall situation might require that strong forces be committed on open terrain.

A company would normally begin its advance by deploying one and a half or two of its three platoons as skirmishers, with the remainder following in platoon or squad column. When the skirmishers had reached a point where they could engage the enemy by fire, a dense skirmish line would be formed and the firefight would begin, with the aim of winning fire superiority. Once fire superiority had been attained the advance by fire and movement would begin. One element would give covering fire while the other bounded forward to a favourable firing position. The size of the advancing unit depended on the effectiveness of the enemy fire. If that fire was weak, not much covering fire would be needed and large groups – platoons or half-platoons – could bound forward. If the fire was strong perhaps only a squad or even an individual soldier could advance. German doctrine emphasised that the infantry firefight could easily be hours long and drawn out, and could not be rushed. The difficulty inherent in attacking a deployed enemy, given the lethality of modern weapons, was fully recognised.

Time and again, both the regulation and tactics experts highlighted that every tactical situation was unique and that uncertainty would be the norm. They therefore warned repeatedly against any attempt to apply cookie-cutter solutions to tactical problems. The best corrective against such a tendency was training outside the Kaserne, on the ground.

Testing Infantry Doctrine

Since the work in the 1850s and 1860s of the modern Prussian army's first great tactical trainer, Prince Friedrich Karl, German tactical doctrine was developed and tested in the field through troop exercises at the major training areas (MTA). The 1906 infantry attack doctrine, based on the lesson learned from the wars in South Africa and Manchuria, was also tested by the Combat Gunnery School in Spandau and in major exercises. One such test was a brigade attack over open ground described by Lieutenant-Colonel Breitkopf of the Bavarian Combat Gunnery School.[50] The exercise was conducted at the Lechfeld MTA, which is a dead-level plain made up of gravel covered by tufts of grass (it is now a Luftwaffe airfield). The description of this attack was presented as a lecture and was published as a FOUO (For Official Use Only) document within the Bavarian army.

The attack over flat, open terrain was the most difficult mission in pre-war infantry tactics.[51] There was some doubt that, in the face of modern firepower, it was even possible at all. Breitkopf warned that this exercise was to present only one example of how such an attack might be conducted. The inevitable changes caused by the situation, enemy, terrain, weather and so forth would lead to other tactical decisions, methods and procedures being employed. He opposed any application of a standard tactical procedure (*Normaltaktik*) as well as pretty but unrealistic 'parade-ground' tactics. On the contrary, the most important factor on the modern battlefield was the initiative of the subordinate leaders.

In this exercise the brigade was assumed to be in the centre of a corps attack, that is, there were brigades attacking to its right and left. The *Exerzier-Reglement* said that a brigade would have taken about thirty minutes to deploy from a march column.[52] At the beginning of the exercise the brigade was in a covered assembly area 2,100 metres from the enemy front. The exercise began with the attacker sending out reconnaissance patrols, which had to penetrate the defender's security elements.

For the sake of simplicity, and so as to be able to isolate and test the infantry battle, the effect of artillery fire was not considered in this exercise. It was assumed that the defending artillery was in large part suppressed by the attacking artillery, and that the attacking artillery caused as many casualties among the defender's infantry as the defending artillery caused among the attacking infantry. The German army was, however, not doctrinally optimistic about the ability of the attacking artillery to suppress the defending artillery.[53] Breitkopf also pointed out that in actual combat everything would happen much more slowly than in an exercise: one hour of movement and firing in the exercise might require ten hours in actual combat.

The brigade plan was to deploy its two regiments abreast, ten companies on a 1,500-metre front. Each of the four front-line battalions committed two or three companies in the first line, leaving a second line made up of the battalion reserves, six companies. In the third line were the four companies of the regimental reserves and in the fourth line four companies of the brigade reserve.

The first task was for the attacking infantry to close within medium rifle range in order to begin the fight for fire superiority, which in this exercise meant crossing the 900 metres of open ground between 2,100 and 1,200 metres from the enemy position. The *Handbook* said that the concern at this stage, given the highly lethal combination of the defender's small-arms, MG and artillery fire, was to avoid casualties: this meant dispersion.[54] Breitkopf said that live-fire tests against moving targets (rows of targets on multiple target sleds) representing a dense skirmisher line had resulted in casualties of 28 per cent. A more open skirmisher line would also take 28 per cent casualties, but because there were far fewer targets in it, it would take much longer and require a far greater expenditure of ammunition to attain the same absolute number of hits. Based on the characteristics of defensive rifle fire at long range[55], the optimal attacking skirmisher line would have intervals of five to six metres between soldiers. The lead companies, on a front of 150 metres, should therefore advance in successive waves of skirmisher lines of twenty-five men each. The waves followed 300 metres apart. Such dispersion would slow movement, but the tactical situation did not demand a rapid advance. At about 1,200 metres from the enemy position, the first wave was to stop and begin to establish a firing position. However, it would not open fire until at least three more waves had arrived, giving one-metre intervals on the firing line, or the strength of one platoon. Reserves would follow dispersed and moving by bounds.

At 0900 the lead ten companies formed up in the attack position behind a low rise with a dense skirmisher line (about one and a half platoons) in front. The troops were given their instructions concerning the conduct of the attack. At 0930 the first wave of skirmishers with five- to six-metre intervals began the forward movement at a run. The enemy opened (simulated) fire. Umpires designated where this fire was ineffective and caused no casualties; the advance was continued at a walk. Otherwise, it was conducted by bounds. The advance became irregular, as some units made rapid progress and others did not. If troops took casualties while lying down, then they were in the beaten zone of the enemy fire and advanced quickly to move out of it. At every halt the NCO and officer leaders attempted to re-establish order and encourage the troops.

At 1000 the lead elements approached to within 1,200 metres of the enemy position and began to establish a firing line by digging in with entrenching tools and by utilising all available cover, and were joined by the following waves. The attackers did not open fire until 1130, when a dense skirmish line had been formed. The supports and reserves remained covered and concealed in the attack

position, 900 metres to the rear. With the beginning of the firefight the first support waves moved out at a walk to within 300 metres of the firing line and then
took cover. When it was necessary to replace casualties to maintain the strength of
the firing line, supports moved forward in open skirmisher lines by bounds. The
reserves also moved out at 300–400 metre intervals, in a single line and at a walk
so long as they did not take effective fire. If they received effective fire and began
to take casualties, they were to move forward by bounds.

The enemy fire on the brigade left flank was less powerful, and the brigade
concentrated its reserves there as the most likely place to penetrate the enemy
position. The right-hand regiment, which was taking more effective enemy fire,
was informed that the brigade reserve would not be committed in its sector. At
1300 the situation was as follows. Of the twenty-four infantry companies in the
brigade, nine and a half had been committed to the firing line. The battalion on
the left had experienced the least resistance and had committed only four platoons of twelve platoons (one and a third of its four companies), its neighbour on
the right had committed seven platoons (two and a third companies), and the two
battalions of the right regiment nine platoons (two and two-third companies)
each. Most of the regimental and the brigade reserves were not receiving enemy
fire. The brigade commander was told that the overall situation now required
that he press the attack. At 1310 he issued the order to the battalion commanders
to begin forward movement; at 1320 this order reached the front-line company
commanders; at 1330 the firing line increased its rate of fire. The front line now
began to advance using fire and movement.

Breitkopf noted that the most productive bound was that conducted by an
entire platoon at once, but enemy fire might make it possible for only half-platoons, squads or individuals to bound forward. The smaller the bounding group
was, the more rifles were available to cover it by fire. On the other hand, the
smaller the group, the shorter the bound, in order to avoid masking the supporting fire. Breitkopf noted that the Gunnery School had conducted live-fire
exercises in 1906 to test the effectiveness of defensive fire against small groups of
moving targets bounding forward at irregular intervals. The ability of the defending squad and platoon leaders to direct fire against small attacking targets was
degraded. Individual fire was less effective against poor and irregular targets than
unit fire and the strength of the defensive fire in general against such targets was
reduced by 50 per cent. On the other hand, a 1903 live-fire test, using large quantities of ammunition, showed that if the attacker tried to low-crawl eighty metres
he was exposed to enemy fire for 105 seconds, more than three times longer than
a thirty-second bound, and that low-crawling was very fatiguing. Low-crawling
was, however, four times more effective for short distances than bounding forward.
Breitkopf said that recent combat and numerous tests had shown that attempting
to move across open terrain, without fire support, in order to begin the firefight at
close range, was hopeless.

The most important task in an attack over open ground was the firefight at medium range (approximately 800–1,200 metres). Using his rule that actual combat took ten times longer than live-fire training, Breitkopf said that crossing the ground from 1,200 to 800 metres from the defensive position would take three to four hours. It was therefore important to move as quickly as possible in the area from 1,200 to 1,000 metres from the defender and bring plenty of ammunition. The attacker's fire could be effective, particularly since the defending line was stationary. A live-fire test in 1903 (using the older Type 88 munitions) involved an attacking group moving in short bounds, who crossed the area from 1,200 to 1,000 metres from the defenders in twenty-two minutes, while in the process their fire hit one-third to one-quarter of the defenders (head-sized targets). In 1905 and 1906, tests using the modern Type S munitions showed that the attacker's fire was 40 to 50 per cent more effective.

Breitkopf then cited Japanese experiences with this form of attack in Manchuria during the Russo-Japanese War. A brigade of the Japanese 5th Division began to advance 1,800 metres from the Russian position; at 800 metres it began to use fire and movement, bounding with platoons, half-platoons, squads and individuals until it got to within 300–500 metres of the Russian position, where it dug in. The advance took three hours and the unit suffered 17 per cent casualties. Another Japanese battalion at Mukden needed three and a half hours to move by individual and squad bounds to within 400 metres of the Russian position. Failure to conduct movement by short bounds could be catastrophic: the Japanese 3rd Guard Regiment attempted to attack with six or seven companies in the first line, moving in long (80-metre) bounds. The regiment was stopped 600 metres from the Russian front with 43 per cent casualties.

In our exercise the left and right elements of the left-flank battalion took little effective fire and were able to bound by platoon, even though the middle of the battalion hung back. These forward elements took up firing positions and under their covering fire the battalion centre advanced by squad and individual 25-metre bounds. The next battalion on the right committed two reserve platoons to the firing line and held the last two platoons ready to do the same. The important thing, Breitkopf said, was to carry the attack forward. There were no attack formations or predetermined sequences of movement. It was irrelevant as to who sprang or crawled forward first. Even the smallest unit used moments of fire superiority to go forward. Rearward units then strove to get forward too. Support and reserve leaders watched the situation on the firing line and pushed their troops forward whenever they found it necessary or advantageous. The regimental reserve companies advanced to replace the battalion reserve companies that were now committed on the firing line. As the reserve companies of the left-hand regiment were committed, they were replaced by the brigade reserve companies.

By 1630 the entire brigade firing line had fought to within 400 metres of the enemy front line. Enemy fire was inaccurate and individual enemy soldiers could be seen moving to the rear. Doctrinally, the assault should begin as soon as the enemy has been weakened enough to permit it. Breitkopf noted that determining when this has occurred is frequently not easy. The effectiveness of infantry fire at short range, Breitkopf said, is fully recognised and requires no further comment. In Manchuria the Japanese had often begun the assault only to be met by strong Russian defensive fire which forced them to halt at close range in front of the Russian position. At Colenso, in South Africa, instead of assaulting General Buller ordered the withdrawal, at the same moment that the Boers were considering abandoning their position.

If the assault was stopped, it was absolutely necessary for the troops to hold the terrain that they had won.

The regulation, Breitkopf noted, did not mandate a particular method for conducting the assault. The important thing was to finish the enemy off with the bayonet. If the leaders on the firing line decided to assault, they made this known to the battalion or brigade commanders through a pre-arranged signal. If the decision was made by the brigade or battalion commanders in the rear, the signal 'Fix Bayonets' was sounded. The firing line began rapid fire and all supports and reserves moved forward quickly. The assault would probably not be conducted by the entire line at once, but by each element as soon as the opportunity presented itself. Once an element began its forward rush, it continued its movement until it had broken into the enemy position. Sections of the firing line that occupied favourable positions remained in place to continue to give assaulting elements covering fire.

In Manchuria, Japanese assaults differed according to their estimate of the enemy resistance. They began 350, 300 or 250 metres from the Russian position and attempted to break into the position in one rush. If the Russian position had not been sufficiently weakened (was not *Sturmreif*) the Japanese would stop and resume rapid fire. Frequently the battle would then go on for hours. Sometimes the Japanese attack would stall 500 or 400 metres from the Russian position. The Japanese did not lack courage or energy, but the morale and physical force of the soldiers on the firing line had been exhausted, and because the Japanese often deployed operationally on too broad a front, they lacked the supports and reserves necessary to give new impetus to the attack. In these circumstances, the Japanese had no other choice but to wait for darkness in order to bring up additional forces. The Russians often withdrew from their positions during the night, without waiting for the Japanese to renew their assault.

In the exercise, the decision to conduct the assault was first made on the left flank of the front line at 1645. The signal 'S S S' (*Sturm, Sturm, Sturm* – assault, assault, assault) was given to the rear and was picked up all along the firing line. The assault was made at 1700 and was successful: the enemy abandoned his position. The retreating enemy was pursued by fire. The assaulting forces prepared the position for the defence; troops not necessary in the defence were pulled back and reorganised to serve as reserves.

Introduction of the magazine-fed rifle had led to widespread concern that the troops would quickly fire off all their ammunition. Breitkopf said that combat experience had shown that this was true only for poorly-trained troops, such as the Turks in 1877–78; troops in the Chilean War (1891) managed to fire off their basic load of ammunition (180–200 rounds) in thirty-five to forty minutes. On the other hand, well-trained Japanese troops with an assault load of 160 rounds (120 rounds basic load, 40 additional rounds for the assault) never ran out of ammunition. The Japanese also employed well-trained carriers to bring ammunition forward in combat.

In the German army the regimental combat load of ammunition was 340 rounds per man. This was divided into an individual basic load of 150 rounds (120 rounds in the ammo pouches, 30 in pack); 70 rounds in the company ammunition wagon (this ammunition was distributed in bandoliers as the assault load before the attack); and 120 rounds in the unit trains.

In Manchuria, Breitkopf said, much to everyone's surprise, 86 per cent of the casualties were caused by rifle fire, 11 per cent by artillery fire and 3 per cent by the bayonet. (Such casualty figures led pre-war theory to underrate the effectiveness of artillery fire.) Breitkopf's conclusion was that Manchuria confirmed the rule that improvements in weapons and increases in the size of armies lead to a lower percentage of casualties overall, but casualties in individual units would reach the highest levels of those in previous wars. This, he maintained, supported the German emphasis on rifle marksmanship and tactics based on rifle fire.

The German army began the First World War with a tactical doctrine that spotlighted the dominance of firepower on the battlefield. Artillery support was essential, but the battle could only be won if the German infantry drove off the enemy infantry and took the enemy position. This could only be accomplished if the German infantry, through fire and movement, could close with and destroy the enemy. These infantry tactics have been adopted by nearly every combat-effective infantry force today. The sole difference is that today the volume of infantry firepower has been vastly augmented, with magazine-fed bolt-action rifles being replaced by automatic assault rifles, light and medium machine guns, grenade launchers, light and medium anti-tank missiles and hand grenades. In spite of all this firepower, it is still recognised that if the enemy is determined, it will be obligatory to destroy him with 'close combat', if necessary, with the bayonet. That German tactics have triumphed is due to the fact that they succeeded on the battlefield. There were competing tactical systems that failed, such as the British artillery-dominant tactics used on the first day of the Somme, Pershing's US Army human-wave assaults in 1918 and French defensive tactics used in 1940.

The surest route to success, the *Exerzier-Reglement* said, was to combine a frontal attack with an attack on the enemy flank.[56] The goal was not merely to push the enemy back, as was the case with a frontal attack, but to cut off the enemy's line of retreat and destroy him. An enveloping attack would not enjoy surprise: the enemy would detect its approach. Therefore an attack on the enemy front was necessary to fix the enemy forces in place, preventing the enemy either from shifting his troops to meet the attack on the flank or from withdrawing. Coordinating the two actions would be difficult. It was important that the frontal attack not be defeated before the flanking attack could be effective. On the other hand, troops in contact could not be shifted to attack an enemy flank. At a minimum, the flank attack had to be made by unengaged reserves. The most productive flank attack was made by operational manoevre, by troops whose approach march led them to the enemy flank.

Defence[57]

The *Exerzier-Reglement* said that infantry firepower in the defence was very strong and therefore required fewer troops. In a well-prepared position a division might hold a nine-kilometre front, three times the frontage it would occupy in the attack. An infantry company would usually defend a trench 150 metres long. The defender was rarely able to choose a defensive position on its merits alone; usually the overall situation determined the line on which he must defend. The defence was capable only of holding a position. The offensive alone could bring victory. The *Handbook* emphasised that only enough forces should be committed to the defence as were absolutely necessary to hold the position, in order to create the largest possible reserve for the counter-attack, in particular, the best response to an enemy envelopment was a counter-attack.

The principal requirements for a defensive position were an open and long-range field of fire and freedom of movement in and behind the position. The artillery position would be at least 600 metres behind the infantry line of defence. Artillery would like to be able to conduct observed fires out to 4,000 or 5,000 metres range; infantry needed a field of fire out to medium range (700–1,200 metres). Good fields of fire immediately in front of the position were also important. The weakness of a defensive position lay in its flanks, so long as these were not covered by terrain obstacles or other troops: a good defensive position had to possess at least one secure flank. It was seldom going to be possible to find a defensive position that was strong everywhere, and particularly not if the position was a long one. Favourable terrain could be weakly held, unfavourable terrain must be more strongly held. In organising the position, the defender observed priorities of work. First priority was to clear fields of fire and to determine ranges. Then fighting positions were dug and communications cable laid down.

The *Handbook* noted that, given the lethality of modern weapons, field fortifications were particularly useful but required considerable time to construct. The defence was to consist of battalion battle positions built around company strongpoints, with the intervals between the strongpoints being covered by fire, and not a continuous line of trenches. Immanuel provided an exhaustive discussion of a formidable position fortified according to German doctrine, including wire obstacles. Field fortifications lost much of their effectiveness if they were observed by the enemy, so they had to be well sited in the terrain and camouflaged: 'what can be seen, can be hit' applied to the defender, too. Security patrols must prevent enemy reconnaissance patrols from approaching the position. German doctrine called for the organisation of one defensive line: strong forces in the security zone in front of the main line of resistance, such as the French habitually used, might confuse the enemy as to the real location of the main line of resistance, but could also lead to defeat in detail and would obstruct the fire from the main position. In allocating forces in the defence, it was important to maintain a strong reserve (*Hauptreserve* – the same term used in fortress defence). In pre-war doctrine, troops did not occupy the entrenchments until an infantry attack was anticipated, but rather were held in a covered and concealed position to the rear. It was felt that keeping the entrenchments strongly manned merely gave away their position and led to needless casualties due to the resulting enemy artillery fire. An important advantage of the defensive position was that it allowed the stockpiling of rifle ammunition; if remunerative targets presented themselves at long range, they could be engaged. Machine guns, which occupied little space but produced high volumes of fire, were seen as powerful weapons in the defensive. They needed to be dug in, concealed and protected by obstacles and supporting infantry positions. Night defence required aiming posts and aiming bars to direct fire at predetermined directions, as well as night security patrols and listening posts.

Initially, the defending artillery would engage the attacking artillery. If it appeared that the defending artillery would lose the artillery duel, it would cease fire, the gun crews would take cover, to resume firing when the attacking infantry advanced, and the priority of fires would be changed to engage the attacking infantry. Artillery fire would mass on an enemy penetration.

The defeated force would find withdrawal during daylight to be very costly. If the infantry were engaged in a close-range firefight, withdrawal might be impossible. Generally the withdrawal would have to be conducted under cover of darkness.

Pursuit and Delay[58]

Defeating the enemy on the battlefield would result in only half a victory. The defeated force would generally be disorganised and practically helpless. But without an energetic pursuit, the enemy would quickly recover. The pursuit should crown this victory with the complete annihilation of the enemy. The admonition to conduct a ruthless pursuit probably appears in every doctrinal manual ever written. German doctrine added a more realistic appraisal of the prospects for conducting a pursuit. It noted that military history offers few examples of ruthless pursuit and as a consequence, few battles of annihilation. The defeated enemy was, in spite of his fatigue, able to make truly remarkable marches in retreat. The attacker had just survived a tremendous ordeal and was exhausted; the natural tendency was for him to relax. The attackers would also be disorganised, low on ammunition and hungry. Key leaders would have been killed or wounded. The *Handbook* made the prescient observation that, given the immense size of the modern battlefield and the nature of combat, it was also going to be difficult both to recognise the extent of the victory and the condition of one's own troops: the victor could not begin the pursuit until he knew that he had won the battle. The *Handbook* obviously felt that forewarned was forearmed, because, having said this, it reiterated the need for ruthless pursuit.

Initially, the pursuit was conducted by fire. The victorious force would overrun the enemy position and advance far enough to put fire on the retreating enemy. If the combat had taken place in a town or woods, this meant advancing to the opposite edge of town or the far side tree line. Machine-gun and artillery fire were particularly effective in pursuit. If the enemy moved out of range, a general pursuit along the entire line followed in order to prevent the enemy from reorganising or establishing a new defensive position. The artillery would advance by bounds.

The infantry was the arm least suited to conducting a pursuit, which was primarily a matter for cavalry and artillery. The truly effective pursuit would be a 'parallel pursuit' developing out of an envelopment, in which the pursuer moves on roads parallel to those of the retreating forces. This allows the pursuing forces to occupy blocking positions at critical choke points (such as bridges) in the enemy rear. The most important and most profitable cavalry mission was the conduct of the pursuit.

The victorious troops and leaders would be tired. Motivating them to conduct an immediate pursuit was very difficult. The leaders were instructed, if necessary, to act with severity towards their own troops in order to press the pursuit: 'whatever collapses [men or horses], lays where it falls'; the remainder presses on. The *Handbook* noted that by this time it was probably dark. The defeated force would conduct a night march in order to break contact. It was therefore necessary that the pursuit also be continued during the night. The entire force would not be able to continue the pursuit. The infantry would finally be worn out. Cavalry would continue the pursuit until it encountered occupied towns or defensive positions. It would then maintain contact. Cavalry units conducting parallel pursuit would continue to advance so as to be able to block enemy lines of retreat on the following day, when the pursuit would be resumed in order to place fire on the enemy and, if possible, block his routes of withdrawal.

Retreating forces would use rearguards to delay the pursuit. The objective of delaying operations is to slow the pursuer down and to allow the retreating force to break contact, either in order to withdraw or to redeploy elsewhere. The *Exerzier-Reglement* emphasised providing rearguards with strong artillery which would fire at long ranges, forcing the enemy to stop, take cover and deploy. Rearguard infantry would also fight at long ranges in broad formations. The infantry would withdraw before becoming decisively engaged.

The Major Training Area

An army fights the way it has been trained; the quality of that training is decisive.[59] The German army's victories in August 1914 did not occur because of its formal barracks square discipline, nor its tactical doctrine, nor *Auftragstaktik*, but because of the superiority of the training that was conducted at the German Major Training Areas (MTA). The number of German regimental histories that mention training, especially at the MTA, and affirm how effective that training was, is quite remarkable. The history of IR 20 expressly connects MTA training with the development of German doctrine.[60] Otto von Moser, a senior serving officer and prominent military writer, said that in 1914 the XIII AK in which he served was a crack unit, one of the reasons for this excellence being the MTA at Münsingen, which was an 'outstanding training area for realistic combat training of troops of all arms, probably the best in all of Germany'.[61]

This is not to say that German training was perfect. There was plenty of criticism that the training areas were too small and that there was not enough time and ammunition, among other things. To some degree, such criticism is inevitable: I can attest from personal experience that aggressive officers and NCOs in combat-arms units can never get enough time, space and ammunition to train with. But whatever its faults, the German army prior to the First World War was one of the best-trained in military history.[62]

In 1911 the German army possessed twenty-eight MTAs: twenty-two large ones and six smaller, comprising 102,328 hectares of land. Each active army corps had its own MTA. In addition, there were three MTAs for the artillery, including the new extra-large artillery range at Grafenwöhr. The German MTAs were big enough to allow infantry and artillery live-fire training without endangering the surrounding countryside.[63] They could accommodate manoeuvres by units up to brigade and division size without concern about manoeuvre damage. The German MTAs had good barracks and were superbly equipped. For example, at MTA Lechfeld in 1901 a target range for light howitzers to practise against field fortifications was built. In 1903 Lechfeld was authorised to buy Müller'schen

Schlitten – target sleds which more effectively allowed the depiction of enemy units advancing by fire and movement. In 1908 the MTA Lechfeld built rifle-fire simulators to depict, realistically, enemy troops firing. Döberitz, outside Potsdam, had a permanent suite of field fortifications to allow practice in their attack and defence.[64] In 1914 electrically-activated pop-up targets were installed at MTA Grafenwöhr.[65] Every German infantry unit spent at least one three-week time block in the summer conducting highly realistic range firing and tactical exercises. Artillery, cavalry and engineer units also spent a similar period of time at the MTA. Many units were able to squeeze in additional weeks at the MTA for company training during the spring.

Since 1893 the German heavy artillery had dedicated firing ranges at the MTAs at Thorn and Wahn.[66] These permitted exceptionally realistic training from a broad palette of tactical situations and terrain, including firing from covered positions and adjusting fire using only the map. These MTAs were large enough to allow artillery battalions and regiments to conduct live fire as tactical units. The targets were realistic. The heavy artillery emphasised quickly but methodically adjusting fire onto the target, followed by a devastating fire for effect: 'dumping a crushing mass of ordnance on the target'. The heavy artillery also held a *Kaiserpreis* live-fire competition, which for every battery might end in firing '100 rounds from the 15 cm guns at 4,000 metres in 20 minutes, with effective fire distribution and accuracy, against a half-covered enemy battery'. For twenty years preceding the war the German heavy artillery had conducted outstanding live-fire and tactical training. The German army began the war with heavy artillery that was not only materially superior to any other in Europe, but was integrated into the combined-arms team. The momentum this training generated would allow the German artillery throughout the war to offset Allied numbers of guns and masses of munitions with its tactical and doctrinal superiority, which culminated in the 'hurricane bombardments' of 1918.

German doctrine and training worked synergistically. German doctrine was efficient because it was developed and tested at the MTAs. In turn, the doctrine did not remain a dead letter but was intensively practised by troops at the MTAs.

In combat at the company level, the well-practised German battle drills resulted in greater German combat power: more effective fire combined with better and faster movement. At the leadership levels from battalion to division, German commanders arrived at a more accurate estimate of the situation and acted decisively.

German Field Training[67]

Tactical training with troops (as opposed to training without troops, such as terrain rides and war games) was conducted from the individual to the army level at the local training areas, major training areas and manoeuvre rights areas. Aside from training for the attack and defence, tactical training principally included road-marching, first aid, outpost duty and patrolling, field fortification and living in the field.

Most field training was individual, and almost all individual and squad training was at home station. In the last years before the war, such training in IR 109 emphasised tactical movement by squads, the use of the entrenching tool, the loss of company commanders, platoon and squad leaders and monthly night exercises. Some platoon and company training could usually be accomplished at the local training areas. In the winter, it might be possible to train on frozen fields near the garrison.

Training from company to brigade levels was conducted during an annual three to four-week period at the Major Training Area in the summer. At the MTA the mornings would be occupied with field training, the afternoons with combat gunnery range firing. Live-fire exercises were conducted at squad, platoon and company levels. MTA training would include the *Bataillonsbesichtigung*, the battalion tactical test and the *Regimentsbesicthigung*, the regimental tactical test, both conducted by the corps commander. Five to six days annually were devoted to the regimental manoeuvres at the MTA, four to five days for the brigade manoeuvres. Division and corps training took place during the two-week corps manoeuvre period in a manoeuvre rights area at the end of the training year in September.

An excellent appreciation for the scope of German tactical training can be gained from a book of exercise scenarios by a Generalleutnant Liebach.[68] For eight days of battalion training at the MTA Liebach he proposed: two attacks on a deployed enemy (including combat in woods); advance guard; two meeting engagements; counter-attack in the defence; night attack on a fortified position. Other missions were intermixed. For six days of regimental training he proposed: an attack on a deployed enemy; two meeting engagements; delay and breaking contact; envelopment and parallel pursuit; night attack on field fortifications. Brigade training, covering a four-day period, was similar. Liebach's programme is most heavily weighted in favour of meeting engagements; the defence is hardly mentioned. The scenarios for the tactical training tests at battalion, regimental and brigade levels would be similar to the training scenarios.

An idea of the high quality of German field training (*Felddienstübungen*) can be gained from reading training after-action reports (*Gefechtsberichte*) for these exercises. The exercise could be opposing force, against a notional enemy designated by flags, or a tactical exercise without troops. The exercises might last only half a day, but were carefully prepared and conducted. As in all German training, the exercise director determined the general situation (*Allgemeine Kriegslage*) and the situations for Blue and Red. After the exercise, the Blue and Red commanders submitted after-action reports. These reports described the situation, information on the enemy, orders received, troop-leading procedures and commanders' decisions, movements and 'combat', including a well-drawn sketch. The exercise was then reviewed and carefully commented on by the two higher echelons: for a company-level exercise, by the battalion and regimental commanders. The conduct of the exercises themselves was of a tactically high standard. These field training exercises demonstrate the importance that the German army attached to tactical training.[69] Subsequent to actual combat actions the German army would require after-action reports in order to understand what factors influenced the fight and to develop lessons learned. An unintended consequence is that modern historians can use these excellent analyses of combat actions which were included in those German war diaries, written by officers who had been trained in peacetime to write after-action reports.

IR 127's regimental history gives an impressive list of the regiment's tactical training.[70] In the LTA the regiment conducted night training exercises against IR 180 and road marches for the regimental trains. At the MTA the regiment conducted combined-arms live-fire exercises and, in 1910, a firepower demonstration put on by the field and heavy artillery. The regiment had a fetish for fortified positions. Its parent unit, the 51st Brigade, built a position reinforced by field fortifications in the Black Forest and then spent three days attacking and defending it. The regiment conducted attacks on a permanent fortress, 'Fortress Hugo', built at the Münsingen MTA, and also practised attacking permanent fortifications during the fortress exercises at Ulm in 1907 and 1913. When trench warfare came, the German army was far better prepared for it than was any other European army.

Many peacetime corps commanders enjoyed immense reputations as tacticians and troop trainers: Prince Friedrich Karl first of all as commander of III Corps before 1866, then Schlichting as commander of XIV Corps,[71] and later Bülow as commander of III Corps. The IR 20 regimental history gives an impressive account of Bülow's training.[72] He conducted battalion live-fire attacks with war-strength units, an Elbe river crossing and a live-fire attack, including heavy howitzers, on a dug-in position. To ensure variety, the corps exchanged Major Training Areas, and was able to train at four different MTAs.

Such men working at the MTAs initiated innovations in German tactical doctrine, which were later integrated into the regulations as well as German Truppenpraxis. In this manner, Schlichting was instrumental in the changes which were written into the 1888 *Exerzier-Reglement*, including the emphasis on *Auftragstaktik* and the meeting engagement, and Bülow tested the principles for the 1906 *Exerzier-Reglement*, including fire superiority and fire and movement.

No trainer was more honoured than Count Haeseler, a student of Friedrich Karl and commander of XVI Corps in Metz. Haeseler led XVI AK from its creation in 1890 until 1903.[73] He had no interest in anything (particularly the parade-ground) that did not promote combat effectiveness. The regimental history for FAR 70 said that the spirit of Count Haeseler was: 'Training in the field as often and as long as possible, both day and night, and in conjunction with other arms!' Haeseler's particular interest was mobility: all three arms marched long distances cross-country and conducted long night marches. Haeseler's artillery went places that field guns had never gone before. The Mance valley in the old 1870 battlefield was considered untrafficable for individual guns; at the end of Haeseler's command it was being traversed by large artillery units. Artillery manoeuvred with fully-loaded ammunition caissons. Haeseler had a field ploughed to accustom the artillery to movement across the furrows. Haeseler's infantry marched unheard-of distances. He threw out outmoded concepts and revolutionised training. For example, he required that both infantry and artillery train for 'danger close' artillery support (shells falling 300 metres or less from the infantry). Every battery live-fire test included support of an infantry attack or defence down to the closest ranges. Pop-up targets that appeared suddenly multiplied the artillery fire-control problems. In August 1898 Haeseler conducted a six-day siege exercise at Metz that the historian of IR 135 said was 'famous'. By the turn of the century men like Haeseler ensured that German training was the most realistic and capable in the world.

At the end of the training year, after the crops had been brought in and there was less concern over manoeuvre damage, each corps conducted a one or two-week field training exercise (FTX) on farmland in the corps area that had been designated a manoeuvre rights area.[74] These were generally opposing-force exercises, with one division manoeuvring against the other, or a corps manoeuvre against a notional enemy (marked with flags) with the corps commander being the exercise director in both cases. These exercises had considerable advantages: the troops manoeuvred in unknown terrain; combined-arms tactics could be practised; in an opposing force exercise there was a real 'enemy'; in a manoeuvre against a notional enemy the entire corps operated together.

In the 1870s and 1880s these exercises were leisurely affairs which were over each day by noon, followed by a comfortable bivouac or billets with the local population. The regimental bands would play and the troops could relax. In the 1890s exercises became more realistic, and a manoeuvre 'day' might last forty-eight or seventy-two hours. The *Kaisermanöver* became especially tough, particularly because of the long forced marches.

The division, brigade and regimental after-action reports for the XII Corps manoeuvre from 18 to 22 September 1913 survive.[75] The after-action reports were structured in a manner similar to that used for a war diary, including the attachment of orders and situation reports. These after-action reports give considerable insight into the German tactics just before the war. The XII Corps exercise deployed the entire corps against a notional enemy marked by flags. On 18 September a meeting engagement was played. The initial contact was between the corps cavalry brigade and an enemy cavalry brigade. The advance guard infantry battalion went over to the defensive and dug in, to give the following brigade time to deploy. An enemy attack was defeated by IR 103's infantry and machine-gun fire and supporting artillery fire. The strength of the artillery fire in particular allowed the division to go over to the offensive. On one occasion the infantry could not advance, on another occasion it could not withdraw because of enemy artillery fire. On the morning of 19 September the corps pursued. IR 102 attacked enemy forces on high ground while IR 103 attacked the town of Eiserode, which had been prepared for defence. The field artillery and corps heavy howitzers, advancing by bounds, supported the attack. IR 103's attack stalled and the brigade reserve was committed in its sector. By 1230 the enemy was wavering and the 63rd Infantry Brigade, which had gained fire superiority, conducted the assault, which succeeded, but at the cost of very heavy casualties: IR 102 was practically destroyed and the remnants(!) of IR 103 had to be withdrawn. II/IR 102's after-action report portrays a doctrinal infantry firefight. The two leading companies, 5th and 7th, took fire from Eiserode and returned that fire at 1,000 to 1,100 metres range. They then began to advance by bounds. 6/IR 102 was committed to reinforce the two leading companies, followed by 8/102 and the attached engineer company. The battalion then conducted the assault, whereupon the umpire declared that both II/102 and the defending battalion were no longer combat-effective. The enemy conducted a counter-attack against the 64th Brigade, which went over to the defensive. The attack was stopped in good part by concentrated artillery fire. The cavalry brigade defeated an enemy cavalry charge by a mixture of dismounted fire and mounted counter-attacks. On 22 September two enemy cavalry charges against the advance guard were unsuccessful. The advance guard was also fired upon by dismounted cavalry and bicycle troops. At another point, the corps commander halted the advance in the woods, fearing that if the main body left the cover of the trees it would be exposed to enemy artillery fire. All in all, this appears to have been an excellent FTX.

The British Army

The British Expeditionary Force consisted of six infantry divisions and a cavalry division. Each infantry division had three brigades of four battalions; each division had twelve infantry battalions. A battalion at war strength numbered about thirty officers and 1,000 enlisted men with two machine guns. The division also had four artillery brigades; each brigade included three batteries for twelve light batteries total. Each battery had six guns. Three artillery brigades had 8.4 cm (18-pound) field artillery pieces which could only fire shrapnel, and did not possess a high-explosive shell. Shrapnel was practically worthless in counter-battery fire, as the German Model 96 n/A gun crews were protected by the armoured gun shield. One divisional artillery brigade had 11.7 cm light howitzers. There was also a battery (four guns) of 12.8 cm (60-pound) heavy guns. British and German infantry divisions were therefore of comparable strength in artillery.

Almost all the British cavalry was concentrated in the cavalry division and an independent 5th Cavalry Brigade. The cavalry division consisted of four brigades, each with three regiments. A regiment, with three squadrons, had twenty-five officers and 526 enlisted men. The cavalry division also had twenty-four machine guns and four artillery batteries (six guns each, twenty-four guns total) equipped with the 7.6 cm gun. The British cavalry division had four times as many MG and twice as many guns as a German cavalry division. The total British cavalry force (five brigades), supporting four/five infantry divisions, had 7,890 enlisted cavalrymen. A German cavalry division had 4,128 enlisted cavalrymen; HKK 2, supporting twelve infantry divisions of the 1st Army, had 12,384 cavalrymen. The BEF had a much higher ratio of cavalry to infantry than its German opponents.

Many British military histories assert that 'the verdict of history' is that the 'British army was well-trained and well-led'.[76] This was true only at the individual soldier level. Nor is one of the best-written British regimental histories in full agreement with this evaluation. It says that 'the majority of the men in the ranks were young soldiers of less than three years service or else reservists who only a fortnight before had been in civil life. For a week [after landing in France] they had been harassed and deprived of sleep, marched and counter-marched, and they were already tired and footsore when they were called on to face an enemy of overpowering strength.'[77]

Some units in Ireland had been pulling security duty for months and had not trained at all during this time: by modern military standards they were not deployable. The history of the 2/King's Own Yorkshire Light Infantry (KOYLI) said:[78]

The ten months spent in Portobello Barracks at Dublin had been as trying and unsatisfactory a period as any that the battalion had hitherto experienced in its history. Throughout the time every available man had been employed on picket duty, chiefly in guarding the tram termini. Dublin was seething with unrest. It was unsafe for soldiers to walk alone in many parts of the city. Political rancour was at its height ... Ulster was an armed camp; the other provinces were in a frenzy of excitement. Picket duty near some improvised guardroom, a monotonous service only enlivened by the routine of daily inspections, was varied by detachment duty to Ulster or elsewhere ... There was not even the relief which battalion or brigade training might have offered. Orders for training were no sooner issued than they had to be cancelled.

The higher up one went on the chain of command, the more serious became the deficiencies in professional competence. In the last half of the nineteenth century the British army prepared solely for colonial warfare. Only in the last few years before the First World War did the British attempt to prepare for mobile continental warfare against a first-rate enemy. This was too late. The deficiencies in troop-leading in the cavalry division and at the corps and army levels were serious, indeed nearly fatal, and were made good only by the skill and courage of the rifle companies.

Most histories of the pre-war British army focus entirely on Haldane's creation of a viable expeditionary force: the doctrine and staff training for that force are given short shrift.[79] The British General Staff was not organised until Haldane's reforms from 1906 to 1909. The first modern doctrinal manual, Field Service Regulations – Operations, was not written until 1909. There was not enough time to practise these procedures – the British army held only two army-level manoeuvres before the First World War, in 1912 and 1913. II Corps, which was to conduct almost all of the fighting in August 1914, did not even exist until mobilisation.

One of the few books to deal with British pre-war doctrine is Bidwell and Graham's *Firepower*.[80] Their description is not a pretty one. In effect, the British army did not have a functioning tactical doctrine, and British manuals did not provide for combined-arms tactics. The British emphasis on regimental (actually battalion) autonomy worked against combined arms, and would continue to do so through the Second World War. The artillery manual did not establish priorities for artillery fire. There was confusion concerning what constituted 'fire superiority' and the conduct of fire and movement. There was no tactics manual for the machine gun. Just before the war the British army shifted from the old eight-company Napoleonic battalion organisation to the German-style four-company battalion, each company with four platoons. 'The platoon was something quite new. On paper a fully mobilized battalion headquarters was over 200 strong, but no one in high places seems to have thought of really organising it for battle. It was left for individual commanders to do what they liked.'[81] In effect, the British had plagiarised the German tactics regulations without understanding them. Ascoli implicitly says that tactical training got short shrift because British excellence at rifle marksmanship and artillery gunnery were 'born of the British passion for field sports', which Ascoli obviously meant as a compliment.[82]

The fundamental problem was that while the British army did not officially have a continental mission, it did have one of imperial policing which occupied the attention of half the force. Under the Cardwell system, each battalion at home was twinned with a battalion overseas. They were rotated over long periods, some fifteen or twenty years. In addition, the home battalion changed station every three years or so. The home battalion was continually receiving recruits who had to be given basic training. Drafts to keep the overseas battalion up to strength had priority over training the battalion. Together, this ensured that training with a full-strength home battalion was practically impossible. A representative battalion on 4 August 1914 had only twenty-two officers and 486 enlisted men assigned.[83] If allowance is made for the normal housekeeping and guard duties, it is clear that there were not enough soldiers present for duty to conduct realistic platoon and company tactical training. Battalions were continually changing brigades, which made stable brigade-level training impossible. There were simply too many innovations, and too little time and training opportunities to become familiar with them. Major-General A. L. Ransome, who was with the Dorsets before the War, said: 'In the current tactical training of the serving infantry soldier great emphasis had been placed on the attack; the defence was seldom practised. When it was, dispositions were inevitably linear.'[84] The Cheshire regimental history said: 'Before the war, in order to foster the offensive spirit, retirement as an operation of war was ignored during training.'[85]

The British army therefore concentrated on individual training, particularly individual rifle marksmanship. The Worcestershire regimental history says that marksmanship competition was a matter of adding up individual range-firing scores; the company with the highest additive score won.[86] These were fired on standard ranges against bulls-eye targets. In the German army, live-fire qualification courses were conducted tactically at platoon, company and battalion levels.

German regimental histories are full of references to peacetime training, in particular unit training at the MTA and the *Kaisermanöver*. British regimental histories that discuss peacetime operations at all usually concentrate on the exploits of the unit sports teams. A notable exception is again the Worcestershire regimental history, which says that after the South African War 'more modern methods of training' were introduced 'and the severe "Kitchener test" was instituted as a criterion of efficiency'. This test consisted of 'a long forced march in full kit by the whole battalion, followed by an attack practice'. This hardly meets German standards for tactical training.

An army fights the way it has been trained to fight. Doctrine and training must correspond to the most likely missions that the army will have to perform. The British army focused on offensive operations; in the first three weeks of the war it would conduct positional defence and withdrawals under pressure, missions for which it was poorly prepared. Aside from the effectiveness of individual training, the British army did not execute the defence/withdrawal missions well, and almost all the casualties would be the consequences of a poorly organised defence and badly conducted withdrawal.

Each British infantry battalion had to be brought to war strength through the addition of some 400–500 reservists. 2/King's Own Yorkshire Light Infantry required 615. In no way was their training and physical fitness equal to that of serving soldiers. Ransome described an unnamed regiment (probably the Cheshires) on the march to Mons:

> I can only describe the battalion in front of us as being in 'pear-shaped' formation, with the pear's stalk leading. Its colonel and the adjutant rode at the rear, striving to get the mass of humanity into some semblance of order, but all the time more and more men, reservists, no doubt, dropped out and seated them-

selves at the road-side ... Count Gleichen, our Brigadier, wrote later of these
early marches: 'Stragglers, I regret to say, were already many, all of them reservists
who had not carried a pack for years.'

According to Ransome, some of the reservists had left the army before there was
a requirement to fire fifteen rounds per minute, and none had the practice necessary to meet this standard.[87]

In order to preserve the political fiction that the British army was not preparing for a war against Germany, the official history said that 'The study of German
military organisation and methods was specifically forbidden at war games, staff
tours and intelligence classes, which would have provided the best opportunities
for such instruction'. It goes on to say: 'Ignorance of the German Army proved a
serious handicap in the early part of the campaign.'[88] The official history cites as
an example German machine-gun crews that were carrying the gun by the four
legs of the gun mount and were taken to be stretcher-bearers and were not fired
upon. British misperception of German tactics was so serious that the BEF had
literally no idea what the Germans were doing.

Another example illustrative of British ignorance of German tactics regards
British troops regularly reporting that advancing Germans 'fired from the hip'.
Such a manoeuvre is unlikely, as anyone who has ever fired a bolt-action rifle
while trying to move forward can attest. German training, on the other hand,
emphasised carefully conducted aimed fire. How can this contradiction be
explained? The solution is simple: the pencil drawings by Döberich-Steglitz
show the Germans advancing by fire and movement. While one group of
German troops provide covering fire, the other group bounds forward, carrying
his weapon by his side at 'trail arms'. The British, who could not see the prone
German riflemen firing, thought the running men were firing. It is truly amazing
that the authors of the British official history did not correct this misperception:
they did not understand German tactics either.

British tactics at Mons and Le Cateau had several distinguishing characteristics
in common. The British spread their forces along the front with no main point
of effort; the British right flank was weak and poorly positioned; and the British
conducted a static defence, with no attempt to conduct defensive manoeuvre.

The German pre-war evaluation of the British army was balanced and accurate.
No senior German officer thought that the British were a 'contemptible little
army'. The German army had reluctantly seen the period of conscription reduced
from three years to two, and envied the British for their long-service volunteers.[89]
Except for the China expedition and the uprising in German South-west Africa,
the German army had no combat experience since 1871. The Germans therefore
acknowledged the value of extensive British overseas combat experience for both
officers and men. The German official history quoted a prescient 1914 memoran-
dum concerning the British army:[90]

The British Expeditionary Force is a first-rate opponent. The officer corps is drawn from the best classes, is united and has excellent morale. The best-trained come from the military schools, but even these sometimes lack thoroughness. Since the Boer War the demands made on the officers have increased, and more is being done to improve their military education. Nevertheless, sport still remains in the forefront of their interests.

Individual marksmanship and use of the terrain are good, fire control deficient. The cavalry is very good at dismounted combat, but its equitation is not quite good enough for coordinated mounted movements of large bodies or for the mounted charge. The horse and field artillery are justifiably considered to be the elite ...

Movements of large bodies of troops are conducted slowly and ponderously; the senior leadership shows significant deficiencies. An opponent who attacks quickly and with determination will often be presented with opportunities for success.

Conclusions

The German army had been preparing for modern warfare since 1888, the British since 1908. The German General Staff was the best in the world; the British General Staff had just been established. The German army practised combined-arms tactics in realistic field-training and live-fire exercises; the British did not.

A professional military evaluation could only conclude that the German army would move faster and hit harder than the British, and that the British should have been wary of a test of strength in the open field.

The German 1st Army in Belgium

German War Plan

At the beginning of the war, the Germans had no idea what the French and Russians would do, but a more-or-less coordinated Franco-Russian attack was the most dangerous course of action they could have taken.

The Germans were certain the Russians would deploy an army in Lithuania (the Niemen Army) and one north-west of Warsaw (the Narew Army). The Russians could attack either when their active-army units had deployed or wait for the reserve units. The Germans deployed one army (the 8th) with nine divisions in East Prussia. Even with active-army units alone, the Niemen and the Narew Armies would each be as strong as the German 8th Army; Russians would outnumber the Germans in East Prussia by at least two to one. When the Russian reserve divisions arrived their numerical superiority would be even greater. The Russian reserve divisions would be followed in about two months by the divisions stationed in the Russian Far East. From the outset, the Austrians would also be outnumbered two to one.

From 1909 on the German intelligence estimates had been warning that Russian mobilisation and deployment were speeding up, and it appears that the Germans expected the Russian attack between the fifteenth and twenty-fifth day of mobilisation.

The Russians began their mobilisation on 30 August, their first day of mobilisation being 31 August. The French and Russians had agreed in 1911–13 to launch simultaneous attacks on the fifteenth day of mobilisation, which was 14 August. This meant that the Russians would attack at the earliest possible time, with just the active-army divisions. The Germans were faced with the probability

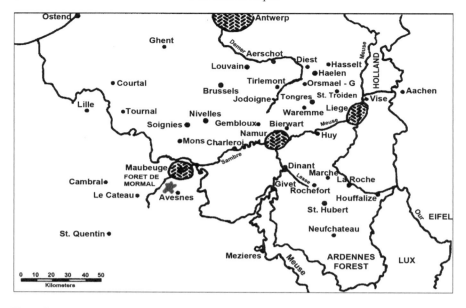

Fig. 6: Operations area.

of having to transfer forces from the west to the east by the thirtieth day of mobilisation (24–31 August).

The Germans initially committed sixty-eight divisions against France. The
numerical odds for the Germans in the west would be no better than even. The
Germans thought the French would deploy sixty-three divisions in the west, initially leaving three divisions and the equivalent of two divisions of mountain
infantry on their Alpine border with Italy.[1] The Belgians had six divisions, and
intervention by the six-division BEF was considered likely, for a total of seventy-
five enemy divisions.

The Germans thought that the French could attack into Lorraine, or into both
Lorraine and the Ardennes (that is, on both sides of Metz), or into Belgium. It
was also possible, but unlikely, that the French could await the German attack and
conduct a defensive-offensive operation.

The French launched a corps-sized attack towards Mühlhausen (Mulhouse)
in the upper Alsace on 7 August, which meant to the Germans that the French
intended to launch a general offensive as soon as possible. In conformity to their
agreement with the Russians, the French began their offensive with two armies
into Lorraine on 14 August.

Since at least 1906 the Germans had expected that the British would take
the French side in a war against Germany and send an expeditionary force to
the continent. The BEF could land in Denmark or north Germany in order
to threaten the German fleet base at Kiel and cut the canal from Kiel to the
Baltic. The Germans initially deployed two reserve divisions in north Germany

for coastal defence. The BEF could land at Fortress Antwerp to reinforce the Belgians. It could also land on the Channel coast, at ports from Calais all the way west to Le Havre, to reinforce the French. The BEF might then assemble at Lille or at Maubeuge.

The German war plan was laid out in the *Aufmarschanweisungen* (deployment orders), which were issued to the army commanders on the first day of mobilisation, 2 August 1914.[2] In the west, the 7th and 6th Armies would defend the German left flank in Lorraine and Alsace, while fixing the opposing French forces in place and preventing their transfer to the French left wing. The 5th Army was deployed behind Metz, the 4th in Luxembourg, the 3rd in the Eifel – opposite the Belgian Ardennes – the 2nd to the south-east of Aachen, and the 1st to the north-east of Aachen. This deployment maximised the use of the German rail assets in the available deployment space in order to produce the fastest possible deployment.

If the French attacked only in Lorraine, the German 5th Army would advance through Metz to counter-attack against the French left flank. The 4th Army would protect the rear of the 5th. The missions of the other armies were not specified, but elements of the 2nd and 1st Armies would probably have been moved by rail to Lorraine.

Otherwise, the German right wing would begin its advance through Belgium on the seventeenth day of mobilisation (18 August), with the 5th, 4th and 3rd Armies in the Ardennes and the 2nd and 1st Armies in the Belgian plain north of the Meuse. The German intent was to win the first battle, which would probably be fought in Belgium or on the Franco-Belgian border, beginning no later than the twenty-second day of mobilisation (23 August). The results of this battle would require a new set of orders, and the *Aufmarschanweisungen* did not speculate what the Germans might do beyond the first battle.

Preparations had been made to shift seven corps by rail. Since the Russians began their attack on 14 August, the Germans could reasonably expect a crisis in the east by 24 August. If the Germans won the first battle in the west, they could either shift forces to the east to reinforce East Prussia or, if East Prussia was secure, continue the attack in the west, with the intent of attacking the French fortress line on the Franco-German border from the front and rear and breaking it. This would open the interior of France to invasion.

There is no indication that the German leadership expected any kind of decisive victory. Moltke seemed to anticipate initial German tactical victories, which would give Germany territorial gains as bargaining chips, followed by a negotiated peace. This was the reason why he placed such a priority in keeping the Russians out of East Prussia. The German High Seas Fleet, instead of seeking a battle with the British Grand Fleet, remained in port as a 'fleet in being'.

The 2nd Army would conduct the principal German attack. It consisted of six corps (Guard, Guard Reserve, VII AK (Armeekorps), X AK, VII RK

(Reservekorps), X RK) and was commanded by the senior German general officer, Karl von Bülow, who initially would be given control over the three right-wing armies; the 3rd Army, with four corps, would attack south of the Meuse on the left of the 2nd Army.

The 1st Army consisted of six corps (II AK, III AK, IV AK, IX AK, II RK, III RK) and was deployed to the right of the 2nd Army with the primary mission of covering the German right flank. The 2nd Cavalry Corps (Heereskavalleriekorps 2 – HKK 2) would usually be operating in the 1st Army sector. The Germans were attacking into Belgium north of the Meuse with a total force of twelve corps and three cavalry divisions.

British Official History and War Planning

The tendentious character of the British official history is evident in the first twenty-five pages. It strains to show that the German army significantly outnumbered the French, and that the Germans were the aggressors. The French were supposedly outnumbered because the Germans mobilised 5 million trained men, the French only 3.5 million.[3] Even if this were true, it is meaningless. The only number that counted was the size of the field armies. As the German official history notes, the French field army amounted to 2,150,000 men, the British 132,000 and the Belgian 100,000: 2,382,000 in total. The entire German field army numbered 2,147,000. In addition, the British official history does not mention the size of the Russian and Austrian armies, and this omission was not accidental. In the east, the Russian army numbered 2,712,000 and the Serb 285,000, for a total of 2,997,000. The Austrian army fielded a total strength of 1,400,000. Altogether, the Entente put 5,397,000 men in the field; the Central Powers 3,547,000.[4] The British official history also asserts that the Germans had nearly as many reserve corps as active corps, which is absurd;[5] and it never compares the number of Entente and German divisions in the west, for that would demonstrate that it was the Germans who were outnumbered.

This is disingenuous. The size of the respective peacetime armies was a matter of public record; the number of reserve units mobilised was not going to change the balance of power significantly. The real problem for the Entente was not the number of reserve units that the Germans raised, but the fact that the German reserve units frequently fought as well as the French active-army units.

It seems clear that the British decided to commit the BEF to the left flank of the French army because they knew the Germans were massively outnumbered; they thought that the Entente would win and that the war would be short.[6] The British wanted to be on the winning side. The British and French would stop the Germans in the west, and in the east the Germans would go down under a flood of Russian manpower.

Kitchener, appointed minister for war on 7 August, did not believe in the premises of British pre-war planning: he did not think the Germans would be quickly defeated. He planned from the outset to raise an entirely new army, which required the greatest possible amount of equipment and numbers of trained officer and NCO cadre. There was no prior planning to facilitate creating this army, and last-minute decisions usually have unhappy consequences. On the one hand, 'the second pair of boots were withdrawn from most of the units of the expeditionary force', leaving it 'with only one pair of boots per man – a shortage which was to have most trying effects', that is to say, on the retreat some men were barefoot, or nearly so.[7] On the other hand, most of the trained personnel were committed with the BEF. High-intensity combat with an enemy as capable as the German army led to crippling cadre casualties. General Ransome cites one example, which serves to stand for the whole: 'The Dorsets deployed with five officers who were "P.S.C." (passed staff college), just the sort of capable and trained officers needed to control a mass army. Two were killed in 1914, two were wounded and the fifth badly wounded and taken prisoner.'[8] It should be no surprise that through 1916 poor British staff work led to outright disasters. The destruction of entire units at Mons and Le Cateau, such as the Gordon Highlanders, including the loss of forty-three irreplaceable sergeants and corporals, made the reconstitution of the unit at its previous level of efficiency impossible. The casualties suffered from 23 August to 26 August 1914 had a long-term effect on the efficiency of the British army disproportional to their numbers.

The fact that Russia was the first great power to order general mobilisation, on 30 July, first day of mobilisation 31 July, has always been a great problem for Entente apologists. Mobilisation meant war. The Germans could claim that they mobilised only after the Russians had done so, and in self-defence. The British official history makes the astounding assertion that the Russians ordered general mobilisation because an issue of a single minor German newspaper, the *Berliner Lokalanzeiger* (Berlin Local News), had printed on 30 July that the Germans had ordered general mobilisation, and though the Germans quickly denied it, the Russians had already begun to mobilise and the damage had been done.[9] Even if true, this would only prove that the Russians were guilty of gross, indeed criminal, negligence. It would still not change the fact that the Germans mobilised in self-defence. In any case, German historians soon discredited this story, and how it survived the 1933 revision of the British official history is mystifying.

Edmonds also says, cryptically, that 'Significantly, Turkey also ordered mobilisation on the 31st July'. Why Edmonds thought this was significant – Turkey did not enter the war until 29 October 1914 – is unclear. It would seem evident that Turkey, like Germany, mobilised because Russia mobilised first – not a fact that would reinforce Edmond's assertion that Germany was the aggressor.

The Belgian Army

Belgium introduced universal conscription on 30 August 1913. Both militia and conscript service were only for a year, so that in peacetime Belgium never had more than one year-group under arms; a brigade had 1,500 men and a company 60, which would have made tactical training impossible and individual training difficult.[10] Conscription was to eventually produce an army of 350,000 men.[11] In 1914, however, the Belgian field army was supposed to be about 110,000 strong.

When Austria declared war on Serbia on 29 July, the Belgian army began partial mobilisation, recalled the three youngest year-groups of the militia back to the colours, ordered horse purchases and began uploading equipment. At 1900 on 31 July the army was formally mobilised, first day of mobilisation 1 August, a day before France and Germany.

The Belgian Army consisted of six infantry divisions and a cavalry division. On paper, the infantry component of the 1st, 2nd, 5th and 6th Divisions was strong: three brigades, each brigade consisting of two infantry regiments, each of three battalions, or eighteen infantry battalions as opposed to twelve in a German division. There was also a divisional artillery 'regiment' with three batteries (Belgian batteries had only four guns) and a cavalry regiment. Each infantry battalion had only one machine gun (pulled on a dog cart) so the Belgian division had eighteen MGs as opposed to the German twenty-four. Each infantry brigade had an organic artillery section with three batteries. The 3rd and 4th Divisions had four brigades (twenty-four infantry battalions) and were of comparable infantry strength to the German corps.

For some reason, the mobilised Belgian infantry divisions did not approach anywhere near their authorised strength. The four 'normal' infantry divisions had only 14,000 infantrymen, or 775 a battalion, far below the European standard of 1,000.[12] There should have been seventy-two field artillery pieces, but in fact there were only forty-eight. The overstrength 3rd and 4th Divisions had only 18,500 infantry and sixty cannons.

The cavalry division was weak: two cavalry brigades, each with two regiments of four squadrons, sixteen squadrons (2,500 cavalrymen) as opposed to twenty-four squadrons (4,080 cavalrymen) in a German cavalry division. The Belgian cavalry had no MGs; a German division had six. The Belgian cavalry had an artillery section with three batteries (twelve guns, the same as the Germans) and a half-strength (450 man) bicycle 'battalion'. Belgian training was nowhere as good as the German, and the Belgians knew it. The assembled Belgian field army in reality included 93,000 infantry, 6,000 cavalry, 324 light artillery pieces (no howitzers) and 102 MGs. The German 1st Army and HKK 2 were three times as strong.

The overstrength 3rd Division mobilised in Liège, the 4th in Namur, the 1st in the north-west in Flanders, the 2nd at Antwerp, the 6th at Brussels and the 5th in the south-west at Mons-Tournai. Belgian mobilisation could not have escaped the attention of German intelligence. France, then Germany, declared general mobilisation on the afternoon of 1 August, first mobilisation day 2 August. At 1900 on 2 August the German ambassador in Brussels demanded free transit over Belgian territory, with twelve hours to answer. The Belgians replied that they would oppose any violation of their neutrality. On 3 August the Belgian leadership decided to orient their field army towards Germany and assemble it behind the Gette River, and troops began moving on 4 August. The garrison of Liège was reinforced by the 3rd Division, that of Namur with the 4th Division.

On the night of 3–4 August it 'was ascertained without doubt that German troops intended to cross Belgium by force'. The order was given to block the roads and execute demolition of critical points in the rail lines and bridges. Belgian troops were told not to oppose the entry of French troops onto Belgian territory. These measures were all taken well before the German troops entered Belgium on the morning of 4 August. On 5 August the mobilisation of the Belgian army was completed, and by 6 August it was combat-ready. There were only 18,000 volunteers for the regular army, few enough in a country that conscripted a very small proportion of each year-group, and therefore had a large number of available men. German troops in Belgium were surprised to find so many men of military age wandering about.

The Belgian army was not strong enough to hold a line from the Dutch border to Namur, so deployed behind the Gette from Diest on the left to Jodoigne on the right. Eventually, this line would be held by the 5th Division on the left, the 3rd in the centre and the 1st on the right. The 2nd Division was in reserve at Louvain, the 6th behind the right flank about 12 km to the south. The cavalry division screened to the front. There was a considerable gap of 30 km between the right flank of the Belgian field army at Jodoigne and Namur, which the German cavalry would find and exploit.

On 4 August the Belgian government sent a note to the British and French governments, announcing that it would cooperate with them to resist the Germans 'and at the same time to guarantee the maintenance in the future of Belgian integrity and independence'. The intent of the Belgian policy was to preserve Belgian national independence, and not just against the Germans. A French war aim was surely to be the occupation of the left bank of the Rhine, and the Belgians were announcing that they were not going to be included in this project.

The Belgian plan provided for two contingencies. In the first, the Belgians would be faced with superior German forces. The Belgian army would defend for as long as possible, in the hopes that the French and British would arrive. The Belgian Army would be 'the advance guard of the French and British armies'. In the second contingency, the German forces would be equal to the Belgian, that is, the Germans would have no more than two corps north of the Meuse. The Belgians would then attack when a favourable moment presented itself. It was not a foregone conclusion that the Germans would, as they did in fact, send twelve corps north of the Meuse. The Belgians might well hope that the Germans would not be very strong north of the Meuse, or that the Germans might be slowed by Liège until the French and British arrived, and that a defence along the Gette would spare the heart of the country from a German invasion.

This strategy also allowed the Belgian government to minimise Belgian casualties, which would be popular domestically. On the other hand, heavy casualties were certain to strain the already difficult relationship between the Dutch-speaking Flemish and the French-speaking Walloons. The Germans inadvertently kept Belgian casualties low by occupying Belgium before the majority of young Belgians could be conscripted: Belgium mobilised only 267,000 men during the entire war. The Belgian strategy was successful: Belgium kept her sovereignty and the only countries to suffer fewer fatal casualties in the Great War than Belgium (13,715) were Portugal (7,222) Greece (5,000) and Montenegro (3,000).[13]

These low casualties were a source of significant friction between Belgium and the Entente, both during and after the war. It was therefore in Belgium's interest to emphasise German atrocities and the hardships of the German occupation, particularly forced labour, to show that Belgium too was suffering at the hands of the Germans.

Heereskavalleriekorps 2

The Germans employed four Heereskavalleriekorps (HKK – cavalry corps) in the west, with two or three cavalry divisions in each HKK. HKK 3 was deployed in Lorraine, HKK 4 and HKK 1 in the Ardennes, and HKK 2 in northern Belgium. Spreading these reconnaissance assets uniformly along the front was a strong indication that the Germans had no idea what the French intended to do.

German cavalry operations in 1914, which consisted principally of reconnaissance and counter-reconnaissance, receive little or no attention in histories of the Marne campaign. This is a grave error. The failure of the French high command to identify the direction of march and strength of the German right wing has generally been explained by their stupidity. The French were not stupid: they could not see the German right wing because the German cavalry screen in the Ardennes had blinded the French cavalry reconnaissance, and the Belgian cavalry division was outnumbered and outclassed by the German cavalry.[14] At the same time, the German cavalry accurately reported French, Belgian and British locations and movements. In the initial battles all five German right-wing armies enjoyed complete operational and tactical surprise, which was a major factor in German victory. German cavalry operations are therefore of the utmost importance, and German cavalry patrolling, especially long-range patrols, are still instructive for modern soldiers.

HKK 2, with the 2nd, 4th and 9th Cavalry Divisions (Kavallerie-Division – KD) and five Jäger Battalions (3, 4, 7, 9, 10) would generally operate in front or on the right flank of the 1st Army. HKK 2 conducted an accelerated deployment and began its rail march on 2 and 3 August, without waiting for the reservists to arrive. It was commanded by Generalleutnant Marwitz, the peacetime General Inspector of Cavalry, and was organised as follows:

2 KD
5th Cavalry Bde (Dragoon Regiment 2, Ulan R 3)
8th Cav. Bde (Cuirassier R 7, Hussar R 12)
Leib (Lifeguard)-Hussar Bde (Hussar R 1, Hussar R 2)
Machine Gun Section 4
Horse Artillery Section FAR 35

4 KD
3rd Cav. Bde (Cuirassier R 2, Ulan R 9)
17th Cav. Bde (Dragoon R 17, Dragoon R 18)
18th Cav. Bde (Hussar R 15, Hussar R 16)
MG Section 2
Horse Artillery Section FAR 3

9 KD
13th Cav. Bde (Cuirassier R 4, Hussar R 8)
14th Cav. Bde (Hussar R 11, Ulan R 5)
19th Cav. Bde (Dragoon R 19, Ulan R 13)
MG Section 7
Horse Artillery Section FAR 10

HKK 2 was a powerful and mobile all-arms force: 7,500 light infantry, 12,600 cavalry (which could dismount 9,500 riflemen: 17,000 riflemen total), with 48 machine guns and 36 7.7 cm guns.

The principal activity of HKK 2 was patrolling. This was demanding work. The patrol leader usually did not have a map, and the patrol was most assuredly in 'Indian country'. The messengers carrying back reports faced an especially difficult task, with only a general idea of the route to follow and unable to speak the local language. But there was adventure and freedom, and the boldest cavalrymen eagerly desired to go out on patrol. The history of Dragoon R 19 waxed poetic when discussing the allure of patrolling: 'the excitement of the patrol sharpened the senses, and made the young officer and trooper more receptive to the magic of the French summer night, and the beauty of the centuries-old castles and gardens seen in passing.'[15]

HKK 2 crossed the border on 4 August, with 2 KD and 4 KD to the north of Liège and 9 KD to the south. The Jäger battalions participated in the attack on Liège and did not rejoin HKK 2 until 13 August.

The Germans had no idea what enemy forces they would find in Belgium, and there was concern that the French and British would move quickly and in strength to reinforce the Belgians. The mission of HKK 2 was to reconnoitre with 2 KD as far as Antwerp and 4 KD to Charleroi and the Sambre. 9 KD's mission was to conduct reconnaissance south of Liège as far as the Ourthe.

The first task was to capture intact the Meuse bridges at Visé, north of Liège. This was to be accomplished by a column which would race ahead of the cavalry, composed of the 1st Company 9th Jäger Battalion and an engineer detachment loaded onto trucks, and the bicycle company of 9th Jäger Battalion.[16] The column found all the roads systematically blocked by overturned vehicles, downed trees and blown bridges. Road signs had been taken down. Civilians caught at this work were fired upon – two were hit. The column barely arrived in Visé ahead of the cavalry, and the bridges had already been blown.

Hussar R 15 was the advance guard for 4 KD, and sent three long-range patrols to the Meuse.[17] One of the patrol leaders reported that the first half of his mission passed without incident; 'the only unusual thing was that the inhabitants of the towns looked at us with curiosity, shaking their heads and making fun of us, as though no one thought that the war was serious'. They then encountered civilians blocking the roads with wagons, equipment and fallen trees, who ran and hid in their houses when the hussars approached. The patrol leader sternly ordered them out to explain themselves. The inhabitants, who spoke perfect German, said that a gendarme had told them to do it. The patrol leader said that if the barricade was not gone in two hours, the town would be tried by court martial. As he left, he saw the civilians begin to clear the road. In a larger town numerous civilians shouted their dissatisfaction, which the patrol ignored. They then saw a Belgian cavalry patrol race out of the town towards the Meuse at full gallop, while a Belgian lancer stepped out of a house carrying a case of beer. He dropped the beer and jumped on his horse but the patrol captured him, which caused 'extraordinary agitation' in the crowd. As they reached the heights above the Meuse they heard a massive detonation – the Belgians had blown the bridge.

It had been originally intended that both cavalry divisions would cross the Meuse to support the reconnaissance squadrons, but the Belgians had destroyed all the Meuse bridges outside Liège. The German bridging material had not arrived by the night of 5–6 August and some of the cavalry's aluminium pontoons were wrecked by Belgian artillery fire, so the reconnaissance squadrons went across the Meuse unsupported and without the usual bicycle infantry or light radio stations.[18] The absence of the radios would be felt severely: messengers from the reconnaissance squadron seldom got through to the KD and the reconnaissance squadrons were completely in the dark concerning the situation at Liège.

2 KD would employ 4th Squadron, Hussar R 12 and 3rd Squadron, Dragoon R 2 in the reconnaissance mission, 4 KD 4th Squadron Dragoon R 17 and 2nd Squadron Dragoon R 18. They crossed at Lixhé near the Dutch border, under some fire from Fort Pointesse. Usually the troopers crossed on the remaining pontoon boats with the horses swimming alongside. German reconnaissance would initially fall on the cavalry alone: according to the history of Dragoon R 17, there were no reconnaissance aircraft available.

2 KD Reconnaissance Squadrons

4th Squadron Hussar R 12 was given the mission of conducting deep reconnaissance to Antwerp. After crossing the Meuse, 4/Hussar R 12 sent out three long-range reconnaissance patrols, with their objectives from Diest to Tirlemont. Patrols were usually ten to twenty troopers strong, subdivided into three sections of three to seven men, the sections well dispersed and moving by bounds from one piece of cover to the next.

Throughout the campaign, fast, long-range movement allowed the German cavalry to appear where it was not expected, leading Belgian and French civilians to think the patrol was British. In addition, civilians had difficulty distinguishing German cavalry uniforms from British. The patrols often used the opportunity to gain information from the inhabitants, as well as food and fodder.

One patrol reported being mistaken for British by the inhabitants, but they soon got wise. The patrol was shadowed by bicyclists and saw patrols of Belgian gendarmes. The patrol secured its bivouac with detachments led by NCOs, one of which was attacked during the night and a trooper wounded. On 6 August another long-range patrol, also shadowed by bicyclists, was ambushed and lost six troopers.

4/Hussar R 12 had to manoeuvre around Belgian security forces in order to advance. Its bivouac was fired upon throughout the night, but it lost only a horse. The Belgians withdrew before daylight. Messengers returning with reports had a hard time getting through and several were lost.

On 7 August the hussars were again shadowed by bicyclists, who fired on them with carbines. Belgian stragglers from Liège were captured, and told the squadron the route that had been taken by the Belgian 3rd Division out of the fortress, which the squadron commander decided to follow. The squadron was fired on in a town; dismounted cavalrymen chased the Belgians off, at a cost of two KIA and one MIA. Continuing on, the hussars ran into a platoon of Belgian cavalry; the squadron took up a position in a sunken road and drove off the Belgians with rifle fire. The squadron then encountered Belgian infantry approaching in skirmisher lines on three sides, which it took under fire. Covered by heavy rain, the squadron broke contact and bivouacked in a brushy area surrounded by a swamp. A sergeant and five troopers were sent back with a report.

The next day, 8 August, the squadron continued its advance. It cut telegraph and telephone lines and then happened onto a Belgian battery. The squadron commander acknowledged that it would have been better to have remained undetected, but this was an opportunity too good to be missed. The squadron dismounted and opened fire and the Belgians fled, leaving several baggage wagons behind. Avoiding Belgian cavalry, the hussars attacked a railway station, forcing the trains there to leave and taking three prisoners, who confirmed the withdrawal route of the Belgian troops from Liège. In the next town an armoured car drove into the squadron's arms. Its occupant was a British bank officer from Brussels who was wearing the uniform of a Belgian Guard Civique officer, and was carrying dispatches. Taking the armoured car along, the squadron continued the march north-west, followed by numerous bicyclists. The hussars dismounted, occupied a circular defensive position and were fired on by superior Belgian forces, which did not venture an actual attack. The reason for this soon became evident – the Belgians were awaiting the arrival of an artillery battery, which soon unlimbered and opened fire. The squadron mounted up and moved under cover to a new position. The Belgians waited for the squadron to show itself, but instead, after dark, the hussars reoccupied their original position and bivouacked.

By 9 August the squadron had been patrolling for four days and had reached the area of Hannut, 45 km from Liège and about halfway between Liège and Louvain. The squadron had no news of the location or situation of other German forces. The armoured car had been hit and was unusable. The squadron was transporting the sick and wounded and was almost out of food, and several exhausted horses had been replaced by bicycles. The squadron commander decided to return to the division.

On the way the hussars ran into automobiles loaded with Belgian troops, whose fire they avoided by moving through a town. They then encountered a Belgian bicycle company, which blocked their route. The bicyclists pursued them through two more towns, until the hussars dismounted and held them off with rifle fire. The hussars lost several horses, but casualties in personnel were light. The situation was grim; the squadron was hot, tired and in no condition to fight through the 25 km to the Meuse. But at 1600 the Belgian cyclists began to withdraw. The reason for this was soon evident: the main body of HKK 2 had just crossed the Meuse, and a patrol from Hussar R 2 appeared in the Belgians' rear. The 4/Hussar R 12's long-range patrols returned on 8 August.

The main body of the 4th Squadron had been engaged by gendarmes, cavalry, infantry on foot, and unidentified shooters on bicycles and in automobiles. One patrol reported being fired on by civilians in Hasselt, the other by civilians in Waremme. The third patrol had been broken up and the patrol leader apparently killed. Out of a strength on 6 August of 147, on 10 August the squadron counted 3 KIA, 9 KIA or POW, 7 WIA and 42 MIA.

On 5 August 3rd Squadron, Dragoon R 2 crossed the Meuse as the second reconnaissance squadron of 2 KD. The dragoons bivouacked in the rain at Glons, east of Tongres.[19] Three long-range patrols were sent out on 5 August, one of which, with ten dragoons, charged a group of thirty Belgians and took them prisoner. A second shot at a low-flying aircraft and forced it to land, but was prevented from taking the crew prisoner by superior Belgian forces. The patrol established that there were strong Belgian forces at Waremme, but both of the messengers bringing this report were shot. Belgian forces were also seen 6 km south of Tirlemont. This patrol was continually shadowed by bicyclists.

On 6 August the squadron reached Tongres and broke up a group of franc-tireurs. During the entire night a patrol observed Belgian troops marching on the Liège–St Troiden road. On the 7th the squadron reconnoitred Orthee, 6 km south of Tongres, and picked up thirty-eight troopers from the reconnaissance squadrons of Dragooon R 17 and 18, which had been scattered by the Belgians. The dragoons spent the 8th avoiding Belgian forces: they were fired on at Tongres 'apparently by Garde Civique'; later, two troopers of the point element were killed, and then the squadron had to avoid a squadron of Belgian cavalry. It had a stroke of luck when it intercepted a Belgian supply column with food and horse fodder. On the 9th a security detachment was engaged by bicyclists and infantry: one man was killed, one wounded and one captured. The squadron joined up with the regiment at Tongres.

On 7 August Dragoon R 2 sent a patrol to St Troiden, which made the entire trip, a distance of 100 km, in sixteen hours. Lifeguard Hussar R 1 sent a reconnaissance squadron to the Gette River on 9–11 August, which found it to be heavily defended.[20]

The 2 KD patrols reported the withdrawal of the Belgian troops to the west, Belgian cavalry on the Gette between Diest and Tirlemont, and infantry moving west towards Louvain. This was invaluable information, for it not only established where the Belgian army was, but also that no French or British troops had been seen. Nevertheless, this was less than had been hoped for. As the war diary of HKK 2 noted, the long-range patrols had not been able to pass beyond the line Diest–Huy, less than halfway to the objectives, Antwerp and Charleroi.[21]

4 KD Reconnaissance Squadrons

4th Squadron Dragoon R 17 had the mission of reconnoitring towards the Sambre and Charleroi. The squadron sent out three long-range patrols; they were the first German cavalry to swim the Meuse. Initially these patrols and two from 2nd Squadron Dragoon R 18 moved together for the sake of security. Civilian bicyclists raced in front, announcing that 'The British are coming!' This allowed the patrol to advance all the way to the west side of Liège, where the patrols split up.

4th Squadron, Dragoon R 17, which followed the patrols, was not so lucky: it took fire. The squadron dismounted, swept through a village, and determined that the shooters had been civilians, who were captured. The squadron had not taken any casualties, so the squadron commander only warned the priest that if it happened again the village would be burned down. The regimental history said that for civilians to fire on soldiers was 'treacherous murder'. Dragoon R 18 had moved to the sound of the firing and the two squadrons bivouacked together near Wihogne, between Liège and Tongres.

On 6 August one of the long-range patrols infiltrated through the Belgian security forces and made contact with Belgian troops at Wassaiges on the Mehaigne River, about 40 km west of Liège, as did the second patrol somewhat to the north. The horse of the first patrol leader was killed and he was taken POW; the same fate befell the officer and NCO of the second patrol and a trooper was wounded. The third patrol, further to the east, found that all the bridges over the Mehaigne, as well as the crossroads, were guarded. When they passed through a town, the church bells were rung.

The two reconnaissance squadrons sent out two more patrols, which were also broken up and their leaders captured. A messenger returned to 4 KD with a report that they had found the Liège–Brussels road packed with Belgian troops: the Belgians were evacuating their field forces from Liège.

Hussar R 15 sent a long-range patrol with an officer and fifteen men towards the Gette River on 10 August.[22] The patrol had gone only 10 km when it encountered a Belgian security detachment. It manoeuvred 3 km to the left to bypass it, and was fired upon by Belgian bicyclists. The patrol leader ordered a mounted charge and captured 'about 8 to 10' Belgians. It then saw a group of twenty-five to thirty Belgian cavalry, apparently a staff. The patrol leader ordered a second charge, but his men took fire from infantry on their left and had to retire, losing the officer and one trooper killed.

Liège[23]

The Belgian fortress of Liège consisted of twelve permanent fortresses constructed between 1888 and 1891 in a ring around Liège on an average of 8 km from the city centre and 2.5–3.5 km apart. In common with fortress doctrine at this time, the mission of Liège (and Namur) was to serve as obstacles to enemy movement (*places d'arrêt*), to support friendly movement, and to provide bridgeheads on the Meuse. To 'arm' the fortress, that is, to put it in a proper state of defence, field fortifications had to be dug between the permanent fortifications. If Liège remained in Belgian hands, the German 1st Army might have to transit Dutch territory, potentially bringing the Netherlands into the war against Germany. The Germans therefore decided to launch a *coup de main* against Liège on the night of the fourth day of mobilisation (5–6 August) with peacetime-strength units, which meant 2–3 OFF and 130 EM per rifle company,[24] probably 600 EM per battalion, 1,800 per regiment, for a total force (six brigades, four Jäger battalions) of about 25,000 infantry, roughly the same strength as that of a single German corps. The intent was to attack before the intervals had been properly fortified, penetrate through the gaps between the forts and seize the city centre, which was not fortified. The Germans hoped that the forts would then surrender.

The attack on the intervals was carried out on the night of 5–6 August. Unfortunately for the Germans, the Belgians had mobilised on 1 August and had five brigades (ten regiments) of field troops in Liège, the 3rd Infantry Division and the 15th Infantry Brigade, to hold the intervals between the fortresses. Since the Belgians units were mobilised and the Germans were at peacetime strength, the defending Belgian field force was just as strong, if not stronger than, the attacking German force. Five of the six German brigades were thrown back. Only one, led by Erich Ludendorff, who assumed command of the 14th Brigade when the brigade commander was killed, had penetrated to the centre of the town by the morning of 6 August.

The attack on Liège had taken the Belgians by surprise; they had expected that the Germans would wait to complete their deployment before attacking, and had not anticipated an *attaque brusquée*.[25] The Belgians seriously overestimated the strength of the attackers at seven corps, 300,000 men, and suspected that the Germans had secretly mobilised these corps.

The Belgians had also received reports that strong German cavalry – the estimates varied from seven regiments to two divisions – were across the Meuse.[26] The commandant of the province of Limbourg reported that the Germans had already occupied Tongres. This was, in fact, only the 3rd Squadron Dragoon R 2. The German cavalry was operating behind Liège in an area 30 km broad and 20 km deep; each time German cavalry entered a town, its presence had surely been reported. When the Germans cut the telephone and telegraph lines they added to the confusion. The Belgians reported the German cavalry activity to the British and French, and the report reached the personal attention of the president of France.

It appeared to the Belgians that German cavalry not only threatened to cut off the reinforced 3rd Division in Liège, but that the left flank of the main army, assembling behind the Gette, was also in danger. This caused the Belgians to withdraw all their field troops from Liège while they still could, leaving only the garrisons of the permanent fortifications. Half of the mobile garrison was ordered out of Liège on 6 August; the other half assembled on the west side of the fortress and would leave that night.

There would be no counter-attack against Ludendorff's isolated brigade. The route into Liège was open for the rest of the German attack force. The task of the German siege artillery was considerably simplified. Belgian fortresses began to surrender at once. The Germans could soon move artillery into Liège itself, which made Belgian counter-battery fire impossible. While the big 42 cm guns are credited with the destruction of the Liège forts, it was the more prosaic but also more mobile 21 cm mortars that did most of the work. At 0930 on 16 August the last fort, Hollogne, fell. The taking of Liège has been attributed to Ludendorff. That his bold action succeeded was due in great part to the work of the German HKK 2 cavalry reconnaissance squadrons.

The Belgian cavalry division and a brigade from the 5th Infantry Division were ordered forward to cover the withdrawal from Liège. This infantry marched directly onto 4th Squadron Dragoon R 17 and 2nd Squadron Dragoon R 18, practically surrounding them. The squadrons tried desperately to break out, gradually losing cohesion in the process. One group entered Waremme: 'The small town was swarming with highly excited civilians, some of whom opened a wild, poorly-aimed fire at us with hunting weapons from behind barricades.' The real danger for the Germans was not fire from Belgian civilians, but the cobblestone street made slippery by horse manure, which caused many galloping horses to fall. The 2nd Squadron Dragoon R 18 attempted to conduct a mounted charge, but was stopped by hedges and wire.[27] The two squadrons returned to their regiments in small groups. One of these, with thirty-three men, encountered a group of Belgian infantry and took thirty-five prisoners without suffering any loss. The 2nd Squadron Dragoon R 18 lost 6 KIA, 3 OFF and 69 EM POW. The squadron was dissolved and the remnants divided among the other squadrons.

Between 7 and 14 August the German 1st Army completed its rail deployment to the area north-east of Aachen.[28] III and IV AK deployed by 11 August, II AK by 12 August, followed by III RK and IV RK. On 10 August OHL ordered the 1st Army to begin the forward movement of the active-army corps on 12 August, a day ahead of schedule. On 13 August all three active corps began to transit Aachen. On that day Fort Pontisse, which dominated the Meuse crossing point at Lixhé, fell, and on 14 August the 1st Army could begin crossing undisturbed. On 15 August the 1st Army penetrated about 15 km into Belgium, to Tongres. IX AK was detached from the 2nd Army and attached to the 1st Army, which now consisted of four active and two reserve corps. IV RK consisted of only 14 RD; 13 RD was completing the reduction of Liège. On 16 August the army closed up on this line. By 17 August the four active-army corps had advanced to St Troiden to close on the Belgian army, while the two reserve corps had reached the Meuse at Visé and to the south.[29]

The German official history says that the 1st Army was a day ahead of schedule. In fact, the only unit of HKK 2 or the 1st German Army that was held up by the Belgian forts at Liège was the 9 KD, which wanted to cross from the south bank of the Meuse to the north bank on 10 August, but had to wait until the X AK put a bridge across the river on 14 August.

The 1st and 2nd Armies occupied forward assembly areas on the west bank of the Meuse while the rest of the German armies conducted their rail deployment.

The 3rd Army, in particular, took longer to deploy because the rail net in the Eifel, the German part of the Ardennes forest, was relatively thin. The German army's rail deployment was completed by 17 August.[30] On that day, OHL issued the final orders for the advance of the German right wing to begin on 18 August.

This brings us to the first case in which the official British history gave politics and propaganda precedence over military professionalism and historical accuracy. Edmonds emphasised that Britain had entered the war in order to honour its treaty obligations to defend Belgian neutrality.[31] This was in keeping with British wartime propaganda. It was therefore useful to claim that German disregard for international law and Belgian neutrality had been appropriately punished: the heroic resistance at Liège had 'rendered transcendent service to the cause of Belgium's allies' by delaying the German attack for four or five days.[32] This gave the French and British forces time to deploy to meet the German right wing.

Edmonds justified this claim by saying that the Germans had begun arriving in their assembly areas on 7 August. Had Liège offered no resistance 'there seems no reason why the II, III and IV Corps should not have reached the above line (forty miles, or three marches, west of Liège) on the 10th and completed their concentration there on the 12th or 13th – four or five days earlier than was the case'.[33]

Edmonds says that Bülow's memoirs state the Germans wanted to begin the advance on 13 August, but because Liège had not fallen this was not possible. In fact, what Bülow actually reported to OHL was that if the advance were to begin on 13 August, then he would go around Liège to the south and leave IX AK to cover the siege artillery. Bülow was actually saying just the opposite of what Edmonds contended: that in fact, for the 2nd Army Liège was not an obstacle.

Edmonds' version of the German deployment was a complete fantasy, constructed out of whole cloth, created to support British propaganda and a satisfying myth. When the real German deployment was made known, Edmonds could not change the British official history without major damage to both the British propaganda position and the credibility of the official history, so he didn't. Later historians uncritically accepted Edmonds' fantasy because it told them exactly what they wanted to hear.

The authoritative Anglophone history of the Marne campaign is Sewell Tyng's *The Campaign of the Marne*, which says that the German right wing could not advance until 17 August 'when the last of the Liège forts had fallen'.[34] The most influential popular book on the Marne campaign is Barbara Tuchmann's *The Guns of August*, which says that Liège held up the German advance by two days.[35]

Complete ignorance concerning German mobilisation, deployment and planning is still common among Anglophone historians, especially of the 'German war guilt' school, which apparently believes that the German army magically appeared on Germany's western border at the declaration of war. Annika Mombauer, a prominent representative of the 'German war guilt' school, contends that 'by the fifteenth day of mobilisation the German troops were expected deep in French territory'.[36] In fact, the Germans didn't conclude their rail deployment inside Germany until 17 August and it took them another five days, until 22 August, to march across Belgium to the French border, much less deep into France. But Mombauer's absurd assertion appeared in a refereed journal, *The Journal of Strategic Studies*, that is to say that the editor and two or three other 'experts' who evaluated and approved it also believed it to be true. The responsibility for this deplorable state of affairs can be laid at Edmonds' feet.

The second element of the Liège myth is that the Germans suffered astronomical casualties attacking Liège. The Belgian official history says that the Germans admitted losing 42,712 men in the attack; where this admission is to be found was not stated.[37] A book on the Meuse forts says: 'Row after row of Germans were shot down by rifle and machine-gun fire ... bodies were piled several deep. The myth of the invincible German army had been shattered and a [unnamed] Cologne newspaper reported at the end of August that 53,000 Germans had been killed at Liège.'[38]

The twelve infantry regiments and four Jäger battalions that participated in the attack on the night of 5–6 August, at peacetime strength, probably included 25,000 infantrymen in all. According to the second figure above, every attacking German was killed twice, and 3,000 were killed three times. The total German casualties were probably below 3,400.[39] On the other hand, the 14th Brigade took 1,500 prisoners. Given the fact that the Belgian 3rd Division also lost significant numbers of killed and wounded on the night of 5–6 August, and that the garrisons of all the permanent fortresses were killed or captured, total Belgian and German casualties were about equal.

Franc-Tireur

In the march across Belgium the German army encountered little opposition from the Belgian army. Instead, it had to fight its way through the resistance by the Belgian civil population. Even though the Belgian regular army was nowhere in the vicinity, German bivouacs were frequently fired upon, and German cavalry was often ambushed. Practically every German regiment reported being attacked by Belgian civilians, known as *franc-tireurs*. Dragoon R 19 (9 KD), for example, reported being fired upon in the town in which they were bivouacking during the night of 5–6 August 'by weapons of all kinds, from roofs and gardens and hedges outside the town'.[40] The troops were 'gripped by a limitless bitterness'. A security outpost was also fired on. The squadron commander and a patrol went to check on them and found both men dead. As they tried to retrieve the bodies, they took fire themselves. A senior sergeant reported 'the shooting lasted a while, but soon we had pulled several of these assassins out of their hiding places'. The next morning several Belgians 'that had been caught with weapons in their hands' were tried by court martial and shot. The sergeant was on the firing squad: 'It was awful', he wrote. Most German units gave up on bivouacking in the comfort of towns because it was too dangerous, and spent the night in the open where it was easier to maintain security, but the troopers had to sleep in the rain and mud.

Civilians or soldiers on bicycles often shadowed German cavalry. The Germans often could not distinguish between the two and were therefore reluctant to fire on bicyclists. When German troops passed near villages, the church bells would sound the alarm and flags were raised on church towers in warning. The Dragoon R 18 history complained that on 19 August it did not meet any enemy regular forces, but lots of *franc-tireurs*.[41] The patrols avoided towns and moved cross-country to stay off the roads, but on the occasions when they did get near roads people in automobiles or on bicycles would fire on them. On 20 August Hussar R 11 caught three civilian bicyclists with a sketch of the regiment's position.[42] They were tried by court martial and presumably shot. On the same day two Belgian civilians gave a report concerning German troops to a patrol of Uhlan R 5, apparently believing them to be British.[43] Lomas printed a picture in Mons of a Belgian boy scout walking between two British cavalrymen, with a British ammunition bandolier over his shoulder and a Lee-Enfield rifle under his arm. Lomas noted that 'equipped as above this one [boy scout] would incur the considerable wrath of any German soldier who met him and would hardly escape the firing squad'.[44]

The Germans soon discovered that many Belgian and French troops wore civilian clothes under their uniforms, something that was impossible in the strictly disciplined German army, and they suspected the Belgian soldiers were fully prepared to take off their uniforms and become *franc-tireurs*. On 20 August Hussar R 11 found three sets of French officers' uniforms, and made the not unreasonable assumption that their owners were operating in civilian clothes.

Civilian opposition was limited almost exclusively to the French-speaking Walloon districts of Belgium. The German troops got along quite well in the Flemish areas, north German Plattdeutsch being very similar to Dutch. The 1st Army troops also had less trouble with French civilians than Belgian ones.[45]

Belgian civilian resistance may have come from three groups: the Belgian active Garde Civique (Civic Guard), the 'inactive' Garde Civique and armed civilians.[46] The Garde Civique was organised in towns of over 10,000 and in the fortresses, the inactive Garde Civique in the smaller towns. Both were subordinate to the Ministry of the Interior and responsible for peace and order, enforcement of the laws, defence of national independence and protection of the borders.[47] The active Garde Civique was made up of men between the ages of twenty-one and forty. Ostensibly, it numbered about 46,000 armed men in 1913, but little definite can be said about it because the Belgians have no records whatsoever concerning its organisation or activities. The active Garde Civique had little military training, the 'inactive' Garde Civique none whatsoever. Coordination between the Interior Ministry and the War Ministry concerning the employment of the Garde

Civique seems to have been minimal at best. There is no evidence of a chain of command above the local level and little even at the local level.

On 5 August the Belgian government armed 100,000 'inactive' Garde Civique.[48] There is no indication that these people had any discipline, uniforms, leadership or training. The Ministry of the Interior issued a proclamation on 1 August, calling on Belgians to resist an invasion and help the army in any way possible, and on 5 August published instructions on the conduct of the Garde Civique. If weapons were unavailable, the Garde Civique was told it should arm itself. Since uniforms were unavailable, it was necessary for members to wear something to identify themselves as combatants. The Garde Civique was supposed to have been disbanded on 18 August, but Hussar R 15 reported disarming Garde Civique members on 20 August.[49]

There is evidence of *franc-tireur* activity in the contemporary Belgian press. The IR 89 history noted that an article in the 14 August issue of the *Burgerwelzyn*, the entire population of Herstal – men, women and children – were described as having fought the Germans, an action which the newspaper found praiseworthy.[50] The Jäger 7 history cited a story in a Liège newspaper concerning the German attack against the headquarters of the Liège garrison, in which it said that, 'From a neighbouring apartment building civilians armed with pistols fired on the German soldiers'.[51]

The German army was desperate to establish good relations with the Belgian population, for both political and military reasons. The German cavalry posted notices warning against civilian resistance. If the German units were able, they searched the towns they entered for weapons and confiscated any they found. Each cavalry regiment carried gold coins in order to be able to pay for goods in cash. They would continue to pay in gold until the middle of August, by which time it was clear that the population was hostile. The German troops then began issuing requisition receipts.[52] When they were fired upon by Belgian civilians the German troops were outraged: in German eyes, soldiers fought soldiers in the open field and civilians were not involved. They noted that the Geneva Conventions provided that soldiers be uniformed or easily identified. Civilians firing on troops were conducting 'ambush and murder like highwaymen'.[53] If sufficiently provoked, the Germans would take reprisals, which ran the gamut from burning down the houses they had received fire from to shooting captured *franc-tireurs*. The historian of Jäger-Bataillon 3 said that the troops detested deeply both the *franc-tireurs* and the job of punishing them.[54] The 1st Army gave a collective sigh of relief when it left Belgium for the interior of France and the *franc-tireur* attacks ceased.

Relations between the German troops and Belgian civilians were not always bad, especially in Flemish towns. On 21 August Jäger-Bataillon 3 received a warm welcome in Nefelle: the inhabitants fed the battalion on the street 'in a marvellous manner'.[55] The local girls engaged the Jäger in conversation and fed them various delicacies, to the joy of the Jäger and their commander alike. German soldiers who bivouacked in Belgian and French towns frequently got along well with the inhabitants. It may not sound very bellicose, but the German troops went shopping whenever they could, and the shopowners were happy to do business.

The Hussar R 10 regimental history tells of bivouacking in Heure le Romain, a small town in eastern Belgium, on 15 August.[56] A sergeant on the regimental staff and the bandmaster were given a room above a shop, where they bought beer, schnapps, cigars and bread, then went out to make further purchases at another store. They found it packed with soldiers and the owner and his wife were at their wits' end because they only spoke French. As befitted old soldiers, the sergeant and the bandmaster knew enough French to get by in such situations; they were even able to convert currencies. They helped the shopowner for two hours, then bought themselves 'a bottle of good red wine for 80 Pfennig'. The shopowner thanked them with much shaking of hands and before they left he made them drink a glass of sherry 'to their health'. Then he gave them his calling card and asked that they get in touch after the war. That night they went to the local pub to receive the unit order, taking the son of their householder with them as a guide. While they waited, they bought the young man a beer and conversed as best they could. The sergeant said that, except for the language problem, they could have been in a Gasthaus on a training exercise in the Altmark of Prussia. On 22 August Jäger-Bataillon 3 'lived off the land' in fine style, taking the opportunity to order dinner in the 'well-appointed pubs' where 'the prices were very reasonable'.[57] On the next day Jäger-Bataillon 3's luck continued. Not only was the population very friendly and fed the troops well, but the pubs had 'relatively good-tasting beer'.

Sordet's Cavalry Corps

The pre-war calculation of the Deuxième Bureau, the French General Staff intelligence department, was that the Germans could attack as of the thirteenth day of mobilisation.[58] Expecting to find the Germans in the northern Ardennes, Sordet's Cavalry Corps of three divisions was sent into Belgium on 6 August and reached the area west of Liège on 8 August. On 9 August he found nothing at Marche. Neither he nor French aerial reconnaissance could find any German forces as far east as the Ourthe River because there were no German forces there, nor would there be any there until around 15 August. Sordet's cavalry had moved ten days too soon. Nor did the Belgians provide much useful information.[59] By 12 August Sordet had moved to Neufchâteau but still made no contact; he then pulled back to the west bank of the Meuse on 15 August and was attached to the 5th Army. Sordet reported that it was impossible to supply the cavalry in the Ardennes and that air reconnaissance was unreliable in the dense woods. His cavalry corps had conducted an eight-day march without obtaining any information concerning the German forces. In order to find the German 3rd, 4th and 5th Armies, the French cavalry would have had to advance across the Belgian Ardennes to the border with Germany and Luxembourg, and it was unable to do so.[60] The German deployment was not completed until 17 August and the German right wing armies did not begin their general advance until 18 August. The French had great difficulty understanding why the Germans were not as far to the west as they expected them to be, and this led to the assumption that there were no Germans in the northern Ardennes at all.

9 KD

9 KD was to cover the left flank of the Liège attack force and reconnoitre to the south and east of the Meuse. On 4 August 2nd Squadron Hussar R 8 was sent on reconnaissance towards Givet with instructions to establish whether the French 5th Corps was assembling there and if it was advancing into Belgium.[61] It was given 10,000 gold marks to purchase food and fodder.

A patrol with fifteen troopers was sent out, led by Lieutenant Humann, who was to become the squadron patrol-leader par excellence. Humann was given 1,000 gold marks to buy provisions. The patrol spent the first night bivouacked in a wood in pouring rain. The next day, the patrol cut telephone lines as it advanced. It charged a Belgian cavalry patrol, which fled, leaving a wounded Belgian and a bearskin cap behind. The patrol again bivouacked in a wood and on 6 August entered Dinant, where the hussars were taken for British and greeted warmly. It approached to within fifty metres of the railway bridge where it took MG fire from French troops and quickly withdrew. A horse was killed, but the rider requisitioned a bicycle as a replacement, an expedient that the German cavalry would use frequently. The patrol then crossed to the west bank of the Meuse at Lesse, south of Dinant, in broad daylight. It encountered a French squadron that was conducting 'a routine peacetime route march' and ambushed it. On 7 August the patrol observed considerable troop movements in Givet. At dawn on 8 August it re-crossed the Meuse 5 km north of Givet before a French outpost could react, and on 9 August rejoined the squadron.

A second patrol, led by Lt Schell, found it difficult to advance because the roads were blocked with 'every imaginable obstacle'. The point also took fire from *franc-tireurs*, but there were no casualties. The patrol had soon sent back so many messengers that it returned to the squadron for reinforcements and started out again on 7 August. It bivouacked near the town of Laroche and observed considerable bodies of French troops advancing on two roads into the town. While on reconnaissance the next day, it encountered a French cuirassier squadron, which pursued the hussars and dispersed the patrol. Two hussars were lost and after several hours Lt Schell could assemble only four troopers. Nevertheless, that night he continued to observe French troop movements. The next day Lt Schell attempted to return to the squadron, moving cross-country. The patrol had to hide to avoid observation by a column of thirty city buses loaded with French infantry. However, attempting to pass through a village, which could not be bypassed, the patrol was surrounded by French troops and captured.

A third patrol was sent out on 5 August. On 8 August this patrol encountered several squadrons of French cavalry and was also captured. These two patrols had the bad luck to fall afoul of Sordet's French Cavalry Corps.

On 5 August at Plainvieux south of Liege a squadron of the Belgian 2nd Lancer Regiment charged superior German cavalry and lost 75 per cent of its strength. It would probably have been opposed by a unit of the German 9 KD but it is not possible to discover which German cavalry regiment was involved.

2nd Squadron Hussar R 8 advanced on 5 and 6 August to 10 km north-west of Marche, about 100 km from its start point. Several civilians approached the squadron bivouac and were detained until the squadron moved on. Sordet failed to detect the hussar squadron, though they must have passed within 10 km of each other.

On the night of 5–6 August Hussar R 11 and Cuirassier R 4 were attacked while bivouacked.[62] 4th Squadron Hussar R 11 was located in a large farm that had electric lighting. The squadron commander reported that 'suddenly the lights went out. At the same moment furious firing began from all the windows and doors of the surrounding houses. There was so much light from shotguns, rifle-fire, and bursting hand-grenades that the entire village took on a pale yellow colour.' Lieutenant Wolff-Metternich of Cuirassier R 4 said that the attack began exactly at 2300.[63] Hussar R 11 evacuated the towns and assembled at a bridge over the Ourthe River. One hussar had been killed and three wounded. Cuirassier R 4 fought until the next morning. Wolff-Metternich spoke excellent French, so he conducted the interrogation of the villagers, who fingered the parish priest as the ringleader, though he denied it. Twenty-three villagers were executed, but the division commander refused to have the priest shot, saying that he did not want to begin the campaign in such a manner.

On 7 August the colonel commanding Hussar R 8 was riding down a road with his orderly when an engineer sergeant directly to his front was shot by a bullet fired from an isolated house in a nearby wood. The colonel heard the sergeant, lying in a pool of blood, repeat: 'Not dead yet. Not dead yet.' A nearby patrol from Hussar R 11 broke down the doors of the house and herded the occupants outside – a dozen men, women and children – and lined them up against a wall, enraged and shouting to the colonel, 'Can we? Can we?' The colonel calmed the patrol, ordered the release of the women, children and two old men. Three men were transported to the 9 KD headquarters, where they were tried by court martial and shot.[64] The house was burned down.

Wolff-Metternich was carrying an order from 9 KD to the 13th Cavalry Brigade at 1100 on 7 August. He had just entered a sunken road when he heard a blast and a load of buckshot whizzed past his head.[65] He pushed through a hedge and saw a trembling civilian sitting ten paces in front of him, grabbed a shotgun from his hands and broke the stock over his head. Then he noticed that it was a brand-new weapon with a shell ejector. 'Too bad that it was now kaput.'

9 KD sent Sergeant Triep, who spoke excellent French, under flag of truce to Fort de Boncelles to demand its surrender. Approaching the fort, he was stopped and blindfolded and led inside, where he was stripped naked and forced to stand with his arms outstretched at his side. The Belgian soldiers around him said, 'We should shoot the dirty Prussian' and called him a pig. This berating went on 'for hours'. The commandant refused to surrender and Triep got dressed and left the fort. After Boncelles was pounded by German artillery into submission, Wolff-Metternich noted in his diary that the fort should have surrendered when it had the chance.[66]

On 9 August Hussar R 11 sent a reconnaissance squadron towards Dinant. The squadron commander noted, 'Finally, a good mission'.[67] The squadron, reinforced with a light radio station and a platoon of bicyclists from Jäger 10, moved out that night and also sent out four long-range patrols. The squadron was stopped on the Lesse River by French security forces. On 10 August the squadron was able to establish that the French were withdrawing, leaving security forces along the Marche–Dinant railway line. The long-range patrols made frequent contact, took casualties and had to return individually or in small groups. It was suspected that the inhabitants reported their location to French and Belgian forces. The patrols began seizing any bicycles they found and rendering them unserviceable.

Dragoon R 19 sent out a patrol under Sgt Siemers on 9 August north-west of Laroche in the Ardennes.[68] While chasing a French dispatch-rider the patrol turned a corner in a town and ran straight into a squadron of dismounted French cavalry. Two dragoons were lost, but the rest of the patrol escaped. Undeterred, Siemers hid beside the road to observe the French. After a while, not only did this squadron ride past him, but also an entire French cavalry division. He reported this to 9 KD. On his return he was promoted and in September received one of the first Iron Crosses.

The 9 KD bivouacs on 5, 6 and 7 August were miserable. It rained in buckets. The local inhabitants were unfriendly and a castle gardener, of all people, was captured in the possession of a military rifle. On 13 August a lieutenant in Hussar R 8 found a telegraph hidden in a house; the telegraph roll contained information concerning 9 KD. The supply vehicles could not come forward because the roads were blocked. The troopers soon learned to forage during the day so that they had rations and fodder that evening. The reservists arrived on 8 August and 9 KD was now full-strength. From 9 to 13 August the division marked time until the X AK engineers could put a bridge across the Meuse so that the division could cross to the north side and join HKK 2. On 13 August Hussar R 11 found a Belgian carrier pigeon station, with messages from Belgian fortresses such as Liège, Namur and Antwerp. The messages went to division HQ, the pigeons into the frying pan. Hussar R 11 also searched the town of Fraiture, confiscating a number of rifles and bicycles. The rifles were used to arm the supply troops. Horseless troopers were assigned bicycles and formed into a bicycle detachment, which was turned over to Jäger 7 because they lacked cross-country mobility.[69] Nevertheless, 9 KD continued to patrol, the reports coming in, as the division General Staff officer said, 'just like in a manoeuvre'.[70]

The Advance into Belgium

The 8th Cavalry Brigade supported the 34th Infantry Brigade's attack on Liège on the night of 5–6 August by holding the bridgehead at Lixhé, but was withdrawn to the east side of the Meuse on 7 August. On 7 August the reservists began arriving. These were far fewer than for infantry regiments – Hussar R 12 received only 61 reservists, to bring the regiment up to 717.

On 8 August HKK 2 began crossing the Meuse in earnest. Although by now the engineers had put a pontoon bridge in the water, it was so unstable that it could only be used dismounted, single file, and 2 KD took all day in crossing. At 0600 on 9 August 2 KD moved from Tongern and did not bivouac until 2300, just short of St Troiden. Aside from the capture of three Belgian cavalrymen, there had been no contact. At 1100 on 10 August 2 KD entered St Troiden, seized all the weapons, destroyed the telephone and telegraph apparatus and captured 130 Gardes Civique. Dragoon R 18 captured three Belgian officers in civilian clothes who were trying to conduct reconnaissance in an automobile.[71] Uhlan R 9 spotted a mass of Belgian cavalry 2 km to the front, deployed and charged. The Belgians ran, with Uhlan 9 in hot pursuit at a gallop for several kilometres, but the Belgians could not be overtaken.[72]

Reconnaissance Squadrons

On 9 August Hussar Regiment 16 (4 KD) sent 1st Squadron on reconnaissance towards Namur, reinforced by a half-company from Jäger Battalion 9 and a light radio station.[73] When the hussars crossed the Liège–St Troiden road they found it 'literally covered' with uniforms and equipment thrown away by the Belgian troops withdrawing from Liège. The squadron bivouacked in a town near Waremme. It was not possible to establish radio contact with the KD.

The commander of 4th Squadron Hussar R 15 arrived in a staff car, saying that his squadron and forty Jäger were being sent as reinforcements.[74] 1/Hussar

R 16 interrogated the supervisor of a railway station and learned that 5,000 to 8,000 Belgians had been transported towards Tirlemont during the night of 9–10 August. Three long-range patrols were sent out: two were broken up and their leaders captured, but the third 'adapted itself quickly to Belgian methods of combat' and gave good service – but only on close-range patrols. Both squadron commanders and a Jäger, armed with carbines, took the staff car on a reconnaissance to determine if there was a Belgian position at Bierwart (17 km north-east of Namur). They found that there was no position there, were ambushed by *franc-tireurs*, but shot their way out without casualties.

4th Squadron Hussar R 15 arrived on 11 August; 1st Squadron Hussar R 16 was having difficulty due to the terrain and *franc-tireurs*, so the two squadron commanders decided to join forces. For the next week these two squadrons, joined later by a squadron from Cuirassier R 4, would conduct a highly-successful reconnaissance-in-force. 4th Squadron reconnoitred towards Bierwart. Material found in the post office indicated that the French left wing was expected at Namur. A patrol sent to the Meuse valley was turned back by enemy security forces before reaching its goal. When enemy cavalry and bicycle troops advanced, 4th Squadron withdrew. This was reported to the KD using 1st Squadron Hussar R 16's radio.

The next day both squadrons advanced on Bierwart and took the town after a two-hour battle. From letters, Belgian dead and prisoners, it was determined that the Belgian 8th Brigade was on the Meuse at Namur, that the French left wing was at Dinant and Givet, and that French security detachments were as far east as Huy. This was reported by radio. On the morning of 13 August, Belgian infantry attacked out of the fog. The cavalry security patrols had become involved in a firefight and were unable to report, so the Belgians were able to march right up to the Jäger providing close security and the Germans had to withdraw 200 metres. Here the Jäger took up a firing position and the cavalry manoeuvred against the Belgian rear, which caused them to withdraw in turn. The hussars reoccupied their bivouac, but withdrew once more when stronger Belgian forces approached. 1st Squadron Hussar R 16 lost 5 KIA; 4th Squadron Hussar R 15 2 KIA, 10 WIA, 16 horses dead and 42 missing. The light radio had been severely damaged.

At 1700 the hussar squadrons encountered 100 Belgian bicycle troops at Bonesse on the Mehaigne River (20 km north-north-east of Namur). The hussars allowed the Belgians to approach to close range, enveloped the Belgian flanks, killed eleven men and captured seventy-nine bicycles, which were used to replace lost horses.

On 14 and 15 August the two hussar squadrons destroyed rail and telegraph lines, searched rail cars and mail for intelligence and shot it out several times with Belgian security forces. On 14 August they determined that the Belgians did not have strong forces east of Bierwart, but had dug in behind the Gette from Tirlemont to Jodoigne. Between Jodoigne and Namur were only security forces.

It was not possible to establish radio communication with 4 KD, so the next morning a lieutenant carried the report to 9 KD and IX AK on a motorcycle. On the 15th the two hussar squadrons pushed into the gap between Jodoigne and Namur and confirmed that it was not defended. The report was given to a lieutenant and a sergeant, who, travelling by different routes on bicycles through the *franc-tireur*-infested countryside, both reached 4 KD.

HKK 2 directed the hussars on 16 August to resupply from 9 KD, which also provided a new light radio, and continue their reconnaissance towards Charleroi. They thoroughly destroyed the main Namur–Brussels railway line at Gembloux, about 15 km north-west of Namur. In this area the hussars began making contact with French cavalry patrols. That evening they came upon a squadron from Cuirassier R 4 withdrawing before superior enemy forces. The three squadrons bivouacked together.

During the night 4th Squadron Hussar R 15 sent out two patrols on bicycles (!). One of these five-man patrols was wiped out by French cavalry, except for a trooper who escaped and evaded in civilian clothing.

Orsmaël-Gussenhoven

On 10 August at 1240 the advance guard of 2 KD, 1st Squadron Hussar R 12, took fire from a small village west of St Troiden, which was swept clear by dismounted hussars. Enemy cavalry, estimated at four squadrons, was reported to the front, and the 2nd Squadron moved down the road at a trot towards the next village, Orsmaël-Gussenhoven, which lay on the west side of the Gette. The east side of the river was lined with meadows divided by barbed wire and hedges. High trees and bushes limited visibility. The 2nd Squadron took fire, dismounted and deployed to both sides of the road. The hussars encountered a barricade on the far side of the Gette bridge and the regimental commander dismounted 5th Squadron and deployed it to the right of the 2nd. The 1st Squadron, following the 5th, took fire from the right front, dismounted and moved in that direction, to the right of the 5th. By now, a sharp firefight had developed. The hussars advanced between the houses and along hedges, through wire fences and ditches. The terrain made control difficult and the regiment split into small groups. Two more rifle platoons were formed from horse-holders. The 2 KD commander committed two MGs and the 3rd Squadron, Cuirassier 7 between the 1st and 5th Hussar R 12.[75] The cuirassiers advanced using fire and movement with two platoons on line, one in reserve. The 2nd Squadron stormed the barricade while 5th Squadron Hussar R 12, 3rd Squadron Cuirassier R 7 and 1st Squadron Hussar R 12 waded the man-deep Gette and attacked into the town. Following German doctrine for combat in built-up areas, hussars and cuirassiers pushed to the far edge of the town, in time to engage withdrawing Belgian

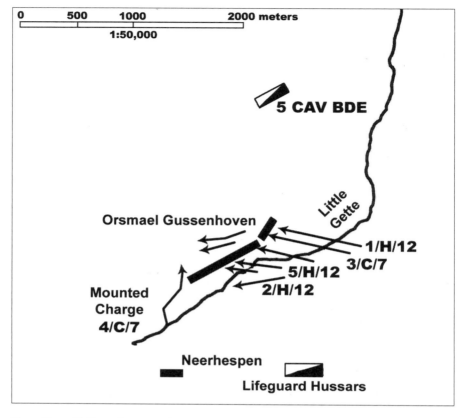

Fig. 7: Orsmaël-Gussenhoven, 10 August 1914.

cavalry with pursuit fire at 600 metres and capture thirty-five horses of the
Belgian Lancer R 3. At the same time, the point platoon of the 4th Squadron,
Cuirassier R 7, reinforced by a patrol from the 5th Squadron, was approaching from the town of Neerhespen to the south. The point platoon leader saw
about thirty dismounted Belgian cavalry in a field of grain firing towards the
east, deployed his troops behind a hedge and then ordered a mounted charge
with the lance, which succeeded completely: the Belgians were killed or taken
prisoner. As the Belgian main body fell back from Orsmaël-Gussenhoven, two
batteries of the 2 KD Horse Artillery Section of FAR 35, which had been
observing the action from the north, now quickly moved forward, unlimbered
and opened pursuit fire on the fleeing Belgians. The hussar regiment had lost 3
officer candidates and 12 EM KIA, 3 OFF and 13 EM WIA; the cuirassiers had
one man killed in the charge.

In their first action of the war, the hussars and cuirassiers had conducted a
model battle, combining excellent infantry tactics, MG and artillery fire support
with a small but effective mounted charge.

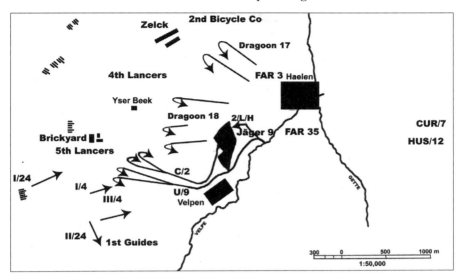

Fig. 8: Haelen, 12 August.

Haelen

HKK 2's mission was to find out what enemy forces, French and British in particular, were in the region of Leuven and Brussels. Up to 11 August HKK 2 had not been able to push reconnaissance elements west of the Gette, so the commander of HKK 2, Marwitz, decided to use his whole cavalry corps in a reconnaissance in force to break through the Belgian screen. Because the crossings of the Gette were so strongly held, Marwitz swung the corps to the north on 11 August in order to cross at Diest. On 12 August 4 KD was on the road to Diest, with 2 KD following.

A cavalry patrol found Haelen held by the Belgians; the patrol leader had his horse shot from under him, his NCO was killed.[76] The 4 KD advance guard and the Jäger 9 bicycle company had encountered the 3rd Company of the Belgian bicycle 'battalion', reinforced with MGs, that was attached to the Belgian cavalry division.[77]

Jäger 9 straddled the road into Haelen with Jägerkompagnie 7 on the left.[78] The Belgian troops were well hidden, their fire heavy and accurate, so the commander of Jäger 9 waited for artillery support before attacking. Two guns of the horse artillery battery unlimbered 600 metres from the town and after ten minutes' fire the Belgian MGs had been driven off – as the Jäger 9 history noted, this was the one correct solution to a small tactical problem. The Jäger took the bridge before it could be completely destroyed, and swept through the town to the west and north sides. The German horse artillery forward observer could see a Belgian battery at 2,000 metres range, firing in the open.

The Belgians deployed with the 1st and 3rd bicycle companies, two dismounted squadrons of the 4th Lancers and two of the 5th in the centre near Yser
beek farm. To their immediate left was a horse battery supported by two squadrons of the 5th Lancers, with the other two about 1,500 metres to the north-west.
A squadron of the 4th Lancers and two platoons of the 2nd bicycle company
held Zelck, two squadrons of the 2nd Guides were about 1,000 metres south-east
of Velpen, three of the 1st Guides in the Bekkolm woods.

The dismounted elements of Uhlan R 9 and Cuirassier R 2 swung south
of the town, where it was then decided to throw a bridge across the Gette to
speed the passage of the river. Greiner, the commander of 4 KD, also ordered a
reconnaissance squadron forward. Hearing that Haelen had been so easily taken,
Marwitz ordered the 17th Brigade (six squadrons) into Haelen. The Belgian artillery noticed all the dust and started firing into the town, initially to little effect.
Nevertheless, it was impossible to keep the 17th Brigade in the town, blocking
the road: the horse artillery in particular needed to pass through to set up on
the west side. Somehow the notion had also taken hold that the Belgians were
withdrawing.

The chain of responsibility becomes muddy at this point: it is nearly impossible
to determine what Marwitz, the HKK 2 commander, told Greiner, the 4 KD
commander, to do. No one wanted to claim ownership of the subsequent fiasco.
The official history gives a sanitised version of the battle.[79] Poseck's German
Cavalry is vague. It seems that Marwitz thought the Belgian forces west of Haelen
were weak and that he wanted 4 KD to move quickly to Diest. It cannot be determined whether Marwitz ordered 4 KD to charge or Greiner did it on his own.
It is clear that Greiner did not properly prepare the attack with reconnaissance
and fire support: this could be due to pressure from Marwitz or Greiner's own
over-confidence. The 17th Brigade commander wanted to attack dismounted;
Greiner thought that would take too much time, so without any reconnaissance,
he ordered an immediate mounted charge to take the Belgian artillery.

The 17th Brigade charged with Dragoon R 17 on the right towards Zelck,
which deployed 2nd Squadron on the right, Lifeguard Squadron on the left, 3rd
Squadron followed 2nd, and 4th Squadron, since Liège only a platoon strong, was
in 4 KD reserve.

The 2nd Squadron commander wanted to pass through the small town to
his front (Zelck), swing left, deploy and attack the artillery. He had no way of
knowing that the road into the town was barricaded and the town defended
by the Belgian bicyclists. The squadron commander later wrote that the road to
the town was lined with deep ditches and wire fences, so the squadron had to
advance in a column of fours at a gallop. He saw the barricade and the squadron
began to take machine-gun and rifle fire: 100 metres from the town his horse was
killed; he received a leg wound and was later captured. About 90 troopers continued the attack into the barricade and even through it; only 15, whose horses

were killed in front of the barricade and were able to hide and escape during the night, returned.

The Lifeguard Squadron had a similar fate. It took artillery fire as it left Haelen. The squadron encountered a broad ditch that could be crossed only by a bridge. Shortly after crossing the bridge, the squadron commander was killed. Belgian dismounted cavalry appeared on the right and left. Ditches, wire and sunken paths prevented an organised deployment. The charge became a disaster. The Dragoon R 17 commander, riding with the 3rd Squadron and seeing the wreckage to his front, halted 3rd Squadron and returned it to Haelen. Dragoon R 17 lost 9 OFF and 159 EM KIA, WIA or MIA, and 165 horses.

Dragoon R 18 attacked to the left of Dragoon R 17. It moved out of Haelen in squadron column, 4th Squadron leading. 1st Squadron, next in line, deployed on the right, 3rd Squadron in the middle. The attack came up against a tile-and-brickworks – industrial buildings surrounded by wire – which stopped the charge cold and presented standing targets to the Belgians. The survivors ran for Haelen. The regiment lost its commander, the adjutant and 39 EM KIA, 5 OFF and 31 EM WIA and 68 EM POW. The remnants were organised into two squadrons. The horseless dragoons made themselves mobile with bicycles and operated with the Jäger.

The 3rd Brigade crossed the stream on the pontoon bridge and attacked to the left of Dragoon R 18, with Cuirassier R 2 on the right and Uhlan R 9 on the left. The 3rd and 4th Squadrons of Cuirassier R 2 almost immediately ran into an uncrossable sunken road and had to veer left. The 3rd Brigade began to take heavy fire from the arriving Belgian 4th Infantry Brigade. Both cavalry regiments had to struggle through the defile between the sunken road and the town of Velpen. Uhlan 9 was fortunate enough to find a hollow where the regiment could organise and deploy into attack formation. The 3rd Brigade charged. Uhlan R 9 was now on the right and Cuirassier 2 on the left, attacking north–west towards the brickyard. It too encountered the wire around the brickyard and raced back to Haelen. Cuirassier R 2 lost 8 OFF, 77 EM and 272 horses. Uhlan R 9 reported on the evening of 12 August a loss of 4 OFF, 121 EM and 311 horses, but several troopers had attached themselves to the Jägers and returned later, some several weeks later. The regiment also reorganised into two squadrons.

Once the way through the town was free, the Horse Artillery Section FAR 3 moved on. The west side of Haelen was under MG and rifle fire. The battery commanders reconnoitred positions while the section adjutant brought the guns forward individually, at a gallop.[80] The horse artillery forced the Belgian gunners to leave their guns. The Germans were helped by the fact that the Belgian artillery fired off a lot of ammunition but shot badly: too far to the right with the shrapnel bursting too high. The 4 KD artillery did not, however, have enough time to engage the Belgian infantry and MGs before the cavalry charged. After the charge, the horse artillery turned on the barricades and chased the Belgian bicyclists away. Machine gun Detachment 2 set up with the Jäger and opened fire.

The Belgian official histories say that in spite of this fiasco the Germans (that is to say, Jäger 9) were winning – the Germans captured Yser beek farm – when the 4th Infantry Brigade (seventeen companies and three batteries) began to arrive at 1500, after a 25 km, seven-hour forced march in 'torrid heat'. I/4 and III/4 attacked towards Velpen, II/24 covered the right flank, I/24 was sent to Yser beek farm, and the last battalion was kept in reserve.

The HKK 2 front was now being held by Jäger 9, supported by a mix of HKK 2 units: the 4 KD's MG section (Garde Maschinengewehr Abteilung 2), the dismounted Lifeguard Hussar brigade from 2 KD, and both 4 KD and 2 KD's Horse Artillery Sections.

The Belgian infantry battalions entered Velpen, supported by its three batteries of artillery, and were met by fire from well-camouflaged MG which stopped the Belgians in their tracks. Supported by their MG, the Jäger counter-attacked.[81] That was the limit of the Belgian brigade's advance: one reinforced Jäger battalion was able to stop four Belgian battalions. Jäger 9 lost 10 men and 1 officer KIA. Belgian losses were not light. The bicycle companies lost 2 company commanders KIA, 51 EM KIA or WIA. The engineer captain was wounded. The 4th Lancers lost 4 OFF and 18 EM. But the unfortunate 4th Brigade ran into the Jäger 9 buzz-saw and lost 3 of 4 majors and 9 of 27 company-grade OFF, plus 399 EM.[82]

HKK 2 withdrew that evening. The Belgians could not follow due to the exhaustion of the troops, the obstacles of the terrain, but most of all because of the 'hellish fire of the [German] machine guns'.

Marwitz's performance at Haelen was one of the worst by a German corps commander in the Battle of the Frontiers. He did not go forward to see the terrain himself (how long would it have taken him to cater 4 km?), but sent 4 KD on an impossible mission. He did not leave his subordinates enough time to conduct a doctrinal reconnaissance. And in peacetime Marwitz had been the inspector-general of the cavalry! He would have failed one of his own peacetime training tests. His high peacetime rank may have precisely been the problem. There was plenty of pressure from important and influential figures like Friedrich von Bernhardi, the author of *Vom heutigen Kriege* (On Modern War) and a cavalry enthusiast, indeed perhaps from Kaiser Wilhelm himself, for Marwitz to prove that cavalry could actually conduct a mounted charge. Such proof would silence civilian critics of the expensive cavalry arm, especially the Socialists.

By wrecking 4 KD, Marwitz lost an opportunity for the cavalry to show what it could actually do on a modern battlefield. Had he allowed his Jäger, artillery and MGs to drive the Belgians from their positions, his cavalry in the pursuit of defeated troops would have had a field day. He would have broken the Belgian Gette position and offered his corps the opportunity of operating in the Belgian rear. It is also evident that the charge was stopped not so much by Belgian fire, but by natural and man-made obstacles. Had the charge been made across favourable terrain, it might have succeeded.

From 13 to 17 August HKK 2 awaited the arrival of the 1st and 2nd Army. The pause was used to rest and repair equipment. It was possible to provide regular supplies of food and fodder. 2 KD screened the HKK 2 front from a position near Hasselt, reinforced by Jäger 7 and 9; 4 KD was withdrawn to the rear, while 9 KD was arriving from the south.

9 KD

The division crossed the Meuse east of Huy on 14 August. A patrol from Hussar R 11 stopped a Belgian motorcyclist in civilian clothing, who was carrying a letter from the commandant of Liège to his daughter saying that the fort would fall soon.[83]

By 16 August 9 KD had linked up with 4 KD and was advancing east of Namur when an enemy cavalry regiment, estimated to be three squadrons strong (it was the Belgian 1st Chasseurs à Cheval), was detected.[84] Uhlan R 5 and Hussar R 11 deployed to conduct a mounted charge. However, reconnaissance detected enemy trenches and barbed wire. The charge was called off. As the enemy cavalry was mounting, it was engaged by the MG section, then by the horse artillery as it withdrew.

The BEF Lands

Austria declared war on Serbia on 28 August. The British government ordered the army to take 'precautionary measures ... to meet an immediate prospect of war' on 29 July.[85] Germany did not take similar measures until 31 July. Nevertheless, not until the Germans crossed into Belgium on 4 August did the British mobilise their army, first day of mobilisation 5 August. This meant that the British mobilisation was three days behind the French. If the British were to participate in the first battle, they would have to hurry to catch up.

The army in Great Britain was seriously under strength. As has been noted, a representative battalion had 486 EM present for duty on 4 August 1914. The British recalled 70,000 reservists, and on 8 August this battalion had 1,198 EM, 200 men over strength.[86] While all these reservists may not have forgotten their basic military skills, many of them were no longer marching fit, and the complicated deployment – rail move to the port of embarkation, crossing the Channel, second rail move to assembly area – left little time for road-march training.

In cabinet meetings on 5 and 6 August it was decided to send only four of the six available infantry divisions to France; two would be kept in Britain for coastal defence. On 14 August the British headquarters, GHQ, crossed to France and arrived at Le Cateau on the 16th. Beginning on 14 August the troop units began to cross over to land, principally at Le Havre, but also at Rouen and Boulogne. By 20 August, the day the Germans entered Brussels, the British had concentrated between Maubeuge and Le Cateau.

By committing the BEF to the continent to operate with the French army, the British had potentially given the Germans a great opportunity. War between Germany and Britain would necessarily be asymmetrical – in favour of the British. British sea power meant that the German colonies were lost and German overseas trade would be strangled. The German pre-war intelligence estimate made it clear there was no hope that the Germans could effect a landing on British soil or defeat the British fleet.[87]

The only way that Germany could damage Britain was by destroying the British army. The German generals who did so were sure to be national heroes; fame, honour and promotions would be theirs. The sky would be the limit for a successful general – one of Moltke's principal staff officers from 1870–71 had even become German Chancellor – and destroying the BEF would be success indeed. This is the prize that Kluck and Kuhl believed was in their reach, and they were not going to let Bülow deprive them of it.

The British were kind enough to commit their army directly in front of the German *Schwerpunkt*, with the British left flank and lines of communication to the home country hanging in the breeze. Potentially, fifteen German corps could attack seven British and French corps. Only unforced German errors could possibly save the BEF. The first, but most serious, of a series of such mistakes was Kuhl's *idée fixe* that the British would appear at Lille.

German 1st Army Advances

On 17 August General Bülow, the commander of the 2nd Army and the most senior serving German officer, was given operational control over HKK 2, the 1st Army and the 3rd Army. On both 17 and 18 August the German leadership expected to see French and perhaps British forces appear between Brussels and Namur. HKK 2's reconnaissance squadrons reported strong groups of French cavalry arriving from Charleroi on the afternoon of 17 August in the area of Gembloux-Namur. It was important to the Germans to defeat the Belgians before they linked up with the Entente forces.

Air and cavalry reconnaissance had identified four Belgian divisions behind the Gette.[88] Bülow wanted to wait until his army had moved further west before attacking the Belgians. Fearing that the Belgians would withdraw into Antwerp, Kuhl wanted to attack head-on, immediately. This was probably the wrong solution. There was little hope that such an attack would do anything more than push the Belgians into Antwerp. There was, however, a gap in the Belgian line between Namur and Tirlemont and the German cavalry had found and reported it. If the Germans pushed through here, they could conduct a parallel pursuit of the Belgian army retiring on Antwerp. Significant parts of the Belgian army might have been overtaken and destroyed. In the event, Bülow allowed the 1st Army to advance on 18 August, with the caveat that it swing a corps to the north to attempt to push the Belgians away from Antwerp.

The 2 KD was placed under the operational control of the 1st Army and deployed on the Army right flank.[89] The 1st Army ordered II AK and 2 KD to attack on the right towards Diest to turn the Belgian left and cut the Belgian line of retreat to Antwerp. IV AK would attack frontally against Haelen, III AK against Budingen and IX AK on Tirlemont. 2 KD also sent two patrols to reconnoitre the small Belgian fortresses at Diest and Leopold. Moving cross-country, both patrols reached their objectives, but spent the entire night avoiding Belgian outposts and patrols in order to return. Both Belgian security and German patrol techniques were improving, but the Germans still had the upper hand. 1st Squadron, Lifeguard-Hussar R 2 was sent on reconnaissance to determine if the British had landed at Antwerp.[90] One of its long-range patrols reached the line of forts, in part because the locals took them to be British. At Antwerp the hussars played hide-and-seek with civilian bicyclists and streetcars loaded with troops, and were able to report the next day that there were no British troops at Antwerp.

Tirlemont

The Belgians detected the German approach on 18 August and withdrew from the Gette towards Antwerp. In spite of a prodigious march of 35 km, III and IV AK in the centre met no serious resistance. II Corps, on the army right flank, had an even longer approach march and no realistic chance of catching and pushing in the Belgian left. The only significant combat took place on the German left, at Tirlemont.

The Belgians defended Tirlemont with the 22 L (de Ligne – line infantry regiment) to the north-east of the town and 2 L to the north, III/3 L at Grimde to the east, supported by three batteries of artillery.[91]

IX AK attacked on the line Oplinter–Tirlemont with 18 ID while 17 ID followed echeloned to the left. The 18 ID advanced at 0930 with the 35th Brigade on the right, 36th on the left, preceded by combat patrols. When these had established the Belgian position, at 1220 18 ID issued the attack order.

IR 86 was on the division right flank. The regiment deployed I/86 on the right, II/86 on the left, III/86 in reserve. I/86 deployed 1/86 and 4/86 on the first line, II/86 deployed 7/86 and 8/86.[92] The advance did not begin until the troops had eaten lunch. Ditches, fences and barbed wire cut up the pastures and

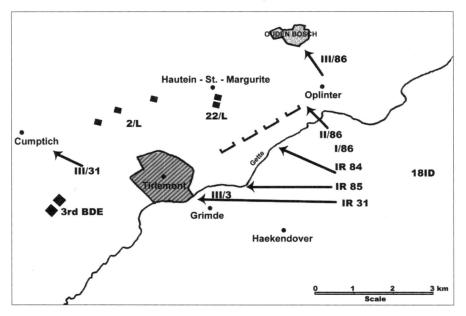

Fig. 9: Tirlemont, 18 August.

meadows and impeded movement. Finally, the troops had to ford the Gette. Behind the cover of the railway embankment the companies deployed from column to skirmisher line. The Belgians were in a dug-in position 700–800 metres distant, across an open field. IR 86 advanced, then returned fire, supported by the artillery. The Belgians were 'miserable' marksmen, a fact that the Fusiliers soon noted:

> They [II/86] could not be held back. 'Fix bayonets!' was sounded and with shouts of 'Hurrah' they broke into the enemy position. At the same time I/86 charged into the burning Oplinter. The Belgian position presented a terrible spectacle. Our artillery had thoroughly smashed it up. Dead and wounded lay thickly together. The majority of the survivors surrendered. A few succeeded in withdrawing to a second position. The units were quickly reorganized. III/86 deployed into I/86; II/86 formed the second line. The leading battalions passed through the Ouden Bosch [wood] while the artillery took the Staffelberg, which rose behind it, under fire. The regiment stormed up the Staffelberg; the enemy hardly resisted, but the first line succeeded in engaging him. Most fled the position in panic; our pursuit fire hit many. The pursuit was ended; the brigade commander was concerned that the men would get completely out of control.

IR 84 attacked on the left of IR 86 with II/84 on the left (6/84 and 7/84 first line, 5/84 and 8/84 second), III/84 on the right (4/84 and 2/84 first line, 1/84 following). III/84 was the 36th Brigade reserve, 3/84 and the MG Company the regimental reserve.[93] Belgian artillery fired on the regiment, without causing any casualties. The 6/84 commander said:

> Advancing under enemy artillery fire in open terrain! As we had practised to excess in exercises in garrison, the platoons assumed the appropriate formation: thin lines, with large intervals between men and intervals between lines, or in single file, first at a walk, then at double-time, the platoons reached the low ground, where the trees provided concealment, if not cover.

The two lead platoon leaders of 6/84 ordered the assault, which the company commander at first considered 'more than rash: reckless and irresponsible'. But there was no holding the troops back, so he ordered a general assault. The Belgians ran and were hit by the German artillery: 'hardly a one of them escaped'. 6/84 took fire from a second Belgian position. The second attack was conducted 'like a peacetime exercise' and this position was taken too. In both, there were numerous dead, all shot in the head. The 6/84 commander said: 'Just like at a combat gunnery range, each man had aimed calmly and in a few minutes any enemy who showed his head above the breastwork was dealt with.' The 6/84 commander now decided that the two lieutenants' decision to assault had been completely correct: the attack had not been disturbed by Belgian artillery, which the German artillery had suppressed. On the other hand, the infantry had advanced so quickly that the German artillery had no opportunity to provide direct support. The 6/84 commander said: 'Thank God! Seven lightly wounded! ... A triumph for our peacetime training!'

7/84 had a similar experience. It passed through the Belgian artillery fire 'just like on an exercise' in thin skirmisher line. Just short of the Gette the lead platoons took fire from a barricaded bridge, but two rounds of German artillery immediately dispersed the Belgians. Since the attention of the Belgians was fixed on 6/84 to the left, the lead platoon of 7/84 was able to cross the bridge and use a covered and concealed approach to within 200 metres of the next Belgian position. The platoon leader could observe 6/84 advancing 'just like on an exercise'. The 'thoroughly nervous' Belgians opened rapid fire against 6/84, which always landed much too short. On the other side, the German fire had 'a quite extraordinary effect. All at once every enemy head disappeared.' 6/84 used this opportunity to execute a long bound forward by platoons. The Belgians resumed their wild fire, but were once again suppressed by 7/84's counter-fire. This repeated itself several times. Then 7/84 saw Belgians running to the rear. These were taken under fire for a short time and then 7/84 assaulted. Once on the first Belgian position, 7/84 received fire from the second position. This time when 7/84 returned fire the Belgians began to surrender. The lead platoon pushed on and surprised and destroyed a small Belgian force digging in.

FAR 9 reported engaging both Belgian artillery and trenches with the 2/9 and 3/9.[94] 2/9 then bounded forward to the infantry firing line. Fire from a single gun at point-blank cleared a barricade in Oplinter. A civilian aimed a weapon at the I/9 detachment commander, but was killed by a lieutenant's pistol shot. 2/39 and 3/39 continually bounded forward to keep the retreating Belgians at 1,000 metres range. In the last engagement a platoon of 2/9 closed to within 300 metres of a Belgian trench, with the gun commanders directing their fire independently. The howitzers of 4/9 initially conducted counter-battery fire, while 5/9 and 6/9 engaged Belgian trenches. The detachment followed the retreating Belgians 'finding many worthwhile targets'.

On the 18 ID left, the 36th Brigade attacked towards Tirlemont north of the Orsmaël road, with IR 85 on the right and II/IR 31 on the left. I/31, III/31 and MG Company 31 were in division reserve.[95] At 1230 the 35th Brigade issued an attack order to take Haekendover. I/31, with only three companies (2/31 was guarding the division airfield), was committed to the left of II/31, with 1/31 and 3/31 on line, 4/31 echeloned behind the left flank. IR 31 advanced in very open order, by bounds, with a half-platoon leading the company and six-pace intervals between skirmishers, 'just like at the local training area'. It was hard work; the troops had to push through standing grain, stumble over fields of sugar beets, across sunken roads filled with practically impenetrable blackberry bushes, and up hillsides so steep 'it was virtually an escalade'. The commander of 1/31 said that Haekendover was probably occupied and ordered the lead platoon to take up a firing position on high ground. The platoon leader found 'wonderful observation': to his front the terrain rose to a low hill at Haekendover, dipped and rose to higher ground at Tirlemont, where he could see figures – probably Belgian soldiers – moving among the houses. The lead platoon advanced to the right of Haekendover and took fire from Belgian troops on the rail embankment. The platoon took cover and returned fire at 600 metres. The second platoon reinforced the first and 3/31 deployed to the right. IR 31's fire was effective; the Belgian fire became inaccurate and died down. The rail embankment was alive with the impact of the German bullets. The battalion commander came forward, calmly smoking a cigar. The Belgian fire was now weak. The platoon leader asked, 'Can I advance, Herr Major?' 'Yes, get going. Attack!' 'Platoon Peters, Bound Forward, March!' The enemy fire increased. The platoon leader said, 'Oh, this wonderful, exhilarating moment! Attack!' The platoon ran as long as they had breath, then advanced at a walk. The Belgians had vanished. They reached the rail embankment and found Belgain dead and wounded. The battalion reorganised in Tirlemont and moved out again, as artillery fire landed. The lead company reached the western outskirts of the town and took small-arms fire; the lead platoon deployed to both sides of the road and returned fire, followed by the rest of 1/31. The Belgians once again held a railway embankment. Several squads of 1/31 climbed a chalk hill which allowed them to fire down on the Belgians. The company attacked by long bounds as the Belgian fire became more intense, but when the company had covered half the distance the Belgians ran.

II/31 attacked to the north of the road. Wet areas and meadows, barbed-wire fences and ditches were difficult to cross while carrying a full pack. 'Remarkably' the Belgians did not defend these obstacles, and not a shot was fired. The floor of the bridge had been ripped off, but the framework was intact and 'the Belgians had been obliging enough to leave the floorboards on the banks of the Gette, so that the bridge was quickly passable again'. On the far bank 7/31 deployed to the left of 6/31, and 5/31 to the left of 7/31 (8/31 was covering the artillery). The battalion moved forward quickly by bounds against Belgian positions that were 'clearly visible' on the east side of Tirlemont. Flanking fire from a farm on the Tirlemont–Oplinter road was quickly silenced by a battery from FAR 9 that set up with the forward line of infantry. Belgian shrapnel burst too high and caused no casualties. II/31 assaulted and took the Belgian position just before 1700, then swept through the town.

The Belgian official history said that the German attack began at 1400. III/3 L defended in place at Grimde until ordered to withdraw at 1630. The Germans had worked their way around the battalion's flanks and it lost almost half its strength trying to pull back. 22 L received orders to withdraw at 1640, which was executed under heavy German artillery and MG fire. The regiment lost 23 of 37 OFF and 900 of 1,800 EM.

At 1700 the 18 ID commander committed III/31 (minus 12/31, but reinforced by 8/31), the MG Company IR 31 and 5/Dragoon 16 to pursue in the direction of Crumpeich to the north-west; the town needed to be taken to facilitate the advance the next day. The MG Company would not find an opportunity to fire; the cavalry was deployed on the right flank. With 11/31 and 8/31 leading, as it left Tirlemont the battalion took fire from the rail embankment to the left front. The Belgian fire was far too high; the battalion suffered few casualties and was able to advance quickly. The Belgians withdrew when the Germans opened fire. 9/31 was committed on the right and the battalion continued the attack to Crumpeich, which was quickly taken. The town had been defended by the gendarme platoon of the 3rd Brigade, which 'lost the greater portion of its strength'.[96] Fifteen Belgian mounted gendarmes had tried, unsuccessfully, to escape through the town. 9/31 took fire from the hills north-west of the town, but it was now dark and the battalion defended in place. Patrols at dawn the next morning found that the Belgians had gone.

IR 86 did not overrate the significance of Tirlemont. The enemy was weaker and had no effective artillery support. A lieutenant and 12 EM were KIA, 60 EM WIA, 12 MIA. IR 86 took 214 POW. IR 84 took 256 POW, captured a standard and 2 guns, at the cost of 3 KIA and 29 WIA. The IR 85 history says little about Tirlemont except for the casualties: 2 OFF KIA and 9 WIA, 219 EM KIA and WIA, 3 Belgian OFF and 471 EM POW.[97] The IR 31 history says II/31

casualties were 1 OFF and 2 EM KIA, 3 OFF (including the battalion com-
mander) and 39 EM WIA; and III/31 casualties were 4 EM KIA, 1 OFF and 27
EM WIA. The Germans lost about 434 casualties in total and took at least 944
POWs.

Tirlemont demonstrated that the German troops were decisively superior
to the Belgians at the tactical level. The German attack had rolled through
the Belgian position; the terrain was a greater hindrance than the Belgian
defence. The Germans fought a combined-arms battle; Belgian artillery was
completely ineffective. The Belgian high command had acted prudently in
refusing to offer battle.

On the operational level, the Germans had succeeded in driving the Belgians
into Antwerp before the French and British had arrived. The bottleneck from
Brussels to Namur was now in German hands. This was not a foregone conclusion. The Belgians had held on to the Gette as long as they could in the hopes
that the French and British would arrive and keep the Germans out of Brussels,
Antwerp and the industry of western Belgium. The principal mission for the
1st and 2nd Armies in the *Aufmarschanweisungen* was to seize this terrain. The
Germans could now seek out the British and French forces.

Reconnaissance, 18 August

Lieutenant Schorlemer with fourteen troopers from Dragoon R 19 set out on
reconnaissance on 17 August.[98] On the morning of 18 August he joined forces
with a patrol from Uhlan R 13. Schorlemer saw a French cavalry outpost, charged
and discovered an entire French cavalry squadron from the 21st Regiment. The
Germans, two officers and twenty-one men, continued the charge straight at the
head of the French column. The French could not deploy and turned in flight,
with the Germans on their heels, who cut down about fifteen, while 'four or
five' French fell from their horses. When the French entered a town the Germans
stopped, collected a prisoner and five horses, evaded a Belgian cavalry squadron
and returned to 9 KD.

At 0800 on 18 August a hussar brought in four horses captured from the French,
one of which belonged to an officer. Papers found in the saddlebags identified
his unit as the 1st French Division de Cavalerie (DC), which on 16 August had
been west of Namur.[99] The horse had been captured just west of Perwez (10 km
north of Namur). Patrols reported French cavalry in the same area, all of which
was relayed by radio to HKK 2. 'And so developed the most interesting part of
the entire reconnaissance.'[100] The three squadrons conducting reconnaissance-in-
force (1/Hussar R 16, 4/Hussar R 14, a squadron from Cuirassier R 4) withdrew
by bounds in front of the advancing French (5th DC), then established a defence
along a railway line, forcing the French to deploy in the open and making them

the perfect target for the artillery sections of 4 KD and 9 KD. 9 KD deployed to conduct a mounted charge against the French cavalry, which was 3 km away. Much to the disappointment of the German horsemen, who complained loudly and often that the French and British would never mix it up in a good old mounted fight, at around 1400 the French cavalry fled the field, leaving behind two guns, two MGs and casualties in men and horses. Hussar R 11 (9 KD) dismounted and attacked a village, capturing an officer and eight men of a bicycle detachment from the French 26 RI.[101]

This was the first time that Sordet's Cavalry Corps had made serious contact with German forces. The French official history says that Sordet, with a Belgian mixed brigade, ran into German forces near Ramilles 'in organized and strongly defended positions with field artillery and howitzers, infantry and machine guns'.[102] Sordet shelled the German positions, then fell back to the west of Perwez. As a consequence of this action, Sordet said it was absolutely necessary that his cavalry be reinforced with infantry.

The German reconnaissance squadrons had established the approach of the French left flank army. HKK 2, the Jäger battalions in particular, had pushed Sordet's Cavalry Corps away before it could gather any information. This was one of the most successful reconnaissance operations conducted by HKK 2 in Belgium.

On the evening of 18 August the 2nd Army believed that the French had an army whose right wing was at Charleroi and moving towards Gembloux. (In fact, the French 5th Army would not reach Charleroi until 20 August.) There was no information concerning the British whatsoever. The German right wing therefore oriented itself on the French army at Charleroi. For the next three days the 1st and 2nd Army swung south-west around the fortress at Namur.[103]

Cavalry Marching

1st Squadron Hussar R 16 had begun its reconnaissance mission on 9 August with 170 EM; on 19 August there were only 68 left. Three of the four officers had been wounded or taken prisoner. Two light radio stations and fifty horses had been lost. The squadron had travelled 333 km in ten days. Nevertheless:

> For everyone, this was a truly satisfying hussar mission: riding alone in front of the armies in enemy territory, always in danger, always alert, ready to fight, your lance in your fist, carbine on your back and a good bottle of wine in the carbine case.[104]

From 18 August to 26 August the German cavalry marched 30–50 km a day, sometimes more. The heat was terrific; to slake his thirst, every trooper carried a bottle of wine, which was to be found 'everywhere'. Foraging for and cooking food was difficult, so the trooper was usually hungry. Hussar R 11 (9 KD), and many other cavalry units, reported living primarily off cans of sardines! Even the tobacco ran out. Occasionally a unit got lucky. On 21 August Hussar R 11 chased off a French requisitioning party that had to leave behind two wagons loaded with bread, butter and eggs, then found masses of hay in the gendarmerie barracks.[105] But this was the exception. Keeping the horses fed, watered and healthy was a constant concern, but the animals held up remarkably well: horse casualties were generally a result of combat and not exhaustion. Morale remained high.

Jäger Mobility

The Jäger were able to foot-march fast and far enough to keep pace with the cavalry. This was an astounding accomplishment. It also gave the cavalry of HKK 2 a trump card – infantry support. Every day was another forced march, often in oppressive heat and humidity.[106] The Jäger usually bivouacked in the open, often having no time to put up their tents. Operating independently, the Jäger had to maintain a high state of night tactical security. Usually the march began at 0500 or 0600, but sometimes as early as 0200. In addition to marching, the Jäger often made or anticipated contact and had to deploy from march column to skirmisher line. Especially at the beginning of the campaign many men were unable to march due to blisters, and the blister plaster was soon used up.[107] The battalions requisitioned wagons to carry the packs and the lame. Thanks to the field kitchens, the food was generally excellent. Bread, however, was in short supply and French white bread, while tasty, was not filling. The combination of bad water and unripe fruit gave almost all of the Jäger diarrhoea at some point. Wine was consumed in vast quantities. Jäger-Bataillon 4 noted that it was astounding how forced-marching allowed the Jäger to drink so much wine with no ill effect. The troops were occasionally disappointed to find that a promising bottle turned out to be cider – sour apple wine.

The experience of Jäger 4 is typical.[108] It crossed the Meuse on 12 August and marched 36 km. On 13 August it ate breakfast from the field kitchens, which had been prepared the day before, cleaned weapons soaked with dew, and then began the march at 0800. By early morning the heat was 'intolerable' and troops began to drop out, especially the reservists. The battalion began to requisition wagons: by 24 August enough wagons had been requisitioned to carry all of the lame. On 14 August forty-seven men were so lame that they were left behind to conduct security duties and did not return to the battalion until October. The march on 15 August was particularly difficult, in spite of being only (!) 32 km long. Downpours of rain alternated with burning sunshine and humidity. Many Jäger were already suffering from diarrhoea. On the night of 16 August the battalion deployed strong security forces on the Gette River. Between 21 and 23 August the battalion covered 110 km, in burning heat mixed with downpours and frequent combat against Belgian rearguards.

The Jäger were continually striving to enhance their mobility. They were favoured in this by their status as independent battalion-sized units, led by innovative young officers and motivated by the self-sufficient Jäger attitude, which gave them an exceptional degree of flexibility. The bicycle companies were usually brought together to form a bicycle battalion. Jäger-Bataillon 4 mounted two more squads on requisitioned bicycles to reinforce it. The most successful battalion in augmenting its mobility was Jäger-Bataillon 7. On 16 August Jäger 7's truck column appeared, consisting of a passenger vehicle and six trucks.[109] It was the only truck column to reach the Jäger during the campaign. It could not lift the entire battalion at once; initially it carried lame troops and the rucksacks, which nevertheless considerably increased the battalion's mobility. At 2300 on 17 August the 3rd Company was loaded onto the trucks to conduct a quick reconnaissance. On 21 August the weather was hot and the battalion had a long march, so the trucks shuttled the battalion a company at a time. Since Jäger 7 was convinced the Belgians were using bicycles to scout the Germans and send reports, all the bicycles in the town of Beeringen were confiscated, the worst ones were broken up and thrown in the canal, the troops kept the best ones 'further increasing the battalion's mobility'. On 20 August a passenger vehicle was stopped at a checkpoint and confiscated, 'giving the battalion good service'. By this time Jäger 7 had gained an unprecedented degree of wheeled mobility.

1st Army March through Belgium

Since the German cavalry corps pushed the Belgian army away, the movement of the German 1st Army was practically a pure foot-march. FAR 75 said that the marching ability of the infantry was 'astounding'. The weather was hot; many of the reservists and horses were not marching fit. New boots caused bloody blisters. The dust was 'indescribable'. By the time the infantry bivouacked, their faces 'were blue-grey from exertion, sweat and dust'. But the next morning they cheerfully began the march again.[110]

Especially at the beginning of the campaign, heavy traffic led to delays in the march. Nevertheless, a distinguishing characteristic of German movement was that the march was completed early enough to give the troops time to rest, even if only for a few hours. The mobile field kitchens ensured that the infantry was well fed; the cavalry and artillery, which did not have them, frequently went hungry. Water for the horses was a constant concern.

The face of war was already changing; FAR 75 said that the greatest disruption to the march was caused by truck traffic. Trucks moving east with wounded men blocked the narrow roads; columns of trucks with up to 100 vehicles, some with trailers, moved west, throwing up immense columns of dust.

1st Squadron Uhlan R 3 and 5th Squadron Cuirassier R 7 (reinforced by 23 bicyclists from Jäger 9) were sent to reconnoitre towards Ostend. They would not return to the 2 KD until the middle of September.[111] The Flemish inhabitants were friendly towards the Germans, but on 20 August the cuirassiers and Jäger received a 'princely' welcome in Bruges because they were taken for British. They were showered with champagne, pastries and other delicacies. By 24 August they were within 3 km of Ostend, detected strong British forces, had a quick firefight and then broke contact and withdrew, frequently encountering British forces, which was all to the good, as finding the British was their mission. The detachment marched 176 km in the next thirteen hours, 'the toughest bicycle tour that I had made until then'.

French and British Plans, 18 August

The German cavalry had stymied Belgian and French reconnaissance. Long-range cavalry patrols had also destroyed the telephone and telegraph lines, making it impossible for the Belgian authorities to report the arrival of German troops. The German 1st Army and a large portion of the 2nd had succeeded in crossing to the north side of the Meuse and marching undetected to forward assembly areas to the west of Liège.

On 18 August the German right wing, the 1st through 5th Armies, began the general advance behind an impenetrable screen of cavalry and Jäger. The infantry pounded behind this screen to cross Belgium in five to six days. The synergistic effect of this security and hard marching was that the Germans gained complete operational and tactical surprise.

On 18 August the French identified two German cavalry divisions at Diest and one at Jodoigne.[112] It was considered possible that the German 1st Army formed the group of forces around Liège, which included elements of the II AK identified near Visé. Only one corps was positively identified north of the Meuse. The 2nd Army, under Bülow, was thought to be on the right (south) bank of the Meuse, lead elements at Huy (although some elements might be north of the river) with VII, IX, X AK and the Guard, followed by three reserve corps. The 3rd Army, with III, IV, XII, XIX AK and perhaps XX AK was at Rochefort.

This was not very accurate. The mass of the German right wing was thought to be south of the Meuse when eight active corps were already to the north of it, about to be joined by four reserve corps. IX, VII, III, IV AK were identified as being south of the Meuse when they were actually north of it. By 17 August II AK at Hasselt was much further west than the French thought, and the rest of the 1st Army was near St Trond. The 3rd Army was credited with being too far to the west, nearly to the Meuse, when it was in fact on the Belgian-German border. The French had failed to identify the Guard Reserve Corps, which counted in German eyes as an active corps. XX AK was not part of the 3rd Army, it was in East Prussia. Nine active corps were identified in this sector, when there were actually eleven; three reserve corps when there were actually five; twelve corps in total when there were actually sixteen.

On 18 August Joffre gave his concept of the operation to the left-wing 3rd, 4th, 5th and British Armies. If the enemy advanced on both banks of the Meuse, between Givet and Brussels, or even further north, the 5th Army, cooperating with the British and Sordet's Cavalry Corps and the Belgians on the left, would block this advance and attempt to turn the German right flank. The decisive attack would be delivered by the 4th Army, which would push the German left into the Meuse and cut the German right wing's lines of communications. The 3rd Army would guard the right flank of the 4th Army. This was the same concept that Napoleon had used at Austerlitz.

If the enemy advanced with only a fraction of his forces north of the Meuse, which seemed on 18 August to be quite likely, then the 5th Army would pivot east, cross the Meuse between Namur and Givet and attack towards Marche or St Hubert. The British, Sordet's Cavalry and the Belgians would deal with the German forces north of the Meuse.

The British mission was to advance on the left of Lanrezac's French 5th Army through Soignies to Nivelles. If the German right wing wheeled south, as expected, then its right flank would not extend far beyond the level of Mons.[113] The BEF would therefore be well placed to take the Germans in the flank. Sordet's Cavalry Corps was moving to the British left flank, and a group of French Territorial divisions was also assembling there.

The BEF would advance in an echelon right formation with II Corps (3rd and 5th Divisions) leading on the left, I Corps (1st and 2nd Divisions) to the right rear. On 21 August II Corps was to reach Bavai, I Corps Landrecies-Avesnes. On 22 August II Corps was to reach Thuin-Mons, I Corps Sambre-Harmignies.

On 23 August the BEF would face east. I Corps would stand fast in the south, facing east, between the Canal du Centre and the Sambre while II Corps crossed the canal and pivoted east. The BEF was having a difficult approach march. The weather on 20 August was 'of almost tropical intensity'.[114] The 2/Royal Scots, which had taken on 500 reservists, reported that the battalion was not marching fit: 'all the men, especially the reservists, suffered severely'. The cobblestones were also hard on the men's feet, and soon the battalion had a number of lame troops.

The *History of the Duke of Wellington's Regiment* reported that the 'fog of war' was very thick. On 20 August the commanding general of the 5th Division did not know anything about the French or even if other British troops or artillery had landed. From 20 to 22 August he had no information on the German forces to pass on to his subordinates.[115]

Defective BEF Troop-Leading

The Cheshires' regimental history reported that the 15th Brigade was visited by
the 5th Division commanding general, Major-General Charles Fergusson, who
'made a short speech in which he emphasised the gravity of the situation they
were likely to have to face, and the necessity for fighting to the last man and the
last round'.[116] The history of the KOYLI said:

> On the 20th August Maj.-Gen. Sir Charles Fergusson addressed each of the bat-
> talions in his division in turn in stirring words. He made use of this expression:
> 'There must be no surrender, men must fight to the last, with their fists if their
> rifles are useless; this will be a war of self-sacrifice; possibly whole battalions, even
> brigades, may have to be sacrificed in order to make it good for the others.'[117]

The BEF didn't have the luxury of sacrificing brigades: there were, on 20 August,
only sixteen infantry brigades in the whole army. Such an attitude assumed that
the war would be short and the first battle would be decisive. If this calculation
were wrong, if the BEF took heavy initial casualties in an indecisive battle, then
the consequences for the entire country would be grave. Bad tactics were to have
serious strategic consequences.

Fergusson's attitude seems to have permeated the tactical thinking of the 5th
Division. It certainly resurfaced at Le Cateau, when, in spite of the fact that the
corps commander's intent was to withdraw, several battalions and batteries were
given orders to defend their position to the last extremity.

Determining the exact nature of the mission, and passing this decision down the
chain of command, is the first requirement of successful troop-leading. Such 'die
in place' orders were completely inappropriate for the situation and mission of the
BEF, and demonstrate a lack of clarity in troop-leading by British senior leadership,
the result of insufficient doctrine and inadequate practice in large-scale exercises.
Instead of good senior leadership, the British troops received histrionic bombast.

On 23, 24 and 26 August the British battalions prepared to defend in place. No
provisions were made to withdraw, either at the operational or tactical level. Yet
the BEF would be forced on all three days to withdraw under pressure. Positions
chosen for defence in place, sited in exposed areas or on forward slopes, which were
unsuitable for a delay and withdrawal, made sure that the withdrawal was the most
costly part of the engagement. Lack of command preparation to withdraw also led
to serious failures in command and control, both in the transmission of orders and
in the willingness of battalion commanders to withdraw on their own initiative.

Such a British 'die in place' attitude suited the German purposes quite nicely.
Even if the errors made by Kluck and Kuhl ensured that the BEF would escape,
at the tactical level several British units would be destroyed when they tried to
match static defence against the German combined-arms attack.

19 August

The Germans knew nothing concerning the British. The German 2nd Army believed, 'A French army group was approaching with its right flank at Charleroi, direction of march Gembloux.'[118] In fact, the French 5th Army was approaching the Sambre, nowhere near being so far north as the 2nd Army thought.

By the end of the day the 1st Army, with four corps on line, had its centre of mass west of Louvain, the two reserve corps about two day's march behind. The 2nd Army, with four corps on line, was north of Namur, centre of mass Perwez. The Guard Reserve Corps was oriented on Namur.

On 19 August HKK 2 continued moving west and by 20 August bivouacked just north of Charleroi. 2 KD had one last fight with the Belgians. South-east of Antwerp the advance guard, 4th Squadron Lifeguard Hussar R 1, dismounted to attack Belgian troops, and was soon supported by the rest of the Lifeguard Hussar brigade, MG Section 4 and the horse artillery.[119] The hussars continued their dismounted attack for 4 km, leaving a trail of Belgian dead, wounded and equipment, as well as capturing the standard of the Belgian III/5 L.

The French 5th Army continued its march north, with the lead elements reaching the Sambre. The Belgian army was withdrawing towards Antwerp. On the evening of 18 August and morning of 19 August the French identified the 9 KD, which it said was covering the advance of II AK at Diest, and 9 KD at Perwez.[120] There was no mention of 4 KD. German columns at Hannut and to the south were presumed to be X AK and IV, IX and VII AK, which were crossing from the south to the north side of the Meuse. X AK may have been identified correctly, but no German troops were crossing the Meuse at Huy and IV, IX and VII AK were between Brussels and Waterloo.

The French pre-war estimate was that the German mass of manoeuvre would concentrate behind Metz, a central position which would allow it to be committed south-west into Lorraine, march straight ahead between Verdun and Toul, or north into Belgium. By 19 August the French were convinced that this *masse centrale* was moving north-west towards the Meuse, which would leave the Germans weak in the Ardennes and vulnerable to a French attack there.[121]

By the evening of 19 August the French had identified the locations of only four German corps north of the Meuse: II at Aerschot, IX at Louvain, X at Jodoigne and VII north-west of Huy.[122] This was essentially correct, except that the last corps was not VII AK but the Guard Reserve. They also identified numerous columns of all arms, which had reached Tirlemont, Jadoigne and Perwez (probably 14 RD). However, the French had not identified the other five German first-wave corps.

The French were relying on the Belgians for intelligence and the Belgians were incapable of providing any. The Belgians complained that at least 10,000 German cavalry had 'inundated' the country, supported by infantry, which could only have kept up if it were transported in automobiles. 'The Belgian reconnaissance could pierce this thick veil only with difficulty.' On 20 August the Belgians identified four German corps: one south of Antwerp, one at Brussels and two north of Namur; all were near major Belgian fortresses and population centres, which made them easier for the Belgians to locate; the other German corps went undetected. The Belgians were probably aware that there were more German forces in the country, but could say neither how many nor where.[123]

An indication of the general ineffectiveness of Belgian reconnaissance and intelligence-gathering is that the Belgians thought on 22 August that Namur was being attacked from the north-east by the VII AK, and the north-west by III AK, while the identity of the unit attacking from the south-east was unknown. In fact, neither corps was anywhere near Namur. The 3rd Guard Infantry Division, whose uniforms were easy to recognise, was attacking on the north-east, and the Saxon 22 ID, also easy to recognise, on the south-east.[124]

British air reconnaissance was no help. The British sent out two machines on 19 August. One became completely lost and flew around near Tournai and Courtai for the entire day, far from any possible German forces. The other flew over Brussels without recognising it.[125]

20 August

The German IV AK entered Brussels; FAR 75 was expressly forbidden to bivouac in a park so as not to damage the grass![126] IX AK on the 1st Army left flank passed through Waterloo. II AK on the Army right was screening Antwerp, waiting for the III RK to relieve it. The 2nd Army finished the day on a line from Waterloo to Gembloux.

On 20 August Bülow's concept was to launch a coordinated attack with all three armies against the French forces on the Sambre-Meuse. This involved the 2nd Army waiting for the 3rd Army to arrive on the Meuse and the 1st Army to come up on the right.

The OHL intelligence estimate issued on 20 August said that the French I CA and II CA, possibly also X CA were on the Meuse between Namur and Givet. To the west there were at most two corps between Namur and Charleroi with three corps plus reserve divisions marching north behind them.[127] This was essentially correct: there were seven Franco-British corps in this sector; the Germans had probably found the BEF but didn't know it. The OHL expected the British to appear at Lille, but was not certain if the British had even landed.

Kuhl was convinced that the British were going to arrive at, or north of, Lille. Over the next three days, the 1st Army's operations were slow and uncertain because Kuhl was never ready to give up this preconceived notion, in spite of ample evidence from cavalry reconnaissance that the British were at Mons.

The French 5th Army had closed up on the Sambre. Sordet's Cavalry Corps was 'extremely fatigued' and each division had lost the equivalent of a cavalry regiment, about 20 per cent of its strength. This was most inopportune, for the French 5th Army was in desperate need of good intelligence and wasn't getting it. The HQ of Groupe D'Amande, the Territorial divisions assembling north and south of Arras, reported that 600,000 German troops were expected in Brussels.[128] Joffre replied that the reports of German forces in Belgium were exaggerated, and the measures the French had taken were adequate. Joffre was both right and wrong: the Germans did not have 600,000 troops near Brussels. However, the Germans had nine corps on the first wave north of the Meuse, not four as the French expected, and the measures he had taken were not adequate to meet this threat.

At 1500 on 20 August GQG transmitted to the 4th Army its concept for its forthcoming attack, the main French offensive, through the Ardennes. Joffre believed that the German army was divided into two masses, one in Lorraine, the second moving on both sides of the Meuse. The latter was the main German attack. In order to make this attack strong enough for a deep envelopment of the French left, the Germans had left few forces in the Ardennes. Joffre still thought that the German mass of manoeuvre, which he had originally supposed to be located east of Metz, was marching through Belgium towards the Meuse to join the German main attack: Joffre told the 4th Army on 20 August that it was not yet time to attack, for the Germans were moving off to the north-west and 'the more troops that move out of the area of Arlon … and Luxemburg, the better it is for us'.[129]

21 August

On 21 August AOK 2 directed HKK 2 to march to the right flank of the 1st Army; it bivouacked north of Mons. The German 1st Army began to swing south-west. The army centre of mass was with III AK at Hal, with IV AK echeloned to its right rear and IX AK to its left front. It was about a day's march behind the 2nd Army, which was also wheeling left, with the Guard Corps west of Namur, with X AK, X RK and VII AK to the west. The 2nd Army instructed Guard Corps and X AK to close up on the Sambre, but remain on the north bank. Nevertheless, the commander of the 2nd Guard Division found the Sambre bridges in his sector lightly held and, with the encouragement of General Ludendorff, the 2nd Army Oberquartiermeister, the 2nd Guard seized the crossings.[130] A general attack by the 2nd Army on 22 August to support the 2nd Guard Division was now inevitable. At 1200 the German heavy artillery opened fire against the Namur forts.

Joffre thought on the afternoon of 21 August that the mass of the German forces in north Belgium had crossed the Meuse near Huy and were still marching north and north-west near Brussels, far from the Sambre. On the evening of 20 August II AK was identified north-east of Brussels, which was correct, but this was because II AK had the mission of screening Antwerp. Brussels had been transited by IV AK on the afternoon of 20 August. IX AK was thought to be south-east of Brussels; the locations of X, VII AK and the Guard were unknown. GQG knew nothing about the German forces south of the Meuse and in Luxembourg. III, XIX and V AK were assumed to be there as part of the German 3rd Army, but their location was unknown. XIX AK had been on the line Houffalize–Neufchâteau in the Ardennes, but its current location was unknown.[131] In fact, there were nine active corps in the first line of German troops in the Ardennes.

The British thought that there were four German corps, perhaps six, on the line Brussels–Charleroi, followed by reserve corps. Three corps were east of the Meuse and the Lesse, covering the movement of even more forces north across the Meuse. The British began their movement north from their assembly areas.[132]

The Belgians had told Lanrezac that three German corps were in the vicinity of Brussels. Lanrezac wanted air reconnaissance on 22 August south of the Meuse from Namur and Dinant to Liège. North of the Meuse he wanted air reconnaissance in the area of Louvain, Wavre and Gembloux, and Huy and Tirlemont. It is clear that Lanrezac thought the Germans were the greater threat south of the Meuse and that the German lead elements were still east of the line Brussels–Namur. Lanrezac also did not know until that evening that the Germans were already across the Sambre.[133]

HKK 2 had hammered Sordet's Cavalry Corps and pushed it out of the way, leaving Lanrezac and Joffre blind. The British and French had been able to detect only the elements of the German 1st Army moving south from Brussels. Four corps of the German 2nd Army had been able to close up on the Sambre completely undetected.

On the British left, the French Territorial divisions of the Groupe D'Amande were arriving between Cambrai and the Channel.[134] 84 Division HQ was at Cambrai, on its left 82 Division (Arras) and then 81 Division (St Omer). These divisions were made up of the oldest year-groups, had little mobility or combat power, and their mission was merely to stop raids by German cavalry. 88th Territorial Division would be ordered to Lille on 22 August.

Joffre thought the Germans were advancing in strength on both sides of the Meuse and told Lanrezac that the first contingency plan for the 5th Army and British army was to be put into effect. On 22 August the 3rd and 4th Armies would attack into the Ardennes.[135] Joffre wanted the 5th Army, supported by the British, to attack the German forces north of the Meuse. Lanrezac replied that the 4th Army would not yet be able to cover his right flank, so he would have to assign a corps to protect that flank. Moreover, the British would not reach Mons until 23 May: the 5th Army would be moving across the Sambre under-strength and alone. It was necessary to wait until 23 August or even 24 August before the

5th Army could attack. His instructions to the 5th Army for 22 August were to close up on the Sambre in preparation for taking the offensive.

In the evening the Belgians reported that II and IV AK had swung south-west, with the latter on the road to Hal.[136] On the night of 21–22 August GQG had identified the location of II AK west of Brussels, IV AK about 25 km south of Brussels, IX AK on its left, south of Waterloo, X at Genappe (actually VII), VII at Sombresse (actually X), the Guard at Tamines, followed by three reserve corps. Almost nothing was known about German troops east of the Meuse.[137] The French had failed to detect III AK and X RK which were in the German right wing first wave.

HKK 2 on 22 August

Unfortunately for the Germans, due to an erroneous air reconnaissance report that British cavalry had been sighted near Courtai on 22 August, HKK 2 had been sent by HQ 2nd Army on a wild goose chase to reconnoitre on both sides of Lille.

However, 2nd Squadron Hussar R 8 was also sent from Soignies in the direction of St Ghislain-Mons. A patrol led by Lt Humann was given Tertre and St Ghislain as objectives.[138] The patrol was continually followed at a distance of 500 metres by young men on bicycles, who the patrol felt were spies, but whom they could not shake off, not by moving cross-country or even with warning shots. There was no way to keep prisoners. Finally the patrol jumped the bicyclists at a bend in the road and roughed them up, 'which helped for a time'. The patrol entered Tertre, where the point element reported 'strangely uniformed men without weapons'. Lt Humann rode forward and observed through his binoculars '15 or 20 British soldiers, who indeed had no weapons, but carried sticks under their arms and were standing or walking around, smoking …The use of security detachments was apparently unknown to the British at this time, or to these British at any rate'. Before the patrol could charge they were noticed and the British disappeared, so Lt Humann withdrew in order to see how much of the canal was occupied by British troops. British silhouettes were seen on the skyline(!) as far as Bardour, which was not occupied. Lt Humann sent a report, requisitioned food and fodder, and the patrol bivouacked in a wood between Baudour and Tertre, observing the roads that led from the north to the British position.

A second patrol from Hussar 8 set out at dawn in the direction of Mons. One kilometre from Soignies they encountered a patrol from Cuirassier R 4, which had the same mission, so together they marched towards Mons. Halfway, in the middle of the town of Casteau, a squadron of British cavalry appeared from a side street, which forced the patrol to beat a hasty retreat. Three members of the

Cuirassier patrol were captured. The British stopped at the end of the town. The German patrols reported this contact, which reached 9 KD at 1030 hours and was immediately forwarded to the 1st Army, arriving there at 1050. The two patrols then met a patrol from Uhlan R 13: the countryside was swarming with German cavalry. The hussars rejoined their squadron, which was about 8 km north of Mons, while the cuirassiers and uhlans continued their reconnaissance towards Mons, this time moving to the west and then south along the Ath–Mons road. They encountered a British infantry security detachment north of Nimy, dismounted, drove it back and sent a second report.[139] The German cavalry patrols had performed superbly: they had identified British infantry on a 20 km front.

Hussar R 15 sent a patrol to Tournai.[140] They entered the town at 0800 and were taken for British, but were soon betrayed by a bicyclist. They moved through the centre of the town to reconnoitre the bridge when French and Belgians sprang up from under the bridge and opened fire, hitting two hussars. The horse of the officer candidate leading the patrol was hit and a sergeant gave him his and went looking for a bicycle. The inhabitants shot at them from the windows with pistols. The sergeant escaped by running through a house, out the backdoor and through gardens. Tournai, he said, was obviously occupied by enemy cavalry and infantry. He made it out of the town and went to sleep in a field, only to be awakened at midnight when the bridge in Tournai was blown.

2 KD reached Grammont, a large city, and made hasty purchases of underwear and boots. Hussar R 12 recorded that 'to everyone's relief' *franc-tireur* activity had ceased.[141]

German Right Wing, 22 August[142]

On 22 August the 2nd Army had four corps engaged in heavy combat with the French 5th Army between Binche and Namur. On the 2nd Army left, the German siege artillery continued the bombardment of Namur, whose defences were rapidly crumbling. The 2nd Army was far ahead of its neighbours: the 3rd Army was still closing up on the Meuse between Givet and Namur, the 1st Army's left flank was bivouacked on the night of 22–23 August at Soignies.

The 2nd Army reported that its left flank was firmly across the Sambre and the French attacks here had not only been stopped, but that the French had been thrown back. The 2nd Army would continue the attack in conjunction with the 3rd Army and the decision would fall on 23 August. Probably because it was concerned about reports of French troop movements near Tournai-Courtai – actually the Territorial divisions unloading – the 2nd Army HQ left HKK 2 far to the right rear of the 1st Army.

Bülow wanted the 1st Army to advance on 22 and 23 August straight south, to pass to the west of the fortress at Maubeuge and closely support the 2nd Army in its attack across the Sambre.[143] The leadership of the 1st Army, still convinced that the British would appear at Lille, wanted to advance south-west in order to be able to retain the option of advancing in the direction of Lille. Bülow insisted the 1st Army advance south, and it did so, but reluctantly and with strong mental reservations.

On the morning of 22 August, the 1st Army was of the opinion that the British had landed six divisions at Boulogne, Calais and Dunkirk on 17 and 18 August, and for some unexplained reason thought they were experiencing 'serious supply problems'. By 1700 the 1st Army aerial and cavalry reconnaissance had shown the entire area on the right flank from Ghent to Lille to be free of enemy troops. The British were therefore not assembling at Lille–Tournai. On the other hand, German cavalry had reported British troops in the area of Mons and prisoners taken by IX AK also reported the British at Mons. A British aircraft had been sighted over Louvain on 20 August and one, coming from Maubeuge, had been shot down by III AK on 22 August. But staff work in the 1st Army was not all it should have been: IX AK aircraft had seen large bodies of troops marching to Bavai and from Bavai to Binche, and columns of vehicles and wagons on the road from Valenciennes to Mons, but failed to report this to the 1st Army. The 1st Army's estimate on the evening of 22 August was that British troops were between Valenciennes and Maubeuge and perhaps even further south. Nevertheless, the 1st Army leadership still thought the situation was unclear and that it was necessary to keep the army deployed so it could fight in any direction, i.e. also towards Lille.

The 1st Army order for 23 August foresaw an easy march day. IV AK would bivouac north of Perluwelz, almost 8 km north of the Canal du Centre. III AK's objectives were St Ghislain and Jemappes, both of which are south of the Canal du Centre: the 1st Army clearly did not believe that the canal would be defended. IX AK's march goal was Mons and its mission was to mask Maubeuge.

In early twentieth-century operational doctrine fortresses were seen as the ideal base for counter-attacks against the enemy flank as he marched past the fort, and the 2nd Army was concerned about a counter-attack out of Maubeuge. The 2nd Army wanted the 1st Army to cover its right flank, and IX AK on the 1st Army left was to mask the north side of Maubeuge. The 1st Army wanted its left flank to be oriented at Mons.

There is little reason to agree with the German official history's repeated assertions that the 1st Army expected to fight the British from Mons to St Ghislain on 23 August, and wanted to extend its right flank to the west in order to outflank the British left. In fact, there is no reason to believe that the 1st Army expected a fight at Mons. Rather, the 1st Army expected only that some British troops would be at Valenciennes–Maubeuge, which meant a fight on the 24th at the earliest. The 1st Army had also not fully renounced the idea that British forces might still appear at Lille.

The 1st Army's principal objective was to be released from the operational control of the 2nd Army. It sent a General Staff officer back to Liège to ask telephonically if it was still subordinate to the 2nd Army; the OHL operations officer, Tappen, said that the 1st Army was still subordinate to the 2nd, and that the 2nd Army's order that IX AK cover the north side of Maubeuge was valid.

At 2050, just after the order for 23 August had been issued, IX AK reported that the enemy was not digging in on the line Mons–St Ghislain, but that the crossings over the Canal du Centre between Nimy and Ville sur Haine were held by the British. At 0200 on 23 August, 4 KD reported: 'There were no enemy forces up to the Schelde – the British were in Maubeuge.' The British were not massing at Lille after all. The German official history said that the British position was now clear except for the position of the British left flank, and that it was necessary for the 1st Army to plan a coordinated attack. It then makes the astounding observation that the 1st Army headquarters still wanted to wait for more information and issued no further orders; in other words, no attack orders for 23 August were given to the corps at all.

French 5th Army and BEF, 22 August

At 2030 on 22 August Lanrezac reported to GQG that 10 CA on the 5th Army right flank had been roughly handled, the commander of 20 DI seriously wounded and the corps had been forced to fall back, which in turn forced the 1 CA guarding the Meuse on its right to retreat.[144] The 18 CA was intact. Sordet's Cavalry Corps was once again exhausted.

The British official history says that on 22 August the BEF thought there was a German corps on the roads to the south of Grammont (about 35 km west of Brussels) and a cavalry division at Soignies.[145] By evening, however, the British had identified VII AK opposite the left flank of the French 5th Army (18 CA), VII RK far to its rear at Nivelles and IX AK at Soignies. II AK was also far to the north, south of Ath. A strong force (actually III AK) was north of Soignies. The British official history made no attempt at evaluating this raw data, which could only lead to the conclusion that there were two German corps (III and IX AK) in the British area of operations, both of which were too far to the east to be able to quickly turn the British left flank. The British had failed to observe the German IV AK, which could turn the British left, and thought that the threat to their left was II AK, which was at least two days' march away.

The French 5th Army sent no report to the BEF. In fact, the 5th Army hardly communicated with the BEF at all. The BEF liaison officer, Spears, was told that 'no information could be given to me without the General's [Lanrezac's] permission, which was not forthcoming', so he had to ferret out the 5th Army's situation himself. He found that the French centre had been driven 'five to ten miles [eight to sixteen km] south of the Sambre'. He reported this to BEF headquarters at 2200 on 22 August.[146] With the French 5th Army on the defensive and two German corps in the BEF sector, Marshal French was fully justified in calling off the attack the next day.

This should have led to a systematic analysis of the new situation. There is no evidence that such a re-evaluation ever took place; Sir John had deployed the BEF on 22 August to attack to the north-east on 23 August; when he called off the attack he merely left the units where they were.

The Mons position served no operational purpose: it was 15 km in front of the French 5th Army and the BEF left flank was hanging in the air: even if the British held Mons and the Canal du Centre on 23 August, it could anticipate having to withdraw on 24 August. The only thing a fight at Mons would produce was unnecessary casualties. It would also give the German 1st Army a day with which to close in on the BEF. The 'school solution' to this operational problem was to withdraw to a new defensive position at Valenciennes-Maubeuge, 20 km to the rear. Here the right flank would be secured by Fortress Maubeuge. There would not have been a fight until 24 August and the Germans could not have threatened the British left until 25 August. The withdrawal would have been executed by establishing rear guards on the canal and to the east, backed up by a cavalry screen 3 km to the rear. The main body should have withdrawn at dawn, the rearguards could have destroyed all the bridges, and once in contact, conduct a low-risk delay and pass through the cavalry, which would cover the general retirement.

At 2300 an officer from the 5th Army appeared at BEF headquarters asking the BEF to attack to the east against the German forces pushing the 5th Army from the Sambre.[147] Lanrezac must have known that such an attack would have been very risky and that the BEF would refuse. By now it was obvious that the 5th Army was going to be beaten, and Lanrezac was probably looking for a scapegoat: he could assert that he had lost because the BEF had refused to give him assistance. Sir John French probably saw this trap, and promised to hold on the Canal du Centre for twenty-four hours. It seems unlikely that Sir John would have ordered a withdrawal from the Canal du Centre on the evening of 22–23 August in any case, but this promise provided a convenient explanation for the otherwise dubious decision to fight at Mons.

4

Mons

Defective BEF Troop-Leading Procedures

On the BEF right at Mons on 23 August was I Corps, facing north-east on a 10 km front. II Corps was on the BEF left, holding 28 km of front; the 3rd Division held an 18 km salient around Mons, to its west the 5th Division held the next 10 km of canal. During the afternoon of 23 August the 19th Brigade (4th Division, III Corps) moved forward to occupy 8 km of canal from the 5th Division left flank to Conde.

The Canal du Centre was about two metres deep and twenty metres wide, a significant obstacle to movement, but was crossed by sixteen bridges in the II Corps sector. The terrain to the north of the Canal du Centre west of Mons was low, filled with drainage ditches, meadows, small woods and farming villages – fields of fire were generally mediocre. As the land rose to the north, it was covered by woods which approached to within a few hundred metres of the canal in the bow north of Mons, to 2–4 kilometres from the canal to the west of Mons. The area south of the canal was covered in miners' cottages, factories, mine heads and slag heaps, which offered good cover and concealment for the defending infantry, but no firing positions for the British artillery.

Mons and the immediate vicinity was the decisive terrain in the BEF position: whoever held Mons won the battle. When the Germans took Mons they would have penetrated the British centre and the British position on the Canal du Centre would be flanked.

The BEF deployment was poor. II Corps, which was most likely to be attacked, had a front three times as long as I Corps, which did not fight at all. The 3rd Division, which held the decisive terrain at Mons, and the sector that was the most difficult to defend, should have been given a narrow frontage, in order to

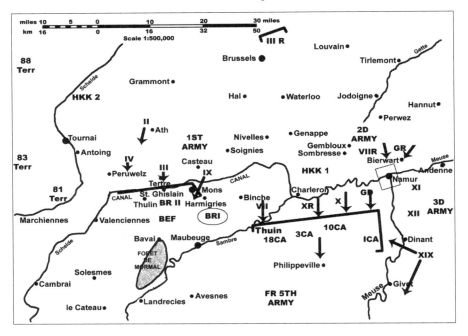

Fig. 10: Situation, 23 August.

allow it to concentrate its fires and hold a strong reserve for counter-attacks. Instead, it was deployed on an 18-km front, nearly twice as long as that of the entire I Corps on its right, and just as long as that of the much stronger 5th Division and 19th Brigade position on its left.

The 5th Cavalry Brigade on the right tried to keep contact with the French 5th Army. The Cavalry Division was echeloned behind the left flank, where it could accomplish nothing. Indeed, the Cavalry Division failed to put out a counter-reconnaissance screen or delay and disrupt the German advance, leaving the field clear for German cavalry reconnaissance.

The concept of the II Corps defence of the canal involved point defences holding the bridges, which were only to be destroyed on order. A security screen held the intervals between the bridges. The infantry battalions could therefore be deployed on much extended fronts. Even if successful, this defence was going to be effective for only one day. When the Germans closed up on the canal and brought forward pontoons and bridging material, they would be able to cross wherever they wanted, and the British infantry would be stretched too thinly to stop them.

In the event, on 23 August the Germans went after the still-intact bridges, which allowed them to concentrate superior force at these points. They were able to seize over half the bridges. By the end of the day the British 3rd Division had been pushed completely off the canal and both the German IX AK and III AK had established sizeable and deep bridgeheads. The fact that the bridges were not blown on the evening of 22 August or the morning of 23 August can only be logically explained if Sir John French still thought that he would need them in the future to conduct an offensive. It must be suspected, however, that logic had nothing to do with keeping the bridges intact; they were retained because there had been no analysis of the BEF's new mission.

The British official history says that at 0230 the commander of II Corps ordered the bridges in sector to be prepared for demolition.[1] This was too late to begin with and bad staff work delayed preparation even further. In the 8th Brigade sector the order reached an engineer company only at 0700, and they did not have time to complete the work. It was often discovered that there were no blasting caps to set off the explosives.

On 23 August Sir John drove off to inspect the 19th Brigade and did not return until the afternoon. There was no army-level control over the battle. I Corps remained unengaged and immobile all day. Command confusion and poor troop-leading procedures were systemic in the BEF. It is impossible for subordinate commanders to intelligently use their initiative if they do not know the situation and mission. As the commander of 2/Royal Irish Rifles said:[2]

> During the retreat and advance I never knew the general position of our cavalry brigades or of the neighbouring infantry divisions; nor had I any idea as to our general intentions at Mons, the Marne or the Aisne; or before and after Le Cateau.

These defective troop-leading procedures must be attributed to a lack of army-level exercises in peacetime.

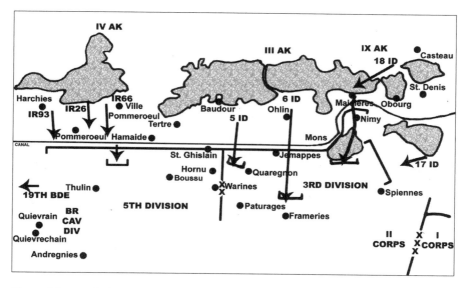

Fig. 11: Mons, 23 August.

Defective German Troop-Leading Procedures

The German senior leadership was just as unprepared for combat at Mons as that of the BEF; the 1st Army order for 23 August was not for an attack, but for a route march to the canal. The 1st Army still adhered to the pre-war estimate that the British would appear at Lille.

Kuhl seemed to believe that he could operate on the basis of his brilliant military insight alone. There were numerous cavalry reports that the British were deployed at Mons and on the Canal du Centre west of Mons that were disregarded. The 1st Army's aviation section did not fly all day, initially because of bad weather, but when the weather cleared in the afternoon the aviation section was apparently forgotten, for it was not given any missions.

The 2nd Army, which had been in serious contact on 22 August, did not order HKK 2 south to outflank the enemy to its front but sent it north-west towards the Schelde River, in exactly the wrong direction, to find the British. This mistake in particular was to have long-term repercussions, for in spite of the fact that HKK 2 would exhaust itself in prodigious forced marches over the next three days, it would never be able to turn the British flank.

At about 0900 on 23 August IV RK reported to the 1st Army that HKK 2 had observed troops unloading at Tournai.[3] This immediately confirmed the preconceived idea at 1st Army Headquarters that the BEF was actually at Lille. Even though there were reliable reports that the British were on the Canal du Centre and that prior to this point no enemy troops had been seen at Tournai, the 1st Army ordered all units to cease forward movement and directed HKK 2 to go to Tournai and determine whether the troops were British or French. Such a decision made no sense. That the British were at both Mons and Tournai was highly unlikely. In any case, the 1st Army's mission was to move south, both to engage the known British force at Mons and to support the 2nd Army. If the British were at Tournai, II AK at Lessines and IV AK south of Ath were in a position to engage them. III AK and IX AK were a day's march away and stopping them was pointless. It also assumed the British would stand and fight at Tournai, and not merely withdraw to the west, where the 1st Army could hardly follow. Even the German official history was critical of this decision. The order did not affect IX AK, which was already engaged. IV AK, which would have had to backtrack if the British were at Tournai, continued the march, but stopped in the early afternoon and began to bivouac, when it received orders to carry on. III AK, which was ready to attack at 1000, did not get permission to do so until 1400, robbing it of four hours of daylight and the chance to break the entire British II Corps position. This was the only significant order the 1st Army issued during the battle, and it ensured only that the 1st Army would not win a decisive victory, either on the 23rd or the 24th. HKK 2 became involved in an unnecessary fight against French Territorial troops in Tournai, which made an envelopment of the British left even more unlikely.

German IX AK Breaks the BEF Centre

Every Anglophone history maintains that the British were outnumbered at Mons. The British official history says that Mons would 'match eight [German] divisions against four [British], and actually in the infantry fight six against two'.[4] Map 7 of the official history shows the German IV, III and IX AK attacking the British II Corps, which actually included two and a half divisions. How the official history arrives at the eight-division total figure is a mystery. Contending that six German divisions attacked II Corps is misleading, because III Corps did not attack until 1400 and IV Corps was not engaged until late in the day. Only IX AK (two divisions) was engaged all day. In fact, the BEF, with four-plus divisions, was just as strong as the engaged German units. Half of the BEF did nothing all day. Sir John French was off on an inspection tour, and nobody in his staff had the wit to bring him back. The commander of I Corps sat tight and did not exercise an iota of initiative.

The most important fact is that German IX AK was able to concentrate 18 ID (a total of 24 battalions, although only a quarter were engaged, and 28 batteries, most of which were engaged) against the three British battalions north of Mons, which had no artillery support, and punch in the British centre.

The British 3rd Division, on II Corps right, deployed the 8th Brigade on the right, south from the Canal du Centre to the east of Spiennes, 9th Brigade on the left, along the Canal du Centre from Nimy to Jemappes, and 7th Brigade in reserve on the south edge of Mons.

4/Middlesex was on the 8th Brigade left, facing north along the canal on a 3 km front in a position that was a death sentence. The canal could be crossed with little difficulty to the east of the 4/Middlesex position. North of Mons the attacker had cover and concealment practically up to the canal bank. Destruction of 4/Middlesex would allow the Germans to penetrate the British position in depth. The two battalions on the brigade right, 2/Royal Scots and 1/Gordon Highlanders, had a 5 km front facing St Symphorien to the north-east. The terrain offered excellent fields of fire over open farmland.

The 8th Brigade had begun to dig in on the night of 22 August, and had prepared section and platoon trenches by morning. Sometime between 0800 and 0900 4/Middlesex and 4/Royal Fusiliers (9th Brigade) to its left began to take artillery fire.[5] The 4/Middlesex history describes the German infantry attack in standard terms for Anglophone histories: at 0900 the German infantry attacked 'in close formation, shoulder to shoulder' to be met by a blast of 'rapid rifle fire' and MG fire, which 'tear gaps in their ranks'. Ascoli quotes a 4/Middlesex private: 'they went down like ninepins until all we could see in front of us was a regular wall of dead and wounded. Above all the noise of rifle fire, you could hear a strange wailing sound and they turned and ran for the cover of the fir trees.'[6]

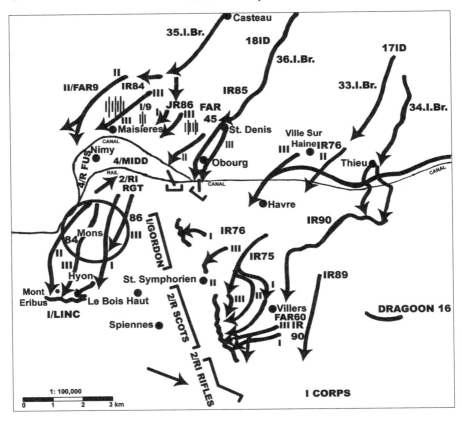

Fig. 12: IX AK, 23 August.

Such accounts differ little from those of British colonial battles, such as
Omdurman or Rorke's Drift. Since the Germans were 800–1,200 metres away,
it is most unlikely that the Middlesex private could have seen 'a regular wall of
dead', and the roar of British rifles and MG and German artillery would have
made it impossible for human voices to be heard several feet, much less a kilometre away. The German accounts contradict this version in every particular. The
Germans, 'foiled in his first attempt, now began to advance more warily, working
across the front in small parties ... From this point, having been taught by bitter
experience the sheer madness of advancing in massed formation, they came on in
extended order.'[7] This was a common British description of a change in German
tactics, which is also not borne out by German accounts.

The Germans were bringing heavy artillery, MG and rifle fire on the battalion, but British rifle fire 'had done its work', which can only mean that it
had inflicted disproportional losses on the Germans, because by any standard the
Middlesex position was crumbling. By 1200 the Germans were getting behind
the Middlesex, who were forced to withdraw. Around 1230 the Middlesex was

reinforced by 2/Royal Irish Regiment, the 8th Brigade reserve, on the high ground south of the railway, but in moving forward the Irish were met by a blast of German artillery, MG and rifle fire. The Irish position offered poor fields of fire, and the Germans quickly pushed in close.[8] The Irish machine guns came under intense artillery fire and one gun was put out of action almost immediately, then the second was put out of action by artillery and German MG fire and all but one man in the MG section was either killed or wounded. The two guns were cannibalised to make one working gun. A company commander was killed. D Company was almost immediately driven back to Hyon by German MG and rifle fire. Company A quickly lost all its officers.

The Middlesex history says: 'By sheer weight of numbers the enemy's infantry, covered by shell-fire, was able to work forward, so that about 2 p.m. both [battalions] … were driven … back to Mons.' The Irish history says that the Germans closed to within fifty yards. The Irish fell back and occupied the next piece of high ground about a kilometre to the south, directly east of Mons, in an open potato field. The Irish immediately came once again under heavy artillery, MG and rifle fire. B Company occupied a trench, which provided no protection against the artillery fire; other troops found protection from rifle fire in nearby houses. The Germans complained that they also occupied a hospital, which was marked with the Red Cross. A section of British artillery attempted to go into action to the left of the Irish but was smothered by counter-battery fire.

As the Middlesex retreated out of the fight, the Germans caught up with them at Hyon and they lost sixty more men. Breaking contact, the remnants of the Middlesex retreated to Nouvelles, 10 km south of their initial position. The Irish pulled back over a kilometre to a position just north of Hyon. After trying unsuccessfully to join the Gordon Highlanders, the Irish retreated a kilometre to the south side of Le Bois Haut, now rejoined by D Company. At 2200 the Irish retreated to Nouvelles, dragging some abandoned artillery with them.

The Middlesex roll call that night showed 275 men present for duty. Casualties were later determined to be 15 OFF (including 1 company commander KIA and 2 WIA) and about 467 EM. Both MG appear to have been lost. 2/Royal Irish Regiment lost 4 OFF and 16 EM KIA, 3 OFF and 57 EM WIA and captured; only 1 wounded OFF and 1 EM escaped. One OFF and 226 EM were MIA, 87 of them not returning to the battalion until 8 September; the rest were probably KIA or POW. Total Irish casualties were 11 OFF and 213 EM; both MG were lost.

It must be remembered in evaluating the British account that the British had no idea what the Germans were trying to accomplish. The British army was forbidden to study German tactics in peacetime. British doctrine was fuzzy concerning the role of fire superiority, which lay at the centre of German offensive doctrine. Nor did subsequent British historians study German tactical doctrine or impartially use German sources. Eighty-six years after the battle, Horsfall and Cave's description of German offensive tactics was still absurd:

The German Army adopted a policy of attacking en masse – just as the French did – advancing shoulder to shoulder in solid blocks of companies and carrying their rifles at the trail; on approaching the enemy they would fire from the hip, regardless of finding a target or taking aim.[9]

No Anglophone historian has ever made a serious attempt to see these attacks from the German point of view. The German perspective is immensely enlightening.

Dragoon R 16 provided a half-regiment to 17 ID and to 18 ID. A patrol from 4/Dragoon R 16 reported at 1845 on 22 August that it had identified British troops at Nimy and Obourg.[10] The bridges were raised and defended by dug-in British troops. Local inhabitants told the dragoons that the British were also on the heights and the rail embankment between Obourg and Mons. Other patrols on 22 and 23 August found bridges east of Obourg intact and unoccupied.

Lt Schoeller, with a patrol from Hussar R 8, bivouacked with Lt Humann's patrol north of Badour until 2400 on 22 August, then set out for Ghlin, which was reached at 0300 without seeing any enemy.[11] Behind them bicyclists raced in all directions. At the Mons city limits they asked two Belgians if the British occupied the town, and they replied in the affirmative, though they could not guess their strength; given the lack of security, the patrol leader supposed that they could not be very strong. The patrol rode a few hundred metres further and saw 300 metres to their front British sentries in greatcoats, standing on the canal bridge smoking and staring at the water, surrounded by children and oblivious of the presence of German cavalry. Lt Schoeller had seen enough, turned his patrol around and saw that the street was black with excited people. Pistol in hand, he broke into a trot and the mass parted to let him pass, shouting curses. He sent off a detailed report.

It is astounding that a German cavalry patrol could penetrate along the principal axis of approach to the British position. The British cavalry had failed utterly to establish a counter-reconnaissance screen. The infantry had not employed outposts. Nor was this an isolated incident.

At 0855 IX AK ordered its divisions, 17 ID on the left and 18 ID on the right, to attack across the Canal du Centre to seize Mount Erebus, south of Mons, and the ground to the east, which was the limit of advance.[12] The 1st Army order to attack was not issued until 0830 and did not reach IX AK until after the corps had issued its attack order. The Army order stipulated the same limit of advance as the corps order had.

The German 18 ID attacked at 0930 with the 35th Infantry Brigade on the right, which deployed IR 84 on the right and IR 86 on the left. IR 86 received its attack order at Casteau.[13] It was told that the enemy – probably British – held Mons with the first defensive position behind the Canal du Centre. The mission was to seize a crossing over the canal and drive the British out of Mons. The regiment swung left into the Forest of Obourg and deployed with III/86 on the left, I/86 on the right, II/86 in reserve. At the treeline, about a kilometre from the canal, the regiment deployed skirmishers. The regiment took fire from Warton Farm, which the British held as an outpost. The British were quickly driven out by fire from 1/86, 3/86 and a platoon of MG. The regiment continued the advance and the British began firing 'like wild' from positions in the houses and gardens south of the canal.

The regimental history observed that the British position wasn't going to be taken without artillery support, which was provided by FAR 45 and FAR 9, the latter a light howitzer unit. The commander of FAR 9 rode forward on reconnaissance in front of the infantry and was pinned down until the advancing infantry rescued him.[14] He was, however, able to identify his targets. The artillery regiment used individual guns or platoons to engage specific targets. Covered by fire from FAR 9's howitzers, IR 86 moved quickly to the canal, but the bridges were raised. Some bold I/86 men ran across the canal gates under heavy enemy fire and lowered the bridges. The regiment crossed. On the other side, the effectiveness of German artillery was clear to see: the German shrapnel had shot the British to pieces. Once across the bridge, the lead battalions deployed again and double-timed across a meadow, past dead and wounded British. The regiment forded the La Haine stream. IR 86 quickly reached the rail embankment 800 metres south of the canal.

On the other side of the railway embankment the ground rose, and the regiment began to receive fire from this high ground, which was returned by both leading battalions. Supported by artillery fire, the skirmishers quickly closed in on the enemy. After half an hour the hill was taken. Dead and wounded British were lying in the trenches, and the regiment took many prisoners: two lieutenants with two squads captured an officer and fifty men. The 18 ID engineers bridged both the canal and the La Haine stream and I/FAR 9 and 1/FAR 45 moved close behind the infantry. 1/FAR 9 found the still-warm beef-and-cabbage lunch prepared by British troops and did not let it go to waste.

The rest of the British retreated southward, with the regiment following on the east side of Mons through gardens, hedges and wire fences. II/86 followed in march column. Suddenly the lead battalions again took fire from a height to the east of Mons; this time artillery fire, as well as small-arms fire from hedges, houses and a castle. One shell killed four men. The castle was sprayed with MG fire to no effect, but was finally suppressed when a platoon (two guns) of 1/FAR 45 was brought into the infantry firing line to provide close support.[15] At 1530 the British were driven off this height, too. In the courtyard of a brewery a platoon from 11/86 captured all the horses of a British cavalry squadron.

II/86 was marching in column through the east edge of Mons when the lead element took fire. A regular panic broke out; troops were firing in all directions. With fearsome oaths the commander of 8/86, still on his horse, re-established order and stopped the senseless firing. Other officers led a few squads forward and forced some bypassed British troops out of positions at the end of town. The regiment bivouacked at Hyon, south-east of Mons.

In a running fight that had lasted all day, IR 86 had crossed the Canal du Centre and punched a hole 3 km deep in the British position. The regimental history says that the Germans won because of their superior German troop-leading and the 'incomparable offensive spirit of the troops, which tradition and training had made second nature'. The regiment lost 30 EM KIA, 6 OFF and 90 EM WIA, but took an officer and 309 EM from 4/Middlesex POW. 'The spirit of victory was overwhelming and was enjoyed to the full.'

IR 84 Attacks 4/Royal Fusiliers

The 35th Brigade deployed IR 84 on the right, against 4/Royal Fusiliers. It is not possible to say much useful about the Royal Fusiliers' side of the fight. The regimental history gives ten lines to Mons, devoted to the fact that Lt Dease and Private Godley won the first Victoria Cross covering the Fusiliers' withdrawal from the canal with a machine gun. Dease was killed; Godley was wounded but said he managed to throw the gun into the canal (nevertheless, IR 84 says it captured two MG).[16] This feat is recounted in every Anglophone account of Mons. What is never mentioned is that while machine guns can be effective as a rear guard, their employment in this manner is an act of tactical desperation: they will usually be lost and could not quickly be replaced.

Horsfall and Cave describe the IR 84 attack on 4/Royal Fusiliers in the standard terms:

> The Germans began their attack ... led by the 84th Regiment in solid blocks ... At a thousand yards the targets could not be missed and their leading sections four abreast were destroyed, causing the whole regiment to retire back into the wood.[17]

On the other hand, there are eleven first-person accounts of Mons in the IR 84 history, including those of the regimental adjutant, and the commanders of I/84, 6/84, 8/84, 10/84, 11/84 and the first sergeant of 10/84, plus the regimental histories of FAR 36 and FAR 9. This is almost too much of a good thing: coordinating these accounts is not easy. The following gives the most plausible synthesis.

IR 84 deployed II/84 on the right, III/84 on the left, I/84 held back as the brigade reserve.[18] III/84 advanced with 10/84 on the right of the road to Nimy, 11/84 on the left. These had been the outpost companies the previous night and had patrolled extensively as far as Maisières. 10/84 advanced with the 1st Platoon in a well-spaced line of skirmishers, followed at a 300-metre interval by the 2nd and 3rd Platoons. 10/84 quickly drove British security forces out of

Maisières, then ascended the reverse slope of a low hill, which gave cover against the British positions on the canal. When they reached the top they began taking heavy MG and rifle fire. The company took cover and 'just like at a gunnery range at home, returned well-aimed fire' at 700 metres range. The 2nd and 3rd Platoons came on line. The enemy was difficult to see, but 'the squad leaders and troops competed in detecting the enemy position'. Bushes along the canal gave an indication of the likely enemy location. The 10/84 commander was ordered to begin the advance, which he thought was premature, as he had not attained fire superiority and the terrain to his front was open. Nevertheless, he ordered fire and movement by squads. Only at this point did 10/84 begin to take casualties. The company commander was hit in the leg and the lieutenant had been killed, so the first sergeant took over. The company advanced to within 80–100 metres of the enemy, when the first sergeant stopped the forward movement and took up the firefight again.

As 11/84 left the west side of Maisières it took heavy fire from the front and left flank, which caused casualties. The reserve platoon was committed on the left. 11/84 advanced by bounds, took numerous casualties, and had to stop 100 metres from the canal.

II/84 advanced towards the rail bridge with 8/84 on the left and 5/84 on the right, followed by 6/84 and 7/84. At 1200 a standing firefight developed. 8/84 sat tight waiting for artillery support. 6/84 and 7/84 took positions in the houses behind 8/84 and fired on the British from there. 5/84 seems to have had an easy time: houses covered its advance to within 600 metres from the canal. A sergeant from 5/84 said that crossing the 'flower-strewn meadow' up to the canal, covered by British MG fire, was not going to be a pleasure, but the company made it, bounding by half-platoons. Somehow the company had drifted to the left and mixed in with 10/84. IR 84 now had 11/84, 10/84, 8/84 and 5/84 on the firing line: the attacking force was no stronger in infantry than the defenders.

At 1130 the howitzers of II/FAR 9 entered the fight, taking ineffective shrapnel counter-battery fire.[19] At 1330 a two-gun platoon from 4/FAR 9, another from 6/9 and a battery from FAR 36 were brought forward in close support; the platoon leader from 6/9 directed his guns from the attic of a house, under heavy British rifle fire. This close artillery support allowed the attack to move forward.

After a long firefight the Germans gained the upper hand. 10/84 reached the edge of the canal and could see the British sandbag positions on the other side, which led to a murderous gunfight at point-blank range. The 10/84 first sergeant organised systematic fire on the British riflemen and MGs and the British fire weakened. In the 11/84 sector, German artillery was effective in suppressing some of the British fire.

Two platoons from 8/84 manoeuvred to the left of 10/84. A patrol from 8/84 led by Sergeant Röver reached the Nimy Bridge. Musketeer Niemeyer swam through heavy fire to the other side and brought back a boat so that the patrol could cross the canal. The patrol occupied a house from which it could engage the British. Niemeyer then turned the bridge back over the canal, but was killed immediately afterwards. A squad succeeded in rushing across the bridge and enfiladed the British position. 10/84 and 11/84 swarmed across the bridge and the fighting became hand-to-hand. The first sergeant of 10/84 says that he bayoneted a British officer in the chest. There was no mention of IR 84 being held up by the MG of Dease and Godley, and as for this MG successfully covering the battalions' retreat, about sixty men from 4/Fusiliers surrendered here and both MGs were captured.

The 10/84 first sergeant said: 'Once on the other side of the canal, we could see what excellent work the company had done. Almost three-quarters of the British in our sector were dead or wounded, and the British sandbags had been completely shot full of holes.' 8/84 charged across the bridge and into a factory complex where it took thirty prisoners. A young German soldier, who was in civilian life a travelling salesman from Hamburg, took charge of the prisoners with the command, in English, 'Gentlemen, please, four and four' and the British formed up in march column.

IR 84 then succeeded in establishing a foothold in the houses of Nimy on the south side of the canal, followed by more brutal house-to-house fighting. The German artillery set the town on fire. IR 84 committed the attached engineer company to the attack, the engineers broke into the houses with axes and the regiment took Nimy. II/FAR 9 crossed the canal and took up firing positions north-east of Mons.

The regimental commander was concerned about the possibility of a *franc-tireur* attack if he entered a large city like Mons, so he sent a lieutenant into Mons to bring the mayor and hostages back with him. After about twenty minutes the hostages appeared, telling the Germans that there were no enemy forces in the city. I/84 was now in the lead, the troops forming a column on each side of the road, observing the windows and doors on the opposite side. In the centre of the city a large group of people had assembled, who kept their distance. Near the southern edge of Mons the point element took fire. I/84 disappeared into side roads and alleys. The battalion commander collected about five platoons on the west side of the town and continued towards the regimental objective, Mont Eribus. II/84 had already drifted off in that direction. In 1914 two German battalion commanders had automatically adopted what would later be known as 'infiltration tactics', bouncing off a defended position and bypassing it to take an objective in the enemy rear area.

In Mons a two-gun platoon of artillery brought forward, protected by volunteers, and their fire cleared the enemy out of the houses and several barricades. Various groups reached Mont Eribus, which was taken without opposition, and the regiment dug in for the night. The field kitchens came up. The commander of 8/84 says that: 'It was characteristic of our men that the first portions were given to the British prisoners.'

IR 84 had lost 1 OFF and 23 EM KIA, 6 OFF and 55 EM WIA, 94 casualties total. The British official history says that the Royal Fusiliers' losses 'did not
greatly exceed one hundred'.[20] Horsfall and Cave say they suffered more than 150
casualties.[21] The Germans took at least 90 POW and reported seeing many British
casualties, so even this number is almost surely too low. The commander of 8/84
wrote: 'The British had fought bravely, but could not withstand our last furious
assault.' He concluded: 'The leaders and troops conducted a difficult attack against
professional soldiers in a prepared position with perfect discipline, great courage,
intelligent use of the terrain, prudence and initiative. On this difficult day the
peacetime training proved itself brilliantly.'

IR 84 had conducted a fighting advance of about 7 km over a ten-hour period.
This was a combined-arms attack in which artillery and engineers continually
supported the infantry. With her sister regiment IR 86, IR 84 had taken Mons
and blown a hole 5 km deep and a kilometre wide in the British defensive position. On the British side, the engineers had again failed to blow up the bridge,
and artillery support was negligible. British battalions were beginning to display
an alarming tendency to loose their machine guns. 'Rapid rifle fire' alone could
not stop the IR 84 attack.

The British had conducted a tactically static, indeed an inert defence. The
division, corps and army commanders did not send reserves to bolster the most
vulnerable and most important point in their line. Still less did they counter-
attack to stabilise the front or limit the German penetration. I Corps had masses
of uncommitted infantry and artillery, which could have been quickly shifted to
assist the defenders of Mons, but nothing was done.

The British did not mow down German troops in rows; indeed, British casualties were higher than German. The Germans advanced by bounds and the
British riflemen assumed that every time a German completed his bound and
took cover, he had been hit. Demoralised German troops did not run to the rear,
as the British reported, but advanced methodically and steadily. This fight was a
useful demonstration of how good combined-arms offensive tactics beats bad
static defensive tactics.

The 36th Infantry Brigade attacked on the 18 ID left with IR 85 against the
right flank of 4/Middlesex, while two battalions of IR 31 were guarding IX AK
HQ and one was in 18 ID reserve.[22] At 0830 IR 85 patrols reported that Obourg
and the Canal du Centre were held by British forces and IR 85 was ordered to
force a crossing. IR 85 deployed on the south side of St Denis with III/85 astride
the road and II/85 on its right. I/85 was brigade reserve in St Denis. Supported by
artillery fire, at 1000 the regiment deployed into skirmishers and attacked, 'with
outstanding verve'. The only criticism the regimental history could make was that
the troops did not wait for the artillery preparation to make an effect. There was
tough street-fighting in Obourg. The bridge was barricaded and the windows in
the railway station had been fortified with sandbags. Two guns from II/FAR 45

were brought forward, and at point-blank range demolished a house that blocked
the line of fire to the railway station. The artillery then silenced the defenders
of the railway station. Two machine guns of the MG Company of IR 31 set up
in the attic of a house and their fire forced the British away from the bridge.[23] III/
IR 85 took the bridge and continued the attack, while II/85 crossed on a footbridge near Warton Farm to the right. By 1345 the two battalions and the MG
Company were across the canal. IR 85 then became involved in a fight against
British troops in trenches on the north-east side of Mons. 6/31 and a platoon
of 5/31 were committed between II/85 and III/85 at 1430. The German troops
closed to within 300 metres of the trench, and at 1700 the British withdrew. Since
it was getting dark, the attack was stopped. IR 85 bivouacked 1,500 metres east
of Mons. IR 85 had lost 3 OFF KIA, 3 OFF WIA and 184 EM KIA and WIA. It
captured 3 OFF and 182 EM from the 4/Middlesex and the Royal Fusiliers, plus
3 MG. 6/31 lost 2 KIA and 13 WIA, took 20 POW and captured a MG.

The 18th Division's attack on Mons offers a number of points of considerable
interest. The most important conclusions to be drawn from it are these:

The Germans concentrated superior combat power at the decisive point. This
is the touchstone of good tactics. The odds were roughly six engaged German
battalions against three British battalions. More important than numbers of infantry, the Germans used some twenty-six machine guns against six (perhaps eight)
British. The German MG tactics, which massed the fire of six guns under the
unified direction of the MG company commander, proved to be superior to the
British system of assigning two MGs to each battalion.

The Germans fought a combined-arms battle; the British did not. One example
is illustrative of the whole: the British engineering effort was so badly organised
that two British engineer companies managed to destroy only one bridge in this
sector; the British engineers had to work under fire and an engineer captain was
captured trying to rig the Nimy bridge for destruction.[24] German capture of
the bridges intact significantly increased German mobility, which is a combat
multiplier of the first order. The German engineer company was immediately on
the spot to bridge both the canal and the stream behind it. The German engineer
commander almost surely did not receive orders to carry out his tasks – the speed
of his work is evidence that he was on the front line, waiting for his opportunity. This was the result of frequent combined-arms field training exercises. The
British engineers displayed no such initiative or professionalism (for example, the
missing blasting caps), which demonstrates the lack of such exercises.

Most important, the Germans made extensive and imaginative use of artillery support; the British artillery was ineffective. The German artillery conducted
both long-range fire support, while frequently sending one or two guns forward
to provide fire support at point-blank range.

In Anglophone accounts of Mons, the British won not because they held the
battlefield at the end of the day – they didn't – but because they inflicted terrible,

disproportionate losses on the Germans. In Anglophone accounts, the Germans attacked in solid blocks and were mown down in rows. This utter nonsense has been taken at face value. To give one more example, from Lomas's *Mons 1914*: '"They went down like a regular lot of Charlie Chaplins" wrote one British soldier to his wife, "every bullet hitting home, sometimes taking two men at one time."'[25] The illustrations on pages 42–3 of *Mons 1914* show lines of Germans advancing bolt upright.

The Middlesex regimental history repeats the common British assertion that the Germans took rapid rifle fire for MG fire: 'That first encounter at Mons gave rise to the legend that [the Germans believed] British battalions were armed with large numbers of machine guns.'[26] There is no evidence to support this in any German regimental history. The British had the standard European allocation of machine guns – two per battalion – and the Germans knew it. The Germans were easily able to distinguish MG fire from rifle fire. The very idea of sustained 'rapid rifle fire' is a tactical absurdity: the rifleman would have shot off all of his ammunition in the first 10–15 minutes of a battle that lasted all day.

The Middlesex history also repeats the common British assertion that 'the enemy had been taught to regard [the British army] as negligible'.[27] This would reinforce the idea that the Germans did not anticipate serious resistance and would attack recklessly. In fact, the most common opinion of the British soldier was given by the FAR 45 history: 'tough old professional soldiers'.[28]

Judging from the terrain and the German accounts, the initial engagements took place at medium range: 800–1,200 metres. At those distances it is difficult to see human figures and conduct aimed fire, much less see one bullet hit two men. According to the German accounts, the Germans had already deployed into skirmisher lines and when the British opened fire and the Germans took cover, they began advancing by bounds and returning fire. The British would have been given fleeting targets and would not have been able to observe the effect of their fire: prone figures would hardly have been visible; still less would it have been possible to determine if those figures were dead or wounded.

Given the lurid descriptions of Germans being mown down in rows, British historians just know that German casualties had to have been far greater than the British. In fact, six attacking battalions of IR 84, 85 and IR 86 (plus four platoons of IR 31) took 425 casualties. The German loss rate was about 14 per cent. Nor did the Germans take 425 casualties in a blast of 'rapid rifle fire' at the beginning of the battle. German accounts make it clear that the initial British fire caused few casualties and that the casualties occurred during the advance in the course of the day: IR 86 was engaged for nine hours and stormed three British trench lines. 6/ IR 31, which was committed at 1430, after the supposed initial blast of 'rapid rifle fire', fought for two and a half hours and took fifteen casualties.

On the other hand, these three German regiments took 600 prisoners! The Germans captured 175 more men than they lost. One British battalion, 4/

Middlesex, took 471 casualties, a loss rate of about 45 per cent. Together with the 2/Royal Irish Regiment – 225 casualties – and 4/Royal Fusiliers – 150 or so – the three British battalions lost at least 845 men, twice as many as the six German battalions combined.

British Right Flank

The rest of the British 8th Brigade held the Mons–Harmignies road, facing generally east. On the left was 1/Gordon Highlanders, with 2/Royal Scots on the right. Each battalion held a front of about 2.5 km. There was a ditch and bank along the road that provided cover and concealment. Unlike the Middlesex and Irish, who took effective German artillery fire all day, the German gunners could not locate the 2/Royal Scots. The Scots were also able to spend the morning improving their positions. However, the commander of the 2/Royal Irish Rifles said that in front of the Scots' position there was dead ground between 1,500 and 300 metres.

At about 1400 the Royal Irish Rifles were sent from the 7th Brigade, the 3rd Division reserve, to reinforce the 2/Royal Scots, which was the right-flank battalion of the 3rd Division. Two companies were sent to extend the position even further to the right flank.[29]

Moving the Irish, the division reserve, in this manner shows that the 3rd Division commander had no idea how the fight was going. The 2/Royal Scots were not even under attack, while the 4/Royal Fusiliers, 4/Middlesex and 2/ Royal Irish were being driven back. It also shows that there was no coordination between I Corps and II Corps, because the 2nd Division of I Corps was immediately south of the 2/Royal Scots; indeed, by rights the entire division should have moved up to cover the II Corps right flank.

IR 76 Attacks 2/Gordon Highlanders

There was a gap between IX AK on the left of the German 1st Army and VII AK on the right of the 2nd Army. In addition, by moving south 17 ID would soon be entering the fire fans of the Maubeuge fortress artillery. Therefore, 17 ID did not seem to be in a hurry to push south; movement across the canal was deliberate and the 33rd Brigade on the right did not cross until 1300.[30]

At this time a dragoon patrol reported two British companies withdrawing south-west across the front of the lead element, I/76. In order to cut the British off, I/76 attacked west. 4/76 soon captured a British officer and nine men, 3/76 took a wagon full of British engineer tools. III/76 moved towards St Symphorien and at 1430 took fire from the town. 10/76 and 11/76 deployed and advanced towards Hyon, but were stopped just beyond St Symphorien by the fire of British troops, 'exceptionally well positioned on the ground'. Although I/76 was making progress, 17 ID remained cautious and ordered IR 76 to stand fast and await the effect of the outflanking attack by IR 75 and 34th Brigade. IR 76 lost 11 KIA and 79 WIA.

III/IR 76 had encountered the Gordon Highlanders. Terraine quotes one Gordie's account of the battle:[31]

> They advanced in companies of 150 men in files five deep ... the first company [?] were simply blasted away to Heaven by a volley at 700 yards, and in their insane formation every bullet was almost sure to find two billets. The other companies kept advancing very slowly, using their dead comrades as cover, but they had absolutely no chance.

IR 76 attacked in skirmisher lines, not solid blocks. I/76 took fifty casualties, III/76 lost thirty-two. Each battalion lost five KIA. IR 76 did not press the attack. The description given by Terraine's Gordie is obviously hyperbole.

The Gordon Highlander regimental history, by Cyril Falls, is much more professional.[32] Falls says that the Germans were advancing by bounds across the front of the Gordons and Scots Highlanders and were unaware of their location. 'The enemy suffered serious loss and was brought to a dead stop 300 yards from the 8th Brigade's trenches.' At 1600 a German company approaching from the north was also pinned down. The battalion was ordered to withdraw at 2100. It had suffered 1 OFF and 2 EM KIA, and 2 OFF and 'about a dozen other ranks' WIA.

IR 75 Attacks 2/Royal Scots and 2/Irish Rifles

17 ID did not order a divisional attack until 1615.[33] IR 75 swung south of St Symphorien, at 1630 saw a column of British infantry 900 metres to the front and then took artillery fire. The lead two companies (9/75 and 10/75) found cover in a sunken road and began 'a lively fire' against the British, but two artillery shells scored direct hits that killed four men and wounded several more in 12/75. Peacetime exercises always began with the 'General Situation'. The commander of 12/75 said that the British had failed to make their known and he was feeling around as though in the dark.

I/75 and II/75 were still about a kilometre to the rear. Several artillery shells landed near 3/75 as it moved forward. The regimental historian said that 'reaction to artillery fire' was a favourite problem in tactical tests and the company commander ordered: 'Pick up the step, double time, march! ... It worked perfectly, actually better than in the tactical tests on the Neuenlander Field.' The company outran the artillery fire without casualties.

II/75 was committed south of III/75 and the MG Company found a position to the left of II/75. In the rolling terrain 10/75 closed to within 100 metres of the British position, but 9/75 and 10/75 were held up by flanking fire from the south. II/75 was having trouble advancing, but by 1900 had approached to within 200 metres of the British position.

The 3/75 commander noted that it was growing dark as his company and 4/75 were ordered to attack south of II/75. He said that the 'complete emptiness of the battlefield' was everything he had expected. In the rolling terrain he had no idea where the forward troops of II/75 were, much less those of the enemy. 3/75 advanced with two platoons forward and the third in support. Moving by bounds, in spite of 'heavy enemy fire', 3/75 reached the first sunken road in good order and with few casualties. The commander of 3/75 said:

> Sunken roads that offer cover in open terrain against infantry fire present a unique situation, this one especially so. It ran along the crest of high ground going north, and the enemy was apparently paying it special attention. Bullets hit the forward slope in massive quantities. It took extraordinary strength of will to jump forward from the protection of the sunken road into the beaten zone. The temptation to leap from this deadly hell back to the safety of the sunken road was very strong.

It wasn't possible to get accurate news of the situation forward, but rumours abounded that the troops on the firing line needed help. The commander of 3/75 gathered 200 men from several units and led them forward: 'Our sense of duty and comradeship with the men of the 75th on the line spurred us forward.' The company commander noted that 'there weren't many long bounds and short rests', as in training; that is, movement was by short bounds with long rests, but the company moved forward nevertheless. Bullets cracked through the air, hit the earth and whizzed through the stalks of grain. In spite of casualties, this group advanced 1,000 metres without firing a shot. They couldn't understand why they didn't reach the forward firing line, when in fact they had passed it in the dark, indeed pulled it forward with them. At 2000 they stopped in dead ground short of the British position. They could hear British voices clearly and see the muzzle flashes. This was the perfect 'assault position'. The 3/75 group now feared friendly fire more than that of the British. To make their position known and to assemble scattered troops, they yelled 'Hurra' and the buglers played 'Fix Bayonets'.

> All of this must have made the British very nervous, for he answered every 'Hurra' and bugle call with a completely crazy rapid fire. Since we were in dead ground, nobody was hit, and gradually we began to feel secure in our assault position. Pretty soon everything was happening just like in training. We

started to dig in and reorganize. The platoon leaders sent in strength reports, as I remember altogether 250 men. Patrols were sent out. Whenever they made a noise, the British blasted away with rapid fire.

At 0200 a messenger arrived from regiment ordering 3/75 to pull back to the sunken road. The company commander says that he 'unfortunately' obeyed. The rest of the regiment had been withdrawn at 2300. Higher headquarters, receiving reports of British forces moving and digging in, feared an attack on the 17 ID left flank, which was 'in the air'. On 23 August IR 75 lost 39 EM KIA, 5 OFF and 232 EM WIA.

Terraine says that IR 75 lost 376 men (it actually lost 271): 'Its [the IR 75] failure persuaded the German commanders that it would be as well to let the British go.'[34] Once again, this is not supported by any evidence of what the Germans were actually doing or thinking. In fact, IR 76 continued to advance even after dark, and was hoping to renew the battle at daylight.

The 17 ID order to attack across the Canal du Centre did not reach the 34th Brigade until 1100. The Brigade initially attacked with IR 90 on the left, IR 89 on the right. The canal was lined with the usual workers' houses, factories and slag heaps. The brigade thought that the canal would be defended, so IR 89 and IR 90 advanced in very open order. IR 90 led with only one battalion, II/90, which deployed with half platoons and wide spaces between skirmishers, followed at 150 metres with successive waves of half platoons: just like in Breitkopf's exercise. IR 89 and IR 90 found the canal undefended, though one town had been prepared for defence.

IR 90 advanced about 2 km and then stopped and distributed lunch from the field kitchens. At 1500 it resumed the advance, turning west. The enemy was thought to be near and the troops were forbidden to sing. At 1630 IR 90 reached Villers St Ghislain and the lead battalion, II/90, deployed and lay down in platoon columns in a stubblefield 500 metres south of the town, facing to the south, where there was supposed to be enemy troops, though no enemy was to be seen far and wide. III/90 deployed behind the left wing of IR 75, I/90 remained in reserve near St Ghislain. An artillery battery set up behind II/90 and opened fire at 1645, which was answered by enemy shrapnel, causing some casualties. Enemy artillery also landed in Villers St Ghislain and started a panic among the baggage horses. I/90 had to change position several times due to British artillery fire.

At 1845 III/90 advanced by bounds to the left of IR 75. Unlike IR 75, IR 90 employed area suppressive fire, beginning at long range (1,200 metres) and aiming at factory buildings, houses and attics, without being able to make out actual targets. I/90 was committed to the firing line. Darkness fell. IR 90 had also approached to within 100 metres of the British. The firing in the darkness became uncontrollable. Buglers played 'General Halt!'; troops cried out

'Cease Firing!' 'Password Altona!' '12th Company here!' or sang '*Die Wacht am Rhein*'. Each time the firing died down, it would flare up again. The din was indescribable and lasted for hours. At 2300 the regimental commander began pulling the troops back to a line about 400 metres from the British position, where they dug in. IR 90 had about 75 WIA and an unknown number of KIA. At 0400 on 24 August the German artillery bombarded the British positions of the previous day. I/90 and III/90 advanced at 0430, only to find the British positions empty.

IR 89 had an easy day on 23 August. It crossed the canal after IR 90. II/89, the lead element, left Maurange, it took fire from British cavalry at 1,600 metres range (!) which was returned. Until 1400 the regiment remained at Maurange and cooked dinner, while I/FAR 60 conducted an artillery duel. The regiment then moved south and occupied Villers St Ghislain.

The 17 ID artillery was strangely inactive on 23 August, for which there is no direct explanation in the artillery regiment histories.[35] The 17 ID artillery was able to engage some British artillery – the FAR 24 history mentions a significant artillery duel with British guns on the Bois du Haut – and this counter-battery fire may be a reason that the 17 ID infantry took so little British artillery fire. It seems that the rolling, open terrain denied the German artillery observation points and battery positions from which it could engage the British infantry. The FAR 24 history mentions that a platoon of 2/FAR 24 was assigned to provide direct support to IR 76. It was able to set up in a fruit orchard at St Symphorien, from which it engaged houses and British trenches to the south-west for the entire afternoon without drawing any British counter-battery fire, even though it fired on British artillery in the Bois du Haut.

The failure of the 17 ID artillery to engage the British infantry was a far more important factor in the ability of the British infantry to hold their positions than was the vaunted British rifle fire. An attack on a dug-in enemy at this time was a combined-arms effort, which required effective artillery support. Where artillery support was forthcoming, as in the 18 ID sector, the British infantry crumbled. The best that can be said for the 17 ID artillery was that the infantry attack had revealed British positions, which 6/FAR 24 was prepared to engage on 24 August.

The tactically significant conclusion to be drawn from IR 75's attack is that the regiment, unsupported by effective artillery fire, was able to deploy from column into assault line, and in four hours cross 1,700 metres of open ground, to within 100 metres of the British line and stay there at the cost of about 10 per cent casualties. The regiment had moved faster, and with fewer casualties, than Breitkopf's test had predicted. If, based on the situation on the night of 23 August, the battle had been resumed on 24 August, the German artillery had found the range and the British would have been overrun.

2/*Royal Scots and* 2/*Irish Rifles*

Two companies and the MG section of the Irish Rifles dug in on a rise to the south-east of the Scots, facing north. The Irish battalion commander said that one company and the MG had a field of fire out to 2,000 metres and were able to provide flanking fire in front of the Scots line, but the other company had a dead zone from 1,000 to 3,000 metres. At 1600 the Germans attacked, and the Scot's commander immediately sent a message to the Irish CO, saying that he needed the two reserve Irish companies or he might not be able to hold.

The Irish history contains the standard descriptions of a German attack:

The leading Germans fired standing, 'from the hip' ... They crumpled up – mown down as quickly as I tell it, their reinforcing waves and sections coming on bravely and steadily to fall over as they reached the front line of the slain and wounded. Behind the death line thicker converging columns were being blown about by our field guns. Our rapid fire was appalling even to us, and the worst marksman could not miss, as he had only to fire into the 'brown' ... gave us a great sense of power and pleasure.

they came on in such bunches. We gave them a burst of rapid firing and wiped out the majority.
(from the *Irish Times*, 8 October 1914).

Excellent as the accuracy of our riflemen was, and deadly as their fire became, it failed to stem the German weight of attack, and countless lines of their infantry moved steadily towards us over the bodies of those we had killed and wounded, displaying both superb discipline and bravery and also the utterly reckless manner with which the higher commands of the German Army regarded human life.

The last account, which emphasised German ruthlessness, was clearly influenced by British propaganda. The account written by the Irish battalion commander was much more professional and accurate:

The German attack developed on the lines usually practised in 1914. Owing to the contour of the ground the enemy attacking the bluff [where all of 2/Royal Scots and all but one company of 2/Irish Rifles were positioned] were invisible from about 1,500 yards until they closed to 300 yards where they were checked. The company flanking the position of the main body of the R. Scots, and the machine guns, however, caused a good many casualties ... German tactics in attack appeared very like our own, in principle. They seemed to make deliberate preparation before launching an attack, bringing up guns and infantry onto the ground. The artillery preparation then began more or less simultaneously along the front of the attack, and where it was thought sufficient effect had been produced the infantry came on with all available machine guns. If the infantry attack did not succeed it was at once abandoned and more preparation commenced.

One of the Irish machine guns was destroyed. Around 1700 a battalion of Grenadier Guards and another of Irish Guards from I Corps appeared in the Irish Rifles' sector, but did nothing. The German artillery had been gradually finding the British position, which by dark 'had become thoroughly unpleasant'. The Irish commander said that the Germans brought up machine guns and attacked again at dusk, but stopped as soon as the British opened fire (this was probably IR 90 arriving). As it became darker the Germans got closer and the Scots conducted occasional 'mad minutes' to discourage any German attack. The Irish commander thought the Germans had withdrawn to cook, leaving an outpost line behind. He would have been alarmed to know that the Germans were still immediately to his front in strength. The Scots began to withdraw at midnight; their casualties were insignificant: 1 OFF and 1 EM WIA, 4 EM MIA; the Irish lost 4 KIA.

The Irish were rear guard and left their positions at 0200. The battalion commander ordered the Irish to abandon their packs, extra ammunition, picks and shovels, because 'The weather was very hot causing considerable distress amongst the troops'. The Irish battalion commander had clearly decided that his primary mission was to move his unit away from the Germans as quickly as possible.

Once again, the British defence relied almost entirely on rifle and machine-gun fire. The British artillery was able to engage only targets deep in the German rear, near Villers St Ghislain. There was no British manoeuvre on 23 August. The left flank of the German 1st Army was being held only by II/90 for most of the day, but both the British II Corps reserves as well as the entire I Corps failed to exploit this situation.

German Night Patrol

Around 2300 Lieutenant Eck, commander of 10/75, led a night patrol with three men to scout out the British positions. The patrol was carefully prepared. The weapons were unloaded, the troops took off their pickelhaube and wore caps, and the company was turned over to the senior lieutenant, who was briefed. They had just left the sunken road when one of the men reported that he had seen a figure and might have heard whispering. 'Such incidents don't cost minutes, but a half an hour', said the 10/75 commander, as everyone strained to see or hear something. Finally they crawled forward at 50-metre intervals, advancing after a low signal. Then contact was lost with one of the men; a man had to go back and find him. Now everybody crawled forward together. A man reported five figures to his front, which turned out to be five sheaves of wheat. They moved forward quickly now, individually, crawling, by bounds. The officer left his pistol, which was a hindrance, preferring to rely on an entrenching tool as a weapon. The sky began to lighten. They were now 200 metres from the British position and heard a rustling, which they believed must be British outposts; the lieutenant thought he saw a cow. Then the rustling was found to be frost thawing on the sugar beets. The patrol had been out for four hours, it was 100 metres to the British position, nearly dawn and there was no way to remain in place or move back unobserved. To prevent the patrol from becoming separated, the lieutenant grabbed one man by the arm, the other two held onto his belt and they advanced upright. Nothing happened. They reached the British position on the road and found it empty. The patrol ran back all the way to the regiment's position and then to brigade headquarters, the lieutenant yelling 'The enemy has gone'; he heard somebody say 'Twaddle!' He arrived at the brigade headquarters just as it was going to begin the preparatory bombardment for the assault.

German 6 ID Attacks British 9th Brigade

The British 9th Infantry Brigade held the Canal du Centre from Nimy to Jemappes. As we have seen, 4/Royal Fusiliers on the brigade right was driven off the canal by IR 84. To the left of the Royal Fusiliers was 1/Royal Scots Fusiliers, and to their left the 1/Northumberland Fusiliers. 1/Lincolnshire Regiment held a backup position to the south side of Mons.

The Scots Fusiliers deployed with security elements on the north side of the canal and all four companies and the battalion headquarters on line south of the canal.[36] The position was strengthened by barricades. A German cavalry patrol appeared 500 metres in front of the Scots Fusiliers and was engaged by a machine gun, removing any doubt the Germans might have had concerning the British location. The German preparatory bombardment began at 1030 and the infantry attack at 1100. The regimental history says, 'The enemy's infantry in great strength advanced from the cover of Ghlin wood, east of Baudour, in a south-easterly direction in a dense formation'. 'Superb target for artillery', wrote Douglas Smith in his diary, 'but we had none at the moment.' The regimental history then gives one of the few accurate descriptions of German infantry tactics in Anglophone literature: 'the enemy spread out into attack formation and, on getting into effective range of our rifles, he continued the advance by alternate rushes of small units ... they were met by a blast of rifle and machine-gun fire. The enemy checked, took shelter, came on, checked again.' The Germans had approached to within 200 metres of the Jemappes Bridge at 1430 when the Scots began to retire. The Germans took the bridge intact and pushed quickly across, forcing B Company to conduct a fighting retreat.

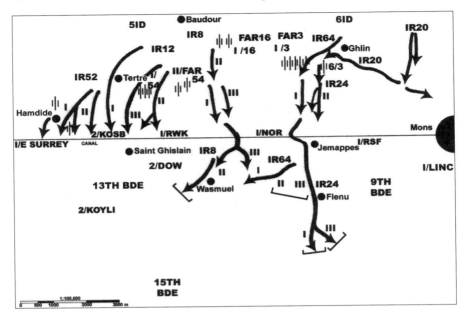

Fig. 13: III AK, 23 August.

The British official history says that two of the three bridges in the sector were not destroyed for lack of blasting caps,[37] which sets a new standard for engineering incompetence. The Scots Fusiliers lost 2 OFF KIA, 'some 100 other ranks were killed or wounded'.

Lt Humann from Hussar R 8 had bivouacked in a wood north of Tertre on the night of 22–23 August.[38] At dawn the patrol rode back into Tertre, where it encountered and chased British cavalry, took fire and lost a man, and rode out again. Having established that the British outposts were still in place, he sent a message that the British were north of the canal and it did not appear that they intended to advance.

6 ID began the approach march at 0600 from Notre Dame Louvignies, about 17 km north of the Canal du Centre. Patrols from the Zeithen Hussars were sent towards Mons and Jemappes.[39] One patrol rode to within ten metres of the entrance to Jemappes without making any contact; British counter-reconnaissance was non-existent. It took fire at 300–400 metres range from two machine guns at the railway station. The patrol was hemmed in by houses and wire fences and British infantry attempted to cut it off. The horse of one hussar was hit and he was listed as MIA. In the next village civilians attempted to block their path. The patrol managed to gallop through it all and report.

At 1000 6 ID deployed at Ghlin to attack Jemappes. However, the 1st Army ordered III AK to wait until it could be certain the British were not at Tournai. The corps did not receive permission to attack until 1400.

6 ID had only three regiments: IR 35 was guarding the army headquarters at Hal and made a 45 km march on 23 August in an attempt to catch up with the division.[40] IR 20 attacked on the 6 ID left, found German troops in Mons and returned to Ghlin. The 12th Brigade attacked on the 6 ID right, with IR 24, holding IR 64 in reserve.[41] The regimental history of IR 24 says that the British II Corps occupied an excellent position, behind a broad canal, with a meadow 5 km deep to the front and houses and mines for cover. IR 24 was short 9/24 and 11/24, which had been held back as the 12th Brigade reserve. The regimental commander issued his attack order at 1000, but was not permitted to attack until after 1400. The regiment deployed at Ghlin with I/24 right of the road to Jemappes and II/24 to the left, the two remaining companies of III/24 on the road. The MG Company would guard the right flank.

I/24 deployed with 1/24 on the right, 3/24 on the left, 2/24 behind the right flank, 4/24 behind the left. II/24 was in a similar formation: 5/24 and 6/24 in front, 7/24 behind the right flank, 8/24 guarding the left.

The regiment waited until the artillery was in position, then moved out, took fire and advanced by bounds, quickly reaching the first houses of Jemappes. The MG Company was periodically able to support the attack with suppressive fire against factory windows. It was difficult for the artillery to conduct observed fire.[42] 6/FAR 39 shelled the Jemappes railway station, 5/FAR 39 and 2/39 the houses. 1/39 and 3/39 did not fire.

Reserve Lieutenant Eger's platoon, 1/24, was on the regimental right flank. The advance started through fenced pastures and ditches as German artillery shells flew overhead. The platoon crossed through a park and as they reached the other side the range estimator was wounded: they had been fired on by a three-man British patrol. The platoon leader took the range estimator's rifle and together with one of his soldiers shot two of the British. The platoon then came to a high wall, which part climbed while others waded a stream that flowed through the wall. Next they encountered a railway line and took fire from a railwayman's house, which caused several casualties. The platoon laid down covering fire while the men crossed the railway line by individual bounds. On the other side they found a position that offered prone protection from British fire. They had also reached the backside of a house that stood just north of a bridge. A door in the rear of the house led only to a latrine. An attempt to go to the front brought intense British fire, which killed one man and wounded two more. Eger and three men climbed to the roof of a stall and into a first-storey window while the rest of the platoon provided covering fire. They searched the building and found that it was a pub. In the common room on the first floor they discovered 'four British NCOs with numerous chevrons on their arms who were completely drunk and made no particular problem when we took them prisoner'. He brought the rest of the platoon through the same window and they began firing on the British troops in the houses on the other side of the canal, without taking casualties. The rest of the company had occupied a glass factory on the other side of the road and were firing from there. The company commander and ten men moved to Eger's house. The company commander then shot several British soldiers. Eger said, 'I was astounded by the calmness and marksmanship of this old soldier and hunter'. Eger tried to storm the bridge with 10–15 men. They made one bound and the British opened fire with a machine gun, which caused several casualties, and they made it back to the house with difficulty. Eger concluded with the remark, 'The British were marvellous marksmen'.

It was clear to the regimental commander that an attack over open terrain and a canal against a well-prepared enemy was impossible for infantry alone. He therefore brought guns from II/FAR 3 forward, which unlimbered behind the cover of houses and were then manhandled by the gunners and men of IR 24 to a position a few hundred metres from the British.[43] One gun was sent to the 1/24 sector. It blasted apart the bridge barricade, which was made out of railroad ties, and then went to work on the houses occupied by British troops. In short order the bridge was in the hands of 1/24.

1/24, followed by all of I/24, crossed the canal and pushed to the south side of Jemappes. The commander of 1/24 felt that his company was no longer under control, so except for Lt Eger's platoon on point he formed the company into squad column and marched them through the town in step. Eger says that this was 'a time-proven method in war' for re-establishing control and discipline.

While 3/FAR 3 and 4/FAR 3 shelled Frameries, 1/24 reached open country again and received machine-gun fire from the left front. Eger and his platoon were able to take cover in an oat field, while the rest of 1/24 took up positions at the train station. 6/FAR 3, which was following close behind, unlimbered behind the slag heaps, manhandled the guns into position and opened fire at a range of 200 metres. Supported by the artillery and the fire of 1/24 and 4/24, Eger was able to take the hill and capture several prisoners. Eger continued the advance and captured several Scots and two sets of bagpipes.

3/24, to Eger's left, had a tougher time. The lead platoon advanced in skirmisher line. Not far from the canal it took heavy fire, but fortunately found cover behind a low rise of land. However, the rucksacks were visible to the British and were 'literally shot up like sieves … the Zwieback (in the iron rations) was pulverized, socks and underwear had hundreds of holes'. The fire was so strong that the other two platoons could not even think of advancing.

Lt Lindenau was a platoon leader in 10/24, which attacked to the right of the road. The company moved out in squad column (one squad behind the other) with Lindenau's platoon in the lead. Wide ditches slowed movement. The platoon reached houses and was ordered to seize the left-hand bridge. Lindenau left the bulk of his platoon in a group of houses and went forward with six chosen men. To his front was a potato field, then a cornfield. In the distance were a railway embankment, houses and a hothouse. Lindenau continued the advance through swampy meadows left of the road. There was no enemy to be seen. Lindenau bounded forward and suddenly several bullets whizzed through the air. With the next bound he found cover in the potato field. He rose to one knee and fired several rounds, which drew heavy return fire and a bullet through his helmet. One of his men was killed, two or three wounded. At his whistle signal the platoon came forward by bounds in skirmisher line. He tried to shout orders, which could not be heard through the din. The two other platoons came up; the company caught its breath and then continued the advance. Lindenau said that only with difficulty could he hold his men back and conduct an organised attack. They waded through swampy low ground. The attack continued at a quick pace until the canal was reached at 1630. The crossings were already in German hands, and the company was ordered to assemble at the north side of Jemappes.

IR 64, which was the 12th Brigade reserve, was ordered to commit a battalion to the right of IR 24 with the mission of seizing a crossing and occupying the high ground south of Jemappes.[44] From the line of departure at Ghlin to the canal lay 3 km of flat and open meadow. III/64 attacked at 1425 with 9/64 and 12/64 forward, 10/64 in reserve (11/64 had been detached). The regimental history says that the skirmisher lines advanced 'just like on the Angermünd training area'. The sound of IR 24's fight could be easily heard, as well as that of the German artillery fire passing overhead. 'Fortunately the enemy did not appear to have any artillery, and III/64 was able to cross the meadow without taking any casualties.' It then encountered thick brush on the banks of the canal, then a barricaded but intact bridge, and took fire from the other side of the canal. At 1545 III/64 stormed the bridge and drove the defenders out of the houses and took the first prisoners. 'The defenders had probably not been very numerous; nevertheless, their casualties were considerable, while thankfully those of the battalion were light.' By 1600 the battalion had passed through Jemappes. I/64 and II/64 came forward. The regiment set up a defence in place.

At 1920 IR 64 was ordered to occupy the high ground north-west of Frameries. It began movement in complete darkness. The march through Flénu was difficult because it crossed with that of IR 24. Zeithen Hussars then reported that the British occupied Frameries. A night attack was out of the question, so the regiment went over to the defence with IR 24 now to the right, IR 64 on the left. IR 64 lost only 2 EM KIA, 1 OFF and 10 EM WIA. The IR 24 history did not mention casualties.

The British 3rd Division, and with it the II Corps, had been defeated; the centre of the division near Mons had been pushed in and it had suffered 1,000 casualties. By nightfall the Germans were behind the units on the division's left and right flanks and they would have to withdraw. The new position on 24 August was also untenable and the entire British army would begin to withdraw again at dawn that day.

The Germans had concentrated three divisions against the British 3rd Division, which was holding both the decisive terrain on the British front and the most vulnerable point on the British line. That the 3rd Division was given the largest and most vulnerable sector in the British line was the mark of extremely poor decision-making, reinforced by command inertia on 23 August at the army and corps levels. That the Germans did not achieve a shattering victory was due solely to the fact that the 1st Army delayed the III AK attack for four hours.

British 13th Brigade Defends St Ghislain

On 22 August the 13th Brigade moved forward to the Canal; 'little, if any, news of a German advance had reached the foremost British troops'.[45] The 13th Brigade deployed two battalions on the canal and two in reserve. 1/Royal West Kent (RWK) would hold 3,000 metres of front and defend three bridges: a railway bridge on the right, a wooden lock bridge (Lock 5) 100 metres to its left and a road drawbridge 1,000 metres to the west.[46] D Company held the bridges on the right, C Company the bridge on the left, the other two companies were in reserve at Hornu, 3 km to the south. Both companies had to cross the canal to get a field of fire. The RWK would be attacked by IR 12. Describing the RWK fight is nearly impossible due to the poor quality of the regimental history.[47] To the left of RWK was the 2/King's Own Scottish Borderers (KOSB). It defended 2,000 metres of canal and the iron road bridge at Lock 4. 2/KOSB would be attacked by IR 52. The 2/Duke of Wellington's was in reserve at Hornu on the right, 2/King's Own Yorkshire Light Infantry (KOYLI) on the left. The 13th Brigade employed all eight machine guns on the forward defensive line. The MGs of the KOYLI were employed between the two battalions, the MGs of the Wellingtons on both sides of the railway bridge in the RWK sector, where they had a fine field of fire out to 1,200 metres.

At 0400 on 23 August Belgian civilians on bicycles reported that they had seen large numbers of German infantry and guns approaching. This apparently constituted the only reconnaissance and security the 13th Brigade enjoyed. At around 1000 the Wellingtons' MG platoon leader opened fire on German cavalry. Not only did they fail to hit the Germans, they had announced where the guns were. The MG platoon leader said:

> The first enemy attack developed about 12 noon … It was not pressed with much determination … Small bodies of the enemy reached the open fields to our immediate front; they, however, were soon checked by our MG and rifle fire; as a result they scattered in small groups behind corn stooks, where they remained for the rest of the day … Practically all of our casualties were a result of enemy shelling. This was very consistent and accurate, particularly after about 3 p.m., when our guns appeared to stop firing, the enemy [artillery fire] then traversed along the general line of the canal continually until nightfall.

An artillery shell landed in front of the lieutenant's MG position at 1500, shattering his arm.

Troops from the German 6th ID had crossed the canal to the east of the RWK and were attacking D Company on the railway bridge in the rear. At 1300 two platoons of B Company Duke of Wellington's reinforced the RWK on the north side of the canal between St Ghislain and the railway bridge. The Wellingtons' battalion commander reported that he could see Germans 'creeping along the hedgerows at from 400 to possibly 700 yards'. When the Wellingtons opened fire the Germans immediately took cover and returned the fire: a Wellingtons captain was wounded in the leg and a soldier next to the battalion commander was killed. The Germans were supported by artillery fire, while the Wellingtons' commander found the lack of British artillery 'most galling'.

The firing ceased at dusk, and the Wellingtons' commander could hear the Germans digging in and hauling artillery forward to close range. The commanders of the West Kents and Wellingtons conferred and agreed that the position would be untenable at daylight and reported this to brigade. At 2155 the Wellingtons were ordered to withdraw to Wasmes.

The KOSB deployed D Company north of the bridge at Lock 4, with the machine guns in the upper storey of a house directly behind it and A and C Companies on the right, connecting to the RWK.[48] B Company formed a security detachment about a kilometre to the front, but withdrew at 1200 without making contact to act as battalion reserve. At about 1300 the KOSB observed IR 12 advancing:

> They were fairly well under cover … Advancing in skirmishing order by alternate bursts over the marshy meadows, occasionally using their nippers to cut wire fencing, they were subject to rapid fire and suffered heavily. But, nevertheless, enough came on to make it necessary to reinforce the troops on the far bank [with part of A Company], especially as those on the near bank had such a poor field of fire.

The German artillery suppressed 'the single and unsuitably placed F.A. battery in support of the 13th I.B.' and then went to work on the British defensive positions in the houses, including the MG, which had to be moved. At sundown the KOSB were ordered to withdraw; B and C Companies had not been seriously engaged.

Of the bridges in the 13th Brigade sector, the British succeeded in destroying the bridges at St Ghislain proper, but failed to destroy the road bridge at Lock 4. The KOSB battalion second-in-command was WIA and later DOW, the surgeon was wounded; there was somewhere between 45 and 100 EM casualties. The Wellingtons lost 3 OFF WIA, 7 EM KIA, 24 WIA and 1 MIA.

German 5 ID Attacks St Ghislain

The 5 ID cavalry reconnaissance squadron, 2/Hussar R 3, reported at 0445 that the British occupied the canal at Ghislain.[49] The division commander personally sent a cavalry patrol, accompanied by an artillery officer and an engineer officer, to reconnoitre the canal and the terrain to the north. The patrol moved along the railway line to St Ghislain and closed to about 50 metres from Tertre when it encountered two British sentries. The patrol took heavy fire; one man and one horse were killed and two horses wounded. Just before he could turn a corner to safety, the patrol leader was slightly wounded in the shoulder. The patrol occupied a farm and continued to observe the British. The patrol leader reported to the division commander, then a medic dressed his wound and left him in a house with a glass of champagne to 'celebrate'. The owner of the house arrived, 'followed by two truly very pretty daughters', took one look at the champagne bottle and said, 'Well, they didn't find the good stuff!' and brought out a better brand.

5 ID attacked at 1400 with IR 8 (9th Brigade) on the left, IR 12 (10th Brigade) on the right. IR 8 attacked with III/8 on the left, I/8 on the right, II/8 following in reserve. Each battalion had a platoon of two machine guns attached. III/8 deployed 12/8 and 9/8 in the first line, 10/8 and 11/8 in the second. The battalion was preceded by an infantry patrol, which took fire from the houses north of the bridge. The patrol reported that the houses were prepared for defence. The battalion commander recognised at once that infantry alone would not suffice, and brought forward two artillery pieces from 1/FAR 18, led by the battery commander, which unlimbered under cover and were manhandled to within a few hundred metres from the first houses. With a few rounds the houses were cleared.[50] The division commander, who was forward with the lead battalion, now ordered the battalion commander to attack the bridge with 10/IR 8. The general was not as good a tactician as the major: the attack was premature and the company was immediately pinned down, and in the resulting firefight several 10/8 soldiers were killed. The battalion commander ordered the artillery pieces pushed forward and their fire cleared the houses.

The commander of 10/IR 8 worked part of his company through houses and backyards until he reached the edge of the canal to the west of the bridge and could fire at the British on the other side. Using 'field expedient materials' he crossed the canal and, together with elements of 1/IR 8 and 2/8, headed west in order to fire into the rear of the British troops at St Ghislain which were opposing IR 12.

While 9/IR 8 engaged the British east of the bridge, other elements of 10/IR 8 (this must have been quite some infantry company!), supported by the artillery and elements of 11/8 and 12/8, stormed the bridge and cleared the barricade on it. The British engineer captain who failed to blow the bridge was awarded the Victoria Cross 'for his dogged determination'.[51]

In British histories, the Germans are able to clear the British from the north side of the bridge because:

> a number of little Belgian girls came down the road and the Fifth Fusiliers nat-
> urally ceased their fire. Thereupon the Germans swarmed forward and, flooding
> over to the western side of the main road, were able to establish themselves
> within two hundred yards of the canal, whence they could bring an oblique fire
> to bear on the defenders of the barricade. The advance party of the Fifth on the
> north side of the bridge was then withdrawn.[52]

Edmonds hastens to say that he is not suggesting the Germans deliberately forced the girls into the street. Terraine, who cites the same evidence, is not so sure.[53] Neither displays any scepticism concerning this unlikely story: an intense fire-fight was going on, to include an artillery piece firing straight down the street, and a group of little girls ran into the middle of it? This sounds like an 'Angels of Mons' story.

I/IR 8 entered Marlette without taking any casualties. It committed 3/8 and 4/8 to support III/8 in taking the bridge. Together they cleared the town south of the bridge in heavy house-to-house fighting and pushed on to take Wasmuel. At the same time 1/8 and 2/8 attacked west to support 10/8 in its fight for St Ghislain.

While the rest of the regiment reorganised in Marlette, 12/8 was sent forward to attack to the south of Wasmuel. The company was joined by elements from I/8 and III/8 until it was the equivalent of two companies in strength. It was also joined by Prince Joachim Albrecht of Prussia, who had been carrying orders and assumed command. The detachment entered a maze of slag heaps, took fire and was unable to advance further. It was pulled back at dark.

The regiment set up a defensive position south of the Valenciennes road. II/IR 8 was immediately opposite British troops that were completely hidden in the closed terrain. 2/FAR 18 set up in the front line. In spite of vigorous patrolling, which led to frequent firefights, the regiment could not determine the outline of the British position. It was an unquiet night, disturbed also by the sound of burn-ing buildings and the screaming of a jammed factory whistle.

The IR 8 regimental historian insisted that the Belgian residents of the town had fired on their troops. Two members of a bicycle patrol had been wounded by buckshot. II/IR 8, which was following in reserve, had been fired on from houses, which were surrounded and burned down. Numerous civil-ians were shot.

IR 8 lost 4 OFF and 29 EM KIA, 6 OFF and 56 EM WIA. All the officer casualties except one were from III/8. The regiment's performance had been outstanding, characterised by aggressive independent action at all levels and the intelligent use of combined arms.

IR 12 attacked to the right of IR 8.[54] The regiment moved out early on 23 August and reached Baudour about 1100. Here a cavalry patrol reported that it had received fire from Tertre and had not been able to advance further. The field kitchens were brought up and the regiment had lunch. The regiment received orders to take Tertre and continue the attack to the canal crossing 2 km west of St Ghislain. On crossing the railway embankment about 400 metres from the first houses of the town III/12 took such heavy fire that the battalion commander brought up two artillery pieces to fire direct support, which drove the British into the town. At the south end of the town III/12 once again took heavy small arms and artillery fire. Supported by a MG platoon, III/12 attacked. The battalion commander and the leader of the point platoon were killed. III/12 cleared the British out of Tertre but received such heavy fire from the houses by the bridge and the canal that it could advance no further. I/12 was committed right of III/12. The regimental commander requested artillery support, but when that was not forthcoming as quickly as he wanted, he committed II/12 on the left. On crossing the railway embankment II/12 took heavy shrapnel fire, but in spite of severe losses the regiment continued the advance. The regiment worked its way to within 200 metres of the canal, where the attack finally stalled and the regiment dug in.

The German artillery was never able to fire effectively on the British positions. It was not for lack of trying. I/FAR 54 went into position 1,100–1,300 metres from the canal to engage the British infantry.[55] It soon began to take British counter-battery fire: an ammunition wagon took a direct hit and blew up. 3/54 bounded forward to get even closer. The slag heaps, houses and bushes offered the British excellent cover and concealment while restricting observation by the German artillery. Nor could the Germans locate the British artillery, which was later found to have set up behind mounds of coal.

IR 12 took the heaviest casualties of any German unit at Mons, especially in officers: it lost a battalion commander, a battalion adjutant, 3 company commanders, 6 platoon leaders (11 OFF) and 62 EM KIA, a battalion adjutant, 2 company commanders, 13 platoon leaders (16 OFF) and 401 EM wounded, 137 MIA, some of whom later returned uninjured to the regiment. This was, however, a loss rate of about 20 per cent; there were other German units during the Battle of the Frontiers which had an even higher casualty rate.

The IR 12 Myth

British accounts of Mons do not much consult German sources, which gives the imagination free rein. For example, Horsfall and Cave say that IR 12 'suffered some 3,000 casualties, inflicted by little more than 300 [British soldiers]'.[56] IR 12, including supply and medical personnel, did not number more than 3,300 men; according to Horsfall and Cave, the regiment was wiped out. In fact, IR 12 lost 490 KIA and WIA. Horsfall and Cave were willing to believe anything if it emphasised the power of 'rapid rifle fire'.

There is one exception to this 'no German sources' rule, and that is the book, mentioned in the first chapter, by a reserve captain, and commander of 2/IR 12, Walter Bloem, titled *Vormarsch* and published in English as *The Advance from Mons 1914*. Bloem was a novelist and dramatist. He didn't miss an opportunity to paint an emotional, exciting picture: according to Bloem, the fight on 23 August had been an epic and heroic battle, the regiment's losses were staggering; it had been thoroughly defeated and his reaction, and that of all the officers around him to the fight on 23 August, was gloom and doom. None of the officers tried to figure out what had gone wrong and how to avoid a repetition of it the next day. That is unprofessional and provides a key to understanding IR 12's problem.

IR 12 had suffered the highest casualties of any German regiment on 23 August but had failed to take a bridge. IR 8 and IR 24 to its left had crossed the canal – IR 24 had penetrated 6 km inland – at much less loss. The regiment on its right, IR 52, which had attacked very late, had also seized a bridge and taken numerous prisoners. Practically every German regiment except IR 12 brought artillery far forward and in every case the artillery support was decisive. Even III/IR 12 used artillery in this manner in Tertre, but when the III/12 commander was killed the trick wasn't repeated.

From Bloem's account it is clear that he and IR 12's other officers don't understand fire superiority. If the initial long-range British fire hit five or six of his men, as he says, then he needed to get his company down, establish a firing line and put some fire on suspected British positions. Instead, Bloem and the rest of the IR 12 commanders tried to advance too fast, in groups that were too large. The number of casualties that this procedure involved should have caused Bloem to slow down, but his reaction was to bull forward. It was therefore even more essential for the regimental commander to get close-range artillery, as IR 52 to his right and IR 8 to his left had done. He did not.

IR 12 also faced a problem that no other German regiment had to confront on 23 August – British artillery fire. II/IR 12 suffered particularly. Elsewhere at Mons the British artillery was practically inert. The only reason the British artillery played a role here was because the guns were brought so far forward that not all of them could be recovered, and two guns had to be abandoned.

Bloem's emotional account was a godsend for Anglophone historians. Few of them spoke German, and here was a German source that was available in English, which told them exactly what they wanted to hear. Following the example of the British official history, John Terraine wrote:[57]

That evening his battalion commander said to him: 'You are my sole and only support ... you are the only company commander left in the battalion ... the battalion is a mere wreck, my proud, beautiful battalion!' Bloem commented: 'our first battle is a heavy, an unheard-of heavy, defeat, and against the English [sic] we laughed at.'

Terraine expressly said that IR 12's experience was typical for German regiments at Mons: 'It was the same story everywhere'. This passage from Bloem is cited by Horsfall and Cave in their *Mons*[58] and David Ascoli in *The Mons Star*.[59] (Ascoli spoke German, but didn't bother to consult other German sources.) To reinforce the point, the British official added a quote from Bloem:

> The regiment was withdrawn a quarter of a mile as soon as it was dark, and spent an anxious night, for, as the colonel [regimental commander] said 'if the English [sic] have the slightest suspicion of our condition, and counter-attack, they will simply run over us.'

This passage was also quoted by Ascoli, with embellishments: Ascoli says it was a battalion commander complaining that his battalion had taken over 600 casualties, when in fact the entire regiment had taken 600 casualties.[60] The British official history used the IR 12 battle to contend that, 'The Germans imagined that they were everywhere opposed by machine guns only, not realising the intensity of British rapid fire'.[61] Terraine quotes Bloem and concluded: 'The Germans were convinced that the British had brought into action great numbers of machine guns; they had never dreamt of anything like the "mad minute" of concentrated rifle-fire which the British infantry had perfected.'[62] There is no support for the 'machine gun myth' in any German literature concerning IR 12's fight – not even in Bloem.

The British historians decided that Bloem's book was representative of the German 1st Army's experiences at Mons as a whole. It was proof that everywhere British rifle fire had cut down masses of German troops, and that the Germans were reduced to demoralised wrecks. It is the basis for the assertion that the German 1st Army took 6,000–10,000 casualties on 23 August. Unfortunately for the British army and its historians, the experience of IR 12 was the exception.

British 14th Brigade

The 14th Brigade defended on the 5th Division left. 1/East Surrey held about 1,600 metres of canal from the railway bridge west of Herbières on the right to the road bridge on the left. The Duke of Cornwall's Light Infantry (DOCLI) was on the brigade left, 2/Suffolk and 2/Manchester were in reserve.

The East Surrey Regiment defended a bridgehead 150–200 metres north of the railway bridge with C Company, while the MG Section was located near the bridge itself.[63] B Company held a shallow bridgehead near the road bridge on the left, D Company held the canal in between, with A Company in reserve behind B. The battalion began digging in at 0600. A Company and a company from the Suffolks were moved forward to help C clear fields of fire and prepare positions. By 1200 the trenches were over a metre (4.5 feet) deep and with a field of fire 300–500 metres. 'Throughout the morning various contradictory orders were received by the Battalion as to the holding of the canal position and as to when a retirement would take place, and owing to the rapid development of the attack it would seem that the officers and men in the trenches on the west of the railway were not aware that retirement might, under certain circumstances, take place before darkness came on.' Command confusion at the brigade level was to cost the Surreys dearly.

At 1300 the Germans began firing at C Company. Elements of A Company and the Suffolks remained to assist the defence. The C Company commander moved forward and was mortally wounded by MG fire. The Surrey history said: 'On the east of the railway the German attack was heavy, their infantry coming on extended at one-pace interval and supported by a large number of machine guns.' The Surreys inflicted 'heavy losses' and their MG fire prevented the Germans from crossing the railway line to attack the western portion of C Company's position. By 1600 the fighting east of the railway line was at close quarters.

At 1800 close-range German artillery fire had forced the KOSB on the Surrey's right to fall back to the south side of the canal. On order, the elements of C Company to the east of the canal crossed to the south side using a barge, covered by fire from A Company on the south bank. By now the two C Company platoons on the west side of the railway line were also under attack. They did not expect to withdraw and did not see the signal to do so. The Germans passed over the empty positions on the east side of the railway line and attacked these platoons in the right flank and rear. The greater part of these platoons were killed or captured. The captain who had assumed command of C Company was wounded and captured; on 24 August he was visited by two German officers, 'who brought him a bottle of wine as a present and complimented him on the fine shooting of his men'. By this time B Company was also under attack by infantry with artillery support, was ordered to withdraw to the south bank and both bridges were supposed to have been blown up. According to Horsfall and Cave the Surreys took 221 casualties.[64]

German IR 52

At 1245 IR 52, the second regiment of the 10th Infantry Brigade, occupied an assembly area in Tertre. At 1300 6/IR 52 was committed to lengthen the right flank of IR 12. They received flanking fire from a brick factory and the railway station east of Hamdide, so 7/52 and a MG platoon were committed against them. At 1600 the 10th Brigade ordered IR 52 to take the bridges south-east of Hamdide. I/52 sent 3/52 and 4/52 and a MG platoon to the right flank of 5/52, and kept 1/52 and 2/52 in regimental reserve.

After a time IR 52 recognised that the British were not only set up at the bridge barricades and the south bank of the canal, but also in bushes and houses on the north bank. An attack on one of these houses failed. A platoon of two guns from 1/FAR 54 was brought forward to engage the British in Hamdide and on the canal at 400 metres range. The British fire became weaker and at 1800 1/52 and 2/52 were committed on the right flank. They reached the brickworks and railway embankment east of Hamdide, swung to the south towards the railway bridge. The British troops in the bushes north of the canal were overrun and seventy-two prisoners from the Surreys were taken. The attacking Germans and retreating British reached the bridge at the same time at 1930. The British attempt to destroy the bridge failed; though damaged, it was still useable and 2/52 stormed across and established a bridgehead. IR 52 lost 3 OFF and 24 EM KIA, 3 OFF and 125 EM WIA and 11 EM MIA, 166 casualties in total.

Terraine's description of the IR 52 fight is a summary of the one in the official history, and is just as tendentious:[65]

> It was the same story everywhere ... at Les Herbières, the German 52nd Infantry Regiment began well by dribbling men in small parties up to the canal bank to drive in the 2nd King's Own Scottish Borderers. Then, after a short bombardment, the same regiment attacked the railway bridge, held by the 1st East Surrey regiment, with two battalions in mass; they were shot to pieces, and decisively repulsed, with small casualties to the East Surreys.

IR 52 did not attack in mass; the regiment took only 5 per cent casualties, which hardly constitutes being 'shot to pieces', and far from being repulsed took seventy-two prisoners and a bridge.

The British still held the canal bank and the bridge north-east of St Ghislain. An attempt by 12/52 to take that bridge was stopped 100 metres from its objective with serious casualties. II/FAR 54 shot St Ghislain in flames. A patrol that night found the undamaged road bridge to the west of the railway bridge and secured it.

II/IR 48 was ordered to attack to the right of IR 52 at 1500.[66] The battalion advanced in a thin skirmisher line (the regiment regularly used three-pace intervals) and made good progress in the bushy terrain, which provided concealment. By dark it was level with the IR 52 right flank, not far from the canal and putting flanking fire on the British positions. The rest of the regiment remained in reserve behind the right flank. The regiment does not appear to have taken significant casualties.

Note: Photo numbers refer to point of view designated by numbered arrows on Fig. 21: Br 5th Division, 26 August, page 231.

Above: 1. Suffolk position seen from the north-east. Trees in centre are at Suffolk monument.

Below: 2. Suffolk position seen from the north.

Above: Infantry advancing by bounds. The squad leader observes the enemy.

Below: 3. Suffolk position seen from the south.

Above: 4. KOYLI position seen from the north-east.

Below: Infantry advancing by bounds. The soldier on the right has his entrenching tool ready. The two soldiers on the left provide covering fire.

Left: A cavalry patrol. The troopers are dispersed and alert, and armed with lance and carbine.

Below: 5. 15th Brigade position seen from the east

Above: 6. Terrain over which IR 36 attacked, seen from the east.

Below: Artillery advancing under fire at a gallop.

Above: 7. KOYLI/KOSB position seen from the north.

Left: Infantry advancing by bounds.

Above: Infantry in the assault.

Below: 8. 15th Brigade and 9th Brigade positions seen from the north.

Left: Troops on the firing line provide covering fire while other troops bound forward. In the centre of the picture is the platoon leader (with binoculars). One of the range estimators observes the company commander to the rear, while a second observes forward. Supporting artillery fire lands in front.

Note: Photo 9 refers to point of view designated by numbered arrow on Fig. 22: BR 3rd Division, 26 August, page 246.

Below: 9. IR 93 attack seen from the south-east.

The III AK Attack

III AK had crossed the canal at three points. 6 ID had penetrated 3 km south from the canal, IR 8 of 5 ID about a kilometre and a half. IR 52 held the bridge at Hamdide. The attack of the left wing of III AK had been halted solely by darkness. The 1st Army's fascination with the possibility that the British were at Tournai cost III AK four hours. If the attack had begun at 1000 instead of 1400, there is no reason to believe that 6 ID, which still had two fresh regiments at its disposal, would not have taken Frameries at least, and thereby have ruptured the entire British position.

British historians contend that by the end of the day the Germans were unwilling to attack out of fear of British rifle fire. In describing the British withdrawal on the evening of 23 August, Terraine wrote: 'The Germans, after the rough treatment they had already received, were understandably slow in following up these determined men.'[67] Once again, Terraine does not support this assertion with evidence of what the Germans were actually thinking and doing. In fact, the German sources show that the Germans continued to advance until they had reached their objectives or darkness set in.

1/Duke of Cornwall's Light Infantry

On 22 August A Company and one platoon of B held the canal from the Surrey's position to the bridge at Le Petit Crépin, and three platoons of B held a bridgehead on the north side of the canal at the bridge.[68] These platoons were well dug in and camouflaged. A MG was positioned to fire down the road. About 400 metres to the front the field of fire was blocked by rail cars standing in a siding.

On 22 August the battalion received a steady stream of reports from British cavalry of the approach of German troops, but on 23 August German cavalry approached unhindered straight up to the Cornwalls' three-man outpost, which ambushed them. The outpost was quite pleased with itself, but most of the cavalry escaped. A second Cornwall outpost engaged another cavalry patrol and, to top it off, a machine gun fired on a third patrol at 700 metres range and hit one horse. The Cornwalls' position was now well known to the Germans. Belatedly, the divisional cavalry went to Pommeroeul, 400 metres to the front, made contact with the Germans and returned, without giving a report to the Cornwalls.

At 1400 the Cornwalls completely changed their defensive dispositions. C Company was brought forward to defend to the left of the bridgehead; three platoons of B Company took the right side. The MG was withdrawn and replaced by that curious but common British defensive position, a breastwork built across the road (this time out of paving stones) and garrisoned with an officer and ten men with orders to hang on for as long as possible and then retire.

The Cornwalls were attacked at 1645. The troops on the breastwork opened fire at 750–800 metres range, naturally at German troops in 'one solid mass and occupying the entire roadway ... every shot must have taken effect'. The Cornwalls then immediately retreated to the south side of the canal and blew up the bridge, passed through 2/Manchester, which was holding a position on the Haine River, and kept moving until they bivouacked at Marliere, just north of Elouges. The Cornwalls' history notes that the Germans were soon across the canal and, supported by artillery, were engaging British troops on the Haine. The battalion had lost one KIA, five WIA. After the Cornwalls had passed over the Haine Bridge, the Manchesters blew it at 1830.[69] They engaged German troops crossing the canal and withdrew to a position north of Wasmes at 2300. The 14th Brigade had given up two significant water obstacles practically without a fight.

German 7 ID

On the evening of 22 August the German IV AK stopped with the 7 ID near Silly and the 8 ID near Ollignies, 25 to 30 km from the Canal du Centre. For any other army, such an approach march followed by an attack on a prepared position would have been unthinkable, but it was well within the capabilities of the German army of August 1914.

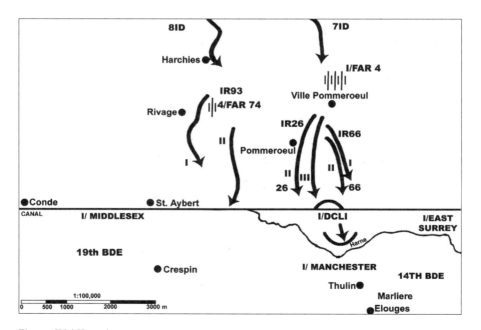

Fig. 14: IV AK, 23 August.

A patrol from Hussar R 8 reached the railway yard at Pommeroeul in the early morning of 23 August, where it took fire, losing one man and a horse killed, one man wounded.[70] Nevertheless, the patrol took cover behind a garden hedge, observed and sent back a report.

7 ID was marching on Ville-Pommeroeul when it received word at 1400 that the British were on the Condé Canal north of Thulin. IR 26 was the advance guard regiment, with 10/III/26 in the lead.[71] As the company left the woods north of Ville-Pommeroeul at 1650 it unexpectedly received heavy fire from the town at close range (probably the British cavalry). 10/26 deployed to the right against a railway embankment, 9/26 to the left of the road, 12/26 to the right. 11/26 was initially kept in reserve, but was later committed on both sides of the road. The commander of III/26 said the deployment of the battalion on terrain that was completely flat meadow, criss-crossed with ditches and hedges, 'was conducted like on the Anger [the local training area] in Magdeburg. It was a joy to see the dash and aggressiveness of our men, in spite of the heavy enemy fire, most of which was fortunately too high'.

III/26, with two MG platoons, was deployed against Ville-Pommeroeul and the canal, while II/26 with a MG platoon attacked on the right towards the railway embankment. I/26 followed III/26. Later 1/26 and 2/26 were deployed to the east of III/26; 3/26 and 4/26 protected I/FAR 4.

FAR 4 deployed I/4 to the left of the road and II to the right, along the south treeline.[72] This position was not satisfactory: it was open to the enemy while at the same time had poor observation of the canal. British artillery fire landed near the exit from the woods. II/FAR 4 moved through the woods to avoid this fire, which caused such a delay that it succeeded in bringing only 4/FAR 4 into position by 1815. I/FAR 4 engaged enemy infantry on the canal. It also combined an analysis of shell craters, enemy fuse range settings and map reconnaissance to estimate the British artillery position and conduct unobserved counter-battery fire, which apparently worked – the British artillery ceased fire.

On the right, I/26 moved through a railway yard, the boxcars still containing British equipment. A platoon leader, Lieutenant Freytag, said the troops conducted themselves well during their baptism of fire. The platoon used the boxcars for cover, but the cars had been uncoupled and there were open spaces between them. The British watched these spots well, and each time the platoon crossed the open areas, with very large intervals between the men, the British opened fire, but Freytag said, 'thank God they almost always fired too high'. The platoon moved through the freight yard, took a breather behind a pile of coal, and made a short 50-metre bound to a factory building that was on the canal. They saw a British trench 500 metres south of the canal. The platoon moved laterally behind a hedge to a house on the north side of the destroyed bridge. Freytag's movement was a model for the use of cover and concealment.

The III/26 attack made good progress until it came up to the canal bridge, which had been destroyed. A standing firefight developed, with both sides using houses and the canal embankment for cover. 10/26 tried to cross the canal on planks that they had brought up, but took casualties and stopped.

The artillery regimental commander, who had already lost two horses to enemy artillery fire, went to the south side of the village on reconnaissance, and ordered I/FAR 4 to displace forward. 1/FAR 4 moved south of the railway line and west of the road, 2/FAR 4 set up on the railway embankment east of the road. Observation was still limited by trees and it was becoming dark, so the two batteries never fired from these positions. The regimental commander therefore ordered a platoon from 2/FAR 4 to manhandle two guns right up to the bridge site and destroy a British MG at 200 metres range. The effect was immediate: the MG ceased fire and the farm the British occupied burst into flames. Covered by artillery and MG fire, Freytag's platoon crossed the canal on 10/26's planks, and was followed by 9/26.

It was now dark. The next goal was the burning farm. Freytag decided that marching straight down the road to Thuin was 'not advisable'. The terrain to the left of the road looked trafficable. After ten steps he encountered a ditch, beyond which was an orchard. Moving quietly through this, he deployed his platoon on line and had them fix bayonets. At a low command the line advanced. The platoon cut through a wire fence, crossed two ditches and reached the farm, which was not occupied. The platoon began to take both enemy and friendly fire, so it lay down in the farmyard and waited for daylight. They were joined by the command group of III/26, 11/26 and elements of 10/26.

IR 66 had followed IR 26 as night was falling.[73] There was 'tremendous' British fire from the canal, but all of it was too high and nobody was hit. (One possible explanation for the British firing too high is that they had set their sights at too long a range.) Crossing the ditches filled with water was difficult, especially for the smaller troops, but by 1900 the regiment had reached the canal. In spite of their exhaustion, the troops wanted to get at the British.

At 2300 Musketeer Hermann Voigtländer swam the canal and established that the British had gone. The bridge train and Engineer Battalion 4 arrived and II/66 crossed on pontoons. It moved 400 metres to the south, linked up with the elements of IR 26 that had crossed and dug in. IR 66 had few casualties; FAR 4 lost 1 EM KIA, 3 EM WIA.

1/Middlesex

Between 1400 and 1500 the 19th Brigade relieved the 5th Cavalry Brigade on the canal to the west of the 14th Brigade, with 1/Middlesex on the right, next to the Cornwalls, and 1/Cameronians on the left.[74] 1/Middlesex deployed B

Company to hold Lock 5 on the right and A Company the St Aybert bridge on the left. The Germans attacked B Company at 1700. German MG fire forced the Middlesex away from the houses lining the south bank, but the Middlesex still kept the Germans from crossing. At 0230 on 24 August the Middlesex withdrew 20 km to the south, to Jenlain. The battalion lost 4 EM KIA, 1 OFF and 12 EM WIA.

8 ID

IR 93 was the advance guard for 8ID on the IV AK right.[75] It moved from Ollignies to the south-west at 0630. At 1500 the regiment had occupied alarm quarters in Basècles and pushed security elements towards the canal at Condé. At 1530 the regiment was ordered to continue the march due south with I/93 and II/93 to Harchies; III/93 would follow after it had collected the security detachments. The 1st Army's indecision had cost the regiment an invaluable hour. As the regiment left the wood to the north of Harchies the cavalry advanced guard squadron 500 metres to the front drew fire from the town and came towards IR 93 at a gallop. The point company, 9/93, deployed and advanced on the town while the other three companies deployed and followed, but the enemy had left and 9/93 occupied the town without firing a shot. Patrols reported that the canal was strongly defended and the noise of battle in the 7 ID sector could be heard. IR 93 was ordered to seize a crossing over the canal. At 1720 the regimental commander issued his attack order. He said that an enemy force of unknown strength held the bridge over the canal 4 km south of Harchies. II/93 would attack frontally against the bridge over the Condé Canal, I/93 would seize the bridge over the Canal d'Antoing at Rivage, and attack the Condé bridge from the west. The MG Company was regimental reserve; III/93, which had just reached Harchies, was brigade reserve. The regimental commander would follow II/93. The terrain was difficult; hedges and small woods restricted visibility and made coordination of the attack problematic. It was growing dark and there was little time for reconnaissance or preparation.

When II/93 was 1,300 metres from the Canal d'Antoing the cavalry took fire. The point company, 8/93, deployed two platoons, which bounded quickly forward. The battalion commander deployed 7/93 and 6/93 to the right of 8/93; 5/93 followed in the middle. The canal was reached on both sides of the bridge and the battalion took its first casualties. A lieutenant with a few men raced over the bridge, which then was raised behind him, cutting him off. A sergeant and a soldier climbed up the bridge and lowered it with their weight. Once the bridge was secure, 8/93 stormed across. The enemy, an estimated platoon, withdrew to the Condé Canal, 800 metres to the south.

The enemy opened fire from the south bank and from houses on the north bank, and the regimental commander committed the MG Company. 4/FAR 74 unlimbered south of Harchies and fired on the houses.[76] With this support, II/93 advanced by rapid bounds in spite of heavy enemy fire. As it approached the canal, the British evacuated the houses and blew up the bridge. The MG Company commander, far ahead of his guns, was shot and killed, as was one of the MG lieutenants. It was not possible to force a crossing without artillery support, but it was by now too dark to direct artillery fire. Bridging material was also necessary. The battle was therefore broken off.

I/93 crossed the Canal d'Antoing unopposed, but found movement slow due to numerous deep and swampy ditches and barbed-wire fences. In addition, it took fire from the right. It reached II/93 only after dark. I/93 took over security on the canals and II/93 bivouacked behind it. The regiment had lost 2 OFF and 11 EM KIA, 1 OFF and 24 EM WIA. 4/FAR 74 had expended 157 rounds.

British Command and Control

There is little evidence in the British official history of command and control above the battalion level during the battle. The 9th Brigade issued withdrawal orders to the Royal Fusiliers at 1400 and to the Scots Fusiliers at 1500; the 8th Brigade also manoeuvred the Royal Irish, but in general British battalions fought where they stood and retreated when they were forced to, without any intervention at the division, corps or army levels.[77] Battalions not in contact stayed on the canal until far into the night.

At 2040 BEF headquarters instructed II Corps to defend on 24 August on a position about 4–5 km south of the canal. The withdrawal was disorganised, with some units not pulling back until midnight, but by dawn on 24 August most of the units were in position.

At about 2400 Lieutenant Spears, the British liaison officer to the French 5th Army, reported to BEF HQ that the 5th was going to retreat early on 24 August. At 2300 the corps chiefs of staff had been summoned to BEF HQ to receive orders. At 0100 on 24 August the Chief of the General Staff gave a verbal order to withdraw about 13 km to a line 11 km long from the west of Maubeuge to the west of Bavai. The corps chiefs of staff were told to work out the details! It was not until noon on 24 August that the corps chiefs of staff could actually meet to conduct the coordination, and by then it was too late; each corps withdrew on its own.[78]

At 0100 on 24 August Joffre belatedly telegrammed the BEF to say the 5th Army would fall back with its left on Maubeuge. In a second telegram he asked the BEF to delay between Maubeuge and Valenciennes towards Cambrai, right flank on Le Cateau. The BEF informed Joffre that it was falling back to a position Maubeuge–Valenciennes.

Evaluation

In British history, Mons is usually accounted a great victory because the BEF inflicted disproportionate casualties on the Germans. British casualties were put at 1,600. Following the example of the official history, British accounts are replete with lurid descriptions of German masses being mown down in rows. IR 12 is made out to be representative of the entire 1st Army. The official history insists that, 'Judged by the units whose casualties are now known, the enemy's losses must have been very heavy'.[79] Later British histories were not so circumspect, and one put German casualties at 6–10,000. Simple mathematics would make even a moderately sceptical historian cautious of these figures, for if true then each engaged German regiment would have suffered between 500 and 833 casualties.

Twelve infantry regiments of IX AK and III AK were seriously engaged on 23 August. Ten of those unit histories state the regiment's casualties and these add up to 1,692. IR 12 was the highest (627), the next highest was IR 75 with 276. Three regiments had fewer than 200 casualties; five more had fewer than 100. IR 90 had about 75 wounded, probably 100 casualties altogether. If one assumes that IR 24 had the same casualties as IR 8 (95), the adjacent unit with a similar situation and mission, then the total comes to under 1,900. Throw in IV AK casualties (about 50), and artillery and cavalry casualties (fewer than 25), and the German 1st Army suffered no more than 2,000 casualties. Instead of the casualty ratio being about 4:1 or 6:1, it was actually 1.25:1. As a proportion of the forces engaged, British losses were far higher than the German: eleven British battalions took roughly the same number of casualties as thirty-six German battalions. British accounts of massacring German hordes were wishful thinking or worse.

Since the disproportionate body count is a fiction, Mons can now be evaluated in terms of real tactics used and military effectiveness. The British army had only begun serious preparation for European war in the two or three years before Mons. It should therefore come as no surprise that the British army demonstrated serious deficiencies. There was little basis for the decision to fight at Mons. The defensive position at Mons was poorly chosen and the allocation of forces downright incompetent. Command and control above battalion level was almost non-existent and there was neither manoeuvre nor any counter-attacks. There was no British combined-arms cooperation; the cavalry division abdicated its counter-reconnaissance mission, the engineers failed to destroy over two-thirds of the bridges and the infantry received virtually no artillery support. The British army fought a colonial battle, relying on rifle fire in a static defence.

At the tactical level the German army showed what forty years of hard and serious work could accomplish. The mission was the most difficult imaginable: hasty attack on a very strong defensive position. The German army executed this mission superbly. The Germans fought a combined-arms battle. Tactical cavalry reconnaissance and security were good. In spite of great terrain difficulties, artillery support was usually decisive, with the gunners frequently bringing their pieces down to ranges that would have made Napoleon's great artillerist, Senarmont, proud. Engineer support was timely. Junior leaders displayed a high degree of tactical skill and initiative. The infantry showed its mastery of fire and movement by repeatedly crossing open ground to capture heavily-defended bridges. By the end of the day the British canal position had been broken along its entire length. The IX Corps commander in particular had concentrated his *Schwerpunkt* against a far inferior enemy force, quickly penetrated the enemy defence on a broad front, taken the decisive terrain, and driven deep into the enemy rear.

It is often contended that German reconnaissance failed to locate the BEF: this is incorrect. German cavalry was unhindered by British counter-reconnaissance, was able to ride right up to the British defensive line and provided excellent reports of the British position.

The German weakness was at the operational level. The 1st Army commander and chief of staff acted on the preconceived idea that the British would be at Lille, even if this idea conflicted with reliable reconnaissance reports, and slowed the Army's movement to the south in order to be able to move towards Lille.

The German official history has clear prejudices in favour of the 1st Army command team, Kluck and Kuhl, and against Bülow, the 2nd Army commander. It states that Bülow attached the left flank of the 1st Army too closely to the right flank of the 2nd, that Bülow prevented Kluck from aiming his left flank at Mons, which in turn prevented Kluck from turning the British left flank. The official history was being disingenuous. In its discussion of operations on 22 August, the German official history admitted that Kluck and Kuhl had no idea where the British left was located.[80] Moreover, IX Corps, the left flank of the 1st Army, was obviously attacking Mons, just as Kluck insisted it should. Nevertheless, Kluck failed to turn the British left flank, not because of Bülow's interference, but because Kluck and Kuhl would not let go of their preconceived idea that the British were at Lille.

In fact, at the end of the day on 23 August, Kluck and Kuhl still thought there were only two or three British divisions to its front, and didn't come to the realisation that the British force numbered four infantry and a cavalry division until the evening of 24 August.[81]

Given the location on 22 August of HKK 2 and the corps of the 1st Army, there was no way the Germans were going to decisively defeat II Corps on 23 August. However, had the 1st Army leadership freed itself of its preconceived ideas and arrived on the night of 22 August at the 'school solution' to this simple operational problem, and attacked without reservation against II Corps with IX, III and IV AK, then on 23 August III AK would have penetrated as far as the British second position, and early on 24 August IV AK would have had bridges across the canal, and the II Corps position on 24 August would have been dire indeed.

24 August

On the morning of 24 August the centre of the BEF line was about 5 km south of Mons. I Corps held roughly the same position as on the previous day, with the left flank being extended somewhat to the west. The I Corps front was now 16 km long. II Corps in the centre held 17 km of front from the south-east of Mons at Nouvelles to Boussu-Bois, the Cavalry Division with the 19th Brigade screened the left flank at Elouges-Audregnies.

At 0200 the I Corps chief of staff informed his commander that I Corps was to cover the withdrawal of II Corps. Nevertheless, by 0500 on 24 August the main bodies of both I Corps divisions, as well as the Cavalry Division and the 19th Brigade, were on the road, while II Corps was still in position: 3rd Division could not begin to withdraw until 0800, 5th Division was defending in place.[1] BEF headquarters was doing nothing to coordinate the withdrawal, which was completely out of control.

The German 1st and 2nd Armies did not communicate with each other on 23 August; the telephone connection did not work and neither sent a liaison officer. This was not only indicative of a poisonous command environment, it would have repercussions for IX AK, which had no idea what was going on in its rear.

The 1st Army's situation report to OHL late on 23 August said: 'Today made contact with the British Army St Ghislain-Mons, will attack tomorrow on the line Condé-Mons. Request cooperation of HKK 2, in the direction of Denain, which unfortunately wants to operate towards Courtai [north-west].' Denain is west of Valenciennes, and would have put HKK 2 in an excellent position beyond the British left flank.

The 1st Army expected the battle to resume in place on 24 August. Its intent was to prevent the British from retreating to the west and push it into Maubeuge.

IX AK was ordered to advance south-west with its right flank on Bavai, III AK with its left flank on Bavai, IV AK 10 km west of Bavai. II AK and IV RK were to begin marching at 0100, II AK to reach Condé behind IV AK, IV RK the west of Ath behind the army left wing. AOK 1 did not issue any further orders to the corps during combat on 24 August.[2]

British II Corps

The 3rd Division was still on the II Corps right, 5th on the corps left. In the 3rd Division sector, according to the British official history, the 8th Brigade, on the division right, had no difficulty in withdrawing at 0800.[3] The 7th Brigade, at Ciply, in the centre almost got away, but 2/South Lancashire was 'enfiladed by machine guns from the slag heaps about Frameries and lost between two and three hundred men'. At 0900 the 9th Brigade at Frameries on the division left also pulled back, breaking contact after some street fighting in the town. German artillery was ineffective. That is all the official history has to say about the 3rd Division. It doesn't mention the Germans at all, other than the boilerplate comment that 3rd Division had 'inflicted on them heavy losses'. Nevertheless, the 3rd Division lost 550 men.

The British official history's description of the 5th Division battle is only seven pages long. It is confusing, and Map 7 for 24 August is worthless, giving the impression that even the official history had an imperfect picture of the 5th Division's fight.[4] It says that three battalions of the 5th Brigade, a 2nd Division (I Corps) unit, held the 5th Division right at Pâturages. The 5th Brigade withdrew before the Germans attacked, but that is not mentioned. The Bedfordshire (15th Brigade), on the 5th Division extreme right, and the Dorsetshire (15th Brigade, but detached to the 13th Brigade), would begin to withdraw at 1100. The next unit to the west was the 13th Brigade, with 1/Royal West Kent at Wasmes, 2/Duke of Wellington's on the rail line north-west of Wasmes, 2/KOYLI to its left, 2/KOSB at Camp des Sarts.[5] They withdrew at an unspecified time, all except for 2/Duke of Wellington's, which didn't get the order and lost 400 men. The British official history says that this battalion stopped IR 66 and IR 26,[6] which were actually at Elouges, 6 km to the west. At this time the 14th Brigade on the 5th Division left, whose sector had been quiet, also withdrew.

On the BEF left, the Cavalry Division withdrew, exposing the 5th Division flank. 1/Norfolk and 1/Cheshire were sent from the 15th Brigade, the 5th Division reserve, to guard the flank and the Cheshires were destroyed in the process. This fight takes up another seven pages, as much as the rest of the entire 5th Division battle.

The British official history's description of tactical combat continued to follow the standard format. German mass attacks were 'mown down', with 'very heavy losses'; they were usually 'thrown back' but sometimes 'checked'. The conclusion was that the Germans were 'severely punished'. The Germans were in awe of British rifle firepower and never pressed the attack. British units usually withdrew unmolested. The entire description of the fight, besides being confused and tactically simple-minded, is wrong.

British 7th Brigade

The British 7th Brigade was the 3rd Division reserve on 23 August and saw little combat. It maintained the same positions on 24 August, with the 2/Royal Irish Rifles on the right at the railway line south of Hyon, 3/Worcestershire in the centre and 2/South Lancashire on the left, with 1/Wiltshire in reserve.

3/Worstershire recorded being bombarded by German artillery all morning on 24 August, with a German infantry attack beginning at 0600.[7] This developed into a standing firefight at about 500 yards range. The battalion was then ordered to withdraw, losing about fifty men in the process. The Worcestershires were opposed by IR 84.[8] Early that morning some of the German artillery had been found to be very far forward and unprotected, so two companies of I/84 were sent forward to cover it. This led to the firefight with the A Company of the Worcestershires. When the Worcestershires withdrew, the I/84 companies conducted salvo pursuit fire, which caused many Worcestershire casualties. The IR 84 history did not mention casualties. Neither IR 84 nor IR 86 advanced until the afternoon.

The South Lancashire position was exceptionally poor; it exposed the Lancashire's left flank and offered the Germans the opportunity to enfilade the entire line.[9] The Lancashires tried to cover this flank by bending back D Company.

The Germans did not even attack the 7th Brigade front, but I/64, which was the left-flank unit of III AK, and was covering the attack on Frameries, occupied a superb position in a railway cutting about 400 metres from the Lancashire's left flank, enfilading the Lancashire line. I/64 was not even primarily concerned with the Lancashires, but was intent on capturing Frameries. Nevertheless, the Lancashire battalion commander was convinced that he was being attacked by two battalions and asked for help from the Brigade reserve. He was ordered to withdraw. The Lancashire commander was also convinced that D Company had 'simply mowed down the enemy' and that it had accounted for 'something like 1,000 Germans', which is absurd. The D Company commander was killed, 12 of the 16 men in the machine gun section were casualties, both guns were lost and A and B Companies had taken 'tremendous' losses. On 31 August the battalion counted 14 OFF and 'about' 400 EM. Since it did not take part at Le Cateau, its losses on 24 August were probably 13 OFF and 580 EM. The MGs were not

replaced until 22 September and 'the absence of this additional fire-power was
felt in all the engagements up to this date'.

IX AK

IX AK was in no particular hurry. The concept of the 1st Army operation was to
turn the British left and push them into Maubeuge. An attack by IX AK would
accomplish exactly the opposite. The situation in the IX AK rear was also unclear.
To the front, the British artillery shelled the German infantry, which led to an
artillery duel. IR 86 noted that it had spent the second half of the night south
of Hyon digging in, and the British artillery had little effect.[10] About 1200 the
British artillery fire ceased and the regiment moved out, fully deployed, to Ciply,
4 km south of Mons. The British had left behind packs and greatcoats; some had
even thrown away weapons, 'which the fusiliers found completely incomprehensible'. On the other hand, the German troops loved the 'magnificent thick British
coats', the British entrenching tools, and the jam and biscuits. IR 89 found two
drums of the Royal Berkshires, which were shipped back to the castle museum in
the regimental garrison town.

The IX AK movement on 25 August would take it around the fortress of
Maubeuge. Apparently in order to avoid observation and fire from the fortress,
IX AK conducted a night march on 24–25 August. Beginning at 2400 IR 86
conducted an exhausting 6 km march to Eugies. IR 90 was assembled on 25
August after two hours' rest but lay in the sun all day and had already made itself
comfortable for the night when the order to move out came. It took six hours for
the regiment to march 12 km, with the column continually stopping and starting.
Exhaustion competed with hunger. At 0200 IR 90 bivouacked in a field as best
it could.[11]

British 9th Brigade

British sources say little concerning the 9th Brigade in its defence of Frameries
on 24 August. The brigade is not even entered on Map 7 of the official history
and receives about ten lines in the official history itself. The histories of the Royal
Scots Fusiliers and Royal Fusiliers are also no help. The description of the battles for Frameries in Horsfall and Cave's *Mons* is incomprehensible for want of
a useful map; the map they use of 'Smith-Dorrien's right flank on 24 August',
copied from the Worcestershire history, shows 5th Brigade positions, but the 5th
Brigade withdrew before the fight.[12]

An exception is the history of the Lincolnshire regiment, which defended
an orchard on the north-west side of Frameries.[13] The battalion held the north

and west sides of an orchard, which meant that during the German attack B Company, on the west side, would be enfiladed from the north. To its front were numerous slag heaps. The German artillery bombardment began at 0400. The German infantry attacked in groups of six to eight men, attempting to move from corn stook to corn stook, but were stopped by the Lincolns' fire. The Lincolns' MGs were quickly knocked out and the section leader killed. The German attack stalled and the Lincolns, who were now the brigade rearguard, were able to break contact and withdraw. They lost 4 OFF and 130 EM; the wounded and the stretcher-bearers were captured, with only the walking wounded escaping. In order to 'march light' the battalion abandoned their great coats and packs, which 'had been a terrible burden in the tropical heat'.

German 6 ID

In the 6 ID sector, the 12th Brigade ordered its regiments to attack towards Frameries at 0330, IR 24 on the left, IR 20 on the right. The terrain was unusual; first the coal and slag heaps and industrial buildings of Flénu-Cuesmes, then 2 km of open ground, finally the mining towns of Pâturages and Frameries, where the British were assumed to be.

I/FAR 3 was to fire support for IR 24.[14] It sent forward artillery patrols, which established that the British had dug in at Frameries, and set up its guns so far forward that they took heavy small-arms fire. FAR 39 went into open positions at 0430 north of the Wasmes–Frameries railway line and immediately began engaging trenches, British infantry in the slag heaps near Frameries and La Bouverie, and the houses in the towns.[15] Target acquisition was not easy; the artillery said the British were masters in the use of the terrain. The British also fired a great deal of ineffective counter-battery, as their shrapnel burst too high.

IR 24 attacked with I/24 on the left of the Flenu–Frameries road, III/24 on the right, II/24 in brigade reserve.[16] I/24 attacked with 1/24 and 4/24 in front, 2/24 in reserve under cover behind the railway embankment. 3/24 was protecting the artillery. III/24 had 11/24 and 12/24 on line, while 9/24 and 10/24 were behind the right flank. The MG Company had used the night to prepare firing positions in the upper stories of buildings, including the station master's house, which allowed them to fire over their comrades' heads. The artillery began its preparatory fires at dawn, the attack started at 0700. It was conducted 'just like on a manoeuvre' – the companies began the firefight at 800 metres, advanced by bounds to an assault position, the reserves came forward and the regiment conducted the assault; except that this time it was live fire. IR 24 said that the British allowed the Germans to close in before opening fire with their machine guns, and then, if necessary, ruthlessly sacrificed the machine guns and their crews in order to cover their retreat. IR 24, attacking across an open field, was at a

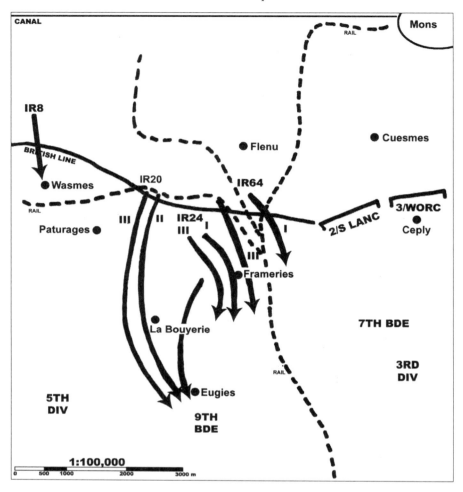

Fig. 15: GE 6 ID, 24 August.

significant disadvantage. The ground was baked hard, causing bullets to ricochet. The regiment was firing into the sun. If this had been an exercise, the regimental historian said the umpires would have given the victory to the British. The first hour of the attack showed how difficult such an operation was in the face of modern weapons, in spite of the fact that, by the standards of the time, it had been preceded by a powerful artillery preparation.

The regimental history faulted the lack of suppressive rifle fire. The troops could not see the enemy, and instead of firing at likely locations, didn't fire at all: it said that the German army had placed too much emphasis on engaging only visible targets. On the previous day some companies had fired only one to three rounds per man, and this 'serious mistake' was repeated today. They should have fired on the edge of the towns, but in the smoke and dust could hardly make them out. The troops were in their first battle and became excited, especially when they took casualties. In addition, the effectiveness of the artillery preparation had been considerably overestimated. In spite of all this, the troops heroically carried out the attack, but it cost 'disproportionally high, bloody casualties'. The FAR 3 regimental history, however, faulted IR 24 for failing to wait until their preparatory fire had made an effect. FAR 36 says that the infantry waited too long after the artillery ceased fire to begin its advance, and the British had time to come out of cover.

The IR 24 regimental history said that it was 'a great good fortune' that the 'superbly trained' MG Company was able to give covering fire. The MG had 'without a doubt' helped the infantry to advance, indeed may have saved the regiment from destruction.

III/24 had a particularly difficult time. The terrain offered no cover. The commanders of both forward companies were killed. I/24 had it little better. The British defence was 'extraordinarily tough'; especially the houses in front of the main position. Having taken one of these houses, the MG Company moved forward several guns, which were able to suppress some of the British fire.

At each firing position the battalions left a line of dead and wounded. By 0945 they approached to within a few hundred metres of the British position at the edge of the towns, but here it appeared that the attack would stall. The regimental commander ordered the commitment of all reserves; II/24 moved forward on the right, between III/24 and II/IR 20. II/24 took artillery fire while moving between the slag heaps: 'not a pleasant position' as the regimental history put it. The battalion deployed and moved forward on the same route taken by III/24 and elements of IR 20, supported by a battery of FAR 39, which deployed in the open to conduct direct fire. The battalion was then hit in the flank by MG fire and pinned down. 8/24 suffered severely, losing two lieutenants killed. FAR 3's shells suppressed this flanking fire.

4/FAR 39 and 6/39 displaced forward, south of the Wasmes–Frameries railway line. After the artillery had softened up the British positions, the regiment rose up in the assault. The British rifles and MGs cut loose, hitting II/24 and III/24 in particular and causing heavy casualties. The German MGs and artillery poured fire on the British positions. Shortly after 1000 I/24 entered Frameries, which they took quickly, without any house-to-house fighting. II/24, III/24 and elements of IR 20 pushed through the gardens and houses of Frameries and La Bouverie to the south sides. Beside each abandoned British machine guns there were eight to ten dead Scots. 'The British fled to the rear, leaving all the streets covered with weapons and equipment, almost as much as the Belgians.' The regiment took few unwounded prisoners. The hardest-hit battalion, III/24, had been reduced from 1,065 men to 560 and only 9 officers.

For the initial attack on Pâturages the commander of IR 20 could dispose of only II/20 and the machine gun company.[17] The regiment moved out from

the railway station at Flénu, 6/20 and 7/20 leading, and immediately took artillery fire, which caused casualties. Nevertheless, the two companies made good
progress and crossed the railway line. In spite of British rifle and MG fire, II/20
advanced quickly by bounds to close range (less than 800 metres). 5/20 was committed, but the advance stalled.

At 0800 I/20 and III/20 were returned to regimental control. I/20 and two
MGs were committed on the right; III/20 reinforced II/20. As they crossed the
railway line they took rifle and MG fire, but no artillery fire. They reached the
firing line and carried it 200 metres further forward. Fire from a mine on the
right flank brought the advance to a halt. The regimental commander, who was
far forward, directed the fire of 2/FAR 39 and some light howitzers against the
walls of the work and the advance resumed. The British fire grew weaker. IR 20
reached the British position just after the British had left.

The regimental commander, who was with the assault line, ordered I/20 and
III/20 to pursue. The heat was 'intolerable' and the advancing troops passed many
pubs in this mining town. Such an opportunity was too good to be true, and the
troops drank beer and 'every variety of schnapps, without causing any bad effects'.
The regiment stopped at La Bouverie. Many British troops had become lost in
the maze of dead-end roads and mines and were captured. A forward security
outpost blocked the valley west of La Bouverie and British troops escaping the
5 ID attack ran right into their arms, including a bicycle messenger with the II
Corps withdrawal order, and the combat trains of the 15th Brigade with the BEF
campaign plan. The regiment bivouacked in Wasmes.

The regimental historian said that the peacetime training had shown itself 'in
the most favourable light'. The regiment had lost 40 KIA, 151 WIA and 10 MIA.

IR 64

IR 64 was assembled along the railway line east of IR 24 while the artillery was
moving into position. All this movement must have drawn the attention of the
British, for the regiment was hit by artillery, MG and rifle fire from Frameries,
which caused some casualties.[18] II/64 took cover behind the railway embankment, III/64 in houses and behind walls, I/64 attacked 'the only correct decision
that would disperse the concentration of artillery and infantry'. With 1/64, 3/64
and 4/64 on line, the battalion advanced east of the Flénu–Frameries railway line,
supported by a platoon of the MG Company, against the Mons–Frameries railway line, which was apparently held by enemy security forces.

At 0600 the brigade attack order arrived to seize Frameries. Since I/64 was
already moving, the regimental commander deployed III/64 to its right, which
deployed 10/64 and 12/64 in the first line. II/64 (5/64 and 7/64) were brigade reserve. III/64 moved out at 0655, supported by two platoons of the MG

Company, 'in perfect order, just like in the training area'. The last two companies were committed and at 0830 III/64 reached the north side of the town. By 0930 they had taken the east side of Frameries. 9/64 and 11/64 pushed into the centre of the town and encountered a 'very well-sited British barricade'. The first attack failed with considerable loss, but with the assistance of a MG platoon the barricade was taken and the south side of the town reached.

I/64 cleared the enemy from the railway line, only to encounter a 1,200-metre long trench system that extended to the high ground north-east of town (the end of which was D Company of the South Lancashire). 2/64 was inserted in the middle of the line and the battalion attacked. It was difficult and bloody: 'the old British mercenaries were excellent shots'. But I/64 was not to be stopped. It received superb support from a machine gun platoon that set up on a high slag heap. The British withdrew by bounds, covered by strong artillery fire, which prevented pursuit. At 1200 the regiment was ordered to defend in place, but resumed the advance at 1600; at 1900 it bivouacked at Warquignies, about 8 km to the west.

The regimental history says that the troops could be proud of their victory; this was the same 64th as that of Alsen and Vionville, names to conjure with in German military history. 1/64, on the regimental left flank, took 100 POW. Four machine guns were also captured. IR 64 lost 4 OFF and 50 EM KIA, 8 OFF and 207 EM WIA, 14 EM MIA. The highest casualties by far were in I/64. As has been noted, Frameries was being defended by the 9th Brigade. Three battalions of IR 64 and one or two battalions of IR 24 were attacking across 2 km of open ground against four British battalions. It is surprising that the attack managed to gain ground at all.

IR 35 had been in corps reserve all day and hadn't fired a shot. 9/IR 35 was given the mission of burial detail in the 6 ID sector between Flénu and Frameries: it buried 169 German and 135 British.[19] This is probably representative of the ratio of casualties: German casualties were 25 per cent higher than the British. There was no general massacre of German troops by British rifle fire.

British 15th and 13th Brigades

On the afternoon of 23 August the Dorset Regiment of the 15th Brigade had sent D Company to occupy a position about 1,000 metres to the north-east of Wasmes, with C Company about 700 metres to the west.[20] The other two companies and the machine guns remained in billets in the rear and were not called forward until after dark. Two platoons of A Company were then moved forward to defend a crossroads to the left of C Company, with the other two platoons and the MGs in battalion reserve; B Company held the left flank. These troops had to occupy their positions in pitch darkness, and the battalion was strung out on a

2-km front. At 0200 on 24 August the battalion was told that it would be relieved in place by troops of the 13th Brigade.

The 5th Division withdrawal from the canal put the 15th Brigade, which had been the division reserve, in the centre of the new line. The 5th Division plan was for the 13th Brigade, which was falling back from the canal, to relieve the 15th Brigade in place. Apparently the intent was to preserve the 15th Brigade as the division reserve. It is hard to understand the logic of this measure. The 13th Brigade, which had been fighting all day, would have to conduct a night relief in place of the 15th Brigade without adequate preparation or coordination. It would have been far more effective to have left the 15th Brigade in place and have the 13th Brigade conduct a rearward passage of lines through the 15th, with the 13th becoming division reserve.

The 13th Brigade relief in place in the dark caused chaos. For some reason, the KOSB, which were to relieve the Dorsets in the brigade centre, did not stop their retreat from the canal at all, but continued the march to the rear. Reading between the lines, it appears the battalion was thoroughly disoriented by the confusing road net, the night march and fatigue.[21] The KOYLI, which hadn't received the order to withdraw from the canal until 2200, was directed in error by the 13th Brigade operations officer to occupy the left flank of the brigade position, so there was no relief for the two forward Dorset companies. There is no indication from the Dorset history that they knew where the KOYLI was.

The Duke of Wellington's moved up to the right of the Dorsets on a front of more than 2,000 metres, with A Company behind the Dorsets, B Company to the right of the Dorsets, D to the right of B and C behind B in reserve.[22] The Wellingtons' history says that British howitzer battery and two 15-pounder guns located near the battalion tried to open fire, 'but they did not get many rounds off before an overwhelming reply by German guns forced them to go back – presumably to find other positions, which, unfortunately, did not exist'. The German artillery fire soon became quite strong, and there was no British counter-fire.

The brigadier came up to the Wellingtons' positions and said 'he could tell me [the battalion commander] nothing new, but that as existing orders went we were to hang on at all costs'. There was a gap between the Dorsets and the KOYLI on their left, which the Wellingtons' commander brought to the attention of the brigade HQ, and which was filled by a company of the Royal West Kents.

The Dorsets' position was dominated by a large slag heap to the north of D Company, and at dawn two or more German MGs positioned there opened a fire on the right half of the Dorsets, which seriously disrupted the defence. Neither artillery nor MG fire could suppress the German MG. German artillery started to fall on C Company. The German MG fire prevented 2/Duke of Wellington's from relieving all but D Company of the Dorsets. The Dorset battalion commander withdrew to Pâturages with D Company, half of A Company, a platoon of C Company and the machine guns and then, on order of the Brigade com-

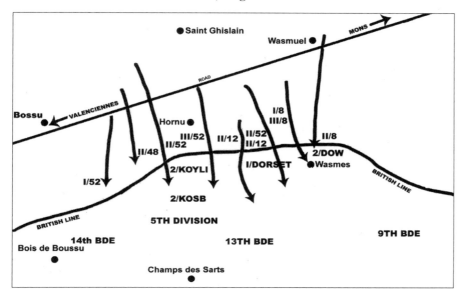

Fig. 16: GE 5 ID, 24 August.

mander, continued the march to Blaugues, 10 km to the south, leaving the rest of the battalion on the front line, a truly strange development.

C Company of the Dorsets was defending a farmhouse on a small rise, which attracted artillery fire. The German MGs on the slag heap were only 800 metres away, and 600 metres to the front were houses which provided the Germans with cover and concealment.

> Good trenches up to the accepted standards of the day were completed before dark [23 August], but they were all on the forward slope and were not provided with any head-cover or protection from flanking fire. In addition to the 120-round basic load, each man was given five bandoliers of 50 rounds each. The men used roots from a nearby field to camouflage the newly-turned earth. This was fairly effective in some cases, but by no means so when a trench had been dug in a stubble field where the roots merely served to make the trench all the more conspicuous.

The packs had been dropped to the rear and the company was unable to retrieve them when it withdrew and they were lost. C Company clearly was on a steep tactical learning curve.

The Germans opened light howitzer fire at dawn, which had 'a considerable moral effect', combined with the MG fire from the slag heap. The Duke of Wellington's, which was to relieve C Company, could not get forward and had taken cover behind another slag heap. The C Company commander decided that his position was untenable, and as the Duke of Wellington's was at hand he could withdraw. This was not executed in an orderly fashion: the company broke up into platoon and smaller groups. One platoon withdrew in front of A Company, masking it. Ransome, the Dorset regimental historian, said the company commander had issued orders that could easily have been executed, but: 'There seems to have been a complete absence of real leadership by platoon commanders.' Ransome admits the battalion had 'seldom' practised a withdrawal under pressure.

The two forward platoons of A Company had organised their position after dark, with the assistance of a detachment of Royal Engineers, including the usual sandbag barricades on the roads leading into the position. Ransome does not comment on this amateurish measure, which only served to advertise the company's location. There were buildings 300 metres to the north, plus slag heaps and railroad cuts, which could provide the Germans with cover. The big slag heap with the German MG on it was 900 metres north-east. This MG fire forced A Company to leave its prepared positions and fall back behind a light railway line about 200 metres to the rear.

On the left, B Company occupied a farm after dark. In the course of the morning German troops managed to occupy railway-line cuttings 300–400 metres to the front. By 1400 the Germans had manoeuvred to the B Company left flank, forcing the company out of their positions, and A Company with it.

The Wellingtons were being pounded by German artillery. A platoon leader said that it 'almost wiped us out'. Elements of the Royal West Kent were sent forward to reinforce the Wellingtons.[23] Before 1200 the German infantry had worked their way around the right flank and were in the battalion rear. The Wellingtons' 12th platoon was sent to protect the flank, but the Germans enveloped and destroyed it in close combat. The reserve company took two direct hits from German artillery, causing several casualties, including wounding the battalion commander. Though no orders for a withdrawal reached the Wellingtons, by 1200 the battalion's position was collapsing and the 13th Brigade was in general retreat.

The KOYLI had a relatively easy day. It doesn't seem to have been shelled, and withdrew just as the German infantry were making their appearance.[24]

The Dorsets lost 3 OFF WIA and POW, 12 EM KIA, 49 WIA and 69 MIA. The Wellingtons lost 4 OFF and 37 EM KIA and DOW, 3 OFF and 35 EM WIA and 2 OFF and 244 EM MIA. KOYLI lost 1 OFF KIA and 27 EM.

German 5 ID

On the III AK right flank III/IR 52, which had not been engaged on 23 August, became the advance guard for IR 12, with 12/52 the point element.[25] The battalion crossed the canal and marched through Hornu, where 12/52 deployed. It took fire and stood fast while a platoon of 9/52 manoeuvred right. 10/52 was committed on the left, followed by the remaining two platoons of 9/52, and their attack initially made good progress, until British pressure forced the left flank of 9/52 back. (They were probably engaged by elements of the British 15th Brigade, but it is not possible from British accounts to know which battalions.) When the bridge was completed the artillery crossed over the canal; FAR 54 went into action along the Hornu–Boussu road. Observation in the mining area was difficult. The division staff, on a slag heap, detected British artillery and directed the fire of 3/FAR 54 against it.[26] The other batteries fired on British infantry in trenches and houses. They received considerable return fire. The observation wagon of 4/FAR 54 took a direct artillery hit and the battery commander was killed, the II/54 section commander and his adjutant were severely wounded. One battery of FAR 54 occupied an open position south of Hornu and engaged the British with direct fire.

The attack slowly gained ground, hindered by friendly artillery fire from batteries north of the canal. At 1215 I/52, plus II/IR 48 and MG Company IR 48, arrived and were committed on the right against the marshalling yard, while II/12 moved up on the left.[27] At 1330 the British withdrew before the German infantry could close.

The units were reorganised and fed. At 1500 the advance resumed, but was stopped at Dour, about 3 km to the south, at 1800. 7/52 was detached to guard prisoners, bridges and railway installations and didn't return to the regiment until 20 September.

IR 48 was impressed by the British defensive positions in St Ghislain, saying that they were 'masterfully constructed'. The town had suffered more from British defensive preparations than it had from the battle. The walls had firing ports on several levels. MG positions were difficult to see. It was clear to IR 48 that the British had profited from their experience in 'small wars'. In the advance south of the canal, every house was searched and a number of British hauled out. The British fired at long range and then withdrew. When the British abandoned their trenches they nearly always left their packs, plus considerable ammunition, large quantities of rations and their wounded. Every pack had shaving gear, good marmalade, tea and tobacco. Most of the marmalade carried the marking 'Made in Germany'. Abandoned trucks with the name of British commercial companies on them were found loaded with rations. A staff car was discovered with maps that went to the east of the Rhine. The regimental historian noted that 'The British had planned for a different direction of march than the one they were forced to take'.[28]

IR 52 lost 1 OFF DOW, 27 EM KIA, 3 OFF and 96 EM WIA, 32 EM MIA. IR 12 did not mention casualties. IR 48 said that their losses were light: 3 EM KIA, 1 OFF and 24 EM WIA. FAR 54 lost 2 KIA, 14 WIA and a considerable number of horses.

Ascoli says, 'The main achievement of their [the German] artillery was the very efficient shelling of their own Brandenburg Grenadier Regiment, [IR 12] which seems to have been virtually wiped out'.[29] This is pure invention. During the entire Marne campaign IR 12 lost 837 casualties out of a strength of 3,400. In the regimental history, 24 August was not particularly eventful.[30]

IR 8 continued the attack on the left flank of 5 ID, supported by FAR 18. On 23 August the MG Company had hauled two guns 100 metres up a slag heap, supported by half-platoons of 5/IR 8 and 6/8.[31] These were probably the guns that vexed the British 13th and 15th Brigades. In proper recognition of the threat that these guns posed, the British artillery began shelling them at dawn, without doing any damage.

Artillery observation from the gun positions was difficult because of the mining works.[32] 4/FAR 18 therefore sent a Forward Observer (FO) team with a telephone 1,500 metres to a slag heap and laid the telephone line to the top. This procedure was disliked in peacetime because it took too long, but now it showed its value. The howitzers of 4/18 could successfully engage enemy trenches, while 5/54 caught British artillery in the flank. IR 8 said that the artillery fire on the MGs on its slag heap ceased at once; FAR 18 lost five WIA. The FO team on the slag heap continued to take small-arms fire, and all movement to the top was exposed. One man was wounded. A medic climbed the slag heap to assist him, was hit in the heart and killed. The wounded soldier bled to death.

I/8 took a factory on the east side of Hornu but came under heavy infantry and artillery fire. It was preparing to continue the attack when it learned that the 10th Brigade (IR 12, IR 52) to the right was making good progress. I/8 was pulled out of the line and moved behind II/8 and III/8 to the regimental left flank. The attack of I/8 was supported by artillery, II/8, III/8 and especially by a MG platoon, allowing I/8 to advance unhindered. II/8 joined the attack, but drew heavy infantry and MG fire. The enemy withdrew before the lead companies, 5/8 and 7/8, could close. 7/8 took the railway station. 5/8 now found itself conducting the pursuit alone but lost contact with the enemy. The company commander then heard firing to the west, so he swung the company in that direction and arrived on the east side of Wasmes, where he found himself on the flank of a British trench. Ignoring the danger of friendly fire, he left an element there and moved the rest of the company in a bow to the south towards a slag heap to the rear of the trench. The company climbed the slag heap and the trench was taken under fire from all directions. About 100 British were hit, the remainder, 2 OFF and 53 EM with 2 MGs, were captured.

BEF Left Flank

The official history said that the 19th Brigade had retired to Elouges during the night. The Cavalry Division had begun to withdraw at dawn, but when it was discovered that the 5th Division was not moving, it turned around and went back to guard its left flank, with the 2nd Cavalry Brigade on the road to Valenciennes, the 1st Cavalry Brigade on the railway to the left, and the other three brigades echeloned to the rear.[33] The Germans appeared in sector in force, and at 0900 the Cavalry Division began to withdraw again, ordering 19th Brigade to withdraw also. The 2nd Cavalry Brigade acted as rearguard. The Cavalry Division was acting like an independent unit, with no responsibility to protect the BEF left flank.

The 5th Division commander now noticed that the withdrawal of the 19th Brigade and the Cavalry Division uncovered his left flank. He sent for the commanders of 1/Norfolk and 1/Cheshire.[34] On determining that the commander of 1/Norfolk was senior, he placed 1/Cheshire under the operational control of the 1/Norfolk commander, told the commander of 1/Cheshire to return to his unit and gave the 1/Norfolk commander the order to hold the Elouges-Audregnies-Angre ridge to cover the withdrawal of the division. The battalions immediately moved out. There was no time to conduct a reconnaissance of the position; the commander of 1/Norfolk deployed his battalion and then placed 1/Cheshire to its left. Both commanders had just enough time to drop their companies off along the road. There were gaps between companies, and irregularities in the terrain prevented them from seeing each other. There was no time to dig trenches; the sunken road gave 1/Cheshires some cover, but no field of fire, which could only be obtained by moving onto the forward slope. Even so, corn stooks and slag heaps hindered visibility. 'Acting in accordance with what he [the 1/Cheshire commander] concluded was the Commander's plan ... [the 1/Cheshire commander] ordered the company commanders to hold their ground at all costs.'

The BEF chain of command in general and the 5th Division and 1/Cheshire commanders in particular had failed this tactics test. The Cavalry Division commander blithely left the 5th Division in the lurch. The 5th Division commander hastily sent a cobbled-together force to guard his left flank. He failed to convey to this force that the mission was to delay, to gain time; instead, the local commander ordered defence in place. The local commanders did not have time to organise a defence. This was a recipe for disaster.

They were attacked by IR 66 in the east, IR 26 in the centre and IR 72 in the west. The action on the left flank is described in the British official history clearly and in detail and supported by Map 8, which is excellent. Horsfall and Cave said that German artillery fire against both the Norfolks and Cheshires was effective, and they took casualties to this fire even before the infantry engagement: a lieutenant and a captain wounded, a soldier killed.[35] The Cheshires' MG section foolishly fired on a German aircraft at 1,800 yards, which they could not possibly hit, but which provided a target for German artillery, and one gun was destroyed. 'The tremendous volume of fire falling on the road almost precluded movement.' A section of 119 RFA was destroyed by German artillery fire.

At 1230 the 9/Lancers and 4/Dragoon Guards conducted a confused forward movement which the official history anachronistically described as a 'charge', which 'seems to have produced some moral effect in delaying the progress of the German attack'.[36]

In describing this 'charge' Horsfall and Cave let out all the stops. They say that this was 'one of the bravest of cavalry charges, one of the epic moments of the war'. 'Nothing can be more fear-inspiring than 400 men, mounted on horses, armed with lances and sabres, yelling and screaming in a mad charge towards you … Spearing or cutting down all who got in their way … scattered the terrified infantry, who had seen nothing like it.' The cavalry were stopped by a barbed-wire fence and tried to escape it by racing along to the right. The two regiments lost 250 men and 300 horses. Once again, the German reaction to this 'charge' is pure invention. None of the German artillery and infantry regimental histories mentions a cavalry charge at all.

At 1430 the Germans had approached to within 'a few hundred metres' of the Cheshires and Norfolks. The German artillery fire was accurate and they had brought forward machine guns, which were enfilading the flanks. The 1/Norfolk commander ordered both battalions and 119 RHA to retire. All but one platoon of the Norfolks, which was surrounded, was able to escape.

The official history reported the Norfolk casualties as 100. The regimental historian said the Norfolks' losses were 4 OFF KIA, 4 WIA and 250 EM. Horsfall and Cave said that 100 wounded had been left behind at Elouges because they could not be moved. The official history clearly under-reported the Norfolk casualties.

None of the Norfolks' bicycle messengers with the order for the Cheshires to withdraw got through the German fire; their adjutant was killed before he could deliver the order. Of the five runners sent to Brigade HQ, only one arrived. The Cheshires sent four messengers to the Norfolks – none arrived; the author of the Cheshires' history says that by this time the Germans were in the battalion rear and the messengers were probably killed or captured.

The Cheshires' commander then began to order a withdrawal, but was wounded and immobilised. The adjutant was captured. The Cheshires no longer formed a coherent defence; the battalion had been broken into fragments. Ammunition began to run low and resupply was impossible. The Germans enveloped both flanks. Of 25 OFF and 952 EM, 18 and 752 respectively were casualties; only 7 OFF and 200 EM remained, with a captain in command.

Horsfall and Cave devote two pages to the destruction of the Cheshires. They describe the fight with the standard boilerplate: 'Fortunately the Germans chose to advance in the same reckless fashion so often employed in the battles in and around Mons – en masse and firing from the hip, with only an accidental chance of hitting someone … The Germans found it difficult to believe that their tremendous casualties had been caused by a few riflemen and vigorously demanded to know where they had hidden the machine guns, as they were sure there must have been many deployed against them.'

This is one-quarter right. The Cheshires hid at least the one remaining func-
tional MG, and IR 72, which destroyed the Cheshires, did not report capturing
any, so the Germans would have been looking for trophies. Otherwise, the
Germans never fired from the hip; IR 72 lost only 252 men, a loss rate of less
than 8 per cent, hardly 'tremendous casualties' (and less than one-third of the
Cheshires' losses); there is no mention in the IR 72 regimental history of the
British possessing a large number of MGs.

German IV AK

As always, the infantry was preceded by cavalry patrols.[37] 1st Squadron Hussar
R 10 sent out a volunteer patrol early on the morning of 24 August. The patrol
leader said: 'I reported [to corps headquarters] with the same eight men as
always, who knew neither fear nor slackness.' The mission was to determine if
the next towns were occupied. The first challenge was getting the horses across
the infantry footbridge. They had practised crossing the Elbe often enough, but
an infantry footbridge was another matter. The patrol leader said that his horse
posed no problem, but one of the others 'went backwards farther than forwards'. Finally everybody was across, the infantry sent their best wishes and the
patrol was off. One hundred metres from the next town (presumably Crespin)
the patrol took rifle and MG fire. The patrol disappeared at a gallop: the enemy
had been found.

The right-flank unit of the German 1st Army was IR 93, on the north side
of the Condé canal south-west of Pommeroeul.[38] During the night it heard the
noise of wagon wheels, which led to the conclusion that the British were withdrawing. The regiment assembled at 0500 and quickly established that the British
had indeed gone. A platoon of engineers began repairing the bridge, which had
been only partially destroyed, and construction was begun on a pontoon bridge.
At 0630 III/93 crossed on the footbridge and took the village of Hensies, 2 km
to the south, without resistance. On leaving the village it encountered a British
patrol and took the first prisoners. The first elements of the main body crossed
at 1030. An IR 72 patrol reported that the French held Crespin to the west and
III/93 was detached to secure the town. On entering the town the battalion took
fire; clearing the town house by house took two hours.

IR 72 crossed the footbridge at 0800. It contained only ten companies, 10/72
and 11/72 having been detached. An officer patrol reported Quiévrain occupied
by the British. At 0915 IR 72 was ordered to take Quiévrain. It deployed and
entered the town, which had been prepared for defence, but the British had left.

FAR 74 moved across the canal at 0830 and by 0935 II/74 was in a position to
overwatch the movement of IR 72; as IR 72 advanced, I/74 bounded forward to
the Quiévrain–Mons road.[39] Before it the terrain sloped somewhat steeply down

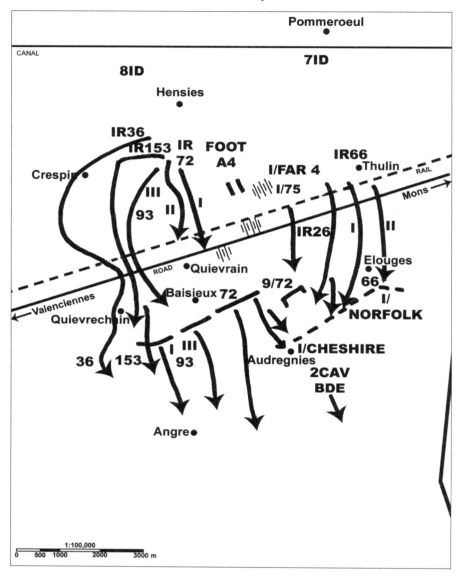

Fig. 17: IV AK, 24 August.

to a wide valley spotted with a few slag heaps, upon which the astonished gunners saw:

> ... a military idyll. 1,000 metres to the left a dismounted cavalry squadron prac-
> ticed flag signals towards the south; in the valley large groups of cavalry with
> horse artillery and a battalion of infantry moved back and forth apparently at
> random. Their conduct was so unconcerned and peaceful that we could not

believe that they were enemy; in any case they had no idea that we were in the immediate vicinity. The section and battery commanders of I/FAR 74 reported that the cavalry did not carry lances and were therefore enemy, but were refused permission to fire out of fear that this was HKK 2 or the cavalry of III AK; the 8 ID cavalry would surely have reported the presence of so large a group of enemy cavalry. To clear the matter up, the section commander sent Lieutenant Thiele of 2/74 forward on an officer's patrol, who quickly established and reported that the troops were British.

What FAR 74 was looking at was almost certainly the 'charge' of the British 2nd Cavalry Brigade.

In the meantime, I/74 had been brought forward at a walk, in order not to draw attention or stir up clouds of dust. There was no time to lay telephone lines from the battery commander's OP to the guns; fire commands would be by voice. 1/74 and 2/74 were deployed in a covered position, but there was no room for 3/74, which had to set up behind hayricks and tall poplars lining the road. The section commander stood on his observation ladder near a railwayman's house; the armoured shield would stop many bullets this day. At 1130, when Lt Thiele made his report, the section commander opened fire on his own responsibility in a target-rich environment; engaging cavalry and artillery 'with visible effect'. The German infantry had begun to advance and I/74 also engaged enemy infantry and machine guns.

3/74 immediately took counter-battery fire from Elouges-Audregnies and suffered heavy casualties in men and material. The hayricks that were being used as camouflage were set on fire by direct hits and two ammunition wagons caught fire. Shells were being fired at a prodigious rate and soon every available man was bringing ammunition to the guns under fire. Gunners were killed and wounded, but the battery kept up the fire. All the officers in 3/74 save one were wounded; an officer from the regimental staff brought an order to the section and stayed to direct the fire of 3/74. The regimental history said, 'What magnificent, unforgettable gunners we had in those days!' II/74 pulled into open firing positions to the left of 3/74, which took some of the pressure off the beleaguered battery. After an hour's artillery duel FAR 74 had gained fire superiority and the British withdrew.

At Quiévrain IR 72 drew water from the wells and then the regiment deployed again, from right to left with 5/72, then 7/72 on the south side of the town, 1/72 and 2/72 in an open field, 3/72 and 4/72 echeloned to the left along the Valenciennes road on both sides of the railway line, and 6/72 and 7/72 in the town. III/72 was guarding the artillery. At 1130 enemy cavalry and artillery north-east of Audregnies was engaged at a range of 1,500–1,700 metres with visible effect. Nevertheless, the enemy was able to set up his artillery on the north side of Audregnies and fire on the regiment. 5/72 and 7/72 moved directly south, 1/72 and 2/72 advanced on Audregnies.

The MG Company reached the south side of Quiévrain at 1100 and the company commander observed that 1/72 and 2/72, which were 500 metres south of the town, were being shelled by enemy artillery. He dismounted two guns from the wagons and ordered them forward to the firing line. The crews moved forward 'just like in training' and the commander of 1/72 motioned that they should join him in a copse. From that position they opened fire on an artillery piece at 900 metres range, which immediately silenced the gun, allowing the infantry to resume their advance. Unfortunately the noise of combat made it impossible to get the forward machine gun to shift fire to an arriving limber team, and the gun got away. The other limber team as well as almost all the gunners were killed or wounded and the caisson captured.

The commander of 1/72 wrote:

> I saw ... our troops to the right of me advance. I went forwards with Elias' platoon; baptism of fire. We were receiving very heavy artillery fire, but had no infantry to shoot at, so we went forwards, almost without firing. An enemy battery stood in the direction of the church steeple at Audregnies. I approached to within 700 metres, but only a squad followed me into the sunken road. Shells flew over our heads. I decided to storm the battery, which probably consisted of two guns. We advanced without stopping, our great hope was that we will get them! Lots of dead horses. They attempted to get the guns away. We were almost there and began shooting again, when a gun pulled by a nag went into the town. Now we were there and found only two caissons. We wheezed further on, but the gun had disappeared into the town. An enemy motorcyclist was hit ... We reached the town at about 1300, at least three-quarters of an hour ahead of the rest, but only with six men; completely exhausted we drank milk, after the terrified peasants had tasted it ... We lay down behind a hedge and shot several Englishmen. I crawled to a wall to orient myself and found a wounded British soldier ... more of our troops arrived.

3/72 and 4/72 decided on their own initiative to attack enemy infantry 1,000 metres to their front. The two companies attacked at a rapid tempo and quickly reached assault distance, but when the signal was given for 'Fix Bayonets!' the British began waving white flags. A field grade officer, several other officers (including three captains) and about 200 unwounded EM surrendered, and two machine guns were taken.

Isolated to the left rear east of Quiévrain was 9/72, which was protecting the artillery, and in the process coming under artillery fire. When the company commander saw 4/72 to his right going forward, he decided to take the mine head to his front. 9/72 was a superbly trained company, and its commander an outstanding tactician. The 3rd Platoon moved out by bounds in two lines, in a very open formation with ten-pace intervals between the skirmishers, covered by the fire of the rest of the company. Such an attack maximised supporting fire. The dispersion required troops who were willing and able to advance on their own initiative. In spite of fire from invisible enemy riflemen and MG, the platoon reached the mine head and captured 5 OFF, 30 EM and 1 MG. Two of the prisoners were French liaison officers who could not get away because their horses had been shot. The 1st and 2nd Platoons now followed, using the same movement formation, and although the enemy fire steadily intensified, they reached the mine head with few casualties. 9/72 now recognised that the main enemy position was 600 metres to their front. The company deployed to both sides of the mine head and took up the firefight. The leader of the 3rd Platoon was killed. The company butcher, who had left the field kitchen and picked up a rifle, was wounded. IR 26 was coming up on the left; the enemy had probably seen this and decided they needed to withdraw; in the face of 9/72's gunnery, a hopeless undertaking. The German troops could see them fall, and a roar went through the company. However, they were not all dead or wounded; some lay down in order to avoid the fire and were captured when 9/72 continued their advance. A sergeant walked the battlefield later and counted 280 enemy bodies.

When the last of these troops disappeared over the horizon, the fight was not over. Enemy troops who were probably unable to retreat across the open ground behind them continued to fire from the 'Three Houses'. The 9/72 commander ordered another attack, with two platoons in the front and one in reserve, using fire and movement, finally assaulting with shouts of 'Hurrah!' About 150 British raised their hands and surrendered. On the ground lay a senior British officer – supposedly the commander of a lancer regiment – who was dying of a stomach wound. He asked for water; only one man in the company had any, but he willingly gave it up.

9/72 had put on a tactics clinic. It had avoided artillery fire, attacked twice over open ground, conducted a successful firefight, taken 250 prisoners and 4 MGs. The cost had not been light: 1 OFF and 17 EM KIA, 48 EM WIA.

I/FAR 75 did not cross over the canal until 1215.[40] It then went into position to the left of FAR 74. It bounded forwards several times, engaging retreating British artillery and infantry, until at 1600 there were no more targets to be seen. II/75 was division reserve and 5/75 captured several lightly wounded British troops hiding in a stook of grain. Watering parties captured more British stragglers.

The IR 72 regimental commander ordered II/72, which was under enemy artillery fire at Quiévrain, to move forward to Baisieux. 5/72 and 7/72 occupied the town without resistance, although it still lay under artillery fire. On the south side of the town the companies fired on enemy rearguards near Angre, and the MG Company engaged artillery at 1,200 metres range. 6/72 and 8/72 moved forward with IR 93 on the right. At 1400 II/72 entered Angre, which was also occupied without resistance. The regiment was now in two groups: II/72 at Angre, I/72 and III/72 at Audregnies, with 12/72 in between. The regimental commander wrote:

> As I rode to I/72 after the battle, I was presented with an unforgettable view. On a green hill the battalion colours fluttered gaily in the wind. The setting sun threw her rays on the Prussian eagle on its shining red background, under which camped a large group of prisoners, khaki-clad British mixed with a few French in their colourful uniforms, and in a ring around them stood our brave field-grey with bright eyes, proud of their fine success. At the bottom of the hill hundreds of captured horses were assembled in perfect order. Over the whole scene stretched the blue evening sky with a few pink clouds, offering a painter the motif 'After the Victorious Battle' that could not be improved on.

The commander of 3/72 wrote in a letter home: 'It was wonderful! Everybody pushed forward with a will. The men were splendid! Even though some could barely crawl afterwards, you didn't notice this during the attack!'

IR 72 lost 2 OFF and 32 EM KIA, 2 OFF and 216 EM WIA. FAR 74 lost 9 EM KIA, 3 OFF, 1 doctor and 49 EM WIA, all but one in 3/74. The regiment had fired 1,340 shells. The damage to 3/74's equipment was replaced at once from the ammunition column.

IR 72 took 1,144 prisoners and three full ammunition caissons. A staff car with four officers from the British 3rd Division drove straight into the arms of the resting IR 72 soldiers at Audregnies, giving the Germans considerable information concerning British positions and orders. All of 3/72 was required to guard the prisoners; instead of delivering them to the rear area, 3/72 had to accompany them all the way to Cologne. IR 72 now consisted of nine infantry companies and the MG Company.

By 1200 IR 93 reached Quiévrain and was joined by III/93, which was ordered to attack to the right of IR 72. It reached Baisieux without opposition, but on leaving the town took artillery, MG and rifle fire from the heights west of Audregnies and the woods north of Angre. It advanced in quick bounds, with 10/93 swinging right towards Angre. II/93 remained in brigade reserve. I/93 had been committed to the left of III/93 and advanced with 1/93 and 2/93 online, 3/93 following in the middle and 4/93 echeloned left. It too soon took shrapnel fire, but continued a rapid advance. The enemy was dismounted cavalry, which quickly vacated its positions. By 1600 the regiment was in the heights and the woods west of Angre. The pursuit was broken off by 1600 and by 1730 IR 93 bivouacked in Quiévrain. The regiment had lost 14 KIA and 77 WIA, mostly from III/93.

IR 153 was committed to the right of IR 93 and took fire from French Territorial troops at Crespin.[41] After a short bout of house-to-house fighting the regiment took the town and pushed south without making further contact. IR 153 lost 9 EM KIA, 30 WIA.

IR 36 was committed to the right of IR 153 and was also engaged with French Territorials, which offered 'very little resistance'.[42] It lost 3 KIA, 6 WIA. Ascoli, who thought that IR 36 had encountered British troops, says: 'A veteran of the 36th Regiment remembers what it was like: "They fired like devils. Simply to move was to invite destruction. In our first attack we lost an entire battalion".'[43] Ascoli didn't cite his sources, so there is no way to tell where this unlikely statement was supposed to have come from.

In the 7 ID sector, elements of IR 26 and IR 66 had crossed the canal in the early morning of 24 August and dug in 400 metres to the south. At 0400, as it began to lighten, II/66 attacked towards Thulin.[44] The battalion took fire from the isolated farmhouses. A small number of enemy troops defended the town energetically; particularly heavy fire came from the church, on which hung a Red Cross flag. The battalion continued the attack towards the railway line, still under heavy fire, and reached it in time to fire on withdrawing enemy cavalry. The brigade ordered that the limit of advance was the Mons–Quiévrain road, so the battalion rested behind the railway embankment. IR 26 on the right moved out at 0640 and by 0700 had reached the railway line.[45] They were ineffectively shelled by British artillery. I/66 moved up behind II/66, FAR 40 deployed II/40 east of the road, I/40 west of it.[46] Men and horses were fed.

At 1215 the two regiments attacked towards Elouges. On the right, IR 26 deployed II/26 on the right and III/26 on the left, I/26 echeloned to the right rear. The terrain in the IR 26 sector contained a large number of mounds of coal and slag, which led to bitter close-range infantry combat. The commander of FAR 40 was riding with and even in front of the forward line of infantry. Thanks to effective artillery support, the attack initially won ground quickly. It then ran into stiff resistance on the Mons–Valenciennes road. Casualties in II/26 were so high that I/26 was sent forward to reinforce it. 1/FAR 40 unlimbered in the III/IR 26 firing line and at 1245 engaged an enemy battery. The infantry attack picked up steam again, moving by short bounds. 2/FAR 40 and 3/40 came on line with 1/40.

South-west of Elouges FAR 40 detected a long line of British artillery, four to five batteries, which was firing at 8 ID at Quiévrain, offering their flank to FAR 40, which opened a withering fire, without receiving any counter-fire in return. The enemy fire weakened, and then the British apparently withdrew.

At 1340 3/FAR 40 and all of II/40 moved forward into the IR 26 infantry firing line, west of the Thulin–Elouges road. The gunners were presented with a wonderful target-rich environment: retreating infantry and MG and British artillery on the high ground west of Elouges. The town was set on fire. In the course of the day FAR 40 fired 223 shrapnel and 91 HE shells. Two lieutenants in 4/FAR 40 reported:

... at Thulin we galloped into position under British infantry fire. We scored great numbers of hits on British artillery and MG using direct fire. Captain Meufel stood on the observation ladder and I observed standing on his wagon. On the next day we marched past the British artillery that we had destroyed: two batteries in position, another while attempting to withdraw; about 200 dead horses.

Finally ... we get the order to support the attack. Hurra! Finally it starts. We gallop past the lead infantry elements and go into battery; the first bullets sail over our heads and smack against the gun shields. Straight ahead is withdrawing enemy artillery in march column. The first rounds strike with colossal effect; the poor fellows, we see ammunition caissons and men blown into the air. The British withdraw in wild flight ... The effectiveness of our fire was frightful. The dead lie in hundreds, horses and men on top of each other; columns of British prisoners pass by continually.

IR 26:

As the staff of III/26 reached the heights north-west of Elouges, it saw the British withdraw in thick columns at 2,000 to 2,500 metres range south in the direction of Baisieux. The commander of FAR 40, LTC Büstorff, who was in the immediate vicinity, was informed. He brought up first one battery into position on the hill, then a second. These batteries shelled the British artillery and withdrawing troops with crushing effect. When we marched through the area the next day we were convinced of the colossal effectiveness of our artillery.

The history of IR 66 shows clearly that this battle belonged to the 7 ID artillery. It says that FAR 40 and FAR 4 held the British positions on the high ground west of Elouges under 'concentric' artillery fire. It continued:

Soon the well-adjusted time-fuses smoked the British out of their trenches and silenced their artillery. When we were still 1,000 metres from their position, the British left their trenches in swarms, effectively pursued by our fire.

The IR 66 historian said that the British rearguards showed their experience in colonial warfare by using the available natural cover; at the initial engagement range of 600–700 metres they were invisible. Nevertheless, the Germans pressed forward, and by 1630 had taken the heights west of Elouges; the British were no more to be seen.

IR 26 lost 2 OFF and 20 EM KIA, 4 OFF and 108 EM WIA, 14 EM MIA, 148 casualties in total. It said that it took 'hundreds' of British prisoners.

In two days of combat IR 66 lost just 3 EM KIA, 1 OFF and 22 EM WIA. It claimed that 'considerable booty in prisoners, machine guns, weapons and horses was brought in'.

IR 27 did not get to fire a shot.[47] The only element of IR 165 which was engaged was the MG Company.[48] At 1530 it reached the railway embankment at Elouges and made contact with 8 ID. The MG Company occupied coal piles, from which it could engage British troops withdrawing in front of the left wing of 8 ID at 800 metres: 'the Tommies went down by rows in the beaten zone of Captain Pfaehlers machine guns, and when the troops later passed by the area, they could convince themselves of the combat power of the MG'.

Casualties

The British official history gives British casualties as 'roughly 250 in the Cavalry Division, 100 in the I Corps, 550 in the 3rd Division, 1,650 in the 5th Division and 40 in the 19th Infantry Brigade'.[49] This is not a very precise accounting, but would mean 2,600 casualties in total. As we have seen, on at least two occasions the official history understated British casualties.

The casualty figures for eleven regiments of German infantry and one of artillery are quite precise: 1,288. The highest casualties were in IR 64 (283) and IR 72 (252). On 23 and 24 August combined, IR 66 lost 26 EM. IR 27 and IR 165 did not take any losses at all. We have no complete casualty figures for only three German infantry regiments. IR 24 lost 500 men in the most heavily engaged battalion, so a total of 1,000 casualties for the regiment would appear to be likely. From the description of the engagement, it would appear that IR 8 took 100 casualties. IR 12, which was hardly engaged, does not seem to have suffered many casualties, probably fewer than 50. The known and estimated losses this brings total German casualties to 2,400. The British and German losses were essentially equal.

Evaluation

On 24 August there was no possibility that the Germans were going to be able to turn the British left flank before the British withdrew. The German IV AK, and elements of III AK, had to bridge the canal and then pass all of its forces through these bottlenecks. The BEF had already decided to withdraw even before the German attack began. The British task was therefore to conduct a delay. In a delay, the mission is to stop the enemy, make him deploy, and then fall back to another position and repeat the procedure. The intent is to trade space for time. It is important not to become 'decisively engaged', that is, not to allow the enemy to approach so closely that the delaying unit cannot withdraw. Instead of delaying, several British units defended in place and became decisively engaged. At Mons the British had the benefit of the canal to stop the German advance; on 24 August there was no such physical obstacle and the British could not prevent the Germans from closing with some of the British units. One British battalion was destroyed in the process and two badly mauled. The British 5th Division was able to break contact because, in effect, it sacrificed its rearguards. What for the British should have been an easy operation, with few casualties, was turned into a desperate fight, with 1,000 more casualties than at Mons.

Cavalry is the ideal arm for conducting a delay. The British infantry should have begun its withdrawal during the night, passed through a cavalry screen and left the cavalry to conduct the delay. This procedure was not followed because of poor and late decision-making at the BEF level. In the event, the Cavalry Division was concerned only with its own withdrawal.

British command and control was demonstrating increasing weaknesses. II Corps was doing all the fighting while I Corps was not engaged. The BEF HQ was making decisions far too late for them to be implemented. Too often, orders did not reach the infantry battalions. There was no coordination of I Corps, II Corps and Cavalry Division movements at the BEF level.

HKK 2

In the early morning of 24 August AOK 1 sought to get HKK 2 to swing south against the British left flank. Then it received reports at 0530 from IV RK that HKK 2 had seen troops unloading at Tournai; at 0830 AOK 1 told HKK 2 to establish the northern flank of these troops and whether they were British or French. At 1100 OHL attached HKK 2 to the 1st Army.[50] At 1145 AOK 1 directed HKK 2 to march through Tournai towards Denain, to the west of Valenciennes and beyond the British left flank.

HKK 2 should have been instructed to bypass Tournai, avoid combat and get south as soon as possible. But even after a day's combat with the BEF on 23 August, Kluck and Kuhl insisted that HKK 2 march through Tournai to make absolutely sure there were no British troops there. Every hour's delay on such a fool's errand reduced the possibility that HKK 2 would turn the British left flank. If there actually was a threat to the 1st Army right flank, II AK and IV RK, following the forward troops, were in a position to block it.

HKK 2 marched back south again, 9 KD moved on the west bank of the Schelde, followed by 2 KD, and 4 KD and the Jäger battalions on the east bank. The operations officer of 9 KD wrote, 'So now we rode south 40 km on the same route we had ridden north yesterday. Considerable grumbling. Twenty-five km trotting on paved roads, passing Tournai to the west'.[51]

At Lamain, just west of Tournai, the advance guard of 9 KD encountered several squadrons of French cavalry, then French infantry and bicyclists. These were Territorial troops from the garrison of Fortress Lille. The HKK 2 advance guard deployed on a hill offering 'observation and fields of fire as far as the eye could see', the three horse artillery batteries and the MG Company were brought forward and everyone opened fire. In ten minutes the French columns, which did not have any artillery support, were broken up. The 9 KD engaged the French at ranges of 1,500–4,000 metres, 'where every foot of the terrain could be observed'. 9 KD dispersed four battalions without receiving a shot in return.

3/Uhlan R 5 and 4/Uhlan R 5 took the town of Rumes with a dismounted assault.[52] Then Uhlan R 5 conducted a mounted pursuit in squadron columns. The point element reported that a train was starting to move away: French troops were seen jumping on (it was a small commuter train that linked two villages). The uhlans took off in hot pursuit and soon overhauled the train; the scene was straight out of a grade-B western. The uhlans rode beside the moving train; some uhlans speared the French with their lances, others fired their pistols, while the French shot back. The squadron commander shot the engine conductor, the engine stopped and thirty-five French soldiers surrendered. The squadron had lost 1 EM KIA, 1 OFF and 2 EM WIA and 4 horses. A sergeant who had been leading the point element arrived; he had conducted a mounted charge and captured eight French. All the prisoners were turned over to the Jäger.

At 1700 9 KD encountered another brigade of French infantry and broke it up with artillery fire.[53] Hussar R 11 dismounted and pursued. One platoon stopped a French locomotive with their fire, capturing a trainload of recently mobilised reservists. A second platoon captured an officer and eighty French troops. In Orchies Hussar R 11 found the route to the railway station was covered with discarded weapons and packs, with fleeing soldiers and mobilised reservists sitting in railcars, waiting for a locomotive. The prisoners were turned over to the Jäger and the march continued.

2 KD entered the fight to the right of 9 KD. 1/Curassier R 7 was in the centre of the division, with Hussar R 12 on its left. The Cuirassier squadron commander observed French infantry escaping and attacked on foot, accompanied by the neighbouring squadron of Hussar R 12. The French were difficult to see because of the close terrain. The German cavalrymen advanced for 2 km in skirmisher line, not bothering to move by bounds because the French fire was so weak. Suddenly they came upon a deep sunken road, full of French troops taking cover from the German artillery fire, who surrendered without firing a shot. Other Frenchmen fled towards a town. A sergeant from 1/Curassier 7 unhitched a horse from a French ammunition wagon, mounted it and galloped after them, threatening the French with a revolver. He returned with 8 POW. The cuirassiers searched the houses and brought in more prisoners. The hussars captured a general.

The two squadrons marched their prisoners back to the 2 KD line – in total a general, 4 OFF and 150 EM. They hadn't lost a man.

4 KD came pounding up, led by Jäger bicyclists, followed by Jäger 10, 3 and 4; the Jäger were keeping up with the cavalry quite nicely.[54] On the morning of 24 August Tournai had been thought to be unoccupied, but the bicyclists had taken fire. Jäger 3 attacked Tournai from the north-west; Jäger 4 from the north-east, Jäger 10 from the east on Jäger 4's left.

Jäger 10 attacked with 1/Jäger 10 on the left against a cemetery wall, and 3/Jäger 10 on the right against a defended building, which turned out to be a hospital. Eight hundred metres from Tournai they began to receive fire but calmly continued the advance, climbing pasture fences and jumping ditches. A squad was sent to deal with French firing on the left flank, and they chased off French cavalry. The squad lost contact with the company, but continued the advance, crossed a chest-deep water-filled ditch and passed through a small wood, to appear behind French cavalry engaged with their company, and opened fire. The French defence in front of 1/Jäger 10 collapsed. 3/Jäger 10 took the hospital. Jäger 10 was now faced with a line of defended houses across 300 metres of open field. The observation was poor and it was difficult for the artillery to support the Jäger. A gun of Horse Artillery Section 3 unlimbered and the gunners and Jäger manhandled it to within 100 metres of the French and opened fire. 'That did wonders. The small-arms fire died down. The French began to quit. In masses they came onto the road with their hands up.' The horse artillery history said: 'Working with such outstanding troops as the Jäger battalions made a powerful impression on the artillerymen.'[55]

The houses on both sides of the road still had to be cleared. A number of French soldiers were pulled out. Others had changed into civilian clothing, but many had done the job too hastily and could be recognised by a piece of uniform that they still wore. One Frenchman was found working industriously on a cobblers' lath, given away by his red trousers. Jäger Kümmel from the MG Company could not be found. He was not a good garrison soldier, but in the field he was outstanding. He reappeared, coming out of the city beaming with pride, an axe in one hand and a pistol in the other, herding four prisoners in front of him. First he got a good chewing-out for unauthorised absence, then praise for his courageous conduct. He was the first in the company to be awarded the Iron Cross.

Jäger 4 attacked the rail depot. The only avenue of approach was an underpass that was blocked with a barricade. About 300 metres beyond that was French infantry behind a park wall. The barricade was cleared away and the firefight taken up, but no advance was possible until the MG had established fire superiority. The Jäger pushed the French out of the area of the railway station and they fled towards Tournai.

A platoon of 4/Curassier 7 was attached to Jäger 4, and the cuirassiers galloped in hot pursuit down a chestnut-lined allée, passing wounded Frenchmen who surrendered.[56] The cuirassiers broke their weapons and rode on, leaving them to the Jäger. The French ran into the town and disappeared around a corner. The cuirassiers reached their hiding-place, an enclosed farmyard; as they were about to beat down the gate the French opened it and surrendered. Eight cuirassiers had captured 100 French.

Jäger 4 was ordered to evacuate the town so that the artillery could soften it up. Seeing the French fleeing in disorder, the battalion commander ignored the order and pushed on into the town, captured the bridge and then moved out to the south-west side. Jäger 4 took several officers and 150 EM prisoners.

Jäger 4 lost 1 EM KIA, 1 OFF and 7 EM WIA. The battalion requisitioned wagons to carry the packs and the footsore Jäger. The bicycle companies were formed into a bicycle battalion, so two squads of 2/Jäger 4 were mounted on requisitioned bicycles.

Jäger 3 advanced in skirmisher line, taking fire, which caused no casualties.[57] It quickly rounded up 250 prisoners, all men over the age of forty who appeared glad to be captured. Some of the French tried to hide in the bushes and change into civilian clothing. Unfortunately, the field kitchens had come to this spot and in the process of waiting for lunch some of the Jäger, wandering around the immediate area, nabbed the French in the act. A French general with his staff was also captured, and the general 'had the great honour to be invited to eat from our company field kitchen'.

The French had intended to create a force of Territorial Divisions between Douai and Lille. On 23 August the 81st and 82nd Territorial Divisions were to retake Tournai and the 88th Territorial Division was to detrain 12 km south-east of Lille. During the night of 23–24 August two battalions of the 82nd Territorial had reoccupied Tournai. These were defeated by Jäger 4 and the cuirassiers, while 9 KD pushed the 81st Territorial Division back to Lille. During the night of 24 August the French evacuated Lille, possession of which would have been of great assistance to the French during the Race to the Sea. The first French attempt to put an army on the German right flank had failed.

HKK 2 now put on a display of cavalry – and Jäger – mobility. HKK 2 had already marched 40 km. The Hussar R 8 history said the regiment marched another 20 km to Marchiennes, 18 km north-east of Valenciennes, by 1800, where there was no warm food or bread, straw or good water. It rested for three hours, sleeping in the roadside ditches, then resumed the march. By 0500 on 25 August it had moved 30 km more, 100 km in 36 hours, a rate that even mechanised units could be proud of.

The Jäger held the pace. Jäger 10 hoped that there would be enough time in Marchiennes to rest and for the field kitchens to come up. In vain! The order was 'Route march. March!' 'If the OHL had heard our curses, we would have been convicted of insubordination in the face of the enemy. But … our Jäger spirit won through.' From 2330 to 0300 the battalion rested where it stopped on the road; in short order the whole battalion was snoring. Then it resumed the march.

The German III and IV AK were now dead on the heels of the British II Corps. The superior German command and control system would allow the Germans to move faster than the British and catch up with II Corps. HKK 2, a fearsome combination of operational mobility and tactical combat power, was pounding south. If HKK 2 found the II Corps left flank, the jig was up for the BEF. Unless the Germans made a serious unforced error, the entire Entente left flank was in danger. But Kluck and Kuhl were just the men to snatch failure from the jaws of victory.

25 August

The BEF HQ issued orders at 2025 on 24 August to continue the withdrawal another 25 km to a position to both sides of Le Cateau.[1] Since the Forest of Mormal was thought to be untrafficable from north to south, I Corps would move to the east of the forest, II Corps to the west. That day most of the 4th Division arrived by train at Le Cateau and was directed to move to Solesmes to cover the withdrawal. When that was accomplished, the 4th Division was to move to the left of II Corps. In the meantime, Sordet's Cavalry Corps was moving to the west behind II Corps, crossing II Corps' line of withdrawal and delaying its movement.

German 1st Army

German air reconnaissance kept the German 1st army well-informed on 24 August concerning the British withdrawal from Condé–Mons in a south-west-erly direction.[2] IX AK aircraft reported the withdrawal of the British I Corps to the west of Maubeuge. French troops south of Valenciennes were also seen with-drawing. IV AK air reconnaissance reports made at 1530 on 24 August reached the 1st Army at 2200 and showed that instead of standing and fighting, the British were withdrawing towards Bavai. Late that evening the 1st Army sent a report to the 2nd Army: 'After heavy combat, 1st Army has driven two or three British divisions back in the direction of Curgies-Bavai. The main enemy position is presumed to be on the line Bavai-Valenciennes. The 1st Army will attack on 25 August and turn the enemy left flank. HKK 2 will operate against the enemy rear.' IV and III AK would attack frontally while II AK would turn the BEF left, with HKK 2 sweeping far to the west, south of Denain.

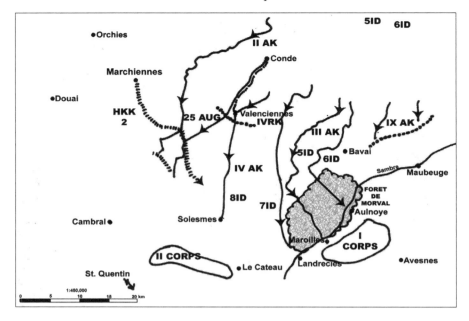

Fig. 18: 25 August, the 1st Army turns south-east.

To this point, Kluck and Kuhl had been convinced it was engaging two to three British divisions. Captured orders now showed that it had engaged four infantry and one cavalry division, obviously the mass of the BEF. It was only now that they decided it was a certainty that British units would not appear at Lille.

At 0200 on 25 August, however, a III AK air reconnaissance report reached the 1st Army, saying that 'The overall impression is that there is a general withdrawal towards Maubeuge'. The German official history said:[3]

> This air reconnaissance report, which contradicted all of the numerous previous reports which had come in during the entire day, did not justify drawing the conclusion that the entire British army was in full-scale retreat to Maubeuge. However, the Army headquarters accepted the unlikely impressions of this aviator as established fact. Even if the idea that the British were withdrawing to Maubeuge was correct, maintaining the previous direction of march to the southwest would have effectively pushed the British in that direction and begun their encirclement. The Army headquarters, on the contrary, believed that the corps must immediately be turned in southeast, towards Le Cateau–Landrecies–Aulnoye.

The new orders, issued at 0700 on 25 August, directed the army to turn southeast: the army marched half-left. HKK 2 was to move in the direction of Guise (south-west of St Quentin), II AK to the west of Le Cateau, IV AK to Landrecies,

III AK to Maroilles. The 1st Army was now facing east while the British withdrew south. In effect, only one German infantry division (8 ID, IV AK) was pursuing II Corps.

Had the 1st Army merely continued the march on 25 August in the only logical direction, south-west, then early on 26 August the British II Corps would have been attacked by III and IV AK, while HKK 2 enveloped its left flank: II Corps would have been destroyed. By turning the 1st Army south-east, Kluck and Kuhl ensured that only three brigades of IV AK would attack II Corps. Instead of turning the II Corps flank, HKK 2 attacked II Corps frontally. Nevertheless, on 26 August II Corps was going to take a fearful pounding.

By 1100 on 25 August air reconnaissance reports unanimously showed Kluck and Kuhl that the British were not withdrawing towards Maubeuge, but were moving in the direction of Le Cateau. At 1130 new orders were issued: the left wing of IV AK was directed towards Solesmes, III AK was to turn south.

The 1st Army counter-order accomplished nothing: none of the major units even mention receiving it, much less implementing it. The IV AK order issued at 0730 directed 8 ID on the right to march to Pommeroeul, halfway between Le Cateau and Landrecies, and 7 ID to Landrecies. IV AK changed nothing and continued the march. III AK had to march through the Mormal Forest: it would have been impossible to turn the corps around in the woods. By dark, the lead elements of 6 ID on the right had reached Hachette north-west of Landrecies, 5 ID on the left had taken the Sambre Bridge at Aulnoye.

The German official history does not paint a pretty picture of the German 1st Army's posture on the evening of 25 August. The only unit that could turn the British left flank, II AK, was far to the rear. Kluck and Kuhl had continually criticised Bülow for wanting to ball up German forces against Maubeuge. Now they had massed the 1st Army on an absurd north–south line along the Sambre, with the enemy escaping to the south-west. If the 1st Army continued the march forward, it would collide not with the enemy but with the 2nd Army. Kluck and Kuhl could be sure that every post-war class at the General Staff academy would have a good laugh when studying their manoeuvre of 25 August.

At the end of the day, the 1st Army HQ moved forward to set up in Solesmes. Finding it still occupied by the British, it had to bivouac in a small house north of the town. It lost contact with the corps and had great difficulty transmitting the order for 26 August.

Air reconnaissance on 25 August had located British columns on the roads from Bavai to Le Cateau, Landrecies and Avesnes.[4] The French Territorial troops south of Denain were also detected. It appeared that it would be impossible to catch the British on 26 August. Kluck and Kuhl clearly recognised that their south-eastward movement on 25 August had allowed the British to escape. They reported to OHL on the evening of 25 August that it would try to block the British retreat 'between Cambrai and St Quentin', that is, on 27 or 28 August at best. The 1st Army issued a march order for 26 August, not an attack order. II AK was to march to the south-west of Cambrai, IV AK to the canal halfway between Cambrai and St Quentin, III AK south-west of Le Cateau. IV RK would march to Cattenières, the left flank of the BEF on 26 August.

III AK

IR 48 was the advance guard for 5 ID.[5] It was marching on secondary roads and was well into France before the regiment was aware of it. The residents of Le Quesnoy watched curiously as the troops filed past. The owner of an orchard passed out 'wonderful pears, which we accepted with thanks and were eaten with pleasure. The contrast with the fanaticised Belgians was a relief'. The regiment requisitioned wagons to carry the troops' packs.

As the regiment reached the east side of the Forest of Mormal, the hussar patrols took fire. 9/48 easily drove the British from the railway station and the Sambre Bridge. 5 ID HQ had not expected further British resistance and had sent the quartering parties to Maroilles ahead of IR 48. The quartering party, which was made up of rear-echelon types, took fire and raced back in complete confusion, having 'unintentionally provided the regiment with useful intelligence': the British occupied the high ground north of Maroilles, probably not very strong, though they could be reinforced. 10/48, 11/48 and 12/48 advanced in a broad front against Maroilles, 9/48 in reserve, I/48 echeloned to the right rear, II/48 to the left rear. The attack was difficult. The one possible avenue of approach was to both sides of the road across wet meadows overgrown with low bushes. This restricted IR 48's visibility, while the British could look down on them and cover their movement with 'well-distributed fire'. It grew dark, making artillery observation difficult, and the fire from II/FAR 18 landed ineffectually south of the town. IR 48 asked that a gun be brought right down to the firing line and an artillery lieutenant volunteered. The gun was manhandled forward, in spite of British MG fire. German troops searched a nearby hamlet and found several British soldiers, but also set some houses on fire, illuminating IR 48. The cannon did good work, suppressing the British MG. Shortly after 2300 the British fire was sensibly weaker. The companies were able to advance and took prisoners. A group of British soldiers put down their weapons and put up their hands. The III/48 adjutant went forward to receive their surrender, but the British took up their weapons and shot him dead, whereupon III/48 stopped taking prisoners. British losses were heavy; where the cannon fired, bodies lay atop each other. In spite of the mass of ammunition the British had expended, IR 48's casualties amounted to no more than the III/48 adjutant and 20–30 KIA and WIA.

The account of this action in the British official history has no resemblance to that in the IR 48 history.[6] The British version is confused, but apparently two groups of British hussars were supposed to have held up the Germans in Mariolles for half an hour, and fell back only when the Germans brought up a cannon. The Royal Berkshires arrived, found that the Germans had fallen back to the bridge, attacked unsuccessfully to retake it, lost sixty men and went over to the defensive.

IR 24, which was the 6 ID advance guard, reported contact with the British rearguard on 25 August only once.[7] The advance guard artillery, I/FAR 3, was engaged twice, against bicycle troops and a French march column.[8] The British threw away 'ammunition, web gear, weapons, ammunition boxes, boxes with biscuits, broken-down wagons, discarded packs lay by the road in piles'. I/FAR 39's supply vehicles did not arrive, but the artillerymen were able to compensate from the British supplies left at a railway station.[9] The principal source of excitement that day was crossing the border into France.[10] IR 64, which was in the division main body, did not see action that day, but marched from 0300 until midnight. It bivouacked on the road at the west end of the Forest of Mormal.[11] The rear of the column, IR 35, did not even enter the forest.[12] The road was clogged with vehicles, which caused traffic jams and frequent halts.

Landrecies

IR 27 was the advance guard regiment of 7 ID.[13] During its march on 25 August it was delayed several times for short periods by dismounted cavalry. Around 1800 it was ordered to seize the Sambre Bridge at Landrecies. It was not known whether there were enemy forces there; the British were thought to be retreating. When it became dark the distance between the advance guard and main body was reduced to 300 metres. The troops were tired. At the edge of Landrecies the point took very heavy and completely unexpected close-range rifle and MG fire from the hedges and houses. IR 27 and her sister regiment, IR 165, had broken through at Liège, so they were experienced night fighters. The regimental commander deployed 9/IR 27 and I/27 to the right of the road, but they could not advance due to a combination of enemy fire, darkness, hedges and wire fences. The regiment had suffered from friendly fire at Liège, and the troops continually called out to each other 'Don't fire!' The machine gun company came forward to provide fire support and the troops slowly made progress. 6/27 and 7/27 were committed to the right of the road and they stormed a British MG, but one company commander was severely wounded and a lieutenant killed. The enemy held fast and further advance was impossible. Flanking fire gave the impression that the British were trying to surround the advance guard.

The initial British fire also hit the artillery battery, hussars and brigade staff marching behind the advance guard company. The hussars turned around and escaped at a gallop. Some of the gun teams of 1/FAR 4, the leading artillery battery, were shot down. The gun crews took cover in the roadside ditches. 1/FAR 4 could not get into firing position because of exploding ammunition in an overturned and burning caisson.[14] With help from the infantry, 3/FAR 4 cut lanes in the bushes on both sides of the road and hauled guns across the ditches. They then cut more lanes in the hedges and opened fire, drawing small-arms fire in return. The vegetation and terrain prevented 2/FAR 4 from coming into a firing position.

The commander of IR 27 sent the adjutant to the rear to get reinforcements and at 2200 IR 165, which had just stopped to bivouac, was sent forward. II/165 was to deploy to the east of the road and I/165 (two companies) and III/165 to the west. I/165 and III/165 immediately encountered a thick hedge, reinforced with wire 'that stood like a wall'.[15] It proved impossible to go around the hedge and took half an hour of hard work to cut through it, only to be immediately faced with a second, if possible even thicker, hedge: 'The composition of which can only be judged by those who know Belgian hedges from personal observation. In any case they are harder to break through than a thick, massive wall.' II/165 had a similar experience. Since it was also pitch dark, the regimental commander halted both battalions.

At 2400 the British also began to fire with artillery. Small groups of IR 27 that had made it through the hedges tried to advance but were stopped by flanking fire. At 0130 the commander of IR 27 ordered a 1,000-metre withdrawal, IR 27 to the right of the road, IR 165 to the left. The troops moved with difficulty through the waterlogged meadows, hedges and fences. A patrol from IR 165 succeeded in dragging back an immobilised artillery piece. Finally the position was reached, security put out and the companies organised; the troops dozed as best they could. At about 0300 the British evacuated their position, leaving behind 25 dead and a machine gun that had apparently received a direct hit from an artillery shell.

IR 27 lost 1 OFF and 34 EM KIA, 5 OFF and 82 EM WIA, but 4 of the officers stayed with the regiment. The regimental histories of IR 165 and FAR 4 did not report any casualties. The FAR 40 history says that the commander of 1/FAR 4 was severely wounded.

The British official history is more colourful, but little of it agrees with the German accounts.[16] It says that the security outpost was provided by the 3rd Company of 3/Coldstream Guards. The Germans tried to trick the guardsman by answering their challenge in French, and were able by this means to come right up to the outpost and rush it, knock down an officer and seize a MG. The British were able (somehow) to throw the Germans back with rifle fire and recapture the MG. 'Charge after charge was made by the enemy without gaining any advantage.' The security detachment was reinforced by unnamed units (presumably the rest of 3/Coldstream) and also by 2/Coldstream Guards. The Germans illuminated the battlefield by setting hay ricks alight with incendiary bombs. The British reported that the Germans withdrew after midnight when the German guns were hit by a single round of artillery and knocked out, losing three artillery officers and sixteen artillerymen dead.

The odds were three attacking German battalions against two defending British. The Germans had been stopped by a combination of British fire, pitch darkness and Belgian hedges. The 3/Coldstream Guards lost 120 casualties. From reading the German and British accounts, it is remarkable that German and British losses were essentially even, although the British account claims the Germans took far heavier casualties.

British I Corps

The British official history may not have been impressed with the IR 27 attack at Landrecies, but the commander of the British I Corps, Sir Douglas Haig, most certainly was. Haig was with the 4th Guards Brigade at Landrecies, and the IR 27 attack caused him to panic. At 2200 I Corps reported to GHQ by telephone: 'Attack heavy from the north-west can you send help?' GHQ told II Corps to send the 19th Brigade at least, an absurd idea which the II Corps commander immediately shot down. Haig was evidently convinced that the Germans were manoeuvring to turn his left flank, for he decided to have the 1st Division support the left of the 4th Guards Brigade, and he suggested that the troops at Le Cateau move to Landrecies. At 0135 Haig reported that the situation was 'very critical' and that he was reinforcing his left with every man at his disposal. The official history concludes that GHQ told I Corps that it would have to retreat south, not south-west. This meant the BEF would be split into two halves for the foreseeable future and the right flank of II Corps would be wide open. IR 27's attack may not have been a tactical success, but it was a distinct operational gain for the German 1st Army.

German IV AK

IR 66, with the 7 ID main body, had a less eventful day. It passed over the British position at Elouges and the road to Audregnies, which showed the regiment the effectiveness of German artillery fire and the extent of British losses.[17] Dead horses lay by shot-up gun limbers, there were abandoned vehicles, dead and wounded British troops. The regiment marched until 2200. III/66 rejoined the regiment, having marched from Brussels.

A battery commander of FAR 40 spoke with a German infantry officer, who said, 'I take my hat off to your guns, I wouldn't have thought it possible: when an enemy skirmisher line appeared, your shrapnel fire landed on it immediately. The British also took your fire in the flank and fell like hares. Their retreat became panic flight'.[18] A FAR 40 lieutenant wrote, 'We went past the scene of our work yesterday. Donnerwetter! What a sight!'

At 1500 IR 72 was detached from the main body of 7 ID to act, with 1/FAR 74, as a covering force to the right.[19] Approaching the village of Verchain, the point element saw red trousers. The regiment deployed on a ridge about 2 km north-east of the town, but the effort was wasted, for as the skirmisher line approached the town about 150 French surrendered. The regiment now marched in column with security to the front. As the point entered the village of Saulzoir, it saw on the shady village square packs lying on the ground and weapons stacked in tripods. It then heard many voices at the village pub. The regimental commander and his adjutant dismounted their horses and entered the large public room and found fifty French soldiers, who were initially surprised, but readily followed the colonel outside, where IR 72 was waiting. He asked one of the soldiers, who were Territorials, why they had not offered any resistance, and the Territorial replied: 'Why fight? We didn't want this war at all and were forced to leave our families and businesses. Why should we get ourselves killed?' Such affairs became a common occurrence that day as IR 72 took between 600 and 800 prisoners; in two days IR 72 had taken 1,750–1,950 POWs. The regiment, still on its own, continued the march. It stopped at 2200 and bivouacked in the town of St Python, just north-west of Solesmes. Patrols searched the houses and found large numbers of French troops, who were taken prisoner.

IR 153 was the advance guard of 8 ID.[20] The regimental commander was Duke Ernst of Sachsen-Altenburg, who was actually a major-general but who insisted in personally leading his Thuringians into combat. A platoon of FAR 75 marched with the point, the rest of the battery with the advance guard battalion. This proved to be a very useful arrangement; at 1400 a few rounds from the guns quickly drove off a French detachment.

Air reconnaissance showed that the British were trying to escape; the highest priority was marching long distances quickly. The regiment requisitioned farm wagons to carry the rucksacks; the increase in the size of the regimental trains had to be accepted. In spite of occasional light contact that the advance guard made (FAR 75 with the advance guard expended ten shells), the main body of 8 ID could maintain an uninterrupted march.

At Vendegies, 8 km north of Solesmes, the point took heavy fire. In pouring rain the regiment deployed to attack, II/153 on both sides of the road, I/153 to the right, two companies of III/153 to the right rear, two on the road, where the advance guard battery also set up. Once again the advance guard battery proved its worth; its fire against the edge of the town and the railway embankment allowed the infantry to move quickly to the far side of the town. The regiment took 300 French Territorials POW. 'Almost all older men who had little interest in fighting and who appeared glad to be quickly out of it – they willingly fell into formation and marched off.' The regiment lost 1 OFF and 3 EM KIA, 22 EM WIA.

The regiment's goal was Pommeroeul, north-east of Le Cateau, so at 1700 it set off again. At 1900, after a twelve-hour march, it began to get dark, when the point unexpectedly took fire from Solesmes: the cavalry had not reported that it was occupied by the enemy. The regiment quickly deployed, the lead battalion, II/153, on both sides of the road, III/153 deployed a company to its right and three to the left, I/153 deployed two more companies on the left, while two remained in reserve. The artillery battery and MG Company set up near the road. The duke thought his regiment had encountered a rearguard, which was correct (South Lancashires and Wiltshires of the 7th Brigade, 3rd Division[21]), and wanted to quickly push it out of the way. However, it was now dark, the British were firing with machine guns in addition to rifles, and the troops were encountering wire fences. As a battalion of IR 93 extended the line to the right there were friendly fire incidents. The duke ordered 'General Halt' to be sounded, followed by 'Officers Call', 'as though it were the end of a very long day in a peacetime manoeuvre'. But it worked – the uncontrolled firing stopped.

8 ID ordered a night attack for 2100 – thick columns, unloaded rifles, fixed bayonets – which was called off at the last minute when the duke reported to Division HQ that there were too many wire fences in the way. The troops bivouacked in place, on the wet ground with a bundle of straw under their heads; the duke and the brigade and division staffs slept in the roadside ditch. Patrols were sent out. The 1st Army HQ drove up in their vehicles, intending to bivouac in Solesmes, and had to make do with a farmhouse a short distance to the rear.[22] 8 ID had marched 40 km.

HKK 2

2 KD on the HKK 2 left was to march on Le Cateau, 4 KD in the centre on Solesmes and 9 KD on the right to 12 km south of Solesmes: HKK 2 was clearly swinging south-east on the basis of the 1st Army's assumption that the British were withdrawing to Maubeuge. Their bivouacs on the evening of 25 August would put them directly in front of the British II Corps, instead of on its left flank and rear.

2 KD resumed the march at dawn. 4/Lifeguard Hussar R 2 was advance guard, and had to clear troops of the French 84th Territorial Division out of the town of Bouchain, capturing thirty-five.[23] Lifeguard Hussar R 1 now became the advance guard. A patrol reported several companies of enemy infantry and their baggage to the front. 3/Lifeguard Hussar R 1 went forward to investigate and managed to spring an ambush on the French at 300 metres range, causing significant casualties. The French were able to quickly find cover in a sunken road. They had considerable numerical superiority over 3/Lifeguard Hussar R 1, which had sent off several patrols and now counted only forty men. A French attempt to turn the right flank was beaten off, but French troops who had not been ambushed caused

serious problems on the left. As the casualties mounted, the squadron commander asked for reinforcements. The regiment came forward at a gallop, accompanied by a battery of horse artillery, which immediately went into action. 4/Lifeguard Hussar R 1 dismounted and reinforced the left flank, while 1/Lifeguard Hussar R 1 was held in reserve.

The regimental staff and 2/Lifeguard Hussar R 2 conducted a mounted charge against the French right flank in successive waves of platoons, with each platoon in very open order. The French, completely surprised, surrendered: 4 OFF, 353 EM, 4 MGs, several vehicles and horses. This was a textbook example of effective modern combined-arms cavalry tactics.

2 KD continued the march in pouring rain, with Lifeguard Hussar R 1 providing security on the right flank. It took fire from French infantry, evaded the fire, swung around the enemy position, approached through dead ground and conducted a mounted charge. Some of the French were speared with the lance, others shot with pistols; thirty-five surrendered.

Dragoon R 2 was now advance guard.[24] West of St Hilaire (just north of Caudry) it encountered troops of the French 84th Territorial Division. The regimental commander, Poseck, wanted to attack dismounted but the division commander ordered him to charge. Poseck instructed 3/Dragoon R 2 to charge west of the town while 2/Dragoon R 2 would move through St Hilaire to attack the enemy flank. 1/Dragoon R 2, the point element, had already dismounted and would manoeuvre to the east. 3/Dragoon R 2 charged in one line with wide intervals, taking increasingly heavy fire from houses and hedges. It then fell into a deep sunken road with steep banks and the French could shoot or bayonet them at leisure. A few troopers, including the squadron commander, were able to jump the ditch. Only the flanking platoon did not drop into the ditch. The rest of the regiment was involved in a series of charges and dismounted battles in the open, against isolated farmhouses and in the town, eventually taking more than 140 prisoners. Dragoon R 2 lost 2 OFF and 23 EM KIA, 19 EM WIA.

4 KD patrols were in constant contact with British cavalry patrols.[25] At one point the British Cavalry Division was sighted. 4 KD and 9 KD deployed for a mounted battle, but the British withdrew. 1/Dragoon R 18 was sent as reconnaissance squadron towards Solesmes.[26] Patrols from this squadron sighted British and French troops on the high ground east of the town. Towards evening 1/Uhlan R 9 and 2/Uhlan R 9 were sent towards Solesmes as flank security for the division. In pouring rain and pitch darkness the two Uhlan squadrons ran into the British; a night firefight ensued until the German cavalry retired.

9 KD, the right-hand division, moved out at 0100, while it was still dark. 2/Uhlan R 5 was again the advance guard.[27] It crossed the Schelde canal at Denain, where the residents, believing them to be British, gave them a warm welcome, including flowers and refreshments. Six kilometres further, at Haspres, the uhlans pushed aside French troops, capturing twenty. From this point the

uhlans made frequent contact. The commander of Hussar R 8 personally captured thirty French.[28] Dragoon R 19 stopped at Avesnes-les-Aubert,[29] Cuirassier R 4 at St Vaast. The division had covered only 30 km but was by now worn out. Nevertheless, 9 KD too had caught up with the British.

In the late afternoon a patrol from Hussar R 12 was sent to Solesmes to make contact with the German II AK.[30] 2 KD was apparently badly informed concerning the friendly and enemy situations: II AK was a day's march to the north. The patrol reported that, 'Strong British columns are marching back to the south-west. The supposed II AK is British'. This was confirmed by a second patrol, but was met with scepticism at 2 KD HQ, which apparently thought the British should be much further south, a not unreasonable expectation.

2 KD was now completely exhausted and encountering more serious resistance, so the division stopped for the night. Lifeguard Hussar R 1 bivouacked in Carnières, Lifeguard Hussar R 2 immediately to the north in Rieux. Hussar R 12 spent the night near soaked to the skin and said that neither man nor horse got any rest.

At dawn on 25 August Jäger 10 marched out again.[31] By noon, 'The sun was burning hot, the pack pressed down terribly, but nothing stopped this almost fanatical marching. If we had not had such good-humoured, irrepressible boys in our ranks, three-quarters of the battalion would have fallen out. But the tired jokes made the rounds. Even the officers enjoyed them, though the jokes were often at their expense.' From 1000 to 1400 there was a rest, but around 1100 it began to rain and the Jäger were soaked through. Jäger 10 reached St Hilaire at 2100 totally exhausted. The town was already full of cavalry and bicyclists and the battalion had to bivouac in the wet fields. Jäger 9 was luckier.[32] It reached the town of Rieux, the troops were fed from the field kitchens and the locals gave the Jäger a warm welcome, taking them from their shakoes to be British; the Jäger did nothing to correct their mistake. The same thing happened to Jäger 3.[33] The locals shouted, '*Vive l'Angleterre; coupe la tête des Allemands*' (Hooray for Britain! Cut off the heads of the Germans!). In pouring rain the Jäger were given hot red wine, warm milk, plenty of bread and white flowers from pretty girls. The Jäger by now knew how to play this game and tried to act the part of British soldiers by using expressions such as 'beefsteak'. The battalion marched until 2200, when it reached Boussières. It was still pouring with rain and the troops lay down in the street. The five Jäger battalions were formed into a Jäger Brigade under the commander of Jäger 10. The fact that on the evening of 25 August the Jäger were up with the German cavalry and in the immediate vicinity of the British army is indicative of outstanding training, discipline and, above all, morale.

HKK 2 was about 5 km from the British II Corps. After an epic forced march, HKK 2 had caught up with the BEF.

British II Corps

The British official history summarised 25 August in the II Corps sector as 'a running fight during which the Germans closed in, following the II Corps and the Cavalry Division, so that at night their advanced troops were practically in contact with the British'.[34] 'The further operations of the cavalry had all the characteristics of a prolonged rearguard action.' The German sources show that this was incorrect. The Germans had serious contact only with French Territorials. The only British troops that were in contact were patrols. This is confirmed by the British official history itself, which says that the rearguards were 'little pressed' – because they withdrew before making contact with the German advanced guards. The British cavalry withdrew when shelled by German artillery. The British rearguards and cavalry failed to slow the German advance, allowing the Germans to march until they were right on top of II Corps.

The South Lancashires and Wiltshires (7th Brigade, 3rd Division), the rearguard which had engaged IR 153 north of Solesmes, withdrew after dark. The British 4th Division, which had been in a rearguard position south of Solesmes, began withdrawing to the west of II Corps at 2100. The Cavalry Division had already withdrawn behind II Corps to the south of Le Cateau. There was no British security force of any kind north of the II Corps infantry pickets. Early on the morning of 26 August the Germans would appear without warning directly in front of the British infantry positions.

The British II Corps' goose was now cooked. The British had failed to delay the march of either HKK 2 or IV AK. The advance guard of the German 8 ID was 7 km to the front, HKK 2 even closer. The German march was better organised and conducted than the British: the regiments of the German IV AK marched about 35–40 km, II Corps half that. The British march had been delayed by traffic jams – that is, lack of movement control – in Solesmes and Le Cateau far more than the Germans had been delayed by British rearguards. The German troops bivouacked at a reasonable hour, rested and started early on 26 August, while many British troops exhausted themselves by moving all night. The chaotic conditions in II Corps would force it to defend on 26 August under exceptionally unfavourable conditions.

Le Cateau

Strength of the Opposing Forces

It is an article of faith among British historians that the British were massively outnumbered at Le Cateau. To prove this point, Becke made a detailed comparison of the strength of both sides.[1]

He says that the British had three infantry divisions, an infantry brigade and a cavalry division: 40 infantry battalions, 12 cavalry regiments (plus the two divisional squadrons), 246 guns (41 batteries) and at most 90 MGs (due to losses, actually far fewer).

The Germans supposedly had four corps (II, III, IV, IV Reserve) and probably two cavalry divisions: 102 infantry battalions, 12 cavalry regiments (plus 32 divisional squadrons), 600 guns and 240 MGs.

The British official history once again maintained that at Le Cateau the BEF drove off hordes of Germans who had a 3:1 numerical superiority. Map 11 of the official history shows the BEF being attacked by IV AK, HKK 2, IV RK and 5 ID of III AK. This is completely wrong. The British official history was intentionally distorting the facts to embellish the heroic image of the Battle of Le Cateau. This myth has been uncritically accepted by subsequent British histories.

On the basis of no more evidence than the British official history Map 11, Lomas says, 'Against them [British II Corps], Kluck sent four divisions drawn from III and IV Corps, the three divisions of II Cavalry corps and, later in the day, the artillery and a further division of IV Reserve Corps'.[2] Lomas's map of Le Cateau shows the 1st Division of the IV Reserve Corps (the 1st Reserve Division was actually in East Prussia – the corps consisted of the 7th and 22nd Reserve Divisions) and the 13th and 14th Reserve Brigades attacking.[3] This attack never took place either. Ascoli says:

> [the Germans committed] III Corps (5th and 6th Divisions), IV Corps (7th and
> 8th Divisions), II Cavalry Corps (2nd, 4th and 9th Divisions) and – by early
> afternoon – the entire artillery and at least one division of IV Reserve Corps.
> It should have been more than enough to achieve a crushing defeat. It was not.
> The BEF survived, dealt the enemy another smashing blow, and so lived to fight
> another day.[4]

Ascoli describes how at Le Cateau the remnants of the Suffolk, Manchester
and Argyll regiments managed to hold off the 'newly arrived 5th Division of
III Corps', while the British 4th Division stopped the German 7th Reserve
Division.[5] Neither German division ever reached the battlefield and neither fight
actually took place.

The Le Cateau Myth

The turn to the south-east on 25 August meant that on 26 August the only
German infantry corps that could attack the BEF was IV AK, plus HKK 2. Even
IV AK could initially attack with one brigade of 7 ID. 8 ID had to march to the
west to be in a position to attack that afternoon. The 14th Brigade didn't make it
to the fight at all.

Half of IV RK artillery regiment (three batteries) arrived after noon. One section (three batteries) of the III AK artillery arrived after the British had begun to
withdraw. One regiment (six batteries) of 8 ID (IV AK) artillery and the other
half-regiment (three batteries) of IV RK artillery arrived at the very end of the
fight. None of the IV RK or III AK infantry would be engaged on 26 August.

The brunt of the battle on the German side would be borne by three infantry brigades, three artillery regiments of IV AK and HKK 2's horse artillery,
dismounted cavalry and five bone-tired battalions of Jäger; in total 23 infantry
battalions, 27 artillery batteries (162 guns), 18 cavalry regiments (at least half of
which were at half strength), 6 squadrons of divisional cavalry and 84 MGs.

It was the British who were numerically superior at Le Cateau. The British
had almost twice as many infantry battalions and guns. The Germans probably
had a few more MGs.

The Germans had two advantages. First, the German cavalry dismounted to
fight and the German horse artillery was in the thick of the battle. The British
horse artillery did little; the British cavalry did nothing. Second, as the attacker,
the Germans could mass their forces at the place of their choosing.

The truly amazing thing is that at the very end of its discussion of 'The German
Accounts', the British official history acknowledges in a single paragraph that its

own description in the text of the forces involved was completely wrong. It admits that the Germans had only two infantry divisions and three cavalry divisions and that IV RK and III AK never made it to the battlefield. The British official history then undermines its sole objective statement concerning the forces involved by contending that the Germans had 'the artillery of five divisions and three cavalry divisions' against the artillery of three British divisions 'and some [!] of the guns of the Cavalry Division – which alone made the British stand difficult'.[6] Not only is this wrong, it is deceptive: in fact, as we have seen, the British far outnumbered the Germans in engaged artillery. The British official history did not change its text to accommodate its belated recognition of the actual situation on 26 August. British historians have found it much more satisfying to stick to the heroic myth of the outnumbered but plucky II Corps fighting off Teutonic hordes.

IX AK

IR 90 was ordered early on 26 August to blockade the north-west side of Maubeuge.[7] The work really advanced when the regimental engineer tool wagon arrived in the morning. At 0815 a dragoon patrol reported the approach of French forces, and half an hour later their skirmisher lines were visible, although they were out of range. The regimental historian wrote:

> The fusiliers now had motivation. They took off their uniform blouses and dug until the sweat ran. They fell in love with their trench and flattened the walls so thoroughly, you'd think the general was going to inspect them, and rounded the firing ports and flattened the spoil so that it looked like it had been done by a steamroller.

At 1030 a platoon-sized enemy point element crossed a railway embankment and the IR 90 security element engaged them. The French withdrew, leaving a dozen of their number on the ground.

> Slowly several waves of enemy troops approached. They formed a firing line and poured fire on the IR 90 positions, especially I/90, without doing any damage. The regiment hardly returned the fire: the French would be allowed to approach to a range where he could get a really appropriate reception. The field kitchens sent hot pea soup forward to some trenches … A battery of FAR 60 then brought a quick end to the glory of the French infantry attack. The shells landed in the skirmisher lines and threw them apart. The enemy ran in disorder, in wild flight, until they were out of breath and began walking. But the shells followed them, and in terror they ran back up the slope that they had so comfortably descended.

After a time a French column was seen in the distance, marching back to Maubeuge. In the afternoon the regiment was pulled out of the trenches, which would be occupied by Landwehr. At 1800 the regiment resumed the march south.

British II Corps

At 1930 on 25 August BEF GHQ issued orders for the withdrawal south-west to continue on 26 August to a position 16–25 km to the south at Busigny–Le Catelet.[8] II Corps had issued orders at 2215 on 25 August for the withdrawal on 26 August. The trains would begin to move at 0400, the main bodies at 0700.

The Cavalry Division did not get the orders which stipulated that it cover the II Corps withdrawal until 2300. The Cavalry Division had already retired, badly scattered, behind II Corps. Shortly thereafter the commander of the 5th Dragoon Guards, which had been with the 4th Division at Solesmes, came to the Cavalry Division HQ to report that the 4th Division had withdrawn to the left of II Corps and that the Germans were at Solesmes.

This sorry state of affairs is discussed in every book on Le Cateau. What has never been pointed out is that the commanders of the Cavalry Division and the 4th Division demonstrated a breathtaking lack of initiative. It is the cavalry's job to cover a retreat, period; the idea that the Cavalry Division commander had no inkling, until he received the order at 2300, that his division would have to cover the retreat on 26 August is absurd. The 4th Division commander exercised what the Germans called *Kadavergehorsam* – unthinking (corpse-like) obedience – when he withdrew as previously ordered from Solesmes, without ensuring that someone else would hold this vital position, in the full knowledge that the Cavalry Division was behind him and strong German forces were to his immediate front.

The Cavalry Division commander went to the II Corps HQ and expressed the opinion that unless II Corps and the 4th Division could march before dawn, they would have to fight where they stood. This came as a revelation to the II Corps commander, and he sent for the 3rd Division commander, who said that many of the 3rd Division units were still coming in and that he could not get moving until 0900; in other words, the 3rd Division commander was just now telling his corps commander that he was going to miss his 0700 start time by two hours. In many armies, this sort of thing gets commanders relieved, even court-martialled.

The Cavalry Division commander then said that his division was so tired that it could not fight on 26 August. This truly remarkable statement must be compared against HKK 2's marching and combat performance in the last three weeks in general, and the last three days in particular; on 26 August HKK 2 would cap it all off by taking on an entire British infantry division and a good part of a second division.

Indeed, the British Cavalry Division had completely abdicated its responsibilities; there were no Cavalry Division security or reconnaissance elements to the north of II Corps. The divisional cavalry of both the 4th and 5th Divisions had been taken from them to reinforce the Cavalry Division, so the two flank divisions had no organic reconnaissance assets.[9] On the morning of 26 August HKK 2 and IV AK were going to appear like a bolt from the blue immediately to the front of the British infantry.

The II Corps commander then (0330) supposedly decided to 'strike the enemy hard, and, after he had done so, continue the retreat'. The actual content of his orders was not stated in the official history. This 'decision' may be an ex post facto rationalisation. It appears that the actual decision was to occupy defensive positions and hope for the best.

No decision made at 0330 was going to affect the situation in any case. The II Corps commander gave his orders to defend to the 5th Division commander personally at 0400, which meant the orders to defend would generally arrive at company level about the same time the Germans did. The 14th Brigade west of Le Cateau got the order at 0600, the Germans arriving soon after; the elements east of Le Cateau never got the order at all. The II Corps order arrived at the 4th Division at 0500; the Germans hit the 4th Division battalions before the division order to defend even arrived. As for the 3rd Division, the British official history noted that the 7th and 8th Brigades did not receive either the order of 2215 on 25 August to withdraw, or the order of the morning of 26 August to defend. The only unit in II Corps to receive the order in a timely fashion was the 9th Brigade. If units were in defensive positions when the Germans hit, it was because they had occupied them on their own initiative and in the absence of higher instructions.

The II Corps commander did not determine the course of the battle – the commanders of HKK 2 and IV AK seized the initiative and controlled the fight. The German troops attacked the British at or near their bivouac areas and forced them to defend in place under unfavourable circumstances.

II Corps was lined up along the Le Cateau–Cambrai road. This position had no military rhyme or reason. Nowhere did it offer long-range firing positions. Along the entire front the Germans had covered and concealed avenues of approach to close range with the British position. This was especially true at the weakest point in the British line, the right flank west of Le Cateau. The entire position was on the forward slope and withdrawal involved moving up high ground to the rear, which made the British fine targets for German pursuit fire; most British units suffered the heaviest casualties while withdrawing, in addition to which the retreating units were broken up and lost cohesion, sometimes for days.

Whether the British army had a functioning operational doctrine is uncertain. In any case, it had little practice in operations. Doctrine imposes clear definitions for operations – attack, delay, defence – and then subdivides these categories – meeting engagement, deliberate attack, night attack. This serves to establish the

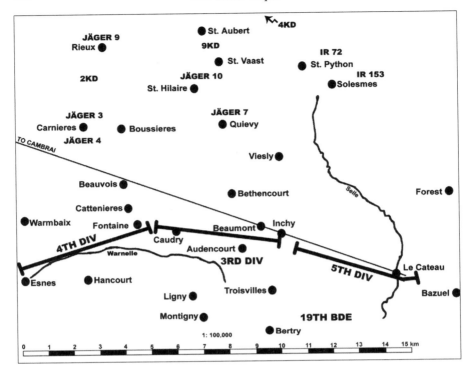

Fig. 19: Le Cateau, 26 August.

requirements for each operation and ensure that each unit acts in doctrinal conformity. Doctrinal clarity is especially important where time is short. No army
has a doctrinal operation called 'occupy a defensive position, strike the enemy
hard [sic], then withdraw'. Smith-Dorrien's intent might have been translated
into doctrinal terms as a 'high risk delay'. The operative concept here is 'delay',
which immediately establishes a set of requirements. Units cannot become 'decisively engaged', that is to say, in such close contact with the enemy that they
cannot withdraw. They therefore need to choose positions with long-range fields
of fire (to engage the enemy at maximum range) and with covered and concealed
routes of withdrawal.

II Corps should have delayed by bounds to the south, with the 5th Division
stopping at the high ground at Busigny (about 10 km to the south-west). This
would have gained time, put distance between the corps and the Germans,
and allowed a defence on much more favourable terrain which commanded
the ground to its front and offered long-range fire against the north side of the
Warnelle ravine, as well as providing covered routes of retreat. It is possible that
the II Corps commander did not order a delay because he thought that the corps
was so disorganised it was incapable of such a complex operation. Whatever his
reasoning, once again, II Corps would conduct an inert defence.

British 4th Division

For reasons that are hard to understand, the 4th Division commander had decided to defend on the north side of the Warnelle ravine, with 12th Brigade on the left at Esnes-Longsart, 11th Brigade on the right south of Fontaine au Pire and 10th Brigade in reserve at Haucourt.[10] In order to withdraw, the forward brigades would have to cross 1,500–2,000 metres of open hillside. There was a gap of 1,200 metres between the 4th Division right flank and the 3rd Division left.

The lead elements of the 4th Division did not begin to reach their positions until 0100 on 26 August. The 12th Brigade on the left was not assembled until 0500. The 11th Brigade did not begin to arrive until 0215 due to a traffic jam caused by 3rd Division supply units. German night cavalry patrols were active, and the 11th Brigade rearguard had several firefights with them.[11] The Brigade then got lost and bivouacked in Fontaine au Pire and the fields to the west. The 10th Brigade took a wrong turn, took German fire, backtracked and did not reach Haucourt until 0430. The 10th Brigade trains also got lost and spent the night at Cattenières – on the German side of the 4th Division front line – realised their mistake at first light and quickly pulled back to Haucourt. Much of this poor land navigation can be attributed to the fact that the 4th Division had only maps for Belgium and Germany and none for France. It is also clear that the British units did not reconnoitre their routes of withdrawal. On the morning of 26 August the 4th Division artillery was not in firing position since it expected to resume the withdrawal at 0700.

For reasons which neither the British official history nor anyone else has explained, GQG had stopped the movement of all the 4th Division service and service support units, as well as the heavy artillery. They were ordered by GQG to retire, and they waited south of the Somme for the division to arrive on 28 August. The only possible logic behind such an order was that GQG decided to solve the traffic control problem by separating the division and its 'unnecessary' service and service support units. The 4th Division therefore did not have most of its signal company, bicyclists, engineers, ammunition resupply units or field ambulances. The 4th Division now had less combat and combat service support than the British army had in the Crimea.

Cattenières

Jäger 4, the advance guard of the Jäger 'regiment' (Jäger 4, Jäger 7, Jäger 9), moved out an hour before dawn at 0400, along with the cavalry advance guard, Dragoon R 2.[12] 2 KD therefore had a two-hour head start on the British 12th Brigade. The 2 KD patrols saw the British at Longsart: entrenching infantry, dense columns of infantry and supply columns. The MG Section of 2 KD (MG 9) went forward at a gallop, along with the Horse Artillery Section of FAR 35. The MG Company commander of Jäger 4 saw this and also brought his guns forward at a gallop. The 2 KD MG Section was in action first, at 600 metres range, firing their seven guns directly from their wagons, a trick reserved only for German cavalry MG sections. They were soon joined by Jäger 4's MG and the horse artillery.

The only security the 12th Brigade established was an outpost at the railway crossing at Wambaix, which did not observe the German approach, probably because of the poor light, intervening high ground and the town of Cattenières. The official history says 1/King's Own was stationary in company column, each company on line, one company behind the other, arms stacked, when shortly after 0600 it was hit by MG fire. The King's Own supposedly returned the MG fire, 'with immediate effect'. The Germans then began to shell the King's Own and they moved to another position and again engaged the MG, 'smothering' them. 'The King's Own, though reduced by some four hundred casualties, recovered themselves with commendable rapidity.'

The King's Own regimental history has a much different tone:[13] 'In the first burst eighty-three men were killed, including the C.O., and over 200 wounded. Men rushed to unpile arms, ammunition was searched for and general mass chaos prevailed.' The MG fire was followed by shrapnel, but the second in command rallied the battalion and brought it under cover on the reverse slope of the hill. The battalion was then withdrawn to Harcourt. There was no mention of heroic resistance; the battalion had been smashed in minutes.

1/Warwickshire had only stopped movement at 0600, in a cornfield just east of Haucourt:[14]

[The Warwickshires] presently saw another British regiment [the King's Own] attacked and driven from the opposite ridge. Spontaneously extending, they dashed forward under Major Christie to the rescue. The attack was thus made without orders and was ill-advised; though a few reached the hedge which marked the crest of the ridge, they were met by so hot a fire that they were forced to fall back with the loss of seven officers and forty men, to a position on the Haucourt-Ligny road below the hill, where they held out throughout the day under an increasing artillery bombardment. The battalion was now split up and out of touch with what was going on around it.

The 12th Brigade was now down to two battalions.

The British official history says that 'for at least an hour and a half the 12th Brigade held its own against the 2nd Cavalry Division and two Jäger battalions backed by numerous artillery and machine guns'. The British official history's account of the Jäger attack bears little resemblance to that of Jäger histories. It says Jäger 4 attacked 'just as the British would have desired – in bunches, firing from the hip'. The fire of 2/Lancashire Fusiliers stopped Jäger 4, 'and the Lancashire

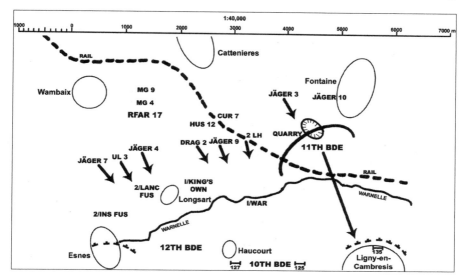

Fig. 20: BR 4th Division, 26 August.

Fusiliers took advantage of the lull to re-form on a better position a short distance in rear'. It maintains that the fire of 2/Royal Inniskilling Fusiliers drove the Jäger 7 back, and that an Inniskilling company commander walked the ground (!) and counted forty-seven German dead on his front alone. Unfortunately for the credibility of this account, Jäger 7 did not withdraw until 1400 and the battalion had only 24 KIA. The British official history's evaluation of the 12th Brigade battle at 1100 was that 'The German attack, delivered by a force of cavalry and Jäger, with a very powerful backing of artillery, had been repulsed'.

In fact, the lack of elementary security precautions had allowed the German MGs to immediately destroy two British battalions. It would have taken some time for the Jäger to catch up with the mounted MG and horse artillery. When they arrived they began a combined-arms attack on the remnants of the 12th Brigade. Jäger 7 deployed on the right, then Uhlan R 3, Jäger 4 in the centre, then Dragoon R 2, Jäger 9 (which moved left to attack the 11th Brigade), Hussar R 12 on the left. The cavalry had already seen hard service, were at about half strength and together might optimistically have dismounted the equivalent of two companies of infantry.

Jäger 7 deployed two companies in the first line, one echeloned to the right rear.[15] The MG Company found an 'exceptionally favourable' position on the left flank. The commander of 3/Jäger 7 on the right flank was killed and two officers wounded. On the other hand, the Jäger enfiladed the Lancashire Fusiliers with MG fire, inflicting severe casualties and forcing them to withdraw, 'which offered the MG an extraordinarily good target'. (The 12th Brigade withdrawal is not shown on the British official history Map 11.) Jäger 7 was then ordered to defend in place.

The Jäger 4 history said that German MG, artillery and rifle fire had caused such heavy enemy casualties that the attack order was soon given.[16] The enemy position was overrun with little loss, numerous prisoners were taken and the British were driven to the south side of the Warnelle. Further advance was impossible because the British had brought up reinforcements (10th Brigade) and superior artillery.

Dragoon R 2 dismounted, crossed the railway embankment and advanced in long bounds to close in to effective rifle range.[17] The 2 KD MG section had already suffered 'serious casualties' by the time the cavalrymen arrived. At 1,200 metres the dragoons began firing, kneeling so that they could see above the sugar beets. The advance was continual and gathered speed. When the left flank got to within 150 metres the British disappeared over the hill in long bounds. The dragoons delivered their pursuit fire standing, 'which allowed few to get down the slope alive'. The dragoons were ordered to defend in place. The British 10th Brigade had entered the fight, and British artillery had begun to fire. 'Further advance was out of the question, the enemy counter-attacked and there were increasing casualties.' Ammunition began to run low and could not be replenished because the horses were 4 km to the rear. The cavalrymen fell back to Cattenières, but the British followed only with artillery fire.

Cuirassier R 7 deployed half of the two available squadrons as dismounts and opened the firefight at 700 metres. At 0830 Jäger 9 passed through it.[18] The cuirassiers then took fire in the left flank that increased in intensity and caused several casualties, including a squadron commander. At 1530, as IV RK was arriving, the regiment pulled back to its horses and was held in reserve at Cattenières.

In less than two hours two battalions of Jäger, three regiments of dismounted cavalry and three batteries of artillery had smashed the King's Own, inflicted heavy losses on the Warwickshire and Lancashire and forced the 12th Brigade to withdraw 1,500 metres.

For the rest of the day the cavalry and the Jäger would hold their ground against a much larger force of infantry supported by superior artillery. Around 1330 the 12th Brigade attempted to counter-attack across the Warnelle but this failed. The British official history makes it clear that the 10th and 12th Brigades were happy to be able to hold their positions and then withdraw.

The Warwickshire battalion commander left for Ligny with a small party, and his group reached St Quentin. The town mayor, who did not want a fight in the town, insisted that before the town supply him with food he sign a document promising to surrender if the Germans appeared; the battalion commander agreed, and was court-martialled and cashiered for it. He joined the Foreign Legion, was wounded, won the Médaille Militaire and Croix de Guerre, was reinstated and later awarded the DSO.

The rest of the Warwickshire battalion, plus groups from other regiments, exfiltrated for two days, avoiding German forces, until it chanced upon Sordet's

Cavalry Corps on 28 August. The wounded, including three company command-ers, had to be left behind and were captured. Most of the battalion was reunited at Compiègne, where it was judged no longer capable of combat operations, and was sent to Rouen and Le Mans to refit. It did not rejoin the brigade until 5 September.

The King's Own lost 6 OFF KIA, 4 WIA, 2 MIA and had 431 EM casualties. The 2/Lancashire Fusiliers lost 'six officers and an uncertain number of NCOs and men killed, three officers and 86 other ranks wounded, six officers and 402 other ranks missing'. The battalion also lost both machine guns, which were not replaced until the end of September. Both battalions had effectively been destroyed. 2/Essex took 141 casualties.[19] Becke says the 12th Brigade as a whole took 1,000 casualties, which is clearly a gross underestimate – the incomplete figures above, which do not include the Warwickshire, come to 940. Becke says the 10th Brigade also lost 1,000 more.[20]

Jäger 4 lost 28 KIA and presumably about 90 WIA; Hussar R 12 3 KIA and 7 WIA; Jäger 7 lost 2 OFF and 22 EM KIA, 2 OFF, an officer candidate and 58 EM WIA, 35 EM MIA. Dragoon R 2 lost 3 OFF and 2 EM KIA, 2 OFF, 3 officer can-didates and 22 EM WIA, 2 of which DOW. Uhlan R 3 and Hussar R 12 casualties were probably comparable to those of Dragoon R 2: 32 men. The total German casualties were around 335, or one-third of those of the 12th Brigade.

Fontaine au Pire

The 11th Brigade was on the right of the British 4th Division line, whose four battalions, indifferently supported by six artillery batteries, would be attacked by three Jäger battalions and the dismounts from three regiments of cavalry, with about the strength of an infantry battalion, effectively supported by one to three batteries of horse artillery. On the other hand, the Jäger and cavalry had twenty-four machine guns, the 11th Brigade only eight.

1/Rifle Brigade had pushed forward its C Company as a security detachment to a position about 500 metres east of Cattenières, and the rest of the battalion was about 1,000 metres to the south-east in support.[21] At dawn (0415) C Company saw German cavalry and artillery approaching. This did not get reported to the entire brigade, because at 0500 the lead German elements fired on the trains of all four battalions located at Fontaine au Pire in front of the combat elements. The trains were completely surprised but the Germans were not present in strength and the trains managed to escape.

There was now a mad scramble by the 11th Brigade to occupy a defensive position. The histories of four battalions give completely contradictory descrip-tions of the unit locations; sorting them out is practically impossible. The 1/East Lancashire history has the most probable explanation for this confusion: 'the distribution of the troops on the ground had not been assigned, so that there was little cohesion between units, and each one eventually fought more or less where it found itself.' In any case, the position was not a good one, as the nearby town of Fontaine au Pire offered the Germans cover and concealment.[22]

1/Rifle Brigade noted that the initial part of the German attack was 'confined to artillery, machine-gun and rifle fire' but concluded that 'no [infantry] attack developed. The deadly rapid fire of the Riflemen was too suggestive to the Germans of their own deadly machine guns'. The British clearly did not comprehend German tactics: the Germans intended to establish fire superiority and cover the movement of the infantry. The Rifle Brigade evidently expected that the Germans would simply get up and charge, ascribing the German failure to do so down to their fear of 'British rapid rifle fire'.

The real character of German tactics quickly became evident: the Germans poured fire on the 11th Brigade while turning both flanks. The 1/Hampshire history complained that they rarely had good targets. Parts of A and C Companies of 1/Hampshires attempted to counter-attack against Jäger 9 to the west but only drew heavy shrapnel fire, which caused casualties; the attack was quickly called off. German infantry also began to press against the front of the line.

The 1/Somerset history said that German MGs worked their way to the right flank of the battalion and their fire enfiladed the line, causing severe casualties. The two companies on the railway line were called forward. The German infantry presented few targets. The Somerset history said, 'a German patrol [appeared] waving a white flag evidently meant to invite the Somerset men to surrender ... The men asked me [an officer] what to do. "Fire on the beggars, range 500 yards."'

At 0800 the Somersets' history says that the battalion's position was becoming untenable and the battalion withdrew to Ligny, sacrificing a rearguard platoon to do so. The absence of medical units began to be felt most keenly. Lacking ambulances, the battalion medical officer collected some carts and put the most severely wounded on them and sent them to St Quentin. A staff officer, for unknown reasons, sent them back to Ligny where they were captured.

By 1000, according to the 1/East Lancashire history, C Company of the 1/East Cheshire, on the left flank, was forced to withdraw to the railway line, where it joined A and B and 1/Hampshire. The only unit on the quarry was 1/Rifle Brigade with parties from East Lancashire.

Jäger 9 had just crossed the Le Cateau–Cambrai road when British forces were reported south of Cattenières.[23] The MG Company was ordered forward at a trot. A company commander called out: 'Beefsteak on the menu!' The battalion deployed and soon was engaged in a firefight at 1,000 metres against the left of the 11th Brigade. The British had the advantage; they held the high ground, where they were well-hidden, and had good observation and fields of fire over terrain which sloped downward across open fields to the Jäger line. Jäger 9 took casualties even as it deployed. The word went out, 'Pay attention and stay under cover!

The British shoot well!' MG Company 4 was already in action and was joined by Jäger 9's MGs. Under the supporting fire of twelve MGs the Jäger reached the railroad cutting. The MG fire grew hot and some of the British soldiers tried to move, but the Jäger were good shots too. Forty-five minutes into the firefight a German battery set up south of the MGs. More British soldiers tried to move and were targets for MG fire. About two hours into the fight British artillery rounds began to land, forcing the battery to change position. Nevertheless, the Jäger felt that the British were weakening. The Jäger began their assault, and in twenty minutes had taken the British position; the British dead lay in their skirmisher line. In this part of the front the British artillery ceased fire.

The Lifeguard Hussar Brigade deployed on the 2 KD left.[24] The hussars were immediately pinned down. Attempts to bound forward resulted only in casualties, and the hussars were unable to make out the British positions. A few hussars put their busbies on the end of their carbines and carefully raised them; this drew heavy fire and the hussars could make out the British position. A squadron commander was killed and his place was taken by Prince Friedrich Sigismund of Prussia. The hussars began to run out of ammunition and it was impossible to bring more across the railway embankment to the rear. When the hussars ran out of ammunition they could do nothing but wait until IV RK arrived.

Jäger 10 attacked on the left. It deployed as it crossed the Le Cateau–Cambrai road, advanced by bounds, pushed back the British security posts and then took fire from the main 11th Brigade position. The British field of fire was ideal and Jäger 10's advance slowed and then stopped. The British infantry shot well, but there was thankfully no British artillery fire. Those Jäger with entrenching tools dug in, the pack was used as a rifle rest. The Jäger fired back, adjusting the *Garbe* onto the suspected British position. Ammunition began to run low. Both sides began to shoot only at movement. Some Jäger took a nap in the hot summer sun. Ammo bearers bounded forward carrying a box of ammo in each hand and five bandoliers around the neck. There were casualties, but the ammunition reached the firing line. Two platoons of MGs were set up near the cemetery at Fontaine au Pire. This resulted in a marked reduction in the British fire. At 1400 the German horse artillery had remunitioned and began hammering the British position; the commander of 1/Jäger 10 ordered an advance. There were few losses: the Jäger had moved into a dead zone for British fire. Some 300 metres to the front was a line of bushes; probably the British position. The British fire had stopped; they were obviously withdrawing and Jäger 10 advanced, taking 250 POWs. There were 150 British dead, mostly hit in the head by rifle or MG fire.

Jäger 3 attacked in the centre. The battalion took fire from Beauvois at 0500 and deployed.[25] The battalion history said that the advance by bounds worked just as it had been practised in peacetime; it was just a lot harder. The intensity of the enemy small-arms fire increased by the minute. At 0900 the terrain and visibility allowed the MG Company to be committed. The guns had to be moved, each crew member also carrying an ammo box, by bounds up a hill, down the other side and then up again through acacia bushes, all under enemy fire. The battalion suffered from MG and artillery fire and ammunition began to run out. Every available man, including the cavalry horseholders, was sent forward with rifle and MG ammunition. Jäger 10's advance allowed Jäger 3 to attack into the British position also. Jäger 3 was impressed by the strength of the British position, the 'masses' of weapons and ammunition they found there, and the execution that the German artillery had done on the British reserves. The German troops had not eaten all day and the British crackers, marmalade and canned food were particularly welcome. Heavy British artillery fire discouraged pursuit and most of the battalion occupied a position in a sunken road and was not relieved by IV RK until 1830.

2/Dragoon R 19 was the advance guard for 9 KD, dismounted skirmishers and spent the day in a firefight with the 11th Brigade, the only 9 KD cavalry unit engaged on foot against the 11th Brigade.[26] The squadron complained that the British would feign surrender, advance and then resume firing.

The Horse Artillery Section of FAR 10 had to support Jäger 3 and Jäger 10 against the 11th Brigade, and the 13th and 14th Cavalry Brigades against Caudry.[27] The section was therefore continually shifting batteries. Initially 2/Horse Artillery FAR 10 and 3/10 supported the Jäger, 1/10 fired on Caudry. In the course of the afternoon 2/10 ran out of ammunition and 3/10 was shifted to Caudry and the Jäger were being supported only by 2/RFAR 7. The horse artillery was in action for twelve hours and the light ammunition column refilled the caissons twice.

There is an unintentional British testimonial to the violence of the HKK 2 attack. II Corps had only the four battalions of the 19th Brigade in reserve.[28] Three Jäger battalions, some dismounted cavalry and a handful of horse artillery guns were putting so much pressure on the four battalions of the 11th Brigade that at 1000 Smith-Dorrien shifted two of those reserve battalions from behind the right wing to behind the 11th Brigade.

By 1200 the Hampshires were being pushed back from the railway line. At 1230 the East Lancashire came under an enfilade of MG fire from the east, which caused 'considerable loss'. At 1400 (East Lancashire history) or 1500 (Hampshire) the 11th Brigade ordered a withdrawal to Ligny. 'As the Hampshire started to retire it seemed, as one officer wrote "as if every gun and rifle in the German Army opened fire".' The downslope part of the retirement was in dead ground, but when the Hampshires moved back up the slope to Ligny they again were visible to the Germans who 'redoubled their efforts'.

> The actual order for the retirement was given verbally to the assembled troops by the brigade commander, and in this difficult position was misunderstood, so that the Brigade moved off together practically in mass, contrary to the intention of the brigade commander. The approach of the Brigade into the open in

this dense formation, as it commenced to climb the long slope towards Ligny, totally devoid of cover, was the signal for a perfect inferno of shrapnel and machine-gun fire from the Germans, causing considerable loss. Companies and platoons became hopelessly disorganised.[29]

The East Lancashire history also said: 'It was only during the latter part of the retirement that the Brigade had any covering fire from the British guns on Ligny ridge, as, through lack of cooperation between infantry and artillery, and until the artillery could see for themselves, they were unaware of what was taking place … The retreat to Ligny was made at top speed – every man for himself.' German pursuit fire was punishing: 'During the withdrawal there were many casualties, and on continuing the retirement over the wide open slope to Ligny the Brigade came under a hail of shrapnel and small-arms fire. There were more casualties, the most serious of which were from small arms fire, for the German shrapnel burst very high and though nearly every man was bruised by shrapnel bullets, very few serious casualties were caused by them.'[30] This is worth remembering when the 11th Brigade's casualties are considered: the Jäger were crack shots too.

The three companies of 1/Rifle Brigade still at the quarry did not get the order to withdraw: 'By now the forward position, enfiladed from both flanks and steadily bombarded from the front, became an inferno of shot and shell.' The Germans had closed to within 100 metres. There was slight respite when the German artillery shifted fire to engage the withdrawing elements of the 11th Brigade as it climbed the south side of the Warnelle ravine. The remnants of 1/Rifle Brigade then fell back too. In Ligny 1/Rifle Brigade could assemble only 200 men.

The 11th Brigade collected around Ligny. The Hampshire reported that 'companies and platoons had become detached'. The brigade was so disorganised that the East Lancashire history said: 'It is impossible to unravel the details of the defence of Ligny.' At about 1600 all four 'battalions' reported beating off a serious German attack from the north-east. The 1/Somerset said that 'battalion after battalion was launched against the village' but the assault broke down at 400 metres range. The problem is that no German unit says it made such an attack. The Jäger made no attempt at any time to cross the Warnelle and by 1500 some of the cavalry regiments were withdrawing. Indeed, no German unit could have made this attack. IR 153 was the right-flank unit of IV Corps, but it was east of Caudry. The lead unit of IV RK, 7 RD, did not reach Haucourt, west of Ligny, until after dark.

1/Rifle Brigade lost 8 OFF and 'some 350 other ranks'. Most of the wounded were captured. 1/Hampshires lost 2 OFF KIA, 5 OFF MIA, the medical officer POW. 46 EM were KIA, 126 EM WIA, the seriously wounded were captured, 186 total casualties. 1/Somerset lost 19 EM KIA, 9 OFF and 150 EM WIA, 100 EM

MIA, 278 casualties total. 1/East Lancashire had lost 1 OFF KIA, 1 WIA, 1 POW and 257 EM. The 11th Brigade had at least 1,090 casualties; Becke says 1,150.

Jäger 9 lost 1 OFF and 12 EM KIA, 48 EM WIA and 10 MIA, 71 casualties total. Cuirassier R 7 lost at least 1 OFF and 4 EM KIA. The Lifeguard Hussar Brigade lost 2 OFF KIA and an unknown number of enlisted men. Jäger 10's losses were 38 KIA, and probably about 120 WIA. All the officers in 1/Jäger 10 were casualties, and the first sergeant was killed. Jäger 3 lost 1 OFF, 2 officer candidates and 13 EM KIA, 2 OFF and 41 EM WIA. The Jäger 3 history said that this was 'low in relation to the results achieved'. Dragoon R 19 lost 2 KIA and 2 DOW. The regimental commander was WIA. The three Jäger battalions and cavalry lost about 350 casualties, one-third of the 11th Brigade losses.

British 4th Division Artillery

Becke's information concerning the 4th Division Artillery was sparse. The artillery was initially in march column and took some time moving and finding firing positions. XXIX and XIV Artillery Brigades supported the 12th Infantry Brigade, XXXII Artillery Brigade was placed in direct support of the 11th Infantry Brigade.[31] Until 1200 the 4th Division Artillery conducted a gun duel with the 'vastly superior' German artillery, mostly by unobserved area fire. 27 Battery, which had set up in the open, claimed to have knocked out a German battery, which is not confirmed by German accounts. It then drew such heavy counter-fire, including a direct hit on a gun, that ammunition could not be brought up and the crews had to take cover; the battery had been suppressed. It resumed fire in the afternoon but drew counter-fire and was again suppressed.

135 RFA (of XXXII) was dug in behind a hedge at Ligny for close defence. All that Becke knew of the other batteries supporting the 11th Brigade was that they 'continued their activity'. Becke knew nothing concerning XIV Brigade at all. At 1400 XXIX Brigade pulled back to escape German artillery fire. When the Germans drove back the 11th Brigade, two howitzer batteries engaged German infantry (probably Jäger 3) and 135 fired on the German infantry occupying the brigade's position, which it described as beating off a German attack. When the British infantry retreated the artillery had little trouble withdrawing (which is the principal topic of Becke's discussion of the 4th Division Artillery), except for 135 in Ligny and 27, which had to leave two guns.

The 4th Division Artillery lost 1 OFF and 2 EM KIA, 1 OFF and 16 EM WIA, and 12 horses. Becke was unable to determine how much ammunition was expended. The overall impression is that the 4th Division Artillery had been caught flat-footed on the morning of 26 August, was a considerable time getting into action, was never able to find good firing and observation positions and its fire for the rest of the day was largely ineffective.

German Reserve Field Artillery Regiment 7

At 0930 I/RFAR 7 was ordered, along with MG Company RIR 27, to move forward at a trot to assist HKK 2. II/RFAR 7 stayed with 7 RD.[32] At 1120 it went into position in the 2 KD sector north-east of Cattenières. The Horse Artillery Section of FAR 35 had just run out of shells and had to retire to remunition, so there was no increase in German artillery firepower. I/RFAR 7 soon found that the position it had chosen was too far to the rear and at 1215 bounded forward through Cattenières and across the railway line to a position halfway to Longsart, where it set up at 1250. It immediately came under British counter-battery fire: 'initially the British fire was not badly aimed, but they soon fired too long, so that the limbers and caissons were under heavy fire'. I/RFAR 7 first engaged two British batteries in the open: 'Our fire must have been on target, for the British tried to bring their limbers forward. The gunners of the 1st Section were having none of that: their devastating fire landed on the British, and the guns stayed there immobile' (probably 27 RFA). The section engaged a broad range of targets: four other batteries, dug-in infantry, infantry in the open, limbers, the tower of the church in Harcourt, which was being used as an OP, and finally the town itself. At 1400 the MG Company of RIR 27 arrived and moved towards Longsart, covered by I/RFAR 7. Shortly thereafter II/RFAR 7 arrived and occupied an open position; speed was necessary, for the British were withdrawing. I/RFAR 7 had expended 1,600 shells (!), II/7 200. I/RFAR 7 lost 2 KIA, 7 WIA; II/7 1 WIA.

The British official history consistently paints a picture of German numerical superiority in artillery: 'the Germans brought up battery after battery, until their line of guns extended from Wambaix to the north of Fontaine [a 5-km front!] and swept the plateau [the 11th Brigade position] with them'.[33] In fact, there were never more than six German batteries in this area, which might have occupied 600 metres of front. The British official history says the attack on the 11th Brigade was made with 'an overwhelming force of artillery'. The history of 1/Somerset says the British artillery was 'outnumbered four to one'.[34] A footnote in the official history says that all of RFAR 7 arrived between 1110 and 1130. In fact, only half of RFAR 7 went into action at 1250, with a princely total of three batteries. Actually, the 11th Brigade, which was supported by six batteries, was never opposed by more than three German batteries. All of HKK 2 was supported by twelve batteries, and they were not all engaged at the same time. They were opposed by the artillery of the British 4th Division (twelve batteries), of which three batteries were howitzers, and at least three batteries of the 3rd Division. Numerical superiority in artillery was on the British side.

What the British official history was actually saying, though it did not know it, was that the German artillery was tactically superior to the British artillery. The numerically inferior German guns provided better close-fire support and counter-battery fire than the numerically superior British artillery. The German

artillery would have been pleased to see the high marks that the British official
history unintentionally gave their work.

British 4th Division Withdrawal

Lomas said that the 4th Division retirement was difficult because 2 KD and 9 KD
had been replaced by 7 RD of IV RK, whose attack on the British rearguard 'suffered severely'.[35] This is still more pure invention. 7 RD didn't even make contact
on 26 August, much less suffer serious casualties.

The 11th Brigade began to retire at 1700. The Hampshires reported that the
Brigade had not been able to reorganise; 'orders failed to reach several parties and
all its units were broken up into disconnected detachments'. The 11th Brigade
HQ could assemble a column of only 700 men, mostly from the 1/East Lancashire.
Three hundred Hampshires were still in Ligny at 1800. The East Lancashire history says, 'The Brigade retired from Ligny in six main parties and many smaller
ones'. The East Lancashires retired in four separate groups, the column with the
East Lancashire commander included only fifty men. The wounded had to be
left behind. When this column reached Clary it found stragglers from all three
divisions. The 11th Brigade CO took command and the 'dejected and unor-
dered' column set off.[36] This column retreated all night, with just a two-hour
halt between 2400 and 0200, and did not stop again until 0700 on 27 August.
1/Rifle Brigade formed a column 'about 200 strong' which marched 38 km until
1000 on 27 August.[37] The battalion had found itself separated from the machine
guns and combat trains. It was reunited with these elements and rejoined the 11th
Brigade on 27 August.

Often, as in the Hampshire regimental history, the lack of a German pursuit is
attributed to the fact that 'the Germans, after the reception they had met, were
in no mood to press forward in pursuit'.[38] This puts myth above serious military
analysis. HKK 2 had marched for three days and the cavalry was still needed to
screen the right flank. IV RK had marched hard all day and arrived at dark. The
German army was deeply sceptical of night operations unless they were preceded by careful preparations and reconnaissance. A night pursuit was not going
to achieve significant results, would merely have tired the troops and carried with
it a real danger of friendly-fire casualties.

In any case, at 0930 on 27 August the German cavalry had already caught up
with the 11th Brigade. German artillery opened fire on the brigade at a range of
1,000 metres, which was the prelude to an attack by dismounted bicyclists and
cavalry. The brigade broke up again: the 1/Hampshire history says that the brigade remained scattered for the rest of the day. The majority of a hastily assembled
rearguard became casualties, including the 1/Hampshire commander, who was
wounded and captured. About 120 Hampshires and other men got separated and

joined the 3rd Division, marching 40 km that day. At this time it was decided to abandon everything except weapons and ammunition. As the history of the 1/Rifle Brigade noted, this was the beginning of the great retreat. The 4th Division did not reassemble until 29 August.

Evaluation

The 1/Somerset historian was convinced that II Corps and the 4th Division had defeated 'vastly superior forces', that the British artillery had been outnumbered 'four to one'.[39] This was the common British perception. For this reason, the 4th Division accepted its massive casualties and the fact that it had been pushed off its original positions and back across the Warnelle, and thought that hanging onto the Egnes-Haucourt-Ligny position counted as 'throwing back the German assault' and a victory. Indeed, Le Cateau was 'an altogether extraordinary military feat'.

This was not an accurate military analysis. The German cavalry and Jäger were inferior in numbers of troops and guns. The Somersets' historian, like all British historians, was satisfied by patriotic myth, failed to consult the German sources, to discover the true situation and force ratio and to ask the hard questions. Why had the British cavalry screen failed, forcing the Somersets to defend a hastily organised, not to say chaotic, position? How were the numerically inferior German troops able to cross 1,000 metres of open farmland in spite of the vaunted 'rapid rifle fire'? How could the Germans fight a combined-arms battle when the British did not? What was the effect of the German superiority in numbers and handling of MG? Instead, the British historians praised the courage of the British soldier. That he was brave and skillful there can be no doubt. Nor can there be any doubt that bravery alone was not enough when faced with the combined-arms tactics of the Jäger, cavalry and horse artillery of HKK 2.

Jäger 10 said, 'in spite of the heavy casualties, the battalion was proud of its tremendous accomplishments'.[40] In three days it had marched 75 km in the heat, fought a difficult battle in Tournai, and then attacked superior British forces across an open plain, with little artillery support, and thrown them out of a good position. Jäger 10 had great respect for the British soldier:

> It was not for nothing that they were known as the 'Sharpshooter Brigade'. These were wily soldiers, tough and tenacious fellows, with iron nerves, even when wounded. They shot well and understood how to use the terrain with such skill that it was difficult even for Jäger to detect them ... Nevertheless our attack succeeded. Captured British officers told us that they thought an attack on their hill to be completely impossible ... We had passed the test and proven our military skills on the open field. We had shown, under the most difficult

conditions, that we could apply in combat what we had learned in training …
When the leaders had fallen, each Jäger squad and each individual Jäger continued the attack. The troops acted on their own initiative, without orders. As
the supporting artillery fire landed the skirmisher line rose on the simple order
of Lt Kirchheim and assaulted the enemy position … The 26th of August is a
glorious page in the history of the battalion. Every Jäger and every officer had
done his duty to the highest standard. The 26th of August is the highpoint for all
the Jäger 10 men of 1914.[41]

This is the evaluation of a well-trained professional officer. That it appears in
a battalion history is evidence of the high degree of military sophistication in
all ranks of the 1914 German army. He emphasised the importance of training in preparing for combat. He highlighted the unit's operational mobility. He
understood the doctrinal difficulty of the attack across the open plain and the
significance of Jäger 10's ability to be able to execute such an operation. The
importance of artillery support was clear. In praising only the individual British
soldier, he implicitly criticised the rest of the system; there was no mention of
British artillery. No matter how good the British professional soldiers were, Jäger
10 and her supporting arms were better.

At no point did any of the Jäger or cavalry histories say that the British had an
unusual number of machine guns or that British rifle fire rose to super-human
levels.

According to Becke, the British 4th Division took 3,150 casualties, HKK 2 in
this sector lost fewer than 700. The disparity can be explained by disasters such as
the destruction of the King's Own, by the effectiveness of German artillery fire
and the ineffectiveness of the 4th Division artillery, by the numbers and handling
of the German MG, and by the deadly German pursuit fire.

The 4th Division, with twelve infantry battalions, had held off with great difficulty five Jäger battalions and four weak brigades of cavalry, the dismounted
equivalent of a bit more than a battalion of infantry. Had Kluck and Kuhl not
turned IV Corps to the south-east, and had IV AK continued south-west, then
on the morning of 26 August 4th Division would have been hit by the German
8 ID, with twice as much infantry and three times as much artillery, and the 4th
Division situation would have been dire indeed.

IR 72 attacks the 14th Brigade

The German IR 72, which had been detached to provide right flank security for
8 ID, had bivouacked at 2200 in St Python, north-east of Solesmes.[42] The regiment had marched 38 km in the heat. It had lost contact with 8 ID, but knew that
the division objective was Le Cateau, so at 0300 IR 72 resumed the march. The

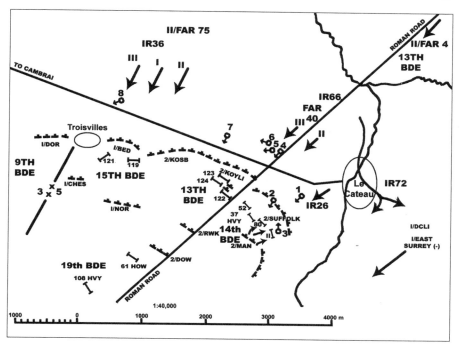

Fig. 21: BR 5th Division, 26 August.

regimental history said that due to the exertions of the previous day it was difficult to get the troops to march with a 'brisk pace' and there were several lame with blisters. As much as possible, wagons were requisitioned to carry packs. At 0500 IR 72 entered Le Cateau, far in front of the rest of IV AK. 8 ID, its parent unit, would swing south-west towards Caudry, 7 ID was 4–5 km to the north-east. A patrol from Cuirassier R 7 took fire and 9/72 pushed what they thought was a British secu-rity detachment out of the way: it was more likely to have been British stragglers or troops strolling around, as none of the British units mention security outposts making contact. The regiment penetrated to the market place without incident, but when it reached the east edge of the town along the Le Cateau–Bazeul road the point took fire.

IR 72 had encountered 1/Duke of Cornwall's Light Infantry (DCLI) and two companies of 1/East Surrey, including the Surrey battalion commander.[43] These units had formed the 5th Division rearguard on 25 August and upon completing that mission had bivouacked at the east side of Le Cateau. During the night they had been told to occupy the defensive positions assigned to them; which positions were not specified. The commander of the Surreys asked where these positions might be, but the 14th Brigade HQ had no idea, so the Surrey commander ignored the order. In the early morning the order arrived to rejoin the main body at a point 8 km south-west of Le Cateau. The two units were formed in march column at

0630 'when suddenly a heavy fire was opened on it from houses in the eastern outskirts of the town'. The Cornwalls' history said the Germans were 100 metres away.

Lomas says: 'The Germans, from the 7th Division of IV Corps, had taken
advantage of the dawn mist to infiltrate their way into and through Le Cateau
itself. The ambush developed into a savage action ...'[44] Everything in these two
sentences is wrong. IR 72 was an 8 ID unit, it did not 'infiltrate' but marched
straight down the road, and there was no 'ambush' by either side.

The British official history asserts disingenuously: 'How the Germans con-
trived to reach the south-eastern outskirts of Le Cateau without being seen, is
unknown.' The Surreys' historian had an answer to this question. He thought
the Germans had penetrated British security by wearing khaki uniforms. The
Cornwalls said 'there were rumours that the enemy's troops were wearing British
greatcoats and caps'. In fact, there had been no British security to deceive. Not
only was there no cavalry security, there were not even infantry outposts.

The initial German fire struck the 14th Brigade signal section and killed the
brigade machine gun officer. Both British battalion histories maintain that they
returned the fire, but the greater part of the troops withdrew at a run to the
south-east. They attempted to form a firing line but the German return fire was
too hot. IR 72 had only nine companies, but had no trouble pushing the six
British companies around. 9/IR 72 and 12/7 manoeuvred against the British
right flank and both British battalions evaded to the south, pursued by German
fire. Eventually they joined the 8th Brigade at Honnechy. The DCLI lost 3 OFF
WIA (2 of which were POW) and about 95 EM.

IR 72 searched the houses and 40–50 British soldiers were hauled out. IR 72
was in a curious position, far in front of the rest of both IV AK and its parent unit,
8 ID. Most of the regiment was east of Le Cateau, oriented to the south and east.
The regimental adjutant climbed in a captured British staff car and reported to
7 ID, 8 ID and IV AK. IR 72 had only 1/FAR 74 for artillery support, because
the rest of I/FAR 74 had gone into position near Viesly to engage targets in the
direction of Inchy. 1/74 engaged targets to the west and south.

Only 7/72, now detached and on the sunken road due west of Le Cateau, 4/72
at the railway station and the MG Company, were oriented west. 4/72, reinforced
by 1/72, engaged and stopped a 'French brigade' (probably 1/Middlesex and 2/
Argyll and Sutherland) on the high ground 3 km south-west of Le Cateau. A
reserve MG was brought forward and engaged British artillery to the west at
1,200–1,400 metres range. IR 72 did not attack west due to the uncertain situation.

British 5th Division

The British retreat through Le Cateau had been delayed for four hours because
Sordet's Cavalry Corps was moving across the II Corps rear area from east to

west.[45] Sordet should have detoured behind II Corps, but probably took the direct route because his troopers and horses were chronically tired. The last II Corps unit, the 19th Brigade, had just exited Le Cateau moving south when the Germans appeared.

The British 5th Division was on the II Corps right flank. The 13th Brigade, in the division centre, faced Le Cateau to the north-east, the 14th Brigade was echeloned towards its right rear and the 15th Brigade was on its left, lined up along the Le Cateau–Cambrai road.

The terrain occupied by the 5th Division was unsuitable for defence. To the east was high ground, which dominated the 5th Division position and potentially provided good positions for German artillery. Both Becke and the British official history are also adamant that the 5th Division thought I Corps was going to occupy the high ground to the east of Le Cateau. That the information that I Corps would do no such thing did not get down to the manoeuvre brigades is a serious breakdown in British command and control. Immediately to the east and north was dead ground which offered German infantry and MG covered and concealed approaches to within a few hundred metres of the 5th Division positions. The sunken Le Cateau–Cambrai road provided the Germans with an offensive strongpoint for MG positions.

The 14th Brigade troops west of Le Cateau did not receive orders to defend in place until 0600, so there was no time to dig in. The idea that the British position was to be held at all costs was widespread in the 5th Division. Where it originated is impossible to determine. 2/Suffolk was told there would be no retreat. Smith-Dorrien, the II Corps commander, took the unusual step of writing a foreword to chapter III of the Suffolks' regimental history, in which he said: 'Someone, certainly not I, ordered that on no account were the Suffolks to retire.'[46] It would have been more accurate to say that Smith-Dorrien did not want to know, for there is no evidence that he made an attempt to find out. This was another catastrophic failure in British troop-leading.

The divisional artillery commander assigned XV Artillery Brigade and 37 RFA (how) on the right, XXVIII in the centre, XXVII (–120 RFA) and 65 RFA (how) on the left, 120 RFA and 61 RFA (how) in reserve, 108 (60-pdrs) in general support. The priority of howitzer and 60-pounder fire was counter-battery, 18-pound guns were to provide direct infantry support.

Many guns were brought up to the infantry front line in open positions. This may have been done because they did not expect to withdraw. Becke said that there was no time to reconnoitre battery positions, so perhaps the guns simply did not have enough time to occupy covered positions. Then again, the British artillery accomplished virtually nothing at Mons, while the Germans brought guns far forward, and that had been very effective. The British gunners may have been copying what they thought were successful German tactical procedures.

The 14th Brigade in the 5th Division right deployed with 2/Suffolk on the right, 2/Manchester on the left, two companies of 1/East Surrey in reserve. The other two companies of 1/East Surrey and 1/Duke of Cornwall's Light Infantry were on the east side of Le Cateau. When the 19th Brigade completed movement it assembled behind the 14th Brigade.

2/Suffolk was already continuing the withdrawal (the 14th Brigade was to be the rearguard) when it was told to stop and defend in place.[47] No attempt was made to find a defensible position: '[the battalion commander] in discussing this state of affairs with his company commanders explained that he had nothing whatever to do with the selection of the position; they were committed to it, and everyone must do the best that he could. He then impressed upon them that there was to be no retirement.' The location given for the Suffolk in the official history map is unlikely and does not match that of the Manchester history. According to the sketch in the 2/King's Own Yorkshire Light Infantry regimental history, 2/Suffolks were oriented to the east, not to the north and east as the official history map shows. It seems that there was as much confusion in the 14th Brigade sector as there was in the 11th.

The 13th Brigade in the division centre deployed 2/King's Own Yorkshire Light Infantry (KOYLI) on the right, 2/King's Own Scots Borderers (KOSB) in the centre, 1/Bedfordshire on the left with 1/Cheshire behind it. The 2/KOYLI commander was given a written order: 'There will now be NO [emphasis in the original] retirement for the fighting troops; fill up your trenches, with water, food and ammunition as far as you can.'[48] The 'no retreat order' was confirmed by a colonel from the II Corps staff, who rode up and repeated it. This would either show that the Corps commander too was telling the troops to 'die in place' or demonstrate that the corps staff was incapable of accurately transmitting the commander's intent to the units.

The KOYLI position was 200–300 metres from the Le Cateau–Cambrai road, which was sunken in places, providing the enemy with 'natural infantry positions'. The KOYLI position bears all the marks of one chosen in haste, with no reconnaissance and no coordination with the neighbouring units. B Company on the right flank was lined up along the Roman road, behind the artillery, oriented south-east towards the Manchesters' position. The MG section was in front of B Company, outside the battalion perimeter, oriented down the Roman road and unable to engage targets to the battalion front. The battalion HQ was much too far to the rear, indeed it was level with 13th Brigade HQ. The KOYLI history said: 'the weak spots of a position taken up in a half-light, and only half prepared, were soon only too apparent.' KOYLI had only its entrenching tools to dig with.

Directly behind the 2/KOYLI was XXVIII Artillery Brigade. Many of its artillery officers were so unfamiliar with the situation and terrain that they thought that Montay was Le Cateau. 122 RFA was in a well-hidden position just west of the Roman road. 123 was in the open, 200 metres to its left front, with 124 at right angles 100 metres behind 123 in order to fire north-west, an awkward position that presented the Germans with the battery's flank.

The commander of XV Brigade told the 52 RFA commander that 'we would fight it out here and there would be no retirement' and deployed his batteries immediately behind the 2/Suffolk. 11 and 52 RFA were deployed in the open and had no time to dig in. 52 had no field of fire directly to the front. 80 RFA had some cover, which prevented it from firing into its assigned sector. Becke tied himself in knots trying to defend this artillery deployment, but there can be no doubt that the XV Brigade commander got a 'no-go' on this tactics test.

Artillery rounds practically never hit a point target. Some landed in front of it, some behind. The technical term for this is 'range probable error' and can be determined with mathematical certainty. By placing the guns directly behind the infantry – 100 metres from the Suffolks – the British artillery commanders were maximising the effectiveness of the German artillery fire: shells aimed at the Suffolks were almost as likely to hit the artillery and vice versa. The gunnery problem for the German artillery was massively simplified. That Becke and the British artillery commanders did not understand this speaks poorly of their qualifications as gunners.

The British official history says that at 0600 both brigades and their artillery came under artillery fire from the north-east and later from the north-west, which 'practically enfiladed the whole of them with the most destructive effect'.[49] This put an end to attempts to dig in.

The origin of this German artillery fire so early in the day is something of a mystery. Aside from 1/FAR 74, there were no German artillery units east of Le Cateau until 1500. The first artillery units of 7 ID, FAR 40, did not begin movement until 0630 or conduct serious fire until 0945. FAR 74 and I/FAR 75 fired in support of IR 153 attacking in the direction of Caudry and IR 93 towards Inchy. II/FAR 75 supported IR 36, attacking Inchy from the north-east, and engaged British artillery 2 km east of Troisvilles, which was certainly XXVIII Artillery Brigade, but did not open fire until 0715. In order to make sure it was not engaging friendly artillery, the section then ceased fire and bounded forward. The British almost certainly got the time wrong, which would be understandable, considering the pounding they were soon to receive.

The Suffolks had just beaten down the sheaves of corn to clear fields of fire and begun digging in when the German shells began to land. The second shell was a direct hit in the middle of a platoon that killed the platoon leader and a sergeant. The battalion commander was shortly thereafter mortally wounded. 'It became immediately evident that their artillery was in vastly superior force to that of the British.' In fact, the German artillery was not more numerous, but it was much more effective.

IR 66 attacks the 14th Brigade

IR 66 provided the advance guard for 7 ID on 26 August. It moved out from Croix, 3 km north-east of Montay, at 0430.[50] It had hardly begun movement when hussar patrols reported the heights west and south of Le Cateau were strongly held by British forces and 7 ID issued an order to attack them. Between 0700 and 0800 IR 66 deployed, with III/66 right of the road, II/66 left, I/66 and the MG Company following.

However, the point company, 6/66, had already pressed on through Montay and up the hill to the south. When it crested the rise 6/66 took 'very heavy' fire, which pinned it to the ground, followed by shrapnel fire. The enemy was initially invisible; only after careful observation with field glasses could the British be discerned.

II/66 followed through Montay, avoiding the British artillery fire in the town and deploying on the reverse slope of the hill (just to the north of the present-day military cemeteries). The range to the British position was about 1,300–1,400 metres, which was too long, so the battalion (minus 6/66, which was still pinned down) ran over the hill and down the open hillside under rifle and artillery fire. In spite of heavy losses they were soon in dead ground and then reached the cover of the sunken Le Cateau–Cambrai road where they were 400 metres from the British position. 'A horrifying battle now began, which dragged on for hours.'[51]

III/66 avoided British artillery fire at Forest, but took more artillery fire on the west side of Montay, which caused casualties. When the British artillery shifted targets, 10/66 advanced by long bounds until it was pinned down by British small-arms fire. 10/66 recognised the British position immediately and returned effective fire, which helped 6/66 on their left. 10/66 also passed ammunition over to 6/66, which had run out. 9/66 came up on the right of 10/66; their approach was a classic use of cover and concealment. A lieutenant wrote:

> We were able to advance on the reverse slope of a hill, then through low ground, where we deployed and went forward in skirmisher line. Infantry fire went harmlessly over our heads. We went along a hedge, then through more low ground; we had found the right place. To our left front was 10/66 in a fire-fight. We needed to make only a bound of 100m to come level with them. Then we crawled to the crest, but we could not see the enemy, though bullets were going past our ears. With one more bound we reached our firing position and saw the British on the other side of the Le Cateau–Cambrai road. We opened fire at 900m range; it was 10 o'clock. We lay in our position for hours and could have stayed hours more; an advance was out of the question. There was hot fire on both sides and it was interesting for the first time to see a firefight develop. There was a continual cracking, rattling, hissing and whistling; an indescribable noise that left nevertheless an unforgettable impression. Our people quickly

took off their packs to use as rifle rests or began to dig skirmisher holes. There were few casualties.

12/66 came up to the left of 9/66, 11/66 also came forward to a covered position behind 12/66. The regimental commander was now at the top of the hill south of Montay, with I/66 and the MG Company on the reverse slope behind him. These units had also crossed through Montay in good order under artillery fire 'as they had never experienced before'. 1/66 and 3/66 were committed between II/66 and III/66. The MG Company also came into action.

The 2nd Suffolks saw the German infantry appear about 1000.

By this time the hostile artillery fire had increased to a pitch of tremendous severity ... Early in the day the enemy had succeeded in getting a number of machine guns into the cutting on the Le Cateau–Cambrai road, immediately in front of the 2nd Suffolk Regiment. By 11 a.m. the fire from these guns had increased to such an extent that the position of the battalion became critical.

At 0945 the 2/Argyll and Sutherland Highlanders and 1/Middlesex from the 19th Brigade moved up to the right rear of 2/Suffolk.[52] At 1000 the Germans brought artillery (perhaps 1/FAR 74) to the east of Le Cateau so that now the troops south-west of Le Cateau were enfiladed from both flanks. The Highlanders and Middlesex were now also under heavy artillery fire. The Middlesex had nothing at all to dig with; the troops had thrown away their entrenching tools during the retreat from Mons. At 1000 the 2/Manchesters were ordered to reinforce the Suffolks.[53]

Until IR 66 pushed forward to the Le Cateau–Cambrai road, FAR 40 could not find suitable firing positions.[54] At 0945 4/FAR 40 galloped into an open position on the hill behind IR 66, immediately drawing counter-battery fire. The section commander wrote that this did no damage because 'the enemy ammunition was apparently bad: there were a lot of duds'. A lieutenant in the battery wrote, 'the shrapnel rattled against the gun shields. We pulled down our heads a bit, but in general felt wonderfully good and safe behind the shields'. In twenty minutes the rest of II/40 went into position and engaged enemy artillery at 4,000 metres range with 'wonderfully effective fire straight into their flank'. 2/40 and 3/40 unlimbered south of Montay, 500 metres behind IR 66, and engaged British infantry at 1,100 metres range. As of 1130 FAR 40 manhandled the guns closer and engaged the British infantry; by 1315 the entire regiment was on the high ground 1,000 metres south of Montay.

The British artillery was little behind the infantry in exaggerating the effects of its fire. The official history said that 'though they [IR 66] attacked again and again, they were driven back by the shrapnel from the artillery'.[55] In fact, German infantry was not 'driven back', either by artillery or small-arms fire, if for no more than the simple reason that running back was an easy way to get killed;

when the Germans received fire, they took cover. 122 RFA said: 'The target generally appeared to be a platoon (a British platoon had sixty men) extended shoulder to shoulder. One round (per gun) gunfire was sufficient for its destruction. The whole platoon would go down "like a target at practice-camp when the rope is cut".'[56] Lomas elaborated on this: 'The 122nd Battery was involved in an extraordinary incident when a platoon of German infantry came over a ridge in close formation. The battery fired a single salvo and the platoon was obliterated.'[57] There is no record of such an incident in the German histories. In fact, the Germans advanced in skirmisher order by bounds; if they all went down, it was because the bound was over or they were taking cover, not because the whole platoon had become casualties. Statements such as these lead to the conclusion that the British histories had little idea of what had actually taken place on the battlefield.

IR 26 had passed through Montay by 1000, took casualties crossing the open ground to Le Cateau and at 1100 passed through the town under heavy artillery fire, where it deployed.[58] The regiment advanced quickly, almost without firing. By 1225 II/26 had reached a hollow road in the British right flank, only to take friendly fire from FAR 4, which the battalion adjutant had to go back to stop. The Germans once again complained that the British feigned surrender: the commander of 8/26 was allegedly killed by this trick, and in consequence 8/26 stopped taking prisoners.

The Manchesters said that 'up to 11 o'clock we seemed to be holding our own ... But as the fight developed on the right front [IR 26] the shallow trenches became quite untenable, the casualties mounted up in an alarming way'. The Suffolks also particularly mentioned German manoeuvre around the right rear, which surrounded the battalion; this must have been IR 26, perhaps elements of IR 72. The terrain here is dead ground for the British position and manoeuvre would have been relatively easy. By 1100 the Germans had exploited dead ground in front of the KOSB position to establish themselves on the south (!) side of the road and enfilade some of the KOYLI trenches.

The German official history says that the IV AK commander issued an order at 1115 that turned the individual fights into a coordinated battle.[59] This is face-saving nonsense. There is no evidence of German command and control above the divisional level. Three of the IV AK brigades were in contact before they received this order and, in spite of the order, the fourth brigade never made it to the battlefield. Furthermore, the IV AK commander had no control over the other half of the German forces, HKK 2, which fought its own battle.

Kluck and Kuhl issued no orders during the Battle of Le Cateau. Snide comments by Becke and Ascoli concerning German generalship on 26 August are beside the point: Kluck and Kuhl had no units to manoeuvre or commit. On 25 August they turned the 1st Army to the left, away from the British II Corps. Turning it back to the south-west would take all of 26 August. They did attempt to wrest control of HKK 1 and send it to the 1st Army right flank, but HKK 1 ignored their order. The vaunted German General Staff was a non-factor at Le Cateau.

As his section moved forward, the II/FAR 75 commander saw that he was positioned on the flank of a long artillery line of at least 23 guns. 'Beside himself with joy', he still wanted to make sure that these were enemy guns, and sent an officer's patrol forward, which went a short distance when it took British rifle and MG fire, which settled the question. The howitzers went into a covered position behind Rambourlieux farm and at 1110 opened fire at 2,200 to 2,500 metres range. 'The effect was what we expected. Although the enemy attempted to escape destruction by changing front and echeloning his guns, indeed tried to bring his limbers forward, he did not come out of these steel jaws. One gun after another was silenced.'

Between 0900 and 1200 FAR 40 and II/FAR 75 had won the artillery duel hands down: the British XV and XXVIII Artillery Brigades were being pounded flat.[60] In 11 RFA all the officers were soon casualties and the battery was reduced to a single gun. 52 RFA lost a gun and the centre two guns were suppressed due to losses in men and equipment. A gun in 123 and two in 124 were destroyed. British claims of putting German batteries out of action and silencing German guns are not borne out by the German regimental histories: the only time the German guns were not firing was when they limbered up to close the range. Both the British and the German guns were firing from open positions. The British were deployed and in firing position while the Germans had to move forward and unlimber under fire. But the Germans had been training for a mobile battle for fifty years; indeed, they had practised it in 1866 and 1870 and mobile warfare would remain the German specialty for the rest of the century. The British artillery was simply outclassed.

Sometime in the afternoon II/FAR 18 (5 ID, III AK) went forward to support 7 ID. The FAR 18 history says almost nothing about its activity.[61] IR 26 says it took friendly fire from III AK artillery. From this, the British official history concludes: 'Apparently the greater part of the artillery of the German 5th and 7th Division was in action against the [British] 5th Division.'[62] In fact, FAR 40 (7 ID) was the only German artillery regiment engaged for the entire day. It was reinforced by II/75. II/FAR 18 (one-quarter of the 5 ID artillery) was in action for the last half of the fight, after the British artillery had been suppressed and the British infantry position was collapsing. FAR 4 (7 ID) arrived as the British were withdrawing.

Between 1200 and 1345 British XV Artillery Brigade had been suppressed and 'had great difficulty keeping any guns in action'.[63] 11 RFA had been destroyed, 80 'had at least two guns in action', 52 had also been reduced to two guns. The limbers and caissons had moved several times to avoid German fire but nevertheless had suffered heavy casualties. 122 was full-strength but had difficulty resupplying ammunition, 123 was reduced to three guns, 124 to two. By 1300 5th Division HQ thought that the right flank might soon collapse.

Becke acknowledged that by 1400 the position of the 5th Division right flank was hopeless. The Germans had fire superiority over XV and XXVIII Artillery Brigades, had established MG on the Le Cateau road 500 metres from the infantry and German troops were outflanking 2/Suffolk.

At this point most British accounts of Le Cateau mention 'two officers of the [Argyll and Sutherland] Highlanders ... bringing down man after man and counting their scores aloud as if at a competition'.[64] This unlikely story does not speak well for the credibility of the British histories.

It was well past time for the British 5th Division artillery to try to withdraw the guns. In XV, 52 RFA was so exposed and its teams so badly shot up that it had to be abandoned. Two guns of 11 and a gun of 80 were also lost, for nine guns lost total, plus a howitzer from 37. In XXVIII Brigade, six teams went forward to try to retrieve the guns of 122. When they came into the open an officer and 8 men were immediately killed, an officer and 15 men wounded and 20 horses lost.[65] Shortly thereafter another team was shot down. Three guns were limbered up, two guns got away, the team of the third was shot down. The teams of 123 and 124 were then forbidden to make the attempt to retrieve the guns. XXVIII had lost sixteen guns and had only two left. The 5th Division direct support artillery had lost twenty-seven guns, almost half.

The MG Company of IR 26 was able to approach through low ground as far as Le Cateau and set up. Half-right the company commander saw a British battery 'too far forward' and beyond the town more British batteries trying to limber up. The MGs engaged the guns and then the British infantry. 'The same ghastly picture ... one develops a taste for MG fire, draws pleasure from its beautiful effectiveness, the way the targets all fall together. The beast slowly awakens inside you.' The MG vehicles came up and the company crossed the battlefield: 'Frightful, indescribable ... We had fired almost straight down the flank of their trenches.' The machine gun was becoming the German infantry weapon par excellence.

With the entry of the artillery and IR 26 into the battle, the commander of II/66 ordered the assault. This was premature. Captain Bonsac, commander of 7/66, was killed leading his company in the attack, just as his father had been killed leading 7/66 at Beaumont in 1870. A squad that charged lost all but one man. Ammunition ran short and had to be brought forward under heavy fire.

Nevertheless, all along the IR 66 line British resistance began to noticeably weaken. The regimental commander committed his last reserve, 2/66. Shortly before 1500 III/66 on the right flank saw British troops withdrawing and opened 'tremendous fire', cutting down the British in groups. III/66 advanced, first by bounds, then in a continuous movement, in spite of British fire, until it crossed the road where it again took up firing positions. II/66 was preparing for an assault on trenches 200 metres to the front when white flags appeared. A British officer gave his sword to a German lieutenant. The Germans then began to take fire from further up the hill. The German lieutenant said that unless this fire ceased he would shoot the prisoners. The British officer signalled and the fire stopped.

IR 66 and IR 26 sounded 'Fix Bayonets!' the battalion colours were unfurled and at 1500 both regiments assaulted. At the same time II/FAR 4, a light howitzer unit, moved through Montay and opened fire from positions on the high ground north of Le Cateau.[66] 4/FAR 4 bounded forward until it was level with the infantry and engaged British columns as they retired towards Beaumont-Inchy. At 1520 4/FAR 40 bounded forward again, under heavy small-arms fire, to a position just north of the road.

I/FAR 4, which was attached to the German 14th Brigade, approached from the east of Le Cateau, where they had a panoramic view of the battlefield, but it was difficult to distinguish friend from foe. I/FAR 4 therefore went into action against British artillery that was trying to withdraw; they could take the British positions in the flank and the effect of their fire was 'massive'. The section tried to bound forward but went too far and got mixed in with IR 26 infantry. It then tried to return to its brigade but was blocked by arriving III AK columns.

The KOYLI machine gun section was in action from 0830 until 1430, by which time one gun had been destroyed and the other gun, probably no longer operational, was broken up. Movement up to or in the KOYLI position was nearly impossible due to German fire. An attempt to reinforce the front line resulted in heavy casualties, including 1 OFF KIA and 1 WIA. Orders could not be brought forward and the troops were pinned to their positions; the KOYLI could not have withdrawn, even if it had received orders to do so.

There was still considerable British fire, but now the British retreat was general. The KOYLI history says: 'There was no surrender. The occupants of the trenches were mobbed and swamped by the rising tide of grey-coated Germans ... Some few of the survivors were bayoneted, but to the credit of the German soldiers, be it mentioned, most of the unwounded were made prisoners and the wounded in the trench were respected ... The action was over by 4.30pm.' The IR 66 history said: 'While some fled from one sheaf of wheat to the other, entire rows stood up and surrendered.' Sixteen officers and 320 EM from 2/KOYLI were captured; 170 of the POWs were wounded. 'A British officer prisoner-of-war ... counted sixty-two dead ... in "B" Company's trenches.'

2/King's Own Scottish Borderers (KOSB) were on the left of the 14th Brigade line.[67] The battalion had dug in 300–400 metres south of the Le Cateau–Cambrai road with their entrenching tools. The battalion was not subject to serious infantry attack. On the other hand, the terrain to the front was rolling and offered the Germans excellent covered and concealed routes of approach and the KOSB do not seem to have done much firing. 'This sector was not shelled so heavily as others, but the reserve company [D] saw a battery of our artillery literally blown to pieces.' At 1430 the German artillery turned its attention to 2/KOSB. Spoil from the trenches was visible and attracted German fire; the battalion took

casualties and had to abandon some positions. At 1500 the battalion was ordered
to retire. Only one platoon of C Company got the order. Since the initial defence
order had said 'No retirement' the rest of C Company held on until surrounded
and 'went into the bag'. During the retreat the battalion took more artillery fire,
which caused further casualties; the battalion commander was wounded and captured and the XO wounded. A lieutenant, trying to rescue a wounded man, was
charged by cavalry, hit on the head and captured. There is no record in the regimental history of 2/KOSB casualties, but Cave and Shelton estimate them at 250.

1/Royal West Kent had dug in as best it could (it had lost its pioneer tools at
Mons) about 600 metres south of the 1/KOYLI and stayed in its trenches until
the remnants of the KOYLI withdrew past it, at which time it also withdrew, not
under pressure. One company commander read the *Daily Mail* or slept through
much of the battle.[68] Apparently no attempt had been made to use any of its assets,
including the MGs and medical personnel, to reinforce the fight at the front line;
one-quarter of the 13th Brigade's combat power sat out Le Cateau, which was
representative of the inert defence that British II Corps fought.

2/Duke of Wellington's had already taken 350 casualties on 23 and 24 August.
It dug in well to the rear, 2,000 metres behind the junction of the 13th and 15th
Brigades, in the same area as 61 RFA (how) and 108 (hvy); the German counter-battery fire intended for them also landed on the Duke of Wellington's.[69] A
captain from this battalion had a good position to observe the effectiveness of the
German fire: 'batteries blown to pieces'. This battalion also withdrew without
making contact.[70]

The two 19th Brigade units to the right rear of the 2/Suffolks, 2/Argyll and
Sutherland Highlanders and 1/Middlesex, engaged German infantry at 1,200
metres range but apparently were incapable of preventing the Suffolks from being
surrounded and overrun. At 1600 1/Middlesex withdrew until 2200, when it bivouacked.

IR 66 and IR 26 were in no condition to conduct a pursuit. They had lost significant numbers of leaders and the two regiments were mixed up and scattered
all over the battlefield. IR 66 had been in combat since 0800 and was exhausted.

Casualties

IR 66 captured 13 artillery pieces and more than 600 POWs. IR 26 captured 12
guns and 8 MGs. FAR 40 made good use of mounds of British equipment: 'rub-
berised ponchos, razors, sleeping bags, shoes, boots – the British soldier was well
equipped down to the smallest details.'

IR 72 lost 1 OFF and 21 EM KIA, 6 OFF and 87 EM WIA, 4 EM MIA. IR 66
lost 5 OFF, including 3 company commanders, and 75 EM KIA; 18 OFF and 398
EM were WIA. IR 26 lost 4 OFF and 57 EM KIA, 12 OFF (including the regi-

mental commander) and 247 EM WIA, 347 EM MIA, most of whom returned to the regiment. The three regiments took some 950–1,000 casualties in total.

2/Suffolk lost 4 OFF KIA, 6 OFF WIA, and 710 EM casualties. At the 2/ Suffolk roll call on 27 August the battalion numbered 111 men and was commanded by a lieutenant. On 28 August the battalion numbered 229 men and was organised as a company and attached to the East Surrey Regiment. 2/Manchester mustered 8 OFF and 339 EM and had lost 14 OFF and 339 EM. Together these two battalions took more casualties than all three German regiments combined. DCLI apparently lost about 100 men. 2/KOYLI lost 18 OFF and 21 sergeants, 22 corporals, 7 buglers and 532 privates (582 EM), which illustrates the loss of cadre that results when a unit is annihilated. 310 KOYLI men were reported POW, of which 170 were wounded. 1/Middlesex (19th Brigade) lost 2 EM KIA, 2 OFF and 36 EM WIA, 74 EM MIA, 'many more probably'. Total British infantry casualties near the Le Cateau area proper were over 1,800 men, nearly twice the German casualties.

FAR 40 had fired 952 shells, lost 2 OFF KIA, 21 EM WIA and only 20 horses. The British XV Artillery Brigade lost 14 OFF, 124 EM, 10 guns and 230 horses; XXVIII lost 6 OFF and 58 EM and 16 guns.

Evaluation

It is difficult to escape the conclusion that the British official histories were systematically trying to make it appear that the Germans were much stronger than was actually the case. Becke says the Germans had probably massed two corps against the 5th Division.[71] Map 11 of the British official history shows the British right flank being attacked by six infantry regiments: IR 153, IR 66, IR 26, IR 72, IR 27 and IR 165. IR 153 was actually about 6 km to the west, and IR 72 engaged only a few companies to the west of Le Cateau. By the time IR 27 and IR 165 arrived the British were withdrawing and neither regiment made contact.[72]

Following the lead of the official histories, Lomas wrote: 'The German attack had been reinforced by their 5th Division of III Corps, and the British forces – four infantry battalions and two Royal Field Artillery brigades – faced the onslaught of at least 12 German battalions and the combined artillery of three divisions.'[73]

The British historians constructed a tactical picture that had strong references to colonial warfare: static defence cutting down hordes of brave but unsophisticated opponents. 'Rapid rifle fire' and artillery fire cut down German troops in rows, threw back German attacks time and again, and the Germans were victorious only because they enjoyed a massive numerical superiority. There was also much emphasis on British pluck, derring-do and the deeds of the winners of the Victoria Cross.

In fact, the odds were practically even. The British 13th and 14th Brigades were being attacked by IR 66 and IR 26. After pushing away six British companies near Le Cateau, IR 72 committed only three or four companies to the west. The comparison forces shows seven German infantry battalions against eight British, six German batteries (FAR 40, later nine batteries when II/75 arrived) against nine British (XV, XXVIII, 37 How, 61 How, 108 Hvy). The British assumed they had been outnumbered 4:1. In fact, IR 66, IR 26 and FAR 40 had hit the British 5th Division so hard that they had the British seeing not merely double, but quadruple.

In six hours the German IR 66 and IR 26, with pulverising fire support from FAR 40, had advanced 4,500 metres by bounds against an equal-sized British force deployed on the defensive, and in a combined-arms attack gained fire superiority, assaulted and overran the British position, taking hundreds of prisoners and capturing nearly half of the defending artillery. The inert linear defence conducted by the British 5th Division allowed the Germans to conduct their attack 'just like in training'.

British 15th Brigade

The 15th Brigade received the order at 0530 to defend in place on a 1,800-metre front. The Dorsetshire Regiment was on the left of the 15th Brigade, 1/Bedfordshire on the brigade right.[74] The Bedfordshire did not dig in on 25 August or the morning of 26 August because it expected to continue the withdrawal. The battalion had just begun to withdraw and had marched about 200 metres on 26 August when a staff officer ordered the battalion to occupy some trenches dug by civilians, adding that II Corps was being sacrificed to save the other corps. The trenches were about 600 metres from the road: 'They had sited the trenches rather badly and had dug them worse. Some of them were about eight feet broad and only two feet deep. Most of them were facing in the wrong direction.' The Bedfords began improving them. The artillery batteries were deployed in covered positions, but 119 RFA and 121 RFA were still too close to the infantry. A battery set up 200–300 metres behind the battalion's trenches. Luckily, fire aimed at the battery never hit the battalion. In the afternoon the battalion began to take MG and rifle fire, which steadily increased. At 1600 it was ordered to withdraw, passing the battery where 'a heap of dead lay around the guns'. The battalion broke up during the withdrawal: 'The CO and I had A and B Companies, or what remained of them, with us; where C and D were we had not a notion.'

1/Norfolk was in reserve behind 1/Bedfordshire.[75] At 1315 it was pulled back to Reumont to cover the 5th Division withdrawal, and at 1630 pulled back again to Honnechy. It engaged German troops at long range (1,400 metres). 1/Cheshire had been destroyed on 24 August at Elouges; the 150 survivors dug in about 500 metres behind the front-line units. The 15th Brigade had done little while its neighbours, the 13th and 14th Brigades, were being destroyed.

IR 36 Attacks the British 15th and 9th Brigades

The British 3rd Division deployed all three brigades on line: 9th on the right, south of Beaumont-Inchy, 8th in the centre between Audencourt and Caudry, and 7th on the left at Caudry. The 3rd Division was the first to be informed that II Corps would defend in place; the division was also fortunate that the German 8 ID had a long approach march. This meant not only that the 3rd Division had more time to prepare, but also that the German 8 ID had less daylight in which to conduct its attack.

The 9th Brigade deployed two battalions on line: 1/Northumberland Fusiliers on the right, 1/Lincoln on the left, about 300 metres from Inchy. Two companies of the 1/Royal Scots Fusiliers were close behind the centre, 4/Royal Fusiliers behind the right rear, north-west of Troisvilles, in reserve.

1/Northumberland dug in with entrenching tools about 800 metres south of Inchy on the forward slope.[76] Their battle was not very eventful, took little fire and hardly saw the Germans. Even though the battalion had to cross 400 metres of open hillside to its rear in order to withdraw, casualties were light.

1/Lincolnshire had some pioneer equipment to dig in with. The battalion took some artillery fire at 0630.[77] The German infantry came down the slope north of Inchy in open order, in successive waves – under British artillery fire, but apparently not under rifle fire – passed through Inchy and set up firing positions on the south side of town. The Germans found good covered and concealed positions 300 metres from the Lincoln trenches. The Lincolns were forced to stay completely under cover. The defence and later the withdrawal, which was ordered at 1530, were successful only because a section of 107 RFA and another from 108 had been dug into the forward slope and provided fire support, though all four guns had to be abandoned. For the Royal Fusiliers the battle was positively restful; the troops even got a hot meal.

IR 36 deployed south of Neuvilly and advanced towards Inchy with II/36 west of the Neuvilly–Troisvilles road, I/36 and III/36 to the east.[78] At 1200 the regiment attacked towards its objective, the Le Cateau–Cambrai road. The regiment complained that the artillery preparation had been inadequate. This was because II/FAR 75 was engaging the British artillery south-west of Le Cateau. II/FAR 75 then engaged Inchy and then the British positions along the road, which were very difficult to locate. Indeed, initially II/FAR 75 did not see the British position at all. IR 36 casualties from British small-arms fire were heavy, and the regimental commander committed all his reserves. At 1500 6/FAR 75 crossed 500 metres of open ground through MG fire to set up 1,100 metres from the British position,

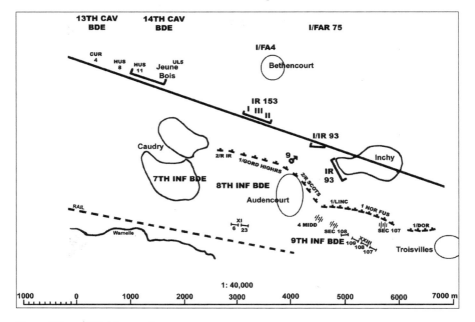

Fig 22: BR 3rd Division, 26 August.

knocking down the houses with direct fire. An officer candidate rode on a bicycle under fire to the IR 36 command post to coordinate fire support. At 1610, 4/FAR 75 bounded forward also. At 1630 the British retreated. All three batteries pursued: 'the enemy continually offered new targets'. IR 36 reached its objective, the road, and then along with II/FAR 75 pushed on to Troisvilles, where they bivouacked.

1/Nothumberland lost 3 EM KIA and 2 OFF and 15 EM WIA, mostly from German shelling of the rear area. 1/Lincolnshire lost 1 OFF WIA (and POW), 3 EM KIA, 40 WIA. There were 50 MIA, most of whom returned to the battalion. 4/Royal Fusiliers apparently lost 1 KIA, 20 WIA. Royal Scots Fusiliers took 3 wounded, only 87 total casualties. IR 36 lost 3 OFF and 48 EM KIA, 13 OFF and 336 EM WIA.

The II/FAR 75 description of the battlefield in this sector does not square with the British description of the battles fought by the 15th and 9th Brigades:

The march over the battlefield and through Troisvilles was an unforgettable and disturbing experience. Dead and wounded, in trenches, in MG positions, between destroyed guns, over limbers, under mutilated horses. Dead, still aiming their weapons, under collapsed walls, behind windows stuffed with mattresses, behind barricades of tables, chairs, cabinets and ladders … weapons, munitions, coats, Scottish caps, medical kit boxes: impossible to count it all. Motor vehicles, loaded with oats, with food, entire trainloads, supply columns, and between them more dead.

The disparity between the British and German accounts is hard to explain. The British reported little contact and took few casualties. The Germans report a tough battle, 400 casualties and many British dead.

Audencourt

The British 8th Brigade in the 3rd Division centre deployed 2/Royal Scots on the right, 1/Gordon Highlanders on the left, and 2/Royal Irish Regiment (RIR), which had lost over 200 men and both MGs at Mons, and the remnants of 4/Middlesex were in reserve. At 0930 C and D Companies of 2/RIR prolonged the left flank of the Gordons, B Company was sent to Caudry, A Company was kept in reserve near Audencourt. One 'company' of 4/Middlesex moved to the right of the Royal Scots, one between the Royal Scots and the Gordon Highlanders north of Audencourt, two in reserve east of Audencourt.[79]

The commander of the Royal Scots was told that 40,000 French were coming to the assistance of II Corps and that further retirement would not be necessary.[80] The Royal Scots deepened trenches begun by French civilians. The regimental history said the field of fire was good and the trenches would be difficult to spot 'if the men kept their heads down'. The regimental history mentioned that the battalion's position faced the town of Beaumont about 500 metres to the front, but failed to say that this provided the Germans with close-range cover and concealment.

The British 8th and 9th Brigades were not significantly engaged until 1200. The British official history attributed this to the fact that 'they [the Germans] were husbanding their strength until their main effort against both flanks of the British should produce its effect'.[81] This is wrong; the German 8 ID did not attack until noon solely because it had to make a long approach march. Once again, the British official history had no idea what the Germans were doing and instead made unjustified assumptions.

IR 153 moved out at dawn, fully deployed, expecting to fight the British at Solesmes.[82] Finding the British gone, the regiment formed march column and moved out again at 0615. HKK 2 reported that it was engaged with British forces along the Le Cateau–Cambrai road and that the British also occupied Bethencourt. At 0900 the regiment deployed with I/153 on the right of the Viesly–Bethencourt road, III/153 on the left, II/153 guarded the artillery. As the regiment left Viesly it took heavy artillery fire, which it passed through moving by bounds. After a sharp firefight Bethencourt was taken at 1000. A bit after 1200 IR 153 attacked between Caudry and Audencourt, I/153 on the right, II/153 on the left, direction of march the church tower at Caudry.

In spite of immediate casualties the companies threw themselves into their first serious battle with well-ordered bounds, just like in the training area. The riflemen demonstrated the marksmanship skills they had learned in peacetime with their first-class accuracy and fire discipline, which was visible the next day in the English dead in their defensive position, shot in the head. But the intense infantry fire from the main British positions, carefully concealed in the sugar-beet fields, which even at 500m could hardly be detected with the naked eye, finally slowed the advance. The MG Company set up on the right flank in the first floor windows of an isolated house and fired over the troops' heads. III/153, in reserve, was committed at around 1600 into a gap between I/153 and II/153.

IR 153 had closed to within assault distance by dark, but IV AK ordered the regiment to wait until the next morning to conduct the assault, when IV RK would be able to cooperate. The regiment spent the second night in a row in a lying in a combat position.

IR 93 was the last regiment in the 8 ID column.[83] When it reached the town of Viesly at 1015 it was ordered to attack Beaumont. The regiment deployed I/93 right of the Beaumont–Viesly road, III/93 to the left, II/93 behind the middle, and advanced in company columns behind a skirmisher screen, using hollows in the terrain to cover its approach. When the church tower of Beaumont came into sight the regiment began to take shrapnel fire – they were sure that the British had a FO in the tower. The regiment deployed into successive lines of skirmishers and advanced by bounds. When it reached the top of the hill north of Inchy it received more heavy shrapnel fire. The Château of Ciermont on the regimental right flank exercised a strange attraction, and both leading battalions moved half-right in that direction, which drew still more artillery fire. II/93 was committed on the left in order to close the gap with IR 36. Two platoons of the MG Company went into position on the crest of the hill and fired over the heads of the forward troops. III/93 had approached to within 400 metres of the town. I/93, through use of the terrain, reached the main road by 1100. I/93 and 4/93 pushed 200 metres south of the main road and established themselves in a sunken road, from where they put effective fire on the defenders, while II/93 and III/93 penetrated into Inchy. British fire was too strong to allow a further advance, and attempts by 9/93 and 12/93 to do so ended with the deaths of the company commanders. The regimental commander was killed by shrapnel fire.

FAR 74 went into action at Viesly at 0800, bombarding the British artillery at Bethencourt, Prayelle and Caudry.[84] The Horse Artillery Section of FAR 10 also fired on Caudry. German artillery bombarded Audencourt and the Royal Scots' history says it 'reduced to splinters and fragments practically the whole of the transport of the 8th Brigade'.

I/FAR 75 provided close support for the infantry attack from a covered position behind a ridge between Viesly and Quiévy that provided good observation over both the enemy and friendly troops.[85] I/FAR 75 fired first on Bethencourt, then Inchy. Some guns were pushed onto the ridge in order to employ direct fire. I/FAR 75 then came under counter-fire from an estimated four covered or half-covered British batteries at 6,000 metres range. I/FAR 75 took up the fight, comparing the azimuths from the battery command telescopes to triangulate the British location. Even as the section was adjusting fire, the British fire slackened. When it fired for effect it observed secondary explosions and at 1200 the British fire stopped completely.

After a 21-km march I/Foot Artillery 4 went into action behind IR 153 and began to pound the British position with 15 cm shells; 3/Foot Artillery 4 fired 239 rounds, 4/4 109.[86]

At 1200 the corps headquarters ordered an attack on the main enemy position along the road between Caudry and Audencourt. The British position was difficult to make out, even at 500 metres distance. At 1230 4/FAR 74 and 5/74 moved forward to provide direct support. At 1530 I/FAR 75 bounded forward by batteries to a position north of Caudry, engaging the British line at 1,200 to 1,600 metres range, many of the guns firing direct from open positions.

At 1700 British troops began abandoning their positions. The MG Company had been set up in the upper stories of buildings in Inchy and engaged them with pursuit fire. It had become too dark to conduct an assault and the regiment settled in for the night. Patrols from IR 93 found at 2300 that the British had withdrawn.

At 1630 the Royal Scots were ordered to withdraw. The position was on a forward slope, suitable only for defence where 'further retirement would not be necessary', but requiring any withdrawal to be executed 'in full view of the enemy' who was 500 metres away in Inchy. The battalion withdrew by company bounds 'and sustained its heaviest losses while carrying out this movement'. The battalion commander was wounded and captured, the D Company commander was killed, two other officers wounded and seven lieutenants were missing. The battalion was so badly broken up and disorganised that no accounting for personnel was possible. Two platoons of D Company had not received orders to withdraw and were captured; D Company mustered 17 men.

The commander of 2/Royal Irish Rifles described the withdrawal from Audencourt:[87]

> At about 4.30 p.m … the bulk of the artillery and infantry that had been defending Audencourt suddenly came streaming down the hill to the railway, then taking the road to Montigny. First came some guns and limbers at full gallop, then guns and limbers etc. covered with infantrymen, then the infantry in complete disorder.

The Royal Irish Regiment had become separated from their pioneer tools and could not dig in properly.[88] They were under close-range small-arms fire from the Le Cateau–Cambrai road all morning, which became more intense at 1330.

At 1400 it appeared that the 7th Brigade had evacuated Caudry. At 1800 the reserve company near Audencourt began receiving MG fire from the left rear; the origin of this fire is a mystery; there were no German units in the area. The lookout reported that there was no more activity in the Gordons' positions to the right. A and B Companies withdrew with the brigade around 2200, C and D did not receive the order and remained on line and were captured with the Gordon Highlanders.

The Gordons' regimental history says that the battalion held 1,000 metres of front 350 metres south of the Le Cateau–Cambrai road between Caudry and Audencourt with a good field of fire.[89] At 0900 the German and British artillery began a gunnery duel, which according to the account of a Gordons officer the Germans won, because they shifted their fire to the Gordons' trenches. They were hardly engaged until 1400, when German infantry appearing at 1,200 metres was supposedly 'dealt with by machine gun', but the Germans somehow managed to reappear, now at 900 metres.[90] The British official history says: 'One subaltern of the Royal Scots reckoned that he hit thirty to forty of them [Germans] himself.'[91] How such an implausible story finds its way into a work that claims to be serious military history is inexplicable. A description from a Gordon officer of German tactics and the effect of British fire was far more realistic than most:

> The command, 'Five rounds rapid at the stubble field 900 yards' produced a cinematographic picture in my field glasses. The Germans hopped into cover like rabbits. Some threw themselves flat behind the corn stooks and when the firing ceased got up and bolted back into the wood. Two or three who had also appeared to fling themselves down remained motionless. The enemy, having discovered that we could be dangerous at even 900 yards, then successfully crossed the stubble field in two rushes without losing a man, and reinforced their men who were advancing through the beetroot fields on our right. Great numbers of troops now began to appear on the ridge between Béthencourt and the little wood. They advanced in three or four sections of ten or fifteen men extended to two paces. Their line of advance was directed on to the village of Audencourt and on the low plateau on our right, so that we were able to pour on them an enfilade fire. They were advancing in short rushes across pasture-land which provided no cover whatever, and offered a clearly visible target even when lying down. Although our men were nearly all first-class shots, they did not often hit the target. This was owing to the unpleasant fact that the German gunners kept up a steady stream of shrapnel which burst just in front of our trenches and broke over the top like a wave. Shooting at the enemy had to be timed by the bursting shell ... But the shooting of the Battalion was good enough to delay the enemy's advance. From the 900 yard mark they took more than an hour to reach their first objective, which was the Route Nationale, 400 yards from our nearest trench. Here they were able to concentrate in great numbers.

The Gordons' history says that the Germans renewed the attack at 1700 'in close formation, but the rapid fire of the Gordons mowed them down'. The British official history's description of the German attack is, once again, tactically wrong: 'for the best part of an hour they swayed backwards and forwards in front of these few isolated groups, probably exaggerating their strength in machine guns, but completely at a loss how to clear them out of the way.' The Germans had not 'swayed' indecisively in front of these 'small groups' (which actually numbered about 1,000 men), they had closed in and stopped only due to darkness; had the British not withdrawn, the battle would have resumed at dawn.

At 1530 (2/Royal Irish says 1645) the 8th Brigade ordered a withdrawal: the Gordons, C and D Companies of the Royal Irish and two platoons of the Royal Scots never got the order. When the Gordons discovered they had been left behind is unclear. When they did, 'A complication which only the British service could have produced now occurred'.[92] The second in command of the Gordons, though junior in regimental rank to the Gordons' commander, was a brevet colonel in the British army. Since the force consisted of more than one regiment, he pulled his British army rank and insisted on taking overall command. None of the British sources expressly say so, but it would appear that the two argued the question for several hours. In any case, this group, about 1,000 strong, did not move until 0030 on 27 August. It marched through Audencourt without making contact. A local man guided them through Montigny towards Bertry.

At 0130 on 27 August IR 153 noticed movement in the British position between Caudry and Audencourt. It was unclear if they were withdrawing or preparing a night attack, so an officer's patrol was sent out. A lieutenant and two men, who the lieutenant had trained as recruits, volunteered for 'a little stroll'. They moved forward to the ditch by the Le Cateau–Cambrai road, watched and listened, then crossed the road. In the ditch on the other side were many British dead. They continued and found a local inhabitant 'anxiously wandering around', who told them that the British had left.

IR 66 had marched south-west until 0100 on 27 August to make room for III AK. II/66 bivouacked at Clary. I/IR 66 and III/66 bivouacked in Bertry, 4 km south-west of Le Cateau.[93] 10/66 had outpost duty in Bertry, and two musketeers were on sentry-go. At 0230 the sentries saw the Gordons' column and alerted the company, which deployed on the edge of the village and opened fire. A British battalion commander, four other officers and 298 EM from three different regiments surrendered with little resistance. In addition, a great number of British lay dead and wounded.

The rest of the Gordons' column was now ordered to withdraw the way it had come and return to Montigny. Instead, it turned south-west, towards Clary. The fire at Bertry had alerted the security platoon from 8/66 at Clary. At 0500 a group of eighty British under an officer approached the sentries and surrendered. The platoon leader detected an enemy column 800 metres away, approaching

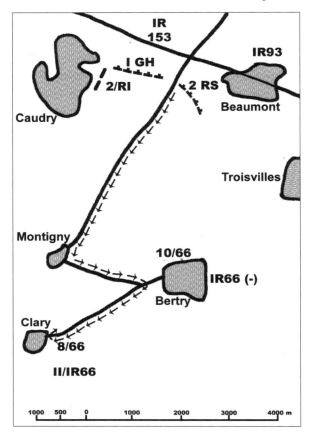

Fig. 23: Destruction of
1/Gordon Highlanders,
27 August.

and waving white flags. He deployed his platoon at the edge of the town. At 400
metres range the British column deployed several skirmisher lines, followed by a
longer skirmisher line. The 8/66 platoon leader feared that the British were going
to overrun him and opened fire. The British fell, ran, crawled into the sugarbeet
fields or opened fire. The other two platoons of 8/66 reinforced. A regular battle
developed which lasted for an hour. The II/66 commander committed 5/66 and
6/66 and two MG platoons. Some of the British fled into a farm and II/66 called
for artillery support. II/66 attacked and took 700 POWs, including several officers, from ten or eleven different regiments of infantry and artillery. Five hundred
of these were Gordons; 2/Scots and 1/Gordons lost their MGs.[94]

IR 153 lost 51 KIA, 250 WIA. IR 93 lost 6 OFF and 112 EM KIA, 9 OFF and
306 EM WIA. The two infantry regiments took 734 casualties. FAR 74 had fired
252 shrapnel and 801 high-explosive shells and lost 3 KIA and 4 WIA.

The Royal Scots regimental history does not give any casualty figure. It says
it received its 'heaviest losses' during the withdrawal and 'Owing to the withdrawal in full view of the enemy their casualties could not have been light'.
Two platoons of D Company were captured. There are no casualty figures for

4/Middlesex. 2/Royal Irish lost their battalion commander and another 265 EM. 1/Gordon Highlanders was destroyed: only three platoons and the battalion transport remained. A month later the battalion was still not combat-effective, and since it was unlikely to become so in the foreseeable future, on 11 September the battalion became army troops, performing POW guard and rear area security missions. IR 66 took 1,100 prisoners on the night of 26–27 August. All the German units that passed through the British 8th Brigade position reported seeing numerous British dead. Becke's figure of 1,000 8th Brigade casualties is therefore far too low. Becke says the British 9th Brigade lost 150 men. The British also lost four guns. 8 ID lost about 1,140 men: the British and German casualties were practically equal.

8 ID was missing IR 72, so it had nine infantry battalions against eight British battalions. The Germans had 19 batteries of artillery, including 4 heavy; the British probably had 10, including 1 heavy. In about six hours 8 ID was able to advance across an open plain and establish itself securely a few hundred metres from the British position. The decisive factor was that the German infantry was not engaged until 1200, which meant that the attack was stopped by darkness. The British weakness was once again defective command and control; the failure to transmit orders resulted in the loss of over a battalion of troops.

British 7th Brigade at Caudry

The British 7th Brigade deployed 1/Wiltshire Regiment on the right, north-east of Caudry, 2/South Lancashire, which had already sustained 300 casualties, with 56th Engineer Company north of the town and 3/Worcestershire to the north-west. The Lancashires did not find their way to Caudry until dawn, completely exhausted. The battalion was clearly shattered and the regimental history devotes exactly one uninformative sentence to its activities at Caudry.[95] The 2/Royal Irish Rifles had got lost, went to Le Cateau and arrived at Caudry only at 0900.

3/Worcestershire had been awakened at 0230 to dig defensive positions with entrenching tools to the north of Caudry, but the tired soldiers had no enthusiasm for it.[96] The 3rd Division had ordered a defence in place sometime between 0400 and 0500, but by the time the orders arrived the brigade was already in contact.

At dawn German artillery fire began to land on the houses. B Company, which was oriented north–south, facing south-west for some unfathomable reason, was caught in an enfilade of German artillery fire and in the rear by MG fire from the north-east. The company withdrew to the town. The other two 7th Brigade battalions moved up to the right of the Worcestershire, not without some confusion; a company of the Wiltshires ended up in the middle of the Worcestershire position. Small parties of German troops appeared to the front.

The 7th Brigade was lined up along the road, making it an easy target for German artillery fire, which was so effective that it caused subordinate commanders to make uncoordinated withdrawals. First C/Worcestershire fell back into Caudry, then two platoons of A Company. The commander of D Company and the Wiltshire company then pulled all the way back to the west side of Caudry. The brigadier sent A Company south-west of Caudry to guard the artillery. This left B and C Companies engaged with German troops and MG at the Jeune Bois. Due to the gap with 11th Brigade on the left, at 0930 these two companies were ordered to withdraw to the west of Caudry. A Company received no orders, but marched south in conformity with the general movement. The withdrawal continued; B and C Companies moved to the railway line south-west of Caudry, with D Company to their rear. An artillery shell scored a direct hit on the 3/Worcestershire HQ; the second in command and the adjutant were badly wounded, most of the signal personnel were killed or wounded. Command and control in the 7th Brigade was collapsing:

> The withdrawal of the two companies was accompanied by a retirement of other troops from the north end of Caudry. No very definite orders as to the length of their resistance seem to have reached the front line. All ranks vaguely knew that a general retreat was in progress. Moved by that knowledge, rather than by the pressure of the enemy, various units of the defending troops fell back from the northern to the southern side of the town. In so doing several units became disordered and there were many stragglers … The movement back became more definite. The field batteries south-east of the town limbered up and moved off.[97]

Then A Company ran into the commanding general of 3rd Division, who ordered the battalion to reoccupy the town. By this time 3/Worcestershire was scattered and the battalion commander had some difficulty assembling a sufficient force, which finally marched into Caudry largely unopposed, but stopped at the town square due to German artillery fire. The battalion was ordered out again at 1630, all the way to the south side of the Warnelle.

The Worcestershire regimental history says: 'That vigorous counter-stroke [which took back Caudry] had the effect of paralysing the enemy around Caudry.'[98] Actually, the attack was tentative, retook only the southern half of the town, and failed to make serious contact with the German cavalry, much less 'paralyse' them. The Worcestershire history then goes on to say, 'At Caudry the enemy had been hit hard', a statement that finds no confirmation in the German cavalry regimental histories.

German 9 KD at Caudry

After another short night in a muddy bivouac in the rain, HKK 2 moved out at 0330. Cuirassier R 4 surprised a band of *franc-tireur* in shocks of rye, charged them and took fifteen prisoners. Shortly after 0600 Caudry was reported occupied by three divisions and HKK 2 deployed.

Map 11 in the British official history has the German 4 KD attacking the north side of Caudry. In fact, the only unit of 4 KD to be engaged was the Horse Artillery Section 3. 4 KD deployed its dismounted cavalry at Herpigny Farm north of Bethencourt. The division tried to advance, but was clearly outclassed.[99] The cavalry took fire from six to eight batteries, which covered the division sector. The three batteries of the Horse Artillery Section took heavy counter-battery fire and the section commander was killed. Fortunately most of the British shrapnel exploded too high and either rattled off the gun shields 'like hail' or hit weakly. Now and again a horse artilleryman would curse: 'Donnerwetter, I just got hit by another one!' Pieces of shrapnel stuck out of the caissons.

The horse artillery ammunition column had its hands full. Almost all the division's shells were fired off and the ammunition column was sent to FAR 74 for resupply. By evening this ammunition had been expended too and the column returned to FAR 74, which refused to give the horse artillery more shells. The column then rode to the 1st Army supply depot at Solesmes, found a motorised ammunition column, reloaded from that and returned in pitch darkness and pouring rain, arriving at the guns at 0100 on 27 August.

The German 9 KD attacked the north-west side of Caudry with the 13th Cavalry Brigade on the right, the 14th Brigade on the left. The 13th Brigade deployed Hussar R 8 on the left, Cuirassier R 4 on the right. This was 9 KD's first serious fight and the units were near full-strength. Nevertheless, the two cavalry brigades would have had no more than 1,800 dismounts against 2,300 infantrymen of the British 7th Brigade.

The cuirassiers dismounted 4th Squadron on the left, 3rd in the centre and 5th on the right, with 1st in reserve. The hussars occupied Beauvois-Beaumont with 4th Squadron and half of the 3rd. The 1st, 5th and the other half of 3rd moved against the heights to the east, from which the regiment was taking fire in the flank. This group drove the British off a position 1,000 metres north-west of Caudry, who left 'numerous coats and maps'. The regiment took particularly strong fire from a factory in Caudry.

A member of 4/Cuirassier R 4 said that they dismounted under fire and with a few bounds forward reached a farmyard. A lieutenant requisitioned bacon and bread and passed them out to the troopers. They crawled individually through a hole in a barn to reach a road ditch 800 metres from Caudry. His group moved by bounds under fire from hayrick to hayrick to reach a position on the left flank.

The British were seldom to be seen. A man from Uhlan R 5 lay down next to him and told 'wonderful stories from the Rhineland'. There were pauses in the fire in which the troops rested. At 1200 the artillery began firing on Caudry and the firefight died down. At 1600 the regiment pulled back.

The Cuirassier R 4 combat trains had an exciting day. They were in St Vaast, preparing to move out, when a captain told the NCO in charge (NCOIC) that there were enemy troops 2 km east of the town. While the NCOIC rounded up some cuirassiers, a sergeant from 3/Cuirassier 4 rode to the group of British troops, who were led by a mounted officer. The cuirassier sergeant motioned to the officer, who waved a white flag. The NCOIC appeared with 10 cuirassiers, who took 37 British POW.

Hussar R 8 deployed two squadrons on line, one in reserve; one squadron was conducting reconnaissance.[100] The hussars immediately got involved in the firefight that lasted until near dark. The British withdrew before the hussars noticed they were gone, but the hussars and cuirassiers compensated themselves by finding 'a great number of British coats, which are very practical'.

The 14th Cavalry Brigade deployed Hussar R 11 on the right, Uhlan R 5 on the left, with the hussar's right flank at Halte Jeune Bois, and at 0600 took up positions along the Le Cateau–Cambrai road. That the hussars could establish themselves without difficulty 500 metres in front of the British 7th Brigade's position does not speak well of British security nor use of terrain.[101] The British made a weak counter-attack, which was easily swatted away, yielding the first prisoners. Hussar R 11 claims to have taken 600 prisoners 'who didn't present a very warlike appearance. They hadn't anything to eat for three days and didn't seem unhappy to have been captured.'

Hussar R 8 took only eight casualties, Cuirassier R 4 lost 2 OFF and 3 EM KIA, 21 EM WIA or MIA. Hussar R 11 lost 4 EM KIA, 14 WIA and 1 DOW. Uhlan R 5 does not mention casualties, but they were probably of the same order as Hussar R 11, so the two cavalry brigades suffered some 75 casualties. Becke says the 7th Brigade took 300 casualties: 3/Worcestershire lost 100 men, 2/Royal Irish Rifles lost 6 EM KIA, 2 OFF WIA and POW, 2 OFF and 29 EM WIA. The Germans overran the Irish supply trains during the confusion of the withdrawal, which 'very considerably increased the hardships of our retreat'.

The German 9 KD recognised that it was not strong enough to push infantry out of Caudry and most prudently did not try, but engaged in a day-long firefight at medium range, attempting to fix the British in place.

No 9 KD cavalry regiment reported that it had advanced much past the Le Cateau–Cambrai road, nor did any say that they had entered Caudry. At most, 9 KD sent patrols into Caudry. The 7th Brigade had been pushed out of Caudry solely by German artillery fire, and it must be suspected that the fire of the 15 cm howitzers I/Foot Artillery 4 played an important role here. The retreat of the 7th Brigade also exposed the 11th Brigade's right flank, forcing it to withdraw.

Casualties at Le Cateau

The British official history says that the British lost 7,812 men and 38 guns. From German regimental records, most German unit casualties can be determined exactly, which allows an estimate of 2,900 total casualties with a high degree of confidence.

British historians have consistently maintained that Le Cateau was a British victory because, as the British official history says, 'they had inflicted upon the enemy casualties never revealed, which are believed to have been out of all proportion to their own'.[102] Lomas says that, 'estimates [of German casualties at Le Cateau] range from 15,000 to 30,000 dead, wounded and missing'.[103] This is based solely on stories of British 'rapid rifle fire' mowing down Germans in rows and blocks.

In fact, it was the British who sustained disproportionally high losses, about two and a half times higher than the German. This was due to German fire from combined arms, pursuit fire, but most of all to the German success at overrunning or surrounding entire British battalions.

Evaluation

The premise of the II Corps operation on 26 August was that it would defend, beat off the German attack and then withdraw. This operation was badly executed. On the right flank the withdrawal was ordered too late, and 2/Suffolk, 2/KOYLI and XXVIII Artillery Brigade were destroyed. In the centre 1/Gordon Highlanders was destroyed and several other units suffered severe losses. On the left, poor security resulted in the destruction of 1/King's Own.

On the night of 26 August the French liaison officer reported to French GQG: 'The British army has lost a battle and appears to have lost its cohesion. In order to reconstitute it will demand to be protected.'[104] He put British losses in his 1927 memoirs at 15,000 men and 80 guns, which may have reflected his understanding of the situation on 26 August 1914.[105]

According to Becke, the 5th Division lost 2,350 men, or about 25 per cent of its infantry, 3rd Division 1,450 (15 per cent) and 4th Division 3,150 (more than 25 per cent). To this must be added 2,500–3,000 'footsore and exhausted' men who had to be evacuated to the forward base at Le Mans for recuperation and refitting.[106] There was so much confusion and disorganisation during the withdrawal from the battlefield that II Corps was not a cohesive combat-capable force for at least two days.

All of this has been buried in patriotic mythology. Ascoli quoted a soldier from 1/Hampshire who claimed that he was firing 'range 1,000 yards and hardly a round was wasted' which, for anyone who has actually fired a military rifle at such long range, is patently absurd.[107] Lomas said that 'it was 26 August, the anniversary of the Battle of Crécy in 1346, when English archers had each fired 12 arrows a minute to destroy their enemy; in 1914, the Short Lee-Enfield rifle would do the same task with 15 aimed rounds a minute': the Mons Myth in a nutshell.[108]

Becke's 'General Comments' concerning Le Cateau are worthless because he wildly overestimated German strength: 'Considering their crushing numerical superiority, their great preponderance in guns and machine guns, and the quantity of ammunition they expended, the amount of success achieved by the Germans in the Action at Le Cateau was astonishingly small. On Wednesday morning, 26 August, the Germans possessed every conceivable advantage, in information, situation, numbers and armament.'[109] In fact, at Le Cateau it was the British who enjoyed numerical superiority and as the defender they could choose the battlefield.

Becke says that the Germans made two mistakes. First, they concentrated against the British right flank when they should have concentrated against the left. This merely proves that Becke knew nothing of the German movements on 25 August. The only unit that had the ability to attack the British left on 26 August was HKK 2, not as Becke thinks, IV RK and II AK. The second supposed German mistake was the German failure to pursue: 'it is clear that the German Commander at Le Cateau was merely *un bon Général ordinaire* for he failed to exhibit real driving energy at this hour.' In fact, the Germans did not pursue primarily because they had run out of daylight; the British could retreat in the dark.

British authors attribute actions or thoughts to the Germans based on preconceived ideas and not proof. Becke says, 'The German leaders felt their way cautiously, weighed the pros and cons, and waited', which is absurd on its face and in any case not supported by evidence.[110] Ascoli criticises Kluck's generalship: he continually asserts that II AK and III AK could have decisively influenced the battle, when they were simply too far away to do so.

The actual German positions, strengths, orders and actions are never considered. Ascoli is convinced that both the German 7 RD (IV RK) and 5 ID (III AK) were present on the battlefield, and constructs elaborate, but non-existent, engagements for both units. The supposed effect of British 'rapid rifle fire' in deterring the Germans from attacking aggressively or launching a pursuit is a favourite topic, not the actual factors influencing German tactics.

The emphasis on German numerical superiority allows British systemic deficiencies to be glossed over. At the army and corps level British command and control and troop-leading was abysmal. There was no coordination between I Corps, II Corps, the Cavalry Division and 4th Division on the night of 25–26 August. Cavalry reconnaissance and security were non-existent. Poor staff work and traffic control were directly responsible for the need to fight at Le Cateau and was the cause of the troops' exhaustion. Troop-leading procedures failed to consider the use of time. The choice of defensive terrain at Mons and Le Cateau was mystifying. Reporting hit rock-bottom on the morning of 26 August, with the Cavalry Division and 3rd Division commanders both presenting the corps commander with most unpleasant last minute 'surprises'. The high casualty rates suffered at Le Cateau were in part attributable to the fact that the staff somehow transformed Smith-Dorrien's order to delay into one of 'die in place'. On 26 August I Corps and II Corps did not communicate with each other, nor did GHQ inform either corps of the other's situation.[111]

In British histories, Sir Horace Smith-Dorrien is extolled as a hero and a great battlefield commander. There is little basis for such an evaluation. Although he had just taken command of the corps and was not responsible for the systemic deficiencies of the British army, nevertheless, on the night of 25–26 August he clearly lost control of the situation. During the battle he did not manoeuvre or counter-attack. The order for the 5th Division to withdraw was given too late.

There is no evidence in the German regimental histories that the German troops had been demoralised by 'rapid rifle fire' or casualties. The Germans knew they had won a significant victory. The IR 93 historian said: 'The battle of Beaumont-Inchy will always be one of the most glorious days in the history of the regiment, which demonstrated that in a frontal attack against an enemy that was heretofore considered unbeatable, the crack troops of the British Army, IR 93 was not merely their equal, it was superior.' FAR 75 said that the battle 'strengthened the self-confidence of the German troops ... all the more so because the British army was made up almost exclusively of long-service active army troops, who were superbly trained and equipped'.

8

27 August

British II Corps Withdrawal

A lieutenant of the 4/Royal Fusiliers wrote: 'Down the roads came a mob. Men from every regiment were there, guns, riderless horses, limbers packed with wounded.'[1] He then said smugly, 'when the rabble had got past' his battalion, which had not been engaged, they 'moved off, marching at attention, arms sloped, fours dressed, etc.'

The Royal Scots history said: 'the road was seen to be lined with men in clusters, some asleep, others "fallen out". The groups embraced men of so many different units and even different corps that a casual onlooker, viewing the variety of badges, would have concluded that the whole organisation of the army had collapsed.' This was not so, the regimental history maintained, because the British army was practising 'organised disorganisation', and the retreat was better conducted than Sir John Moore's retreat to Corunna, which is faint praise indeed. The KOSB history says that the 13th and 14th Brigades were 'a orderly crowd' which was reorganised 'inside of three days', with which the regimental historian seemed to be quite satisfied.[2]

The Gordon Highlanders officer who described German offensive tactics was severely wounded by MG fire.[3] He could not be moved and had to be left behind. German troops passed by: 'Their attitude was distinctly sympathetic; but I was too far gone to struggle with their language.' He pulled his greatcoat over his head and slept. He heard a shout and saw a German soldier, pointing his pistol, who soon recognised the extent of the Gordie's wounds. He gave the officer a drink and pointed to his Red Cross armband. Finding the Gordie was unmoveable, he left to get a stretcher party. The Gordie was concerned that he would not come back. The German medic said: 'I am of the Red Cross, you are therefore my Kamerad and I will come back and I will never leave you.' A German cavalry officer came up, offered him some chocolate and they conversed in French. War in August 1914 could still be chivalrous.

The Royal Scots continued the march until 0900 on 27 August, took a three-hour rest, ate a cold meal of canned meat, marmalade and biscuits, then marched again, had a brief evening rest and resumed the march at 2000 and marched throughout the night. The next morning (28 August) the battalion managed to get some tea and fresh meat, but did not have time to cook the meat. Nevertheless, 'no other unit fared so well that day'. The Royal Scots marched all day on 28 August in the 'scorching sun', and did not get any real rest until that night. The worst blister cases were sent ahead by vehicle.

The official line was that II Corps had delivered the German 1st Army such a 'punishing blow' that the Germans were reluctant to pursue. The details of the II Corps retreat prove the contrary. II Corps had no desire to repeat the action of 26 August and marched night and day for two days to avoid contact, putting so much distance between themselves and the German 1st Army that the Germans had no hope of catching them.

German IV AK

On 27 August the corps mission was to cross the Somme and take Peronne. IR 72 had taken such serious casualties that it was reorganised into two battalions. 1/72 and 2/72 were formed into one company. Nevertheless, the regiment marched at 0400, initially in a broad formation, but when no contact was made formed into march column and covered 30 km, hardly the performance of a demoralised unit.

IR 153 advanced across the Le Cateau–Cambrai road between Caudry and Audencourt at dawn.[4] It encountered abandoned, sometimes shot-up machine guns and 'many, many dead'. The lieutenant that had reconnoitered the Gordons' position that morning spied four British approaching out of a bush. At his command they laid down their weapons and surrendered. One of them, with a short pipe between his teeth, approached the lieutenant and said, 'You are a gentleman' and asked for a match! The lieutenant marched on:

> From a small hill near to the village we saw a disorderly column approaching. Even with my binoculars, I couldn't determine whether they were friend or enemy. I went forward with my patrol. They were British! We moved forward as quickly as we could. Near the train station they went around a corner. We

occupied the rail station and a ditch, 50m from the British. Both sides fire, and then hands appear raised in the air. They want to surrender, we want to go forward and take them prisoner, but they begin firing again! One of my recruits from the previous night falls dead, hit in the head and chest ... We take cover again ... The British try raising their hands again, but this time we are more careful; what do you know, they open fire again, but we don't take any casualties. Now we fire until nothing moves ... We advance, and find mostly the dead, and many groaning wounded rolling in the grass. There are three unwounded in a ditch; we take them prisoner, although they deserved a bullet. But we had revenged our fallen comrade and paid the blackguards for their treachery.

IR 153 found a dead Highlander officer with an English-language version of the French 1:80,000 General Staff map which carried the notation 'Printed at the Ordnance Survey Office, Southampton 1909', which the regimental historian said was evidence of Franco-British cooperation in preparation for war with Germany. In Caudry the regiment captured an officer and fourteen men.

8 ID advanced in two columns, both routes of British retreat. FAR 75 reported:

... both roads offered graphic scenes of the enemy's panic flight: wounded, who had lay in the open all night and again many dead; overfilled field hospitals, guns missing only the breech blocks, munitions wagons filled to the top ... on both sides of the road masses of coats, weapons, packs, webbing, wool blankets ... every piece showed how well the British were equipped into the smallest detail. There was hardly a pack that did not have a shaving kit, sewing kit, first-quality rations.[5]

FAR 75 reported that a great many exhausted British soldiers and stragglers were made prisoner, many lying on the roads, others were pulled out of all kinds of hiding places, proof that the wind had been knocked out of the British troops.

In the church at Caudry were 200 British wounded, guarded by German cavalry. British equipment and weapons were everywhere, and the IR 153 men helped themselves to souvenirs: 'the so-called Scots swords were much prized.' Officers replaced their belts, which glittered, with British leather belts. The IR 153 historian said British coats were 'cozy and fluffy', ideal for drivers and mounted men. Given the rapid advance and the lack of butter, 'the many [British] cases and cans with delicious marmalade, biscuits and all kinds of preserves were most welcome'. The regiment marched in the dust and August heat until dark, then bivouacked and got a decent night's sleep for the first time in three days.

9

Conclusions

Evaluation of British Effectiveness

Armies fight the way they have trained to fight. For a century, the British army trained for colonial war. The short duration of the Haldane reforms was not adequate to prepare the British army for continental warfare. Therefore, at Mons and Le Cateau II Corps attempted to fight colonial-warfare battles.

Due to lack of preparation, the BEF made grave errors at both the operational (army and corps) and tactical levels, the worst of which was ignorance of the enemy. The British were to engage the premier military force of the twentieth century, and should have been much more circumspect. By rights, the BEF should not have lived to tell the tale.

The BEF had to avoid casualties and fight only for a very good reason. Mons performed no useful operational purpose; it gave the Germans a day to close the distance with the BEF, and could have led to a disaster. During the retreat to Le Cateau the BEF failed to delay the Germans with rearguards. Combined with deficiencies in British staff work and traffic control, which by the morning of 26 August caused command and control to collapse, the German IV AK and HKK 2 were allowed to catch II Corps and force it to fight under extremely unfavourable circumstances. Motivated by the pounding it took at Le Cateau, II Corps finally got serious about retreating on the night of 26–27 August, and in two days of continuous movement broke contact.

BEF troop-leading was poor. The army and corps commanders did not issue clear, timely orders. Subordinate commanders did not understand the commander's intent. Confused and uninformed battalion commanders failed to exercise their initiative.

There was no rhyme or reason to the distribution of forces for the defence at Mons and Le Cateau. The most exposed and most important sectors were weakly held. The salient north of Mons and the 5th Division right flank at Le Cateau were indefensible. The positions at Le Cateau offered the enemy covered and concealed avenues of approach and close-range firing positions. Most seriously, while the commander's intent at Le Cateau was clearly to withdraw, most of the positions were on the forward slope, where withdrawal would lead to a massacre.

The British Cavalry Division was an operational liability. Before Mons it failed to perform its reconnaissance and counter-reconnaissance missions. On 24 August it left the II Corps left flank floating in the air. In the retreat to Le Cateau it failed to delay HKK 2 and IV AK; indeed, the cavalry division could provide no useful information concerning enemy strengths or locations. At Le Cateau, citing exhaustion, it did nothing.

The artillery failed to effectively support the infantry. At Mons it was unable to provide fire support at all. During the withdrawal there were no artillery rearguards. At Le Cateau the British artillery was completely dominated by equal or inferior numbers of German guns and was generally unable to put fire on the German infantry. Indeed, it drew German fire onto its own infantry by setting up in their immediate vicinity.

Individual physical fitness was inadequate: many of the troops, particularly the reservists, were not marching fit. From 24 August on, British commanders began ordering their men to abandon equipment in order to 'march light'. On 25 August the British infantry was outmarched and overtaken by infantry of IV AK and the Jäger of HKK 2.

'Rapid rifle fire' was not the battle-winning wonder weapon that British historians have made it out to be. Repeatedly German infantry, supported by artillery and MG fire, was able to cross hundreds of metres of open ground in the face of 'rapid rifle fire', close with the British infantry and throw it out of its position or destroy it in place. The idea that 'rapid rifle fire' was so effective that the Germans took it for MG fire finds no support in German sources.

German Military Effectiveness

German tactical doctrine and troop training proved themselves unequivocally in combat. The BEF escaped destruction at Mons and Le Cateau solely due to egregious errors by the 1st Army commander and his chief of staff.

The organisation of HKK 2, combining cavalry, large numbers of machine guns, artillery and high-quality infantry, was a resounding success and HKK 2 performed superbly, in spite of Marwitz's command failures at Haelen. It screened the strength and movements of the 1st and 2nd Armies so effectively that they gained operational surprise over the BEF and the French 5th Army. The operational mobility HKK 2 displayed on 24 and 25 August is nothing short of astounding. At Le Cateau HKK 2, though heavily outnumbered, delivered a stinging defeat to the British 4th Division and the 7th Brigade of the 3rd Division.

The Germans fought as a combined-arms team, which allowed them repeatedly to successfully execute one of the most difficult missions in modern warfare: hasty attack over open terrain against a deployed enemy. At Mons the German artillery provided effective fire support, often moving to within a few hundred metres of the British positions to do so. At Le Cateau the German artillery engaged, suppressed or destroyed the British artillery, which was generally unable to fire effectively on the German infantry. The massing of six MGs under a company commander allowed a concentration of fire at the decisive place and time. Artillery and MG fire support gave the German infantry fire superiority and allowed it to move across large stretches of exposed ground to close with the enemy. German engineers brought the infantry and artillery across obstacles and assisted the infantry in street fighting.

Day after day the German infantry marched hard. This operational mobility allowed it to appear where the enemy did not expect, and in force. German marches were well-organised: the troops always got some rest at night, even if it was a wet bivouac, and the field kitchens ensured that they got a hot meal.

At Mons the IV AK commander concentrated his *Schwerpunkt*, his main point of effort, against the weakest point in the British line, as did the 7th Division commander at Le Cateau. Tactical leaders of all grades were aggressive and exercised their initiative to utilise covered and concealed avenues of approach and firepower to close with the enemy.

Taken together, these factors produced superior combat power. At Mons all three engaged German corps were able to establish bridgeheads over the Canal du Centre at the cost of casualties that were little higher than those of the defenders. In two days of pursuit III AK caught up with I Corps and forced it to retreat away from II Corps, splitting the BEF in half, while IV AK and HKK 2 were able to overhaul II Corps and force it to fight. At Le Cateau the German troops, although significantly outnumbered, inflicted disproportional casualties on the British and drove them from their position.

Superior German operational mobility and tactical combat power was negated by unforced errors made by the 1st Army commander and his chief of staff. The real culprit was Hermann von Kuhl, the chief of staff; for the army commander, Kluck, was not a General Staff officer and operational decisions were clearly Kuhl's responsibility. All Kuhl had to do was make the obvious staff-school solution to the operational problems at hand and the BEF would have been destroyed. Instead, Kuhl was too clever by half.

Cavalry reconnaissance reports made it clear on 22 August that a large British force was west of Mons. Nevertheless, Kuhl retained the notion that the British would concentrate at Lille for so long that the 1st Army missed its chance to inflict a truly serious defeat on II Corps on 23 August.

The BEF was now in range, only a day's march ahead of the 1st Army or even less. The only correct solution to the operational problem facing the 1st Army on 24–25 August was to continue the march south-west. With HKK 2 coming up on the right, there was every prospect of turning the BEF left flank and forcing the British to fight. Instead, Kuhl decided that on 25 August the British were withdrawing to Maubeuge and turned the entire 1st Army and HKK 2 south-east. This was the wrong solution. Even if the British were moving to Maubeuge, the correct solution would be to continue the march south-west to allow the 1st Army to conduct a deep envelopment of the Anglo-French left.

Kuhl had been one of Schlieffen's star pupils, one of the officers closest to the old master strategist. Schlieffen had continually warned against shallow envelopments, which the enemy could avoid. Kuhl was breaking Schlieffen's cardinal rule.

Throughout the campaign, Kuhl would display a consistent inability to make operationally sound decisions. His mistakes from 5–9 September would be the reason for the failure of the German campaign and the loss of the Battle of the Marne. He would offer the French the 1st Army's unprotected right flank. He then disregarded orders to fall back and defend the German flank in favour of a pointless offensive which allowed the French to pry open the German front.

Had the 1st Army merely continued the march south-west on 25 August, it would not have required Hindenburg and Ludendorff to produce a western Tannenburg on 26 August. Three brigades of IV AK alone had inflicted a severe defeat on II Corps. Had III AK been attacking the II Corps right and IV AK the left, the British would have been facing eight brigades and the result would have been a British disaster. The British left was guarded only by Sordet's cavalry and French Territorials: HKK 2 had already convincingly demonstrated an ability to summarily deal with these and advance rapidly into the British rear, turning disaster into catastrophe.

The destruction of II Corps would not have ended the war, as Tannenberg did not end the war with Russia. The German advance into France was going to run out of momentum and come to a halt on 5 September in any case. But the removal of three divisions would have been a serious blow to the British army.

The Significance of Mons and Le Cateau

The Mons Myth encourages soldiers, policymakers and citizens to believe that doctrine and years of tactical training are unimportant: war is simple and all that an army needs is patriotism, 'field sports', personal heroism and rifle marksmanship. Such a belief, widespread in the British army and British society before the First World War, resulted in the death or maiming of an entire generation of young Britons.

This study demonstrates in detail what happens when an army that has neglected doctrine and tactical training meets up with an army that made a religion of both. The denouement came at Le Cateau, where the German army showed that it knew how to attack a numerically superior enemy force and win.

Reaching such a pinnacle is complex and difficult. Most armies never do. It requires realistic doctrine, combined-arms cooperation, mobility, security and intelligence, troop-leading procedures, and individual initiative, all perfected in long, hard training. There must be an institutional commitment to tactical excellence. These qualities, developed in forty years of peacetime work, were the reasons for German success at Mons and Le Cateau.

Notes

Chapter 1

1 David Ascoli, *The Mons Star. The British Expeditionary Force 5th August–22nd November 1914* (London, 1981), xvi–xvii.

2 A. F. Becke, *The Royal Regiment of Artillery at Le Cateau, Wednesday 26th August 1914* (Woolwich, 1919). Major-General F. Maurice's *Forty Days in 1914* (London, 1919) was a very early attempt to discern what the Germans were doing. It differs little from the other British histories, and serves only to confirm that the Mons Myth had been established by 1918.

3 J. E. Edmonds, *History of the Great War. Military Operations. France and Belgium, 1914* (London, n. d.)

4 Ascoli, *Mons Star*, p. 13.

5 *Military Operations. France and Belgium*, p. 80.

6 Walter Bloem, *Vormarsch* (Leipzig, 1916). Why this got past the German censors is hard to say. Edmonds always referred to this unit as the 'Brandenburg Grenadiers'.

7 Walter Bloem, *The Advance from Mons 1914. The Experiences of a German Infantry Officer*, G. C. Wynne (trans.) (1930).

8 Ascoli, *The Mons Star*, pp. 3–4. Ascoli did not properly cite his sources, but apparently Moore's statement was made during an interview in the late 1970s – perhaps fifty-five years after the fact.

9 John Terraine, *Mons. The Retreat to Victory* (London, 1960).

10 David Lomas, *Mons 1914. Britain's Tactical Triumph* (Westport CT, 2004).

11 See also: Jack Sheldon, *The German Army on the Somme 1914–1916* (Barnsley, South Yorkshire, 2005) which has extensive accounts by individual German soldiers.

12 Jack Horsfall and Nigel Cave, *Mons* (London, 2000). *Le Cateau* by Nigel Cave and Jack Sheldon (London, 2008).

13 *Exerzier-Reglement für die Infanterie vom 29. Mai 1906. Neuabdruck mit Einfügung der bis August 1909 ergangenen Änderungen (Deckblatt 1–78).* (Berlin, 1909).

14 General-Inspektion des Militär-Erziehungswesens (bearbeitet), *Leitfaden für den Unterricht in der Taktik auf den Königlichen Kriegsschulen* (Berlin, 1910).

15 F. Immanuel, *Handbuch der Taktik* (Berlin, 1910).

16 Hein, *Kampfesformen und Kampfesweise der Infanterie* (Berlin and Leipzig, 1914). Falkenhausen, *Der grosse Krieg der Jetztzeit* (Berlin, 1909) offers a comprehensive picture of German strategic and tactical doctrine based on the applicatory method – a case study of a Franco-German war. Max von den Bergh, *Das Deutsche Heer vor dem Weltkriege* (Berlin, 1934) offers an interesting but overly critical view, probably as a warning against making the same mistakes in the newly re-established Wehrmacht. For an excellent, detailed history of the development of European armies from 1900 to 1914, Dieter Storz, *Kriegsbild und Rüstung vor 1914* (Herford, 1992). W. Balck, *Entwicklung der Taktik im Weltkriege* (Berlin, 1920).

17 Ernst von Schönfeldt, *Das Grenadier-Regiment Prinz von Preußen (2. brandenburgisches) Nr. 12 im Weltkriege* (Oldenburg i. O., 1924), p. 26.

Chapter 2

1 Rudolf von Freydorf (ed.), *Das 1. Badische Leib-Regiment Nr. 109 im Weltkrieg 1914–1918* (Karlsruhe i. B., 1927) pp. 17, 742, 754–9; Friedrich von Friedenberg, *Geschichte des Königlich Preussischen Ersten Garde-Regiments zu Fuss: 1871 bis 1914* (Berlin, 1933), p. 173.

2 Bogislav von Studnitz, *Geschichte des Thüringischen Husaren-Regiments Nr. 12 im Weltkriege* (Weimar, 1930), pp. 5–6.

3 Immanuel, *Taktik* II, p. 9. *Leitfaden*, p. 105.

4 Clausewitz, *Vom Kriege*, Book 2, Chapter 3.

5 Immanuel, *Taktik* II, pp. 261–4. *Leitfaden*, pp. 107–10, 122.

6 Freydorf, *Infanterie-Regiment 109*, p. 759.

7 *Leitfaden*, p. 104.

8 *Leitfaden*, pp. 102–4, 145. Immanuel, *Taktik* I, pp. 259–60, 295; II, pp. 10–12, 93.

9 *Taschenbuch des Generalstabsoffiziers* (Berlin, 1914). *Leitfaden*, p. 18. Curt Jany, *Geschichte der Preussischen Armee IV* (Osnabrück, 1967), p. 299. *Anhaltspunkte für den Generalstabsdienst*, p. 318. Freydorf, *Infanterie-Regiment 109*, p. 926.

10 Freydorf, *Infanterie-Regiment 109*, p. 727.

11 Breitkopf, *Die Ausbildung im Gefechtsmässigen Schiessen* (Augsburg, 1907). Voss, *Unsere Infanterie. Ihre Ausbildung und Kampfweise* (Leipzig, 1914); Friedberg, *1. Grenadier-Regiment zu Fuß*, pp. 193–4. Joachim Leder, *Geschichte der 3. Schlesische Infanterie-Regiments Nr. 156* (Zeulenroda, 1930), pp. 4–11. Dieter Storz, *Gewehr und Karabiner 98* (Vienna, 2006).

12 Liebmann, 'Die deutschen Gefechtsvorschriften von 1914 in der Feuerprobe des Krieges' in: *Militärwissenschaftliche Rundschau* 2. Jahrgang (1937) 4. Heft, p. 458.

13 *Exerzier-Reglement für die Infanterie vom 29. Mai 1906. Neuabdruck mit Einfügung der bis August 1909 ergangenen Änderungen (Deckblatt 1–78).* (Berlin, 1909).

14 Ortenburg, *Waffen und Waffengebrauch im Zeitalter der Millionenheere* (Bonn, 1992), pp. 66–73.

15 Döring von Gottberg, *Das Grenadier-Regiment Graf Kleist von Nollendorf (1. Westpreußisches) Nr. 6 im Weltkriege* (Berlin, 1925), pp. 18–19.

16 Cordt von Brandies, *Die vom Douamont. Das Ruppiner Regiment 24 im Weltkrieg* (Berlin, 1930), p. 3.

17 Storz, *Gewehr and Karabiner 98*, pp. 208–9.

18 Doerstling, *Infanterie-Regiment 20*, pp. 10–13.

19 Immanuel, *Taktik* I, pp. 191–2. Byern, *Veranlagung, Durchführung und Beurteilung gefechtsmässiger Abteilungsschiessen und des Prüfungsschiessens für Infanterie und Kavallerie* (Berlin, 1908). Breitkopf, *Vorbereitung, Durchführung und Beurteilung gefechtsmässiger Schiessen in grösseren Abteilungen; Besonderes über gefechtsmässiges Belehrungs- und Prüfungsschiessen. Nur für Dienstgebrauch!* (Augsburg, 1907). Ortenburg, *Waffen und Waffengebrauch*, pp. 144–7. Freydorf, *Infanterie-Regiment 109*, p. 11. Hauptstaatsarchiv Dresden 11359/1389, IR 134, Ergebnisse des Gefechtsschiessens (Results of Combat Gunnery Qualification Firing) shows in detail how combat gunnery was conducted and evaluated in 1913. Hauptstaatsarchiv Dresden 11359/1388 Erfahrungsberichten, Schiessvorschriften 1907–1909 (Lessons Learned, Combat Gunnery Regulation) gives a detailed analysis of the conduct of gunnery and proposed changes. Friedenberg, *1. Grenadier-Regiment zu Fuß*, pp. 177–85.

20 *Exerzier-Reglement … Infanterie*, p. 453; Leitfaden, pp. 27–31, 116–7. *Taschenbuch des Generalstabsoffiziers.* Immanuel, *Taktik* I, pp. 298–307.

21 Robert Bruce, *Machine Guns of World War I* (London, 1997), pp. 12–15.

22 Friedenberg, *1. Grenadier-Regiment zu Fuß*, p. 190.

23 Freydorf, *IR 109*, pp. 776–868. Friedenbach, *1. Grenadier-Regiment zu Fuß*, pp. 159–61. Immanuel, *Taktik* I, pp. 145, 220.

24 Karl Vogt, *3. Niederschlesisches Infanterie-Regiment Nr. 50 1914–1920* (Rawitsch-Lissa i. P., 1931), p. 19.

25 The 1st Foot Guard regimental history says 24 kg (53 lbs), IR 109 – the Baden Guard Regiment – says 30 kg (66 lbs).

26 *Exerzier-Reglement … Infanterie*, pp. 324–51. Breitkopf, *Der Angriff über die Ebene. Nur für Dienstgebrauch!* (For official use only!) (Augsburg, 1907). Immanuel, *Taktik* I, pp. 193–246. Freydorf, *Infanterie-Regiment 109*, pp. 742–3, 753–4. Voss, *Infanterie*, pp. 24–31. Friedenberg, *1. Grenadier-Regiment zu Fuß*, p. 172, which calls this 'Burentaktik', not because the Boers or the British used it in South Africa, but because it represented the German army's 'lessons learned' from the Boer War. It was instituted by an army order on 6 May 1902.

27 *Exerzier-Reglement … Infanterie*, pp. 82–100.

28 *Leitfaden*, p. 15. 'Cover' is protection from enemy fire, which is normally provided by placing a terrain feature, like a hill, between your own troops and the enemy. 'Concealment' is provided by anything that hides your troops from enemy observation, such as vegetation. Concealment does not provide protection against enemy fire.

29 The author of the IR 109 regimental history said that the 'Boer tactics' introduced into the German army after the South African War consisted of conducting the firefight at the squad level. Freydorf, *Infanterie-Regiment 109*, p. 11.

30 *Leitfaden*, p. 22.

31 *Leitfaden*, p. 8.

32 Hein, *Kampfesformen*, pp. 41–2. Breitkopf, *Die Ausbildung im gefechtsmässigen Schiessen. Nur für Dienstgebrauch!* (Augsburg, 1907), p. 39.

33 *Exerzier-Reglement … Infanterie*, pp. 454–65.

34 Moser, *Bataillons- und Regiments*, pp. 105–6, 119, 240–2. Freydorf, *Infanterie-Regiment 109*, p. 14.

35 Friedenberg, *1.Grenadier-Regiment zu Fuß*, pp. 94–5.

36 *Leitfaden*, pp. 32–47, 111–12, 159–61.Voss, *Infanterie*, pp. 25–6. Immanuel, *Taktik* I, pp. 309–64.

37 Moser, *Württemberger*, pp. 216–7.

38 *Exerzier-Reglement … Infanterie*, pp. 451–2.

39 Claus-Just von Lattorf, *Kriegsgeschichte des Brandenburgischen Jäger-Bataillon Nr. 3 1914–1918* (Berlin/Oldenburg, n.d.), p. 21.

40 *Leitfaden*, pp. 93–5.Voss, *Infanterie*, pp. 9–10. Immanuel, *Taktik* I, pp. 88–111; II, pp. 19–20.

41 *Leitfaden*, pp. 53–8, 113–16. G. Ortenberg, *Waffe und Waffengebrauch im Zeitalter der Millionenheere* (Bonn, 1992), pp. 105–10, 157–66. Hauptstaatsarchiv Dresden 11359/1376. No title; eleven-page perceptive discussion of latest developments in artillery doctrine, 12 April 1906.

42 Anon., *Artillerie-Regiment 25*, pp. 61, 438.

43 *Taschenbuch des Generalstabsoffiziers.*

44 Marx, *Geschichte des 3. lothring. Feldartillerie-Regiments Nr. 69* (Berlin, 1927), pp. 10–13.

45 *Leitfaden*, pp. 71–8.

46 Hauptstaatsarchiv Stuttgart M 1/4 Bü 197 … *Gefechtsübungen mit gemischten Waffen unter Beteiligung der schweren Artillerie des Feldheeres. K. P. Kriegsministerium* 2. Juli 1904.

47 *Exerzier-Reglement … Infanterie*, pp. 443–52. Immanuel, *Taktik* I, p. 269.

48 *Infanterie-Regiment 127*, pp. 10–11. *Handbuch*, p. 115.

49 *Exerzier-Reglement … Infanterie*, pp. 362–74. *Leitfaden*, pp. 123–32. Otto von Moser, *Ausbildung und Führung des Bataillons und Regiments* (2nd ed., Berlin, 1912).Voss, *Infanterie*, pp. 27–31. Immanuel, *Taktik* II, pp. 18–22.

50 Breitkopf, *Der Angriff über die Ebene.* Herrmann Vogt, *Das Buch vom Deutschen Armee* (Bielefeld and Leipzig, 1891), p. 38. The Gunnery Schools also set the standards for the annual unit range firing, which was quite similar to that held at the US Army National Training Centers, except that they took place at the Corps Major Training Areas.

51 *Leitfaden*, p. 9.

52 *Exerzier-Reglement … Infanterie*, p. 473.

53 *Leitfaden*, p. 9.

54 *Leitfaden*, p. 9.

55 If a rifleman is aiming at a point target, a host of variables will cause him to miss: jerking the trigger, poor point of aim, defects in the weapon and ammunition, wind, humidity, etc. This is called deflection probable error. The deflection probable error at these ranges is 5½ metres. Almost all of his rounds will impact 5½ metres to the left and right of the target. At closer ranges, the deflection probable error is less, and the intervals between skirmishers can be closed up without an increase in casualties.

56 *Exerzier-Reglement ... Infanterie*, pp. 392–6. *Leitfaden*, pp. 120–1. Immanuel, *Taktik* II, pp. 35–9.

57 *Exerzier-Reglement ... Infanterie*, pp. 397–416; *Leitfaden*, pp. 24–5, 108–9, 136–46. *Anhaltspunkte*, p. 311. Immanuel, *Taktik* II, pp. 40–55, 70, 287–94.

58 *Exerzier-Reglement ... Infanterie*, pp. 417–25. *Leitfaden*, pp. 149–53. Hein, *Kampfesformen*, pp. 110–1. Immanuel, *Taktik* II, pp. 54–6.

59 On the training year as seen from the regimental level, Joachim Leder, *Geschichte des 3. Schlischen Infanterie-Regiments Nr. 156* (Zeulenroda, 1930), pp. 1–11 and Arens, *Das Königlich Preussische 7. Westpr. Infanterie-Regiment Nr. 155* (Berlin-Charlottenberg, 1931).

60 Doerstling, *Kriegsgeschichte des Königlich Preussischen Infnaterie-Regiments Graf Tauentzien v. Wittenberg (3. Brandenb.) Nr. 20* (Zeulenroda, 1933), p. 12.

61 Otto von Moser, *Die Württemberger im Weltkriege* (Stuttgart, 1927), pp. 9–10.

62 For German infantry training, warts and all: Koetsch, *Aus der Geschichte des früheren Kgl. Sächs. 9. Infanterie-Regiments Nr. 133 1881–1918* (Dresden, 1924).

63 Dieter Storz, *Kriegsbild und Kriegsrüstung vor 1914* (Herford, 1992), p. 106. Voss, *Unsere Infanterie*, p. 16.

64 Friedenberg, *1. GRzF*, p. 152.

65 Bayerisches Kriegsarchiv, 1. b. AK (F) 776 Lechfeld. Bayerisches Kriegsarchiv 1. b. AK (F) 778 Grafenwöhr.

66 Kaiser (ed.), *Das Ehrenbuch der Deutschen Schweren Artillerie*, p. 19.

67 Voss, *Unsere Infanterie*, pp. 9–22.

68 Liebach, *Bataillons-, Regiments- und Brigade-Uebungen und Besichtigungten der Infanrterie in praktischen Beispielen* (Berlin, 1914).

69 Hauptstaatsarchiv Dresden 11359/2997, *Infanterie-Regiment Nr. 134 Gefechtsbericht*. Hauptstaatsarchiv Dresden 11359/2998, *Felddienstübung des 10. Infanterie-Regiemnts Nr. 134 am 8. Januar 1914* (Blue's report for the same engagement. Opposing-force exercise. Two Blue companies were to force a river crossing, one red company was to prevent it.) Hauptstaatsarchiv Dresden 11359/1365, *Felddienstbericht des 10. Infanterie-Regiments Nr. 134 am 14. März 1913. Gefechtsbericht Rot* (rear guard and destruction of a bridge). Hauptstaatsarchiv Dresden 11359/1367, *Bericht über das Gefecht des 10. Infanterie-Regiments Nr. 134 in Gegend Glossen 12. September 1912* (Day-long regimental exercise: field fortification, attack, withdrawal, bivouac).

70 Freiherr von Gemmingen-Guttenberg-Fürfeld, *Das Grenadier-Regiment Königen Olga (1. Württ.) Nr. 119 im Weltkriege 1914–1918* (Stuttgart, 1927), pp. 1–2.

71 R. von Freydorf, *Das 1. Badische Leib-Grenadier-Regiment Nr. 109 im Weltkrieg 1914–1918* (Karlsruhe, 1927), p. 10.

72 Doerstling, *Infanterie-Regiment 20*, pp. 10–13.

73 Voss, *Infanterie*, pp. 11–12. Hess; von Breitenbuch, *Geschichte 1. Lothringischen Feldart. Regts. 33. Erster Teil: Februar 1890 bis Oktober 1916* (Worms, 1937), pp. 25–9. Marx, *FAR 69*, pp. 8–9. Anon., *Aus der Geschichte des ehemaligen Königl. Preußischen 4. Lothringischen Feldartillerie-Regiments Nr. 70* (Hildesheim, 1937), p. 10. Wilhelm Dopheide, *Geschichte des 3. Lothr. Infanterie-Regiments Nr. 135* (Berlin, 1940), p. 16.

74 Moser, *Bataillons- und Regiments*, pp. 221–2. Voss, *Unsere Infanterie*, pp. 17–23. Leder, *IR 156*, p. 8.

75 Hauptstaatsarchiv Dresden, Generalkommando XII Armeekorps 11347. *Korpsmanöver des XII AK im Korpsverbande gegen markierte Feind.* The XII AK units were at peacetime strength – I/IR 102 had 10 OFF and 410 EM present for duty – which was considerably less than wartime strength.

76 Shelford Bidwell and Dominic Graham, *Firepower. British Army Weapons and Theories of War 1904–1945* (London, 1982), p. 38.

77 Stacke, *Worcestershire Regiment*, p. 3.

78 Reginald C. Bond, *History of the King's Own Yorkshire Light Infantry in the Great War 1914–1918 Volume III* (London, 1929), pp. 713–14.

79 A half-page of general commentary in Corelli Barnett's *Britain and her Army 1509–1970* (New York, 1970), p. 367.

80 Bidwell and Graham, *Firepower*, pp. 7–58.

81 A. L. Ransome, *"Fine Fighting of the Dorsets"* (1938?), pp. 5, 7.

82 Ascoli, *Mons Star*, p. 84.

83 Ascoli, *Mons Star*, p. 32.

84 Ransome, *Dorsets*, p. 8.

85 Arthur Crookenden, *The History of the Cheshire Regiment in the Great War* (1939), p. 4.

86 H. FitzM. Stacke, *The Worcestershire Regiment in the Great War*, pp. xxiv, xxvi.

87 Ransome, *Dorsets*, p. 8.

88 *Military Operations. France and Belgium 1914*, p. 11.

89 Ernst Zurborn, *Doe Schlacht bei Mons* (Oldenburg i. O., 1919), pp. 22–5.

90 *Weltkrieg* I, pp. 93–4.

Chapter 3

1 T. Zuber, *German War Planning 1891–1914. Sources and Interpretations* (Boydell, 2004), pp. 38–42.

2 T. Zuber, *Inventing the Schlieffen Plan; German War Planning 1891–1914* (Oxford, 2002).

3 *Military Operations. France and Belgium 1914*, p. 15.

4 *Weltkrieg* I, p. 22. Not including 127,000 French troops in Corsica and North Africa, 350,000 Russian troops in Siberia and Turkestan or the British forces in the colonies.

5 Military Operations. France and Belgium 1914, p. 15.

6 Samuel R. Williamson, *The Politics of Grand Strategy* (London, 1969), pp. 362–7.

7 Stacke, *Worcestershire Regiment*, p. 1.

8 Ransome, *Dorsets*, p. 9.

9 *Military Operations. France and Belgium 1914*, p. 25.

10 There are two good contemporary Belgian sources: *La Campagne de l'armée belge (31 juillet 1914–1er janvier 1915) d'après les documents officials* (Paris, Bloud et Gay, 1915). We will call this Belgian official history I. The second is by the Belgian Army High Command, *Guerre de 1914: L'action de l'armée belge pour la defense du pays* (Paris, 1915). We will call this Belgian official history II. There is a US Army War department translation of history II from 1932 at the Army Heritage Center at Carlisle. Also *Weltkrieg* I, pp. 96–100.

11 The date for the completion of this build-up (1918 to 1926) and the number of militia classes (six to eight for the field army and seven or eight for the garrisons of the fortresses of Liège, Namur and Antwerp) varies by source.

12 Belgian official history I, pp. 15–16, 19.

13 Ernest Depuy and Trevor Dupuy, *The Encyclopedia of Military History* (New York and Evanston, 1980), p. 990.

14 French air reconnaissance was ineffective in the heavily wooded Ardennes and the German 1st and 2nd Armies in north Belgium were generally out of range. Frequent thunderstorms and other bad weather also hindered air reconnaissance.

15 Franz Döring von Gottberg, *Das Oldenburgische Dragoner-Regiment Nr. 19 im Weltkriege* (Oldenburg i. O., 1937), pp. 48–9. *Weltkrieg* I, pp. 96–100.

16 Curt Bedinski, *Aus großer Zeit. Erinnerungsblätter des Jäger-Feld-Bataillons Nr. 9. Weltkrieg 1914–18* (Ratzenburg, 1932), pp. 46–9.

17 Trauwitz-Hellwig, *Husaren-Regiment Nr. 15*, pp. 29–40.

18 Paul Freiherr von Troschke, *Geschichte des 1. Großherzoglich Mecklenburgischen Dragoner-Regiments Nr. 17. Band 2 Der Weltkrieg* (Berlin, 1938), pp. 20–1.

19 Albrecht Freiherr von Funck, et. al., *Das Brandenbergische Dragoner-Regiment Nr. 2 im Weltkriege 1914 bis 1918* (1933), pp. 6–8.

20 Anon., *Leib-Husaren-Brigade (1. Leib-Husaren Regiment Nr. 1 und 2. Leib-Husaren Regiment Königin Viktoria von Preussen Nr. 2)* (Berlin, 1929), pp. 5–6.

21 Köhler, *Kürassier-Regiment Nr. 7*, p. 95.

22 Trauwitz-Hellwig, *Husaren-Regiment Nr. 15*, pp. 33–4.

23 The Liège operation was under the control of the German 2nd Army and will only be discussed here insofar as it concerned the 1st Army and HKK 2 operations.

24 Doerstling, *Infanterie-Regiment 20*, p. 18.

25 *Weltkrieg* I, p. 100.

26 Troschke, *Dragoner-Regiment 17*, pp. 26–31.

27 Heribert von Larisch, *Das 2. Großherzogl. Mecklenburg. Dragoner-Regiment Nr. 18 im Weltkriege 1914–1918* (Oldenburg, 1924), pp. 15–19.

28 *Weltkrieg* I, pp. 129–31.

29 *Weltkrieg* I, pp. 214–16.

30 *Weltkrieg* I, p. 137.

31 *Military Operations. France and Belgium 1914*, p. 3.

32 *Military Operations. France and Belgium 1914*, p. 35.

33 *Military Operations. France and Belgium 1914*, p. 35.

34 Sewell Tyng, *The Campaign of the Marne 1914* (London, 1935), p. 95.

35 Barbara Tuchmann, *The Guns of August* (New York, 1962), p. 193.

36 Annika Mombauer, "Of War Plans and War Guilt: The Debate Surrounding the Schlieffen Plan" in: *The Journal of Strategic Studies*, Vol. 28, no. 5, pp. 857–85, here p.873. See my reply, "The 'Schlieffen Plan' and German War Guilt" in: *War in History*, Vol. 14, No. 1, 2007, pp. 96–108.

37 Belgian official history I, p. 30.

38 Clayton Donnell, *The Forts of the Meuse in World War I* (Oxford, 2007), pp. 47, 54.

39 The casualties from seven of twelve attacking infantry regiments and two of four Jäger battalions are available. In the 14th Brigade, which broke through

and captured the centre of Liège, and saw some of the heaviest fighting, IR 27 lost 8 OFF and 40 EM KIA, 11 OFF and 187 EM WIA, 97 EM MIA; IR 165 lost 2 OFF and 34 EM KIA, 5 OFF and 89 EM WIA. The brigade lost 84 KIA and 292 WIA. Even including the 97 MIA, there were only 473 casualties. In the 34th brigade, IR 90 lost 4 OFF and 38 EM KIA, 8 OFF and 139 EM WIA, 22 MIA, 212 casualties in total. In the 11th Brigade, IR 20 lost 2 OFF and 21 EM KIA, 3 OFF and 57 EM WIA, 85 casualties altogether; IR 35 3 OFF and 32 EM KIA, 31 EM WIA, 3 OFF and 21 EM MIA, 90 casualties in the regiment, 175 in the 11th Brigade. IR 74 lost 266 casualties, IR 53 lost 418, Jäger 4 about 100, Jäger 10 lost 58. The losses for IR 73, IR 165, IR 16, Jäger 7 and Jäger 3 are not given in the unit histories or are unclear. I did not have access to the histories of IR 82 and IR 83. After 6 August the Germans took no significant numbers of casualties, as the forts were reduced by artillery fire alone. Slightly more than half the attacking force took 1,700 casualties, so it is not unreasonable to believe that total casualties were 3,400.

40 Gottberg, *Dragoner-Regiment 19*, pp. 29–30.

41 Larisch, *Dragoner-Regiment 18*, p. 35.

42 Anon., *Kriegsgeschichte 1914–1918 des 2. Westfälischen Husaren-Regiments Nr. 11* (Oldenburg i. O./ Berlin), p. 110.

43 Alhard von Burgsdorff, *Das Westfälische Ulanen-Regiment Nr. 5 und seine Kriegsformationen* (Oldenburg/Berlin, 1930), p. 19.

44 Lomas, *Mons*, p. 66.

45 Wilhelm Jürgensen, *Das Füsilier-Regiment „Königin" Nr. 86 im Weltkriege* (Oldenburg i. O./Berlin, 1925), pp. 22–5.

46 The Belgians and their apologists deny that there was any armed civilian resistance whatsoever: Jean Schmitz and Norbert Niewland, *Documents pour server a l'histoire de la invasion Allemande*, 9 vols (Brussels and Paris, 1919–25); John Horne and Alan Kramer, *German Atrocities 1914: A History of Denial* (New Haven and London, 2001); Larry Zuckermann, *The Rape of Belgium: The Untold Story of World War I* (New York and London, 2004).

47 *Weltkrieg* I, pp. 96–7.

48 Horne and Cramer, *German Atrocities*, pp. 128–9. The Belgian official military histories do not mention the Garde Civique, probably because it was subordinate to the Ministry of the Interior.

49 E. von Trauwitz-Hellwig, *Das Königlich Preußische Husaren-Regiment Königin Wilhelmina der Niederlande (Hannoversches) Nr. 15 im Weltkriege 1914–1918* (Wandsbeck, n.d.), p. 43.

50 Ernst Zipfel, *Geschichte des Großherzoglich Mecklenburgischen Grenadier-Regimens Nr. 89* (Schwerin i. M., 1932), p. 38. The author was an *Archivrat* in the Reichsarchiv, that is, a trained historian.

51 Verein der Offiziere, *Das Kgl. Preußische (Westfälische) Jäger-Batallion Nr. 7 (Feldbattalion) im Weltkrieg 1914–18* (Oldenburg/Berlin, 1929), p. 21.

52 Victor Köhler, *Das Kürassier-Regiment von Seydlitz (Magdeburgisches) Nr. 7, seine Geschichte* (Hannover, 1935), p. 100.

53 Ernst Günther von Etzel, *Geschichte des 2. Pommerschen Ulanan-Regiments Nr. 9* (Berlin, 1931), p. 41.

54 Lattorff, *Jäger-Bataillon 3*, p. 20.

55 Lattorff, *Jäger-Bataillon 3*, pp. 22–3.

56 Albert Benary, *Königl Preuß. Magdeburgisches Husaren-Regiment Nr. 10 im Weltkriege 1914/18* (Berlin, 1934), pp. 61–2.

57 Lattorff, *Jäger-Bataillon 3*, p. 23.

58 *Armées Françaises* I, I, p. 40.

59 *Armées Françaises* I, I, Annexe, pp. 166–9.

60 *Armées Françaises* I, I, pp. 134–7; Annexe, p. 272.

61 Oertzen, *Geschichte des 1. Westfälischen Husaren-Regiments Nr. 8* (Paderborn, 1939), pp. 69–81.

62 Anon., *Husaren-Regiment 11*, pp. 88–9.

63 Heinrich Glassmeier, *Geschichte des Kürassier-Regiments von Dreisen (Westf.) Nr 4* (Oldenburg i. O, 1932), pp. 30–3.

64 Oetzen, *Husaren-Regiment 8*, p. 82.

65 Glasmeier, *Kürassier-Regiment 4*, p. 31.

66 Glasmeier, *Kürassier-Regiment 4*, pp. 34–5, 49.

67 Anon., *Husaren-Regiment 11*, pp. 93–102.

68 Gottberg, *Dragoner-Regiment 19*, pp. 34–5.

69 Anon., *Husaren-Regiment 11*, pp. 102–3.

70 Oetzen, *Husaren-Regiment 8*, pp. 83–92.

71 Larisch, *Dragoner-Regiment 18*, p. 24.

72 Etzel, *Ulanen-Regiment 9*, pp. 43–4.

73 August Reimers, *Das Husaren-Regiment Kaiser Franz Joseph von Österreich, König von Hungarn (Schleswig-Holsteinisches) Nr. 16* (Berlin, 1937), pp. 124–6.

74 Trauwitz-Hellwig, *Husaren-Regiment 15*, pp. 36–40.

75 Köhler, *Kürassier-Regiment 7*, pp. 95–6.

76 Troschke, *Dragoner-Regiment 17*, pp. 44–51.

77 Belgian official history I, pp. 8–9; II, p. 34.

78 Bedinski, *Jäger 9*, pp. 72–6. Anon., *Das Kgl. Preußische (Westfälische) Jäger-Bataillon Nr. 7 (Feldbataillon) im Weltkrieg 1914–18* (Oldenburg/Berlin, 1929), pp. 27–33. Jäger 7 participated in the attack on Liège, during which 200 men became separated from the battalion and were attached to HKK 2 as *Jägerkompagnie 7*.

79 *Weltkrieg* I, p. 121.

80 Leopold Hederich, *Die Reitende Abteilung des Königl. Preuß. Feldartillerie-Regiments Generalfeldzeugmeister (1. Brandenburgisches) Nr. 3 im Weltkriege 1914/1918* (Berlin, 1936), pp. 29–36.

81 Belgian official history I, pp. 34–8.

82 Belgian official history I, p. 37.

83 Anon., *Husaren-Regiment 11*, p. 104.

84 Burgsdorff, *Ulanen-Regiment 5*, p. 48.

85 *Military Operations. France and Belgium 1914*, pp. 23–4.

86 Ascoli, *Mons Star*, p. 32.

87 Zuber, *Inventing the Schlieffen Plan*, p. 242.

88 *Weltkrieg* I, pp. 214–17.

89 Bogislav von Studnitz, *Geschichte des Thüringischen Husaren-Regiments Nr. 12 und seiner Mobilmachungsfromationen im Weltkriege 1914–1918* (Weimar, 1930), pp. 18–21. Köhler, *Kürassier-Regiment Nr. 7*, pp. 100–5.

90 Anon., *Leib-Husaren Brigade*, p. 8.

91 Belgian official history I, pp. 42–5.

92 Wilhelm Jürgensen, *Das Fusilier-Regiment „Königin" Nr. 86 im Weltkriege* (Oldenburg i. O./Berlin, 1925), pp. 19–22.

93 *Erinnerungsblätter der ehemaligen Mansteiner. Geschichte des Infanterie-Regiments von Manstein (Schleswiges) Nr. 8.4 1914–1918*, Hülsemann (ed.), Nr. 6, pp. 42–8.

94 Hans-Erich Henning, *Feldartillerie-Regiment Generalfeldmarschall Graf Waldersee (Schleswiges) Nr. 9* (Oldenburg i. O., 1934), pp. 24–8.

95 Bernhard Studt, *Infanterie-Regiment Graf Bose (1. Thüringisches) Nr. 31 im Weltkriege 1914–1918* (Oldenburg i. O./Berlin, 1926), pp. 18–27, 304–5.

96 Belgian official history I, p. 45.

97 Oskar Beltz, *Das Infanterie-Regiment Herzog von Holstein (Holst.) Nr. 85 im Weltkriege* (Heide i. Holstein, 1925, 2nd ed.), p. 14.

98 Gottberg, *Dragoner-Regiment 19*, p. 46.

99 Trauwitz-Hellwig, *Husaren-Regiment 15*, pp. 40–1.

100 Reimers, *Husaren-Regiment 16*, p. 128.

101 Anon., *Husaren-Regiment 11*, p. 106.

102 *Armées Françaises* I, I, pp. 436–7.

103 *Weltkrieg* I, pp. 217–18.

104 Reimers, *Husaren-Regiment 16*, pp. 128–9.

105 Anon., *Husaren-Regiment 11*, pp. 110–11.

106 Lattorff, *Jäger-Bataillon 3*, pp. 20–1.

107 Ernst Neumann, *Das Magdeburgische Jäger-Bataillon Nr. 4 im Weltkriege 1914–1918* (Sporen, Zeulenrode, 1935), pp. 40–2.

108 Neumann, *Jäger-Bataillon 4*, pp. 44–54.

109 Anon., *Jäger-Bataillon 7*, pp. 33–6.

110 Günther Herr, *Das Königlich-Preußische Mansfelder Feldartillerie-Regiment Nr. 75 zu Halle a. d. S. im Weltkriege 1914/18* (Gräfenhainchen, 1934), pp. 26–7.

111 Badinski, *Jäger-Bataillon 9*, p. 82.

112 Ministère de la Guerre, *Les Armées Françaises dans la Grande Guerre, Tome Premier, premier Volume* (Paris, 1923), pp. 434–5.

113 *Military Operations. France and Belgium 1914*, pp. 50–1.

114 John Ewing, *The Royal Scots 1914–1919 Vol I* (Edinburgh, 1925), p. 16.

115 C. D. Bruce, *History of the Duke of Wellington's Regiment [1st and 2nd Battalions] 1881–1923* (London, 1927), p. 61.

116 Arthur Crookenden, *The History of the Cheshire Regiment in the Great War* (1939), p. 1.

117 Bond, *King's Own Yorkshire Light Infantry*, p. 717. Italics in the original.

118 *Weltkrieg* I, pp. 216–17.

119 Anon., *Leibhusaren*, p. 9.

120 *Armées Françaises* I, I, pp. 438–9.

121 *Armées Françaises* I, I, Annexe, pp. 525, 535.

122 *Armées Françaises* I, I, pp. 441–2.

123 Belgian official history I, pp. 38, 53.

124 Belgian official history I, p. 61.

125 Terraine, *Mons*, pp. 61–2.

126 Herr, *Feldartillerie-Regiment 75*, pp. 46–7.

127 *Weltkrieg* I, p. 255.

128 *Armées Françaises* I, I, p. 442.

129 *Armées Françaises* I, I, Annexe, p. 530.

130 *Weltkrieg* I, pp. 346–50.

131 *Armées Françaises* I, I, p. 452.

132 *Armées Françaises* I, I, pp. 446–8.

133 *Armées Françaises* I, I, pp. 450–1.

134 *Armées Françaises* I, I, p. 449.

135 *Armées Françaises* I, I, pp. 446–7.

136 *Armées Françaises* I, I, p. 453.

137 *Armées Françaises* I, I, p. 468.

138 Anon., *Husaren-Regiment 8*, pp. 99–101.

139 Glassmeier, *Kürassier-Regiment 4*, pp. 54–5.

140 Trauwitz-Hellweg, *Husaren-Regiment 15*, pp. 44–6.

141 Bogislav von Studnitz, *Husaren-Regiment 12*, p. 20.

142 *Weltkrieg* I, pp. 364–70.

143 *Weltkrieg* I, pp. 221, 366–9.

144 *Armées Françaises* I, I, pp. 467–8.

145 *Military Operations. France and Belgium 1914*, pp. 63–4.

146 Edward Spears, *Liaison 1914* (London, 1930), pp. 145–6.

147 *Military Operations. France and Belgium 1914*, p. 68.

Chapter 4

1 *Military Operations. France and Belgium 1914*, p. 72.

2 James W. Taylor, *The 2nd Royal Irish Rifles in the Great War* (Dublin, 2005), p. 27.

3 *Weltkrieg* I, pp. 417–19.

4 *Military Operations. France and Belgium 1914*, p. 75.

5 Everard Wyrall, *The Die-Hards in the Great War. A history of the Duke of Cambridge's Own (Middlesex Regiment) 1914–1919. Vol. I 1914–1916* (London, 1926), p. 15.

6 Ascoli, *Mons Star*, p. 63.

7 Wyrall, *Middlesex Regiment*, pp. 15–20.

8 Stannus Geogheagan, *The Campaigns and History of the Royal Irish Regiment Vol. II. From 1900 to 1922* (Edinburgh and London, 1927), pp. 12–15.

9 Horsfall/Cave, *Mons*, p. 42.

10 Dietze, *Das 2. Hannoversche Dragoner-Regiment Nr. 16 im Weltkriege 1914–1918* (Oldenburg i. O/Berlin, 1927), pp. 51–4, 120–2.

11 Oetzen, *Husaren-Regiment 8*, pp. 101–3.

12 *Weltkrieg* I, p. 418.

13 Jürgensen, *Füsilier-Regiment 86*, pp. 22–5.

14 Hans-Erich Henning, *Feldartillerie-Regiment Generalfeldmarschall Graf Waldersee (Schleswigsches) Nr. 9* (Oldenburg i. O., 1934), pp. 29–34.

15 Otto Bene, *Das Lauenburgische Feldartillerie-Regiment Nr. 45* (Oldenburg i. O./Berlin, 1923), p. 21.

16 Michael Foss, *The Royal Fusiliers (The 7th Regiment of Foot)* (London, 1967), p. 107.

17 Horsfall/Cave, *Mons*, p. 63.

18 Hulsemann, *Geschichte des Infanterie-Regiments von Manstein (Schleswigsches) Nr. 84 1914–1918* (Hamburg, 1921–), No. 8, January 1924, pp. 57–82.

19 Henning, *Feldartillerie-Regiment 9*, pp. 33–4.

20 *Military Operations. France and Belgium 1914*, p. 85.

21 Horsfall/Cave, *Mons*, p. 75.

22 Oskar Beltz, *Das Infanterie-Regiment Herzog von Holstein (Holst.) Nr. 85 im Weltkriege* (2nd ed. Heide in Holstein, 1925), pp. 15–16.

23 Studt, *Infanterie-Regiment 35*, pp. 32–3.

24 *Military Operations. France and Belgium 1914*, p. 85.

25 Lomis, *Mons 1914*, p. 40.

26 Wyrall, *Middlesex Regiment*, p. 20.

27 Wyrall, *Middlesex Regiment*, p. 20.

28 Bene, *Feldartillerie-Regiment 45*, p. 21.

29 Taylor, *2nd Royal Irish Rifles*, pp. 24–9.

30 Herbert von Sydow, *Das Infanterie-Regiment Hamburg (2. Hanseatisches) Nr. 76* (Oldenburg i. O./Berlin, 1922), pp. 17–18.

31 Terraine, *Mons*, p. 91.

32 Cyril Falls, *The Gordon Highlander in the First World War 1914–1919* (Aberdeen, n.d.), pp. 4–5.

33 Zipfel/Albrecht, *Geschichte des Infanterie-Regiements Bremen (1. Hanseatisches) Nr. 75* (Bremen, 1934), pp. 43–50.

34 Terraine, *Mons*, p. 103. The official history and Terraine overstate the IR 76 casualties. They say that IR 75 lost 5 OFF and 376 EM. In fact, it lost 5 OFF WIA and 271 EM KIA and WIA.

35 Anon., *Geschichte des Großherzoglich Mecklenbergische Feldartillerie-Regiments Nr. 60 im weltkriege 1914–18* (Hamburg, 1921), p. 19. Pflieger, *Holsteinisches Feldartillerie-Regiment Nr. 24* (Oldenburg i. O./Berlin, 1922), pp. 30–7.

36 John Buchan, *The History of the Royal Scots Fusiliers (1678–1918)* (London, 1925), pp. 286–8.

37 *Military Operations. France and Belgium 1914*, p. 86.

38 Oertzen, *Husaren-Regiment 8*, pp. 100–3.

39 Rantzau, *Husaren-Regiment Nr. 3*, pp. 60–1.

40 Anon., *Das Fusilier-Regiment Prinz Heinrich von Preussen (Brandenburgisches) Nr. 35 im Weltkriege* (Berlin, 1929), p. 26.

41 Brandies, *Infanterie-Regiment 24*, pp. 20–8.

42 Hans Rosenthal, *Kurmärkisches Feldartillerie-Regiment Nr. 39* (Oldenburg i. O./ Berlin, 1923), p. 23.

43 Wilhelm Schlawe, *Feldartillerie-Regiment General-Feldzeugmeister (1. Brandenburgisches) Nr. 3 im weltkrieg 1914/1918* (Berlin, 1935), pp. 23–4.

44 Anon., *Geschichte des Infanterie-Regiments Generalfeldmarschall Prinz Friedrich Karl von Preussen (8. Brandenburg.) Nr. 64 während des Krieges 1914/18* (Berlin, 1929), pp. 12–15. III/8 was actually the Fusilier Battalion.

45 C. D. Bruce, *History of the Duke of Wellington's Regiment 1881–1923* (London, 1927), pp. 62–73.

46 Horsfall/Cave, *Mons*, pp. 51–4.

47 C. V. Molony, *"Invicta". With the First Battalion, the Queen's Royal West Kent Regiment in the Great War* (London, 1923), pp. 20–4. It relies mostly on Bloem,

and repeats the myth that the Germans took British rapid rifle fire for MG fire as well as the myth that the Germans had many more MG than the British.

48 Stair Gillon, *The KOSB in the Great War* (London, 1930), pp. 27–30.

49 Rantzau, *Husaren-Regiment 3*, pp. 58–60.

50 Alfred Rosenberg von Lipinsky, *Das Feldartillerie-Regiment „Generalfeldzeugmeister" (2. Brand.) Nr. 18 1914–1918* (Oldenburg i. O./Berlin, 1922), pp. 18–19.

51 Horsfall/Cage, *Mons*, p. 85.

52 *Military Operations. France and Belgium 1914*, p. 78.

53 Terraine, *Mons*, p. 93.

54 Ernst von Schönfeldt, *Das Grenadier-Regiment Prinz Karl von Preußen (2. branden-burgisches) Nr. 12 im Weltkriege* (Oldenburg i. O./Berlin, 1924), pp. 24–6. Once again, III/12 was actually the Fusilier Battalion.

55 Otto Hensel, *Das Neumärkische Feld-Artillerie-Regiment Nr. 54 1914–18* (Berlin, 1932), pp. 22–3.

56 Horsfall/Cave, *Mons*, p. 87.

57 Terraine, *Mons*, p. 94.

58 Horsfall/Cave, *Mons*, p. 67.

59 Ascoli, *Mons Star*, p. 69.

60 Ascoli, *Mons Star*, p. 78.

61 *Military Operations. France and Belgium 1914*, p. 80.

62 Terraine, *Mons*, p. 94.

63 H. W. Pearce, *History of the East Surrey Regiment Volume II (1914–1917)*, pp. 31–6.

64 Horsfall/Cave, *Mons*, p. 94.

65 *Military Operations. France and Belgium 1914*, p. 81. Terraine, *Mons*, p. 94.

66 Broede, *Infanterie-Regiment von Stülpnagel (5. Brandenburgisches) Nr. 48* (Berlin, 1935), pp. 99–100.

67 Terraine, *Mons*, p. 100.

68 Everard Wyrall, *The History of the Duke of Cornwall's Light Infantry 1914–1919* (London, n.d.), pp. 12–22.

69 H. C. Wylly, *History of the Manchester Regiment Vol. II 1883–1922* (London, 1925), p. 88.

70 Oertzen, *Husaren-Regiment 8*, p. 103–5.

71 Wolfgang von Vormann, *Infanterie-Regiment Fürst Leopold von Anhalt Dessau (1. Magdeburg) Nr. 26. Band I/Das Kriegsjahr 1914* (Oldenburg i. O./Berlin, 1925), pp. 42–8.

72 Friedrich Wilhelm Rübesamen, *Feldartillerie-Regiment Prinzregent Luitpold von Bayern (Magdeburgisches) Nr. 4. Teil I (1 August 1914 bis 31 Juli 1916)* (Magdeburg, n.d.), pp. 57–9.

73 Otto Korfes, *Das 3. Magdeburgische Infanterie-Regiment Nr. 66 im Weltkriege* (Berlin, 1930), pp. 9–22.

74 Wyrall, *Middlesex Regiment*, pp. 18–20.

75 Hans Trützschler von Falkenstein, *Das Anhaltische Infanterie-Regiment Nr. 93* (Oldenburg i. O./Berlin, 1929), pp. 33–7.

76 Konrad von Hippel, et. al., *Erinnerungsblatt des ehem. Königl. Preuß. Torgauer Feldartillerie-Regiments Nr. 74* (Oldenburg i. O./Berlin, 1928), pp. 30–1.

77 *Military Operations. France and Belgium 1914*, pp. 82, 85.

78 *Military Operations. France and Belgium 1914*, pp. 97–8.

79 *Military Operations. France and Belgium 1914*, pp. 91–2.

80 *Weltkrieg* I, p. 369.

81 *Weltkrieg* I, p. 518.

Chapter 5

1 *Military Operations. France and Belgium 1914*, pp. 97–8.

2 *Weltkrieg* I, pp. 429–30.

3 *Military Operations. France and Belgium 1914*, p. 100.

4 *Military Operations. France and Belgium 1914*, p. 101.

5 Ascoli says that 2/Duke of Wellington's was at Pâturages and 1/Bedfords and 1/Dorset at Hornu. *Mons Star*, p. 80. This is at complete variance with the official history.

6 *Military Operations. France and Belgium 1914*, p. 106.

7 Stacke, *Worcestershire Regiment*, p. 6.

8 *Infanterie-Regiment 84*, p. 80.

9 H. Whalley-Kely, *"Ich dien". The Prince of Wales's Volunteers (South Lancashire) 1914–1934* (Aldershot, 1935), pp. 15–16.

10 Jürgensen, *Infanterie-Regiment 86*, p. 26.

11 Anon., *Infanterie-Regiment 90*, p. 40.

12 Horsfall/Cave, *Mons*, pp. 108, 113–14.

13 C. R. Simpson, *The History of the Lincolnshire Regiment* (London, 1931), pp. 12–16.

14 Schlawe, *Feldartillerie-Regiment 3*, pp. 27–8.

15 Rosenthal, *Feldartillerie-Regiment 39*, p. 24.

16 Brandis, *Infanterie-Regiment 24*, pp. 31–7.

17 Doerstling, *Infanterie-Regiment 20*, pp. 47–9.

18 Anon., *Infanterie-Regiment 64*, pp. 15–18.

19 Anon., *Fusilier-Regiment 35*, p. 28.

20 Ransome, *Dorsets*, pp. 12–21.

21 Gillon, *King's Own Scottish Borderers*, p. 30.

22 Bruce, *Duke of Wellington's Regiment*, pp. 73–81.

23 Molony, *Royal West Kent Regiment*, pp. 23–7.

24 Bond, *King's Own Yorkshire Light Infantry*, pp. 720–1.

25 Reymann, *Infanterie-Regiment 52*, pp. 25–6.

26 Hensel, *Feldartillerie-Regiment 54*, pp. 23–4.

27 Schönfeldt, *Grenadier-Regiment Nr. 12*, p. 27.

28 Kaupert, *Infanterie-Regiment 48*, pp. 99–102.

29 Ascoli, *Mons Star*, p. 80.

30 Schönfeldt, *Grenadier-Regiment 12*, pp. 26–7, 200.

31 Schönig, *Leib-Grenadier-Regiment 8*, pp. 59–60.

32 Lipinsky, *Feldartillerie-Regiment 18*, pp. 19–20.

33 *Military Operations. France and Belgium 1914*, pp. 103–4.

34 Crookenden, *Cheshire Regiment*, pp. 5–16. F. Loraine Petre, *The History of the Norfolk Regiment 1685–1918. Vol. II 4th August 1914 to 31st December, 1918* (Norwich, n.d.), pp. 4–5. Petre was a distinguished historian of the Napoleonic Wars.

35 Horsfall/Cave, *Mons*, pp. 124–5.
36 *Military Operations. France and Belgium 1914*, pp. 108–9.
37 Benary, *Husaren-Regiment 10*, pp. 77–9.
38 Falkenstein, *Infanterie-Regiment 93*, pp. 37–9.
39 Konrad von Hippel, et. al., *Erinnerungsblatt des ehem. Königl. Preuß. Torgauer Feldartillerie-Regiments Nr. 74* (Oldenburg i. O./Berlin, 1928), pp. 31–2, 68–71.
40 Herr, *Feldartillerie-Regiment 75*, pp. 54–8.
41 Ernst Schmidt-Oßwald, *Das Altenberger Regiment (8. Thüringisches Infanterie-Regiment Nr. 153) im Weltkriege* (Oldenburg i. O./Berlin, 1927), pp. 47–8.
42 H. Wolff/Hoffmann, *Königlich Preußische Fusilier-Regiment Generalfeldmarschall Graf Blumenthal (Magdeburgisches) Nr. 36 im Weltkriege 1914–1918. Ein Kriegstagebuch* (Eisleben, 1931), p. 9.
43 Ascoli, *Mons Star*, p. 84.
44 Korfes, *Infanterie-Regiment 66*, pp. 21–2.
45 Vormann, *Infanterie-Regiment 26*, pp. 50–2.
46 Ernst Glaser-Gerhard, *Das Altmärkische Feld-Artillerie Regiment Nr. 40 im Weltkriege 1914–1918* (Zeulenroda, n.d.), pp. 29–32.
47 Bernard Werner, *Das Königlich Preußische Inf.-Rgt. Prinz Louis Ferdinand von Preußen (2. Magdeb.) Nr. 27 im Weltkriege* (Berlin-Charlottenburg, 1933), pp. 56–7.
48 Otto Fließ/Kurt Dittmar, *5. Hannoversches Infanterie-Regiment Nr. 165 im weltkriege* (Oldenburg i. O./Berlin, 1927), p. 22.
49 *Military Operations. France and Belgium 1914*, p. 112.
50 *Weltkrieg* I, pp. 404, 418–19, 426.
51 Oertzen, *Husaren-Regiment 8*, pp. 105–7.
52 Burgsdorff, *Ulanenr-Regiment 5*, p. 51.
53 Anon., *Husaren-Regiment 11*, pp. 115–16.
54 Neumann, *Jäger 4*, pp. 56–61.
55 Hederich, *Reitende Abteilung FAR 3*, p. 42.
56 Köhler, *Kurassier-Regiment 7*, pp. 106–8.
57 Lattorff, *Jäger 3*, p. 24.

Chapter 6

1 *Military Operations. France and Belgium 1914*, pp. 118–29.
2 *Weltkrieg* I, pp. 517–19.
3 *Weltkrieg* I, p. 519.
4 *Weltkrieg* I, p. 521.
5 Broede, *Infanterie-Regiment 48*, pp. 103–7.
6 *Military Operations. France and Belgium 1914*, p. 133.
7 Brandis, *Regiment 24*, pp. 39–40.
8 Schlawe, *Feldartillerie-Regiment 3*, p. 29.
9 Rosenthal, *Feldartillerie-Regiment 39*, p. 25.
10 Doerstling, *Infanterie-Regiment 20*, p. 50.
11 Anon., *Infanterie-Regiment 64*, pp. 19–20.
12 Anon., *Fusilier-Regiment 35*, p. 29.
13 Werner, *Infanterie-Regiment 27*, pp. 57–60.

14 Rübesamen, *Artillerie-Regiment 4*, pp. 62–3.

15 Fließ/Dittmer, *Infanterie-Regiment 165*, p. 23.

16 *Military Operations. France and Belgium 1914*, pp. 134–5.

17 Korfes, *Infanterie-Regiment 66*, p. 23.

18 Glasner-Gerhard, *Artillerie-Regiment 40*, p. 33.

19 Gruson, *Infanterie-Regiment 72*, pp. 58–9.

20 Schmidt-Oßwald, *Infanterie-Regiment 153*, pp. 49–52.

21 *Military Operations. France and Belgium 1914*, p. 136.

22 The British official history says that if IR 153 had attacked, it would have hit IR 72, which bivouacked in St Python, just north-west of Solesmes (*Military Operations. France and Belgium 1914*, p. 136). Incorrect; IR 153's attack was set for 2100; IR 72 did not enter St Python until 2200.

23 Anon., *Leibhusaren*, p. 10.

24 Poseck, *Dragoner-Regiment 2*, pp. 21–3.

25 Etzel, *Ulanen-Regiment 9*, pp. 56–7.

26 Larisch, *Dragoner-Regiment 16*, pp. 38–9.

27 Burgsdorff, *Ulanen-Regiment 5*, p. 51.

28 Oertzen, *Husaren-Regiment 8*, p. 108.

29 Gottberg, *Dragoner-Regiment 19*, pp. 51–2.

30 Studnitz, *Husaren-Regiment 12*, p. 22.

31 Jung, *Jäger-Bataillon 10*, p. 75.

32 Badinski, *Jäger-Bataillon 9*, pp. 84–5.

33 Lattorff, *Jäger-Bataillon 3*, pp. 24–5.

34 *Military Operations. France and Belgium 1914*, pp. 125–9, 136–43.

Chapter 7

1 Becke, *Artillery at Le Cateau*, pp. 21–2.

2 Lomas, *Mons 1914*, p. 72.

3 Lomas, *Mons 1914*, p. 70.

4 Ascoli, *Mons Star*, p. 99.

5 Ascoli, *Mons Star*, pp. 109–10.

6 *Military Operations. France and Germany 1914*, p. 210.

7 Anon., *Infanterie-Regiment 90*, p. 40.

8 *Military Operations. France and Belgium 1914*, pp. 140–3.

9 *Military Operations. France and Belgium 1914*, pp. 147–8.

10 *Military Operations. France and Belgium 1914*, pp. 143–9.

11 C. T. Atkinson, *The Royal Hampshire Regiment, Vol. II 1914–1918* (Glasgow, 1952), pp. 7–13.

12 Poseck, *German Cavalry*, pp. 57–61. Neumann, *Jäger 4*, pp. 64–9. Poseck, *Dragoner-Regiment 2*, pp. 23–4.

13 Howard Green, *The King's Own Regiment (The 4th Regiment of Foot)* (London, 1972), p. 109.

14 Charles Lethbridge Kingsford, *The Story of the Royal Warwickshire Regiment* (London, 1921), pp. 130–2.

15 Anon., *Jäger-Bataillon 7*, pp. 38–41.

16 Studnitz, *Husaren-Regiment 12*, pp. 22–3.

17 Poseck, *Dragoner-Regiment 2*, pp. 23–4.

18 Köhler, *Kürassier 7*, pp. 109–10.

19 Cave/Shelton, *Le Cateau*, pp. 178, 181, 189.

20 Becke, *Artillery at Le Cateau*, p. 85.

21 Reginald Berkeley, *The History of the Rifle Brigade in the War of 1914–1918 Vol. 1 August 1914–December 1916* (London, 1922), pp. 11–19.

22 Everard Wyrall, *The History of the Somerset Light Infantry (Prince Albert's) 1914–1919* (London, 1927), pp. 6–11. E. C. Hopkinson, *1st Battalion The East Lancashire Regiment August and September 1914* (Cambridge, 1926?), pp. 10–11.

23 Badinki, *Jäger-Bataillon 9*, pp. 87–95.

24 Anon., *Leib-Husaren*, p. 11.

25 Lattorff, *Jäger-Bataillon 3*, pp. 25–8.

26 Gottberg, *Dragoner-Regiment 19*, pp. 52–3.

27 Schneider, *Feldartillerie-Regiment 10*, pp. 360–3.

28 *Military Operations. France and Belgium 1914*, p. 171.

29 Cecil L. Nicholson, *The History of the East Lancashire Regiment in the Great War 1914–1918* (Liverpool, n.d.), pp. 15–16.

30 Hopkinson, *1/East Lancashire Regiment*, p. 8.

31 Becke, *Artillery at Le Cateau*, pp. 37–9, 52–3, 63–6, 82, 84, 86.

32 Rudolf Werneberg, *Königl. Preußisches Reserve-Feldartillerie-Regiment Nr. 7* (Oldenburg i. O./Berlin, 1926), pp. 26–30.

33 *Military Operations. France and Belgium 1914*, pp. 168–9.

34 Wyrall, *Somerset Light Infantry*, p. 10.

35 Lomas, *Mons 1914*, p. 81.

36 Hopkinson, *East Lancashire Regiment*, p. 20.

37 Berkeley, *Rifle Brigade*, p. 20.

38 Atkinson, *Hampshire Regiment*, p. 13.

39 Wyrall, *Somerset Light Infantry*, p. 10.

40 Jung, *Jäger-Bataillon 10*, pp. 86–7.

41 The same evaluation appeared in the Jäger 3 history: Lattorff, *Jäger-Bataillon 3*, p. 25.

42 Gruson, *Infanterie-Regiment 72*, pp. 61–72.

43 Pearse, *East Surrey Regiment*, pp. 37–9. Wyrall, *Duke of Cornwall's Light Infantry*, pp. 28–40.

44 Lomas, *Mons 1914*, p. 73.

45 *Military Operations. France and Belgium 1914*, pp. 153–64.

46 C. C. R. Murphy, *The History of the Suffolk Regiment 1914–1927* (London, 1928?), p. 29.

47 Murphy, *Suffolk Regiment*, pp. 31–6.

48 Bond, *King's Own Yorkshire Light Infantry*, pp. 722–9.

49 *Military Operations. France and Belgium 1914*, pp. 156–62.

50 Korfes, *Infanterie-Regiment 66*, pp. 24–35. This account of Le Cateau is outstanding.

51 British maps put the 2/Suffolk position too far to the north and east. It is clear from the German accounts of the battle that the 2/Suffolk position was near to the Suffolk monument. This is confirmed by observation on the terrain.

52 Wyrall, *Middlesex Regiment*, pp. 30–3.

53 H. C. Wylly, *The History of the Manchester Regiment Vol. II 1883–1922* (London, 1925), pp. 94–5.

54 Glaser-Gerhard, *Feldartillerie-Regiment 40*, pp. 34–42.

55 *Military Operations. France and Belgium 1914*, p. 160.

56 Becke, *Artillery at Le Cateau*, p. 44.

57 Lomas, *Mons 1914*, p. 76.

58 Vormann, *Infanterie-Regiment 26*, pp. 56–60.

59 *Weltkrieg* I, p. 524.

60 Becke, *Artillery at Le Cateau*, pp. 42–5.

61 Lipinski, *Feldartillerie-Regiment 18*, p. 22.

62 *Military Operations. France and Belgium 1914*, p. 171.

63 Becke, *Artillery at Le Cateau*, pp. 55–9.

64 *Military Operations. France and Belgium 1914*, p. 175.

65 Becke, *Artillery at Le Cateau*, pp. 58–61.

66 Rübesamen, *Feldartillerie-Regiment 4*, pp. 63–5.

67 Gillon, *KOSB*, pp. 33–6. Cave/Shelton, *Le Cateau*, pp. 62–6.

68 Molony, *Royal West Kent Regiment*, pp. 28–33. The West Kent history is a font of military misinformation. It maintains that the Germans caught up with II Corps because 'the Germans moved their advanced infantry in motor lorries' (p. 28).

69 Cave/Shelton, *Le Cateau*, pp. 61–2.

70 Bruce, *Duke of Wellington's Regiment*, p. 90.

71 Becke, *Artillery at Le Cateau*, p. 68.

72 Fleiß/Dittmar, *Infanterie-Regiment 165*, pp. 24–5. Werner, *Infanterie-Regiment 27*, pp. 60–1.

73 Lomas, *Mons 1914*, p. 77.

74 Cave/Shelton, *Le Cateau*, pp. 66–9.

75 Cave/Shelton, *Le Cateau*, pp. 69–70.

76 Cave/Shelton, *Le Cateau*, pp. 94–5.

77 Simpson, *Lincolnshire Regiment*, pp. 18–20.

78 Wolff/Hoffmann, *Fusilier-Regiment 36*, pp. 9–11.

79 Almost nothing is known of 4/Middlesex; the battalion's account of Le Cateau is 36 words long. Wyrall, *Middlesex Regiment*, p. 34.

80 Ewing, *Royal Scots*, pp. 29–36.

81 *Military Operations. France and Belgium 1914*, p. 164

82 Schmidt-Oßwald, *Infanterie-Regiment 153*, pp. 53–9.

83 Falkenstein, *Infanterie-Regiment 93*, pp. 40–4.

84 Hippel, et. al., *Feldartillerie-Regiment 74*, pp. 34–6.

85 Herr, *Feldartillerie-Regiment 75*, pp. 65–75.

86 Max Dobryznski, *Fußartillerie-Regiment Encke (Magdeburgisches) Nr. 4* (Berlin, 1924), p. 23.

87 Taylor, *Royal Irish Rifles*, p. 31.

88 Geoghegan, *Royal Irish Regiment*, pp. 16–18.

89 Falls, *Gordon Highlanders*, pp. 6–7.

90 Cave/Shelton, *Le Cateau*, pp. 112–21.

91 *Military Operations. France and Belgium 1914*, p. 184.

92 Falls, *Gordon Highlanders*, pp. 8–9.

93 Korfes, *Infanterie-Regiment 66*, pp. 36–40.
94 Becke, *Artillery at Le Cateau*, p. 62.
95 Whalley-Kelly, *South Lancashire Regiment*, p. 16.
96 Stacke, *Worcestershire Regiment*, pp. 8–11.
97 Stacke, *Worcestershire Regiment*, pp. 9–10.
98 Cave/Shelton, *Le Cateau*, pp. 136–7.
99 Hederich, *Reitende Abteilung Feldartillerie-Regiments 3*, pp. 46–50.
100 Oertzen, *Husaren-Regiment 8*, pp. 110–11.
101 Anon., *Husaren-Regiment 11*, pp. 116–18.
102 *Military Operations. France and Belgium 1914*, pp. 191–2.
103 Lomas, *Mons 1914*, p. 81.
104 *Armée Françaises*, Volume I, Tome 2, Annexes, p. 429.
105 Huguet, *L'Intervention*, p. 81.
106 Becke, *Artillery at Le Cateau*, p. 85.
107 Ascoli, *The Mons Star*, p. 106.
108 Lomas, *Mons 1914*, pp. 72–3.
109 Becke, *Artillery at Le Cateau*, pp. 73–6.
110 Becke, *Artillery at Le Cateau*, p. 77.
111 *Military Operations. France and Belgium 1914*, p. 201.

Chapter 8

1 Michael Foss, *The Royal Fusiliers (The 7th Regiment of Foot)* (London, 1967), p. 108.
2 Gillon, *KOSB*, p. 36.
3 Cave/Shelton, *Le Cateau*, pp. 118–21.
4 Schmidt-Oswald, *Infanterie-Regiment 153*, pp. 57–9.
5 Herr, *Feldartillerie-Regiment 75*, pp. 78–9.

Appendix I

British Order of Battle

British Expeditionary Force (BEF)
Commander: Field Marshal Sir J. D. P. French
Chief of Staff: Lieutenant-General Sir A. J. Murray
52 Battalions, 38 Squadrons, 57 Batteries (324 guns)

Cavalry Division
36 Squadrons, 5 Batteries (20 guns)

'D', 'E', 'I', 'J', 'L' Batteries, Royal Horse Artillery

1st Cav. Bde: 2nd Dragoon Guards, 5th Dragoon Guards, 11th Hussars
2nd Cav. Bde: 4th Dragoon Guards, 9th Lancers, 18th Hussars
3rd Cav. Bde: 4th Hussars, 5th Lancers, 16th Hussars
4th Cav. Bde: Household Cav, 6th Dragoon Guards, 3rd Hussars
5th Cav. Bde: 2nd Dragoons, 12th Lancers, 20th Lancers

I Corps

24 Battalions, 2 Squadrons, 26 Batteries (152 guns)

1st Division

2nd Division

II Corps

3rd Division

7th Bde: 3/Worcestershire R, 2/South Lancashire R. 1/Wiltshire R,
   2/Royal Irish Rifles
8th Bde: 2/Royal Scots, 2/Royal Irish R, 4/Middlesex R, 1/Gordon Highlanders
9th Bde: 1/Northumberland Fusiliers, 4/Royal Fusiliers, 1/Lincolnshire,
   1/Royal Scots Fusiliers
XXII Arty Bde: 107, 108, 109 Batteries
XL Arty Bde: 6, 23, 49 Batteries
XLII Arty Bde: 29, 41, 45 Batteries
XXX Howitzer Bde: 128, 129, 130 Howitzer Batteries
48 Heavy Battery
'C' Squadron, 15th Hussars

5th Division

13th Bde: 2/Duke of Wellington's, 2/King's Own Scottish Borderers, 1/Queen's
   Own, 2/King's Own Yorkshire Light Infantry
14th Bde: 2/Suffolk R, 1/East Surrey R, 1/Duke of Cornwall's Light Infantry,
   2/Manchester R
15th Bde: 1/Norfolk R, 1/Bedfordshire R, 1/Cheshire R, Dorsetshire R
XV Arty Bde: 11, 52, 80 Batteries
XXVII Arty Bde: 119, 120, 121 Batteries
XXVIII Arty Bde: 122, 123, 124 Batteries
VIII How Bde: 37, 61, 65 How Batteries
108 Heavy Battery
'A' Squadron, 19th Hussars

III Corps

4th Division

10th Bde: 1/Royal Warwickshire R, 2/Seaforth Highlanders, 1/Irish Fusiliers,
   2/Royal Dublin Fusiliers
11th Bde: 1/Somerset Light Infantry, 1/East Lancashire R, 1/Hampshire R,
   1/Rifle Brigade
12th Bde: 1/King's Own Royal Lancaster R, 2/Lancashire Fusiliers, 2/Royal
   Inniskilling Fusiliers, 2/Essex R
XIV Arty Bde: 39, 68, 88 Batteries
XXIX Arty Bde: 125, 126, 127 Batteries
XXXII Arty Bde: 27, 134, 135 Batteries
XXXVII How Bde: 31, 35, 55 How Batteries
31 Heavy Battery
'B' Squadron, 19th Hussars

19th Bde: 2/Royal Welch Fusiliers, 1/Cameronians, 1/Middlesex R, 2/Argyll
   & Sutherland Highlanders

Appendix II

German Order of Battle

Höherer Kavalleriekommandeur 2 (2nd Cavalry Corps – HKK 2)
Commander: *Generalleutnant* von der Marwitz
5 Battalions, 72 Squadrons, 9 Batteries (36 guns)

Jäger Battalions 3, 4, 7, 9 and 10

2 Kavallerie-Division
24 Squadrons, 3 Batteries (12 guns)

5th Cav. Bde: Drag R 2, Ul R 3
8th Cav. Bde: Cur R 7, Hus R 12
Lifeguard Hus Bde: Hus R 1, Hus R 2
MG Section 4
Horse Artillery Section FAR 35

4 KD
3rd Cav. Bde: Cur R 2, Ul R 9
17th Cav. Bde: Drag R 17, Drag R 18
18th Cav. Bde: Hus R 15, Hus R 16
MG Section 2
Horse Artillery Section FAR 3

9 KD
13th Cav. Bde: Cur R 4, Hus R 8
14th Cav. Bde: Hus R 11, Ul R 5
19th Cav. Bde: Drag R 19, Ul R 13
MG Section 7
Horse Artillery Section, FAR 10

1st Army

Commander: *Generaloberst* von Kluck
Chief of Staff: *Generalmajor* von Kuhl
164 Battalions, 41 Squadrons, 138 Batteries (796 guns)

II Armeekorps

24 Battalions, 8 Squadrons, 28 Batteries (160 guns)

I/FAR 15 (sFH)

3 *Infanterie-Division* (Infantry Division – ID)
5th Inf. Bde: Gren R 2, Gren R 9
6th Inf. Bde: Fus R 34, IR 42
Drag R 3
3rd FA Bde: FAR 2, FAR 38

4 ID
7th Inf. Bde: IR 14, IR 149
8th Inf. Bde: IR 49, IR 140
Drag R 12
4th FA Bde: FAR 17, FAR 53

III Armeekorps

I/2nd Guard FAR (sFH)

5 ID
9th Inf. Bde: Gren R 8, IR 48
10th Inf. Bde: Gren R 12, IR 52
First Half, Hus R 3
5th FA Bde: FAR 18, FAR 54

6 ID
11th Inf. Bde: IR 20, Fus R 35
12th Inf. Bde: IR 24, IR 64
Second Half, Hus R 3
6th FA Bde: FAR 3, FAR 39

IV Armeekorps

I/FAR 4 (sFH)

7 ID
13th Inf. Bde: IR 26, IR 66
14th Inf. Bde: IR 27, IR 165
First Half, Hus R 10
7th FA Bde: FAR 4, FAR 40

8 ID
15th Inf. Bde: Fus R 36, IR 93
16th Inf. Bde: IR 72, IR 153
Second Half, Hus R 10
7th FA Bde: FAR 74, FAR 75

IX Armeekorps

I/FAR 20 (sFH)

17 ID
33rd Inf. Bde: IR 75, IR 76
34th Inf. Bde: Gren R 89, Fus R 90
First Half, Drag R 16
17th FA Bde: FAR 24, FAR 60

18 ID
35th Inf. Bde: IR 84, Fus R 86
36th Inf. Bde: IR 31, IR 85
Second Half, Drag R 16
18th FA Bde: FAR 9, FAR 45

III Reservekorps

25 Battalions, 6 Squadrons, 12 Batteries (72 guns)

5 Reserve-Division
9th Res. Bde: *Reserve Infanterie Regiment* (Reserve Infantry Regiment – RIR) 8,
    RIR 48
10th Res. Bde: RIR 12, RIR 52, Reserve Jäger Battalion 3
Res. Drag R 2
Res. FAR R 5

6 RD
11th Res. Bde: RIR 20, RIR 24
12th Res. Bde: RIR 26, RIR 35
Res. UL R 3
RFAR 6

IV Reservekorps

7 RD
13th Res. Bde: RIR 27, RIR 36
14th Res. Bde: RIR 66, RIR 72, Res. Jäger Bn 4
Res Heavy Cav. R 1
RFAR 7

22 RD
43rd Res. Bde RIR 71, RIR 94 (two bn), Res. Jäger Bn 11
44th Res. Bde: RIR 32, RIR 82
Res. Mounted Jäger R 1
RFAR 22

Acknowledgements

I want above all to thank the staff of the library at the University of Würzburg, who obtained hundreds of books for me through the superb German interlibrary-loan system. This book would not have been possible without their hard work and professionalism. Nevertheless, some gaps in my research remained, which I was able to fill at the *Deutsche Nationalbibliothek* (German National Library) in Leipzig and the *Bayerische Nationalbibliothek* (Bavarian National Library) in Munich. Both are superbly run and it is remarkable how much can be accomplished in a few days. The German National Library survived the Second World War without losses and its vast holdings are of exceptional value for research on the Imperial German Army. Gillian Margenson and Wolfram Knoblach were kind enough to put us up while I did my research in Munich. I would also like to thank the librarians at the Princeton University Library, the New York Public Library and the Library of the US Army Heritage and Education Center at Carlisle Barracks, PA.

New Martinsville WV (pop. 4,500), where we live, is a great place to write history. The pace is unhurried. Our car doesn't move for weeks at a time because everything is accessible on foot or with a bicycle. There is also a remarkable depth of local talent. At West Virginia Northern Community College, which is a block from our house, I was able to obtain some British and German books through the determined efforts of librarian Janet Corbett. The College Dean, Larry Tackett, provided invaluable assistance in preparing the photographs. Heather Wetzel, whose bookstore is two blocks away, once again drew the maps.

Publishing with The History Press was a pleasure. I would like to thank Robin Harries, Simon Hamlet and especially my copy-editor, Abbie Wood. I am not the easiest author to work with, but they put up with me. The History Press is a very professional outfit.

Once again my wife, Tina, got to tour another battlefield and sacrificed large parts of several vacations to allow me to work in libraries in America and Germany. She quietly supported this enterprise, for which I am profoundly grateful.

New Martinsville, WV
December 2009

Index